Margaret Heffernan is an award-winning chief executive, author and playwright and blogs for BNET, *Real Business* and the *Huffington Post*.

Further praise for *Wilful Blindness*

'Entertaining and compellingly argued.' *Sunday Times*

'*Wilful Blindness* makes a convincing case that while we are supposedly better informed than ever, we are guilty of frequent and self-destructive acts ... Full of juicy, awkward stories ... Given how so many of us wander around in the warm fug of distortion, it is good to be beaten to attention every now and again.' *Financial Times*

'Writing in clear, flowing prose, [Heffernan] draws on psychological and neurological studies and interviews with executives, whistle-blowers and white-collar criminals. The book made me think long and hard about how the pace and priorities of our daily lives can hinder our ability to live as decently and as truthfully as we can.' *New York Times*

'An engaging read, packed with cautionary tales ... With deft prose and page after page of keen insights, Heffernan shows why we close our eyes to facts that threaten our families, our livelihood, and our self-image – and, even better, she points the way out of the darkness.' Daniel H. Pink, author of *Drive* and *A Whole New Mind*

'A remarkable book ... It is a tour de force of brilliant insights, broad span applications and written in the most engaging style.' Philip Zimbardo

'Uniquely broad in scope, engagingly written. This in-de[illegible] an excellent read.' Albert Band[illegible]

'An amazing book, which highlights beautifully the potential for organisational denial.' Alan Corbett, psychotherapist

'A thoughtful and entertaining treatise on the seductiveness – and consequences – of ignoring what's right in front of our eyes ... Heffernan's cogent, riveting look at how we behave at our worst encourages us to strive for our best.' *US Publishers' Weekly*

'My eyes are now open to the many ways we all choose not to see reality even when it is painfully obvious. Why do we choose to turn a blind eye to the truth? ... Heffernan clearly asks the important questions about why we delude ourselves.' *Forbes*

WILFUL BLINDNESS

WHY WE IGNORE THE OBVIOUS

MARGARET HEFFERNAN

SIMON & SCHUSTER

London · New York · Sydney · Toronto · New Delhi

A CBS COMPANY

First published in Great Britain by Simon & Schuster UK Ltd, 2011
This paperback edition published by Simon & Schuster UK Ltd, 2019
A CBS COMPANY

3 5 7 9 10 8 6 4 2

Simon & Schuster UK Ltd
1st Floor
222 Gray's Inn Road
London WC1X 8HB

www.simonandschuster.co.uk
www.simonandschuster.com.au
www.simonandschuster.co.in

Simon & Schuster Australia, Sydney
Simon & Schuster India, New Delhi

A CIP catalogue record for this book
is available from the British Library

Paperback ISBN: 978-1-4711-8080-4
eBook ISBN: 978-1-84737-771-5

Typeset in Bembo by M Rules
Printed and bound by CPI Group (UK) Ltd, Croydon, CR0 4YY

For my Forward fellows

Contents

Introduction

This book was inspired by a coincidence: I was writing two plays for the BBC about the collapse of Enron just as the banks started to fail. Both debacles attracted eerily similar narratives: nobody could have seen the disaster coming. But that narrative was false. In both cases, experts, economists and ordinary citizens had all identified the danger and tried to sound the alarm. The problem was not that nobody knew what was happening; the real failure was the refusal to pay attention. I called that wilful blindness.

Almost as soon as the book came out, wilful blindness was used in Parliament as an explanation of phone hacking by News Corporation; how could so many phones have been hacked without someone in the executive knowing? Wilful blindness explained Fukushima, the horrors discovered about Jimmy Savile, at Mid Staffordshire NHS Trust, Winterbourne View, Rotherham, FIFA, Tesco, General Motors, Volkswagen, BHS, Hillsborough, Two Sisters, Wells Fargo, Grenfell Tower, Carillion, Harvey Weinstein, Larry Nassar, Barry Bennell, Oxfam, Facebook, Windrush. So many, perhaps even most, of the worst crimes had been committed not in the dark, hidden where no one could see them – but in full view of hundreds or thousands of people who simply chose not to look. And when we woke amazed by the results of the EU referendum and the election of Donald

Trump, we came face to face with what we had tried so hard not to see. Meanwhile, for the last three decades, the known threat of climate change has been ignored with such consistency that it now seems implausible we will be able to meet even the modest ambitions of the belated Paris Accord.

I had first encountered the concept of wilful blindness in the transcript of the trial of Enron CEO Jeffrey Skilling and Chairman Kenneth Lay. Instructing the jury, Judge Simeon Lake explained:

> You may find that a defendant had knowledge of a fact if you find that the defendant deliberately closed his eyes to what would otherwise have been obvious to him. Knowledge can be inferred if the defendant *deliberately blinded himself to the existence of a fact*.[1]

Lake was applying a fundamental legal principle: you are responsible if you could have known, and should have known, something that instead you strove not to see. Skilling and Lay were found guilty because they could have known, and had the opportunity to know, just how rotten their company was. Their claim not to know was no excuse.

Reading this, a chill went down my spine. Having run businesses myself, I knew that there had been times when I had not known everything I could have, and should have. And as the months passed, I continued to see wilful blindness all around me. After the bank bailouts, it was easier to talk about a banking crisis than to acknowledge its rapid evolution into an economic crisis, and then that proved easier to discuss than the fact that we were heading into a full-blown democratic crisis.

It wasn't just business and institutions. Wilful blindness was evident in domestic lives too – in failing marriages: why had she never asked about all those business trips? In hospitals: why had he skipped his check-up? Why had she started smoking? At home: how could so many people have got themselves so deeply into debt? Why was child abuse mostly found in families and perpetrated not by strangers but by familiar people seen every day?

When I mentioned wilful blindness to friends and colleagues, their eyes lit up: they knew exactly what I was talking about. Doctors described unnecessary treatments their patients demanded and got. Lawyers recounted their struggles to forget information their clients should never have shared. Prison workers talked about suicides and accountants all knew that business collapses are preceded by a clean audit. Intelligence chiefs told me they had not connected the dots that led to 9/11 or the Arab Spring, while executives confided that the hardest part of their job, even in a small company, was knowing what was going on. Almost everyone mentioned the Iraq War and global warming: big public threats caused or exacerbated by a reluctance to face uncomfortable facts.

Creative souls also saw that wilful blindness occurs not just when awful choices are made but when imaginative opportunities are overlooked. Technologists expressed their amazement that Microsoft hadn't seen the internet coming, and Google had been blindsided by social networking. Why did people who were so creative at home turn out to be so constrained in their thinking at work? How could seasoned hospitality professionals fail to see the promise implicit in Airbnb? Wilful blindness didn't have to involve a crime, just a criminal waste of opportunity.

Wilful blindness first emerged as a legal concept in the nineteenth century. A judge in Regina vs Sleep ruled that an accused could not be convicted for possession of government property unless the jury found that he either knew the goods came from government stores or had 'wilfully shut his eyes to the fact'. Thereafter, English judicial authorities referred to the state of mind that accompanied one who 'wilfully shut his eyes' as 'connivance' or 'constructive knowledge'.[2] Since then, lots of other phrases came into play – deliberate or wilful ignorance, conscious avoidance and deliberate indifference. What they all have in common is the idea that there is an opportunity for knowledge, and a responsibility to be informed, but it is shirked. Nowadays, the law is most often applied in cases of money laundering and drug trafficking: if you've been paid a large amount of money to carry a suitcase, then you are being wilfully blind if you don't check what is inside.

The law doesn't care why you remain ignorant, only that you do. But I am interested in why we choose to keep ourselves in the dark. What are the forces at work that make us deny the open secrets that stare us in the face? What stops us from seeing that burying knowledge only makes it more powerful, and us so much more vulnerable? Why, after any major failure or calamity, do voices always emerge saying they'd seen the danger, warned about the risk – but their warnings went unheeded? And why, as individuals, companies and countries do we so regularly look in the mirror and howl: how could we have been so blind?

As I've investigated the causes and patterns of wilful blindness, from our daily lives to the boardrooms of global corporations, I could have confined myself to business alone; there's no shortage of material. But it struck me that one source of our blindness at work is the artificial divide between personal and working lives. Business often acts, but doesn't in fact exist, in a vacuum. Every workforce is a conglomeration of individuals whose behaviours and habits started well before they were hired. Individuals, singly and in groups, are equally susceptible to wilful blindness; what makes organisations different is the scale of damage they can cause. The rules and rituals that separate domestic life from work just make it easier to turn a blind eye.

Whether individual or collective, wilful blindness doesn't have a single driver, but many. We can't notice and know everything: the cognitive limits of our brain simply won't let us. That means we have to filter or edit what we take in. So what we choose to let through and to leave out is crucial. We mostly admit the information that makes us feel great about ourselves, while conveniently filtering out whatever unsettles our fragile egos and vital beliefs. It's a truism that love is blind; what's less obvious is just how much evidence it can ignore. Ideology and orthodoxies powerfully mask what, to the uncaptivated mind, is obvious, dangerous or absurd, and there's much about how and even where we live that leaves us in the dark. Fear of conflict, fear of change keeps us that way: almost all employees believe their bosses do not want to hear the truth. An unconscious (and much denied) impulse to obey and conform shields us from confrontation and crowds provide friendly alibis for our inertia. And money has the power to blind us, even (or especially) to our better selves.

In the surprise results of the EU referendum and US presidential election in 2016, all the hallmarks of wilful blindness were evident: citizens ensconced in an echo chamber of like-minded individuals who amplified biases; ideologies prizing confirmation over curiosity and complexity; a lack of constructive conflict; peer pressure to stay silent; power hierarchies that rewarded blind obedience and conformity; metrics that supported an overwhelming preference for the simple over the true. When the world awoke, stunned with surprise, we scarcely recognised ourselves: what had we been missing all along? Since then, the open secret of sexual harassment – in the entertainment industry, in sport, in education, in politics – revealed what we'd preferred to ignore: that sex is a weapon used by the powerful, not just in war but at work.

Of course, wilful blindness isn't always disastrous. Such a behaviour is unlikely to have endured without conferring some evolutionary benefit. Turning a blind eye can oil the wheels of social intercourse when we don't see the spot on a silk tie, the girlfriend's acne or a neighbour's squalor. Ignoring political differences may contribute to office calm. In times of national emergency, blindness can be positively helpful. During the London Blitz, morale was better sustained by dancing and partygoing than by acknowledging the possibility of defeat. And it's far easier for all of us to maintain optimism and momentum by ignoring our own mortality.

Perhaps it is the sheer utility of wilful blindness that sucks us into the habit in the first place. It seems innocuous and feels efficient. But the mechanisms that make us blind to the world also put us in peril. The children who grow up among abusive parents come to maturity feeling crazy, confused and anxious because their reality has been consistently denied. Ideologues, refusing to see data and events that challenge their theories, doom themselves to irrelevance. Companies full of compliant employees take on levels of risk beyond their ability to recover. And all the time that these perils go unacknowledged, they grow more powerful and more dangerous.

Fake news is a convenient scapegoat. It makes it harder to distinguish fact from fiction and offers an alibi for apathy. But the fact that wilful blindness is so pervasive does not mean that it is inevitable. Since the book first appeared, I've been heartened by the many organisations that have taken my thesis to heart, running wilful blindness workshops and thinking hard about mitigating its greatest risks. Most companies are now attempting transformations that aim to reduce the hierarchies, bureaucracies and inequality in which wilful blindness runs rampant. And the most inspiring people in this book have found in themselves the courage to look, a fierce determination to see. That is what makes them remarkable. They aren't especially knowledgeable, powerful or talented and they're not heroes; they're human. But their courage in daring to see reveals a central truth about wilful blindness: we may think being blind makes us safer, when in fact it leaves us crippled, vulnerable and powerless. But when we confront facts and fears, we achieve real power and unleash our capacity for change.

1. Affinity and Beyond

In life one and one don't make two. One and
one make one.
And I'm looking for that free ride to me: I'm
looking for you.

'Bargain', The Who

Meet Rebecca.

The first thing you will notice is that she is very tall – just under six foot. Mid-thirties. Healthy, wholesome and, even today when she's had to bring her two children into work with her, she has plenty of energy.

Meet Robert.

He's tall too – just over six foot. Mid-thirties. Handsome, clean-cut and, despite some looming deadlines, unfailingly polite.

If you meet Rebecca and Robert together, you will notice what all their friends comment on: they look very alike. Not the same, of course; they're not twins. They're husband and wife. And their looks are not deceptive.

'Amazing similarities,' Robert concedes. 'Similarities in background that I didn't notice, but I like more and more. Not rich, not poor. Went to the same university, both in broadcasting, both Christian. But then there are more nuanced things, like the way we both think about family and friends, and believing in hard work. And of course we work in the same industry and,' he looks over at Rebecca and beams, 'wear the unofficial uniform: neat jeans, crisp shirt.' They both laugh.

Rebecca and Robert enjoy the fact that they are similar, because it makes them feel comfortable, safe, located within each other.

'It isn't that we like all the same things,' says Rebecca when she's on her own. 'I love going for walks – and Robert's had to learn to like them! But the skeleton of our lives, that's what we have in common. Very settled home lives, parents still together, parents who were always very encouraging. We didn't think consciously about these things when we started going out, but you look back and see these things, these patterns.'

However, Rebecca and Robert have very little sense that their similarity limits them, narrows their perspective on life or blinds them to a wide array of opinions, experiences and different ways of thinking and being. But the fundamental human preference that they exemplify – for the familiar over the alien, the known over the unknown, and the comfortable over the dissonant – has insidious but important consequences. Embedded within our self-definition, we build relationships, institutions, cities, systems and cultures that, in reaffirming our values, blind us to alternatives. This is where our wilful blindness originates: in the innate human desire for familiarity, for likeness, that is fundamental to the ways our minds work.

Because for all that their similarities are so pronounced, in fact Rebecca and Robert are typical. Most people marry other people very like themselves: similar height, weight, age, background, IQ, nationality, ethnicity. We may think that opposites attract, but they don't get married. Sociologists and psychologists, who have studied this phenomenon for decades, call it 'positive assortative mating'[1] – which really just means that we marry people like ourselves. When it comes to love, we don't scan a very broad horizon.

Gian Gonzaga used to work as a senior research scientist before leaving to join eHarmony, not an online dating site, it insists, but an online 'relationship site'. It depends on the 'science of compatibility' consisting of '29 Dimensions™ that predict great relationships'. But this is not romance, it's business. So eHarmony stands or falls on its success in finding people who really will like each other. Since its inception in 1997, the world of online matchmaking has grown considerably and is now one of the most common ways for couples to meet. In addition, there's growing evidence that the marriages resulting from online dating have a slightly lower rate of breakup.[2]

'We know that people select for appearances, which is why you upload your picture. But our questionnaire goes a lot deeper and that's really based on what we know works. So we ask lots of questions about personality – how neat you are, how punctual – and about values: do you value religion, altruism, volunteering? Values are the things you hold on to even in tough times and they are the things you most want validated by others. Of course interests count too, but they change. You can learn to love walking, but values are really sticky.'

When it comes to marriage, there are cultural differences of course. Married people in the United Kingdom consistently express greater satisfaction than in the US with the amount of consensus they experience in their marriage. They're more satisfied with their family relationship, the way they make decisions and how they take care of household chores. And this striking degree of consensus even affects their sex life: compared with the US and Australia, British couples are the least likely to report that being too tired for sex is a problem for the marriage. All couples, according to eHarmony, want to agree with each other about career decisions, friendships, leisure activities and friendships, but British couples in particular care about family, sharing household tasks equally and about definitions of proper behaviour.

Gonzaga and his wife, Heather Setrakian, don't just practise what they preach – they *are* what they preach. They met while working as academic researchers in UCLA's marriage lab, they're both in their thirties, dark-haired and, according to their friends, both brilliant, witty and wise. The eHarmony system could have matched them, Gonzaga says, except that when his wife filled out her questionnaire she said she wanted someone two years younger.

That questionnaire certainly tests for patience and endurance. It takes at least half an hour to complete – longer if you're seriously committed to finding a mate. The questions are all designed to identify your key values and attitudes – those twenty-nine dimensions – and to match them up with someone else whose dimensions are as close to yours as possible. It may be software but it is, quite literally, matchmaking. It is not looking for opposites or quirky combinations.

'People may have an interest in people who are different from themselves,' said Gonzaga. 'But they don't marry them. They're looking for confirmation, for comfort.'

Gonzaga based his claims on data from 25 million questionnaires. What these tell him is that, whether you're using the wiring in your brain or the software underneath eHarmony's site, we go through life looking for people who make us comfortable because they're so much like us. We may be intrigued by difference – but, ultimately, we reject it.

'For a while, I went out with women who looked different,' Robert told me. 'And women who really were different – sometimes very different indeed. But the turbulence of those relationships really drew me back to the centre. You'd think it would widen the circle but it really didn't. I tried but I found I really didn't love Albanian women! Clearly some Albanian women are wonderful – I have nothing against the Albanians! But I think I learned that you're given a centre of gravity that is immutable. You've been given a set of rules that you return to almost without thinking.'

It isn't that Robert wasn't curious about other kinds of people and other cultures; he was. He wanted, more than many people, to explore beyond his own immediate knowledge and experience. But ultimately he did what most of us do most of the time: he rejected a difference that just felt too great. That puzzled him enough to make him think about it, but not enough to change his mind.

'I wonder if I might feel I am looking at myself when I look at Rebecca,' Robert said. 'Have I chosen myself?'

Robert and Rebecca are well educated and sceptical. They aren't inclined to take much at face value. What makes them unusual is that they were prepared to analyse and talk about the powerful influence that their similarity has had on their relationship. They both acknowledge that it is a source of delight and comfort, but worry that sticking to their own kind narrows their experience of life. By choosing to live and work among people like themselves, are they restricting what they see?

These findings – that we mostly marry and live with people very like ourselves – always annoy people. Confronted by the data, the most common response is a challenge: I'm not like that, my husband's not like that. Why are we so affronted? Because we all want to feel that we have made our own choices, that they weren't predictable, that we aren't so vain as to choose ourselves, and that we are freer spirits, with a broader, more eclectic range of taste than the data imply. We don't like to feel that we're blind to the allure of those who are not like us; we don't like the sense of being trapped by our own identity.

But our minds operate somewhat like eHarmony's software: we go through life searching for good matches and, when we find one, it feels good; the more something is like us, the more we're inclined to like it. And that habit of mind pertains equally to things that really matter (like choosing a partner) and to things that don't matter at all. So when subjects in an experiment were led to believe that they shared a birthday with Rasputin, they were far more lenient in judging the mad monk than those who had nothing in common with him. Just the thought that they shared a birthday made people like him more.

Even when it's something as trivial as our own initials, we stick to what we know best. A meta-analysis of the most severe hurricanes between 1998 and 2005 showed that people were more likely to donate to relief funds if the hurricane's name shared their first initial – so Kate and Katherine were more likely to donate to Hurricane Katrina relief than Zoe was.[3] I've always been baffled by monogrammed towels and shirts (do we really not know who owns the towels in our own homes?) but clearly these familiar letters mean a lot to us.

In other experiments, asked to choose a preferred letter from several pairs of letters, subjects tended, quite reliably, to opt for letters from their own names. What's so interesting about these findings is that the letters themselves are meaningless – nothing will happen as a result of the choices made.

Yet still the participants gravitated towards letters they see, and sign, every day.

When you take this out of the lab and into the real world, the same pattern emerges. Carol, it seems, is more likely to drink Coke while Pete will choose Pepsi.[4] Leo likes Listerine but Catherine prefers Colgate. And while those choices may seem unimportant, it appears that life choices too may be influenced by those initials we love so much. Dentists are overrepresented by people whose names begin with 'D' and there are more people named George than you should expect to find living in Georgia.

Familiarity, it turns out, does not breed contempt. It breeds comfort. In a series of experiments at the University of Michigan in the 1980s,[5] one group of sixty-four students was shown photographs of a male college student once a week for four weeks; the other group of sixty-four saw different faces each week. After the four weeks were up, the two groups were asked to assess how much they thought they would like the people whose faces they'd seen if they were to meet them in the future. They were also asked how far they believed those people to be similar to themselves.

The students who had seen the same face for four weeks believed more strongly that this was a person they would like in real life. They also believed (on no evidence except the photograph) that the face belonged to someone who was similar to themselves. In other words, the familiar face – with no supporting evidence – felt better. Women responded to the experiment in exactly the same way as men. A similar experiment, using irregular octagons, generated the same pattern of responses. What is familiar makes us feel secure and comfortable.

This pertains even when we go looking for emotional experiences, as when we listen to music. It can be hard fully to enjoy a new piece the first time you listen to it; only after repeated hearings does it become a favourite. Part of that may be because if you're trying out, say, Mahler's 8th Symphony for the first time, there is a lot to take in: two orchestras, two choirs and eight soloists over eighty minutes won't create an instant impression. And listening to music is a hugely complex cognitive exercise.[6] Even the White Stripes' 'Seven Nation Army' can take some getting used to. But once we've heard it a few times, we're used to it, like it, can chant it. And then we don't want something different; we want more of the same.

'We score hundreds of attributes of every song and then we find the matches between those songs – and then that's what we recommend to you. Because we know that if you liked one piece of music, you are very, very likely to like another one that shares the same characteristics.'

Tim Westergren isn't talking about dating, but about his company, Pandora Radio. It does for music what eHarmony does for dating. Each song is scored manually by musicians for 400 attributes; there are thirty for the voice alone, capturing everything from timbre to layers of the voice to vibrato. Then that 'score' is matched to other songs that have scores that are as closely similar as possible. Pandora software is doing to music what we do when we meet people: looking for matches. And, when it finds them, people feel very happy.

'God, I love Pandora!' said Joe Clayton, a music fan in Boston. 'I love it. I'm always finding new bands, new stuff that I just couldn't find otherwise – certainly not in any music store. And it's kinda creepy – but in a good way – because they almost never give me something I don't like. Almost never.'

Pandora does, in essence, exactly what Spotify does and what Amazon's and Netflix's and all personalisation software tries to do: to match what it knows about you to what it knows about others like you. But what none of these will do is come up with that serendipitous suggestion that introduces you to something completely different from anything you've ever heard before. I like Bruce Springsteen, Frank Zappa and the White Stripes – but I also adore Handel. And, given my first three preferences, not Spotify or Amazon or Pandora would offer me Handel.

Westergren acknowledges that limitation. 'It's about broadening your selection – but narrowing your taste. If you like jazz, you like more jazz. If you like hip-hop, you like more hip-hop. But Pandora is never going to take you from Springsteen to Handel.'

All personalisation software aims to make our lives easier by reducing overwhelming choice. And they do it the same way that our brain does: by building a profile and searching for matches. It's as though, online and offline, our life is one gigantic game of Snap! This is immensely efficient, a triumphant evolutionary solution to the problem of load balancing. Your brain could not function if it could not segment and prioritise what's familiar (and therefore demanding of less scrutiny) from what's unfamiliar and needs a lot of close attention. This bifurcation allows your brain to take shortcuts, giving an easy pass to what is familiar and concentrating on what's new, different, demanding and even potentially dangerous. So when we find what we like, what's familiar, part of our pleasure is the joy of recognition.

As Westergren says, we are narrowing our taste, reducing the music or books or people that might widen our horizons. Our brains aren't designed to draw us into experiences that are wild and different; there would be little evolutionary advantage in doing something so risky. And so, by focusing in one direction and excluding others, we become blind to the experiences that don't match.

This is not to say that strange, serendipitous things never

flow into our lives. Of course they do. You meet someone at work who introduces you to Handel and you develop a love of baroque music. Or – more likely – your son introduces you to Four Tet. But these encounters are random and risky. Remember Robert's problem with Albanian women.

There's a circle here: we like ourselves, not least because we are known and familiar to ourselves. Ours is the face we see in the mirror each morning, ours is the voice we hear all day long. So we like people who look and sound like us. They feel familiar and safe. And those feelings of familiarity and security make us like ourselves more because we aren't anxious. We belong. Our self-esteem rises. We feel happy. Human beings want to feel good about themselves and to feel safe, and being surrounded by familiarity and similarity satisfies those needs very efficiently.

The problem with this is that everything outside that warm, safe circle is our blind spot.

We aren't just rejecting music that doesn't match; we use these same processes to make important decisions in our everyday lives. When I had my first opportunity, as an ambitious young producer at the BBC, to choose my own team, I hoped to hire people who would challenge me and each other and who would invest the entire project with intellectual richness and vigour. With all that firmly in mind, I selected liberal-arts graduates who were all female, spoke several languages, were under five-foot-seven and had birthdays within the same week in June. In other words, they were all like me.

Did I consciously intend to do that? Of course not. Like hiring managers the world over, I intended to recruit only the best and the brightest and that's what I thought I was looking for. But did I also want people I'd feel comfortable working with, enjoy spending late hours with, people who shared the values of the project? Well, yes.

I was biased, in favour of those just like me. Everyone is biased. But just as we are affronted when told that we're likely to marry and associate with those very similar to ourselves, so most people vehemently reject the idea that they are biased: others may be, but not us. And we consider the people who disagree with us to be the most biased of all.[7]

The recognition that we all fall into these traps, that we are all biased, has led many organisations to adopt 'unconscious bias training'. Such courses hope that making bias conscious will eliminate it. Unsurprisingly, there's no compelling evidence that this works, and some think it exacerbates rather than remediates bias. We've certainly seen no substantive change; despite a great deal of expenditure, articulated goodwill and equality legislation, we still see so few women and ethnic minorities in top roles or in receipt of venture capital and so few male midwives, nurses and teachers. Stereotypes are energy-saving devices – they let us make shortcuts that feel just fine.[8] That's why they're so pervasive and so persistent.

The famous development of blind auditions for new symphony members provided graphic illustration of this point. Harvard economist Claudia Goldin and Princeton's Cecilia Rouse found that when musicians were allowed to audition behind screens, where their gender could not influence the evaluation of their music, women's chances of making it through the first round increased by 50 per cent – and in the final rounds by 300 per cent. Blind auditions have now become standard in the US, with the result that the number of female players in major orchestras has increased from 5 per cent to 36 per cent. Eliminating names and photographs from job applications is a more recent attempt to replicate this impact within other industries where those details alone can determine whose CV gets attention and whose gets binned. The automation of these processes – taking the human element out – might seem to offer real hope here, but it might also just make it cheaper and faster to select with impunity the prevailing stereotype of success.

The financial services industry used to be the poster child for this kind of discrimination, but it has now been supplanted by high tech as the world's centre for power, money – and bias. As venture capitalists started investing vast sums into new businesses, the environment that developed became one, according to Melinda Gates, of 'white male nerds who've dropped out of Harvard and Stanford'.[9] The majority of start-ups were founded by young men with their male friends who hired their male friends to develop business propositions eagerly understood and backed by investors just like them. By 2016, just 7 per cent of partners in VC firms were female and just 2 per cent of their funding went to female entrepreneurs.[10]

And just as German and Austrian orchestras used to insist that Asians could never fully comprehend or perform classical music, the capacity and talent of women in high tech is frequently invisible. Erica Joy Baker recalled one experience when she worked at Google, providing tech support to senior executives. When CEO Eric Schmidt came into the tech support room, he asked for Baker's teammate Frank. When told Frank was otherwise engaged, Schmidt described his technical issue and asked that Baker pass the message along to Frank. What's remarkable about the story is that Erica Joy was sitting in the tech support room because she *was* tech support – and fully capable of resolving Schmidt's issue. But he of course was blind to her abilities: the black woman did not look like the white man's mental model of technical expertise.[11]

The voices arguing in favour of diversity in recent years have not been motivated only, or even primarily, by notions of social justice. The argument for diversity is that if you bring together lots of different kinds of people, with a wide range of education and experience, they can identify more solutions, see more alternatives to problems, be more creative together than any single person, or homogenous group, ever could. But as our biases keep informing whom we hire and promote, whom we are prepared to listen to and take seriously, whom we respect and whom we denigrate, we weed out that diversity and are left with corporate headquarters and sometimes entire industries full of people who perpetuate existing power structures. They aren't exposed to other ways of seeing the world, they lack different experiences to exchange, they don't see other faces or hear other voices. They can't celebrate difference because they are blind to it. Underpowered and overconfident, monocultural institutions and industries fail to serve the world because they don't reflect the world, only the biases of those already in power. From Hollywood to Westminster, Silicon Valley to Shoreditch and from the City of London to Washington DC, this means that they perpetuate their risk of being blindsided – and feel super-comfortable doing so. Which may help explain why Kensington and Chelsea council didn't see that there might be a problem in not fitting sprinklers in Grenfell Tower: no one in the room at the time the decision was made actually lived there. It may also explain why it was so easy to destroy papers relating to the arrival of the Windrush generation: because nobody from Windrush families was involved in the destruction.

What happens at work doesn't stay at work. Just as we choose jobs with people very like ourselves, we choose to live among them also. Opposites don't attract. The psychologist David Myers says that the way we move around and build neighbourhoods mirrors the way we choose our spouses.

'Mobility enables the sociological equivalent of "assortative mating",' he says. Now that many of us have a great deal of freedom to move around, choosing the jobs we like, we also choose the communities we like. And, by and large, we choose 'those places and people that are comfortably akin to ourselves'.[12]

In the United States, Bill Bishop studied this pattern and found that, over the last thirty years, most Americans had been engaged in moving towards more homogenous ways of living, 'clustering in communities of like-mindedness'. He calls this 'the big sort' and what strikes him is how well defended these communities can be. When a lone Republican neighbour, living in a staunchly Democratic part of Austin, Texas, dared to articulate his political opinion in a local listserv, the response he got was unambiguous: 'I'm really not interested [in] being surprised by right-wing e-mail in my inbox, no matter what its guise. It makes me feel bad, and I don't like it.'[13] At first, I thought this was a specifically American phenomenon – until a mother at my children's school dared to send an email to other mothers during the 2010 election campaign. Criticising the local MP provoked a vociferous response: pleas for lost games kit might be fine but an exchange of political views was not welcomed.

'The London neighbourhood where we live,' Rebecca says, 'is lovely. The neighbours are lovely. The family on the other side of us, Paul and Juliet – they are us! Mid-thirties, two boys. Slightly younger but exactly parallel. Juliet doesn't work, but I'm only part-time. The street is full of people like us. Each house is a carbon copy of the same kinds of people.'

When they were house-hunting, Rebecca recalls that they were driven by price, proximity to work, choice of schools. All her neighbours were using the same parameters, so perhaps it isn't so surprising that they'd all end up together. 'I guess you could say that,' Rebecca concedes. 'But there were other places that would have fit the bill. But when we came here, it was more than just functionality. We liked it here – we still like it here. It feels right for us.'

The clustering of likeminded people was visible when I lived in Stockwell, south London, which estate agents at the time called 'a mixed area' – meaning an ethnically mixed and sometimes volatile combination of early Victorian terraces and 1960s council housing. You didn't see much traffic between those two architectures, not a lot of cups of sugar being borrowed. Teachers, professors, business people and TV producers lived in elegant stucco homes; single, sometimes teenage, parents lived across from them. At least we could see each other, but that was about as far as it ever went. It was little different from more recent London housing developments that deliberately provide separate doors, bike storage, rubbish facilities and post boxes: one set is for the rich and one set for the poor, ensuring they never encounter one another.[14] Economic inequality is manifested physically in a single, segregated development.

Now we live in Somerset and I'm struck by the polarisation between city and country. My village neighbours rarely travel to London, and they mostly go as tourists, critical and a little intimidated. But this cuts both ways. An esteemed British playwright wrinkled up her nose, telling me about her sojourn in Dorset. She cut short her time there because, while she liked the scenery, not enough of her city friends came to visit at the weekends. What she'd aspired to was her London life but with roses around the door. She wanted to live in the country, not engage with it. And every year, as more Londoners move down to the country, I watch as they search out fellow *émigrés* who are so much easier to make friends with than the locals.

By following our instincts to cluster together in likeminded communities, walking through our separate doors, we reduce our exposure to different people, values and experiences. We slowly but surely focus on what we know, losing sight of everything else. We may have more choices than ever before, but our narrow tastes have become better defended.

This is trivial when it comes to choosing between Coke and Pepsi. It's dangerous when it comes to like-minded people vigorously amplifying each other's biases in large corporations. It can be fatal when it comes to spending decisions on housing that councillors don't live in and have no connection with. What this means is that bias – that you can't see and don't feel – is profoundly destabilising when it comes to democracy. The Brexit referendum in 2016 showed all of us aspects of Britain we had previously been blind to, none more than the degree to which we were all in bubbles of our own making and design, frequently unaware of and isolated from those who had different experiences and opinions from our own. Like so many, my son was horrified to realise he'd had no serious debates about the referendum because he didn't know anyone who wanted to leave the EU. He was just typical of his age group: 73 per cent of 18–29-year-olds and 70 per cent of university graduates – people just like him – wanted to remain in the EU.

Perhaps more shocking was the revelation that people whose business it is to study and understand community were no less blind. Alexander Betts describes himself as a 'liberal internationalist'. A successful academic, deemed a 'young global leader' by the World Economic Forum and 'one of the top global thinkers of 2016', he confessed himself amazed to recognise that, of the top fifty areas with the strongest leave vote, he had spent 'a combined total of four days in those areas . . . People like me who think of ourselves as inclusive, open and tolerant perhaps don't know our own countries and societies nearly as well as we like to believe.'[15]

Betts is exceptional only in being so open about his own blindness. And the problem is not unique to Britain. The small town in Texas where my father grew up has just one paved street and a small, broken-down convenience store. It has no other facilities and most housing now consists of mobile homes parked on breeze blocks. Such poverty is not new in America and neither is it hard to find; in the richest country in the world, 51 per cent of adult Americans can expect to spend at least a year below the poverty line.[16] But, until Trump's surprise election, almost nobody wrote about it or thought about it. The galvanic shocks of 2016 revealed the same truth: that by living with like-minded people, exchanging views in what is more of an echo than a debating chamber, we have become blind to the needs, concerns, fears and hope, anger and expectation of people not like ourselves. That Brexit, Trump and the 2016 election were such surprises revealed the epic scope of our wilful blindness.

Media companies – old, new and social – understand this perfectly and always have. Readers have always chosen media that they broadly agree with; the business model depends on advertisers being able to match products with specific audiences and outlets. When we buy a newspaper or a magazine, or watch the news, we aren't looking for a fight. Trump voters are no more likely to watch CNN for a challenge than his opponents are to dip into Fox News. All that is new about so-called social media is its capacity to amplify that effect – and to narrow even more drastically what we see and read and hear. Our Facebook pages are littered with amplification and endorsement; they are both a bad place and a lame format for anything approaching discussion or debate. We select both old and new media knowingly, because we feel delight in being disseminated and applauded, surrounded by those who cheer who we are, and what and how we think.

And while this is natural, we now see that it isn't neutral. In what he calls the 'group polarisation effect', legal scholar Cass Sunstein found that when groups of like-minded people get together, they do not just *not* challenge one another, they make each other's views more extreme.[17] (It is worth noting that Sunstein, a professor at Harvard, is married to Samantha Power, also a professor at Harvard, and both served the Obama administration. Even people who write about this behaviour aren't immune to it and being aware of it provides no inoculation against it.) Just as eHarmony reduces your choices, and Spotify and Pandora narrow your taste, like-minded people have the same impact on opinions.

In 2005, Sunstein and some of his colleagues brought together two groups of like-minded people: liberals from Boulder, Colorado, and conservatives from Colorado Springs. In their respective groups, each was asked to deliberate on three topics: civil partnerships, affirmative action and climate change. But before the discussions began, individual participants recorded their private opinions on each topic. And then the groups were mixed up and encouraged to discuss their views.

The group deliberations were consistently respectful, engaged and substantive, but when they were finished, almost every member ended up with more extreme positions than they had held at the start. Conservatives from Colorado Springs who had been neutral on a climate-change treaty now opposed it. Boulder liberals who had felt somewhat positive about civil partnerships became firmly convinced of their merit. What small diversity each group might have had at the outset was, says Sunstein, 'squelched', while the rift between them had grown larger.

Even when presented with a wide range of data and arguments, Sunstein's work demonstrated that when individuals read, they focus on the information that supports their current opinion, paying less attention to anything that challenges their views. Overall, people are about twice as likely to seek information that supports their own point of view as they are to consider an opposing idea.[18] Rather than broadening their attitudes, the very process of discussion renders them blind to alternatives. Just as Robert stopped going out with Albanian women, we stop looking at places or jobs or information or people that will prove too uncomfortable, too tumultuous for our closely held beliefs. We choose the *Guardian* or the *Daily Mail* because they confirm our view of the world, not because they challenge it. We watch the news on Sky or the news on Channel 4 for the same reason. We may think we want to be challenged, but we really don't. Our intellectual, even our moral and ethical homes are just as self-selected and exclusive as our physical homes.

In theory, the internet was supposed to change all of this. Access to the world's store of knowledge was supposed to broaden our horizons and open our minds. After all, online you can meet anyone from anywhere. But while it's true that all of us now have access to more information than ever before in history, for the most part we don't choose to use it. Just like newspapers, we read the blogs that we agree with – Breitbart UK or The Canary – but there we encounter a virtually infinite echo chamber, as 85 per cent of blogs link to other blogs (and ads) with the same political inclination.[19] The transition of the internet, from the PC to mobile phones, has just exacerbated this trend. Reliance on phone apps means that the information we consume is filtered more finely than ever.

In fact, while early founders celebrated the capacity of the internet to bring together those who were far apart in every sense, what makes money online is affinity: bringing together like-minded people whose identity is so specific that they are a well-defined market for higher-priced advertising. What is useful to individuals makes billions for companies profiling and exploiting narrowly defined identities; this is the business model of the internet. It can, of course, be benevolent and pacific. Wherever you live, whatever your age, whether you love orchids, aikido or ideology, you can find and connect to like-minded enthusiasts. In doing so, you gain access to shortcuts: information from people who you trust to be reliable. If you don't know how to lift and split your orchids, orchid aficionados will save you a lot of money and grief. But the same applies to sourcing prohibited drugs, making explosive devices or sharing extremist content. We cling together because it feels comfortable but also because it's efficient. We don't have to learn everything ourselves, the hard, slow way. And we aren't encouraged to have doubts.

Shortcuts reward us in many ways but they lead us astray, because the comfort they produce discourages us from questioning, from thinking for ourselves. Which is what happened when the fraudster Bernard Madoff tapped into a community of investors, all very much alike and eager to pass on what they knew.

'I inherited my account from my dad,' said Irvin Stalbe. I didn't know much about it. I got it when my parents died. They weren't wealthy, they just put a little aside every year. I'd tried investing for myself but I wasn't that good at it, and I just thought: it's steady and it works.'

We spoke in Stalbe's modest apartment in Pompano Beach, Florida. He retired there when he was fifty-five, but had continued to work part-time in a bank, just for the companionship. The money he made from his inherited Madoff account was for extras – vacations, a little gambling – and to pay for his grandchildren's education. What chiefly delighted him was that the financial returns were so stable and regular, there were no surprises. Even though this is never true of any stock market, Stalbe's Madoff fund seemed to be a dream come true.

'When I brought the paperwork to my accountant and he saw the income, he said he'd like to add money to it. So we worked out a way we'd issue statements to anyone who put money in. In the end, I had forty friends and family in the account.'

Did the accountant, did anyone, do any research before they joined, I wondered.

'No, not really. We were in it for twenty-five years, my parents twenty years before me! Over the years, we brought in friends, grandkids, all under my name. For many years, it was wonderful. Of course what I realise now is I should have remembered the golden rule: never put all your money in one place. But at the time, I mean, everyone was in it. We didn't have to worry.'

Madoff's was an affinity crime. He found new victims from old ones, preying on people like himself who knew people like themselves, who didn't ask questions because their level of comfort with each other was so high that they felt they didn't need to do research – they could take shortcuts. Sitting with Stalbe and his family in their Florida sitting room, it's clear that these aren't greedy people. They just wanted the safety of a reliable return and they believed they'd found that in an investment vehicle that they all validated for each other. It is the kind of shortcut we take every day, though few of us pay such a high price for it.

'I'm okay,' Stalbe says. 'I still have some income and I work at my son's take-out restaurant, cleaning tables, working behind the counter. I like to talk to people. But my sister, she's devastated, she has nothing. My sister-in-law, the same thing: ninety per cent of her money was in there. Because of me.'

These days, what distresses Stalbe most isn't his own loss but the fact that he drew in so many others. He's angry with himself because his confidence is what gave them confidence. Everyone felt so at home with each other, they all had so much in common, that no one ever asked any questions. It's that affinity too that allowed Madoff 's fraud to reach such astronomic proportions.

Shortcuts can be very pragmatic but, when you take them, you miss a lot along the way: that's what shortcuts are for. Living, working and making decisions with people like ourselves brings us comfort and efficiencies, but it also makes us far narrower in how we think and what we see. The more tightly we focus, the more we leave out. For while it's been fashionable lately to blame all of this on the internet, Bernard Madoff (like generations of fraudsters before him) didn't need technology to perpetrate his crime. He had human biology on his side.

These blind spots have a physical reality in the brain. Robert Burton used to be chief of neurology at Mount Zion-UCSF hospital. He has a restless mind and is almost allergic to the certainty that our biases give us. He's highly aware that, in its endless search for matches, our brain rejects the information that might broaden our outlook, widen our gaze or make us just a little less certain.

'Neural networks,' said Burton, 'don't give you a direct route from, say, a flash of light straight to your consciousness. There are all kinds of committees that vote along the way, whether that flash of light is going to go straight to your consciousness or not. And if there are enough "yes" votes, then yes you can see it. If there aren't, you could miss it.

'But here's the thing: what does your brain like? What gets the "yes" vote? It likes the stuff it already recognises. It likes what is familiar. So you will see the familiar stuff right away.

The other stuff may take longer, or it may never impinge on your consciousness. You just won't see it.'

We were talking on a beautiful morning in Sausalito, California, overlooking the harbour. It was early, there weren't many people about, but there were a few. Even before his first coffee, Burton eagerly scanned the horizon.

'I'm aware of people moving around, the town starting to wake up,' Burton continued. 'But it's a kind of fuzzy background, it doesn't get much attention from me. But if someone I knew walked across the street, I'd see that at once. Zip – straight into my consciousness, "yes" votes all the way. A perfect match.'

Burton is wary of our love for matches and craving for certainty. It goes against the spirit of enquiry to which, as a scientist, he's dedicated. But mostly he's suspicious of it because he thinks it stops us seeing so much. For him, the development of the neural networks in our brain is similar to the creation of a riverbed.

'Imagine the gradual formation of a riverbed. The initial flow of water might be completely random – there are no preferred routes in the beginning. But once a creek is formed, water is more likely to follow this newly created path of least resistance. As the water continues, the creek deepens and a river develops.'

Burton's is a beautiful metaphor, and a useful one too. The longer we live, and the more we accumulate similar experiences, friends and ideas, the faster and more easily the water flows. There's less and less resistance. That absence of resistance gives us a sense of ease, of comfort, of certainty. Yet, at the same time, the higher the sides of the riverbed grow. As we pursue like-minded people, in like-minded communities, doing similar jobs in homogenous corporate cultures, the riverbed sinks deeper and deeper, its sides climb higher and higher. It feels good; the flow is efficient and unimpeded. You just can't see much.

This is how wilful blindness begins, not in conscious, deliberate choices to be blind, but in a skein of decisions that slowly but surely restricts our view. We don't sense our perspective closing in and might prefer that it stay broad and rich. But our blindness grows out of the small, daily decisions that we make, which embed us more snugly inside our affirming thoughts and values. And what's most frightening about this process is that, as we see less and less, we feel more comfort and greater certainty. We think we see more – even as the landscape shrinks.

2. Love is Blind

> Love to faults is always blind,
> Always is to joy inclin'd,
>
> *William Blake*

The vaccine for German measles was first introduced in 1970 but, in the years before that, getting German measles when pregnant was dangerous for both mother and child. Michael's mother knew this – there were so many doctors in the family – but there was nothing she could do. So Michael was born in 1948 with a congenital heart defect.

Growing up, he was frail and allowed not to do sports. But, as though he knew that his future must depend on brain not brawn, he was so very clever. All his Jesuit teachers knew he was a student to cherish: bound to do well in exams and get into a top university, maybe even become a priest himself. They were disappointed in the last ambition but not the rest, as Michael grew up to be one of those individuals you knew, almost at first sight, was electrifyingly brilliant. That he was also very funny was a necessary saving grace.

On leaving university, he worked in broadcasting, first in radio and then in television. But TV was too stressful and his time there coincided with his first heart valve replacement.

Typically, he confronted the event with bravura that masked fear. Open-heart surgery wasn't something most men in their twenties had to contemplate. Afterwards, when kids in the public swimming pool marvelled at the thick red scar that ran down his chest, he would impress them – and intimidate them a little – by explaining he was a bionic man, with just one little piece of clicking plastic keeping him alive.

Like tuberculars in the nineteenth century, the closeness of death made Michael more alive than other people. Each experience was so vivid, every encounter so vital. When the plastic valve started to fail and another operation was needed, he wasn't so afraid because he knew the drill. For friends, sitting by his hospital bed being regaled with tales of the long-fingered, Porsche-loving heart surgeon Magdi Yacoub was one of the best social scenes in town. But it was becoming clear that, as far as marriage and a family went, Michael wasn't a great proposition. However much women might find him charismatic, attentive and insightful, he was a bad bet. By the third operation, his girlfriend of nine years' standing, Leslie, decided it was time to move on. She took him to tea to explain that, however much she might love him, she had a long life to consider. Walking back to work after their conversation, he thought about the different ways a heart can fail.

But a few years later, back in radio, he fell in love with a colleague, was married and for a time had everything he had ever dreamed of: a good marriage, a stimulating job that earned him respect and the company of writers, artists and musicians who all enjoyed his courage and his wit. He began to think of starting a family, but then became ill again. This time he would need a heart transplant but, before it could be arranged, Michael died at the age of thirty-eight.

Was I wilfully blind when I married Michael? Of course I was. I knew about his heart condition – everyone did. But

I fell in love with him and decided it didn't matter. We were going to live for ever, somehow. Now I know that the fact that we had the same initials, were both expatriates, had gone to the same university and were of medium build made the relationship highly determined. But I might have done the research and discovered his short life expectancy or talked to psychologists about the pain of grieving or read books about the sadness of widowhood. But I didn't do any of those things. I looked away from those sad certainties and pretended that they weren't there.

Love is blind, not, as in mythology, because Cupid's arrows are random but because, once struck by them, we are left blind. When we love someone, we see them as smarter, wittier, prettier, stronger than anyone else sees them. To us, a beloved parent, partner or child has endlessly more talent, potential and virtue than mere strangers can ever discern. Being loved, when we are born, keeps us alive; without a mother's love for her child, how could any new mother manage or any child survive? And if we grow up surrounded by love, we feel secure in the knowledge that others believe in us, will champion and defend us. That confidence – that we are loved and therefore lovable – is an essential building block of our identity and self-confidence. We believe in ourselves, at least in part, because others believe in us and we depend mightily on their belief.

As human beings, we are highly driven to find and to protect the relationships that make us feel good about ourselves and that make us feel safe. That's why we marry people like us, live in neighbourhoods full of people like us and work with people like us: each one of those mirrors confirms our sense of self-worth. Love does the same thing but with infinitely more passion and drive. We think well of ourselves because we are loved and we will fight fiercely to protect the key relationships on which our esteem depends. And that seems to be just as true even if our love is based on illusion. Indeed, there seems to be some evidence, not only that all love is based on illusion – but that love positively requires illusion in order to endure.

When psychologists studied young dating couples, they analysed each partner's view of their beloved, and then compared that with the beloved's own view of him- or herself. What they found was not only that there was a big disconnect – the lover thought better of her beloved than he did of himself – but the relationships were more likely to persist where that idealisation occurred. Individuals were more satisfied in their relationships when they saw virtues in their partners that their partners did not see in themselves. In other words, idealising the loved one helped the relationship endure.[1]

The beneficial effect of these positive illusions went even further. When you love someone, they may even start to adapt to your illusion of them. So there is a kind of virtuous circle: you think better of your beloved, who starts to live up to your illusions and so you love them more. It sounds a little like a fairy tale but kissing frogs may really make them act like princes or princesses. It is indeed a kind of magic: illusions transforming reality. We don't have to love people for who they are but for who we think they are, or need them to be.

So I married a man whom I did not think of as an invalid, and one reason we were happy together was because we lived as though there was nothing wrong with him. This was a benign blindness, without which the relationship stood no chance. And even when it isn't a matter of life and death, this is something everyone does: overlooks the flaws, discounts the disappointments, focuses on what works. Our love for each other allows us, even compels us, to see the best in each other.

This doesn't mean we don't have doubts; of course we do. But such doubts tend to surface only after we have already invested a great deal in a relationship. And that investment – although it is very cold-blooded to call it that – is like our other investments: as the behavioural economists Kahneman and Tversky found, losses loom very much larger than corresponding gains.[2] What that means when you apply it to love life (instead of the stock market) is that when a relationship starts to sour, our fear of losing it may far outweigh any hopes we might cherish of freedom and release. If things go wrong in a relationship, we hang on, trying hard to adapt, or we try to trivialise our worries. We find excuses (he's had a horrible day, or a horrible childhood), we weave alternative interpretations (she didn't really mean it, I must have misunderstood) or we may just minimise the disappointment (it's not a big birthday). We use considerable ingenuity to sustain our illusions, blind ourselves to inconvenient or painful facts. We protect our life with our illusions.

Because our identity and security depend so much on our loved ones, we don't want to see anything that threatens them. So, most of the time that I was married to Michael, I didn't think about his frailty or his heart. We went on walking trips and swam a great deal. I might rationalise that, in keeping him fit, I was keeping him healthy, and perhaps I was. But I was also acting as though my husband were just as strong and fit as anyone else my age. I had to believe that.

Mine was perhaps an extreme case of love masking all physical realities. But even the most educated and logical can be amazed by how little impact rational understanding makes when love is involved.

'I remember my mother calling me up and explaining about the pains she was having in her arm and her stomach that had lasted about twenty minutes,' Dick told me one evening. Dick is a highly experienced, level-headed physician not known for pulling his punches. Like many doctors, he loves the intellectual puzzle of diagnosis and isn't easily second-guessed. 'And she said to me perhaps it was something she ate. And I said, instantly, yes, it must have been something you ate. And I put the phone down.'

As he tells this story, Dick's wife, Lindsey, looks on, bemused. She is also a doctor, but it isn't her parents we're talking about.

'So I hung up the phone and told Lindsey about the conversation and she looks at me and says, "No, it isn't what she ate. She's having a heart attack." And of course she was right! So I was straight back on the phone to her.'

Dick tells his story with wry amusement that he could have got something so simple so wrong. But of course that is why physicians aren't supposed to treat family members – because love blinds them to the realities of the case. This doesn't, unfortunately, stop family members from asking for advice and even, on occasion, free care. And it has proved impossible for professional organisations to prevent doctors treating their own families. The dangers are twofold: either a tendency to underplay the problem (I love you and can't bear for you to be ill) or to overplay the problem (I couldn't bear to lose you so will treat the tiniest symptom). Every doctor I've met has experienced one of those responses; they know they can't do a proper diagnosis and they also know that that isn't a reflection of their clinical expertise.

Our identity depends critically on the people we love, and a central function of family life is to preserve our positive illusions about one another. That is what families are for. The fictional poster child for love blindness in families must be Carmela Soprano, who hovers between knowing and not knowing that her husband is a murderous, adulterous gangster. How can she acknowledge the truth? It would destroy everything she loves: her family, her home, her children, her sense of herself as a good person. For the children, Meadow and Anthony Jr, facing facts is easier; they did not choose their father and don't feel their identity wholly depends on his. But Carmela chose Tony, so for her the cost of facing what she has condoned is too high: not just Catholic guilt but responsibility for 'terrible acts' that she cannot bring herself to imagine. She so desperately wants Tony to be a good father, for her family to be the archetypal American happy family, that most of her physical and psychic energy is devoted to maintaining the illusions that make her life worth living. She is blind to Tony's criminal activity because she has to be.

Carmela's dilemma is extreme but it is also something everyone can relate to; that's why it's great television. So many couples find themselves in predicaments where they fear something bad is happening but prefer not to know. Like Carmela, it feels easier to turn a blind eye and act as if everything is normal. In this respect, fiction is not so different from fact. Although far from the glamorous and affluent wife that Carmela struggles to represent, Primrose Shipman appears, by all accounts, to have denied that her husband Harold was the worst serial killer in British criminal history. She has always maintained his innocence, despite the overwhelming evidence that found him guilty. At the inquiry that followed her husband's conviction, she answered 'I don't know' over a hundred times. Yet no one thought she was being disingenuous. Dame Janet Smith, who chaired the inquiry, described Primrose as 'honest and straightforward'. She had been present at, or immediately after, the death of three of Shipman's patients and had stood by one – Irene Chapman – while her husband went to see another patient. Yet all indications are that she did not see what was going on.

While neighbours were surprised and disgusted by her loyalty, other observers were not. The only psychiatrist to have interviewed Shipman, Dr Richard Badcock, described his tremendous need for control and in his wife he had found a perfectly subservient subject. Primrose Shipman was, after all, entirely dependent on her husband. Cut off by her parents when she became pregnant by Shipman at the age of seventeen, the hasty wedding was the last time she ever saw her father; her mother did not even attend. Barely literate, she earned a little money as a childminder and running a sandwich shop, but, with four children to look after, she was emotionally and financially dependent on Shipman. There's no evidence she had close friendships or other relationships that could have given her the sense of role and place that her marriage, however abusive, provided. At no point in her life does she appear to have had the strength or the independence to be able to see what was happening in front of her eyes.

Most of us will never have to deal with the scale of denial Primrose Shipman needed to survive. The secret we are more likely to uncover is infidelity. Although rates of couples having affairs are notoriously difficult to pin down (for obvious reasons) estimates run between 30 and 60 per cent of marriages.[3] At the time of divorce, 24 per cent of divorces cite infidelity as a proven fact.

'In couples when someone is having an affair, nobody really wants to know,' says Emily Brown. Brown is a marriage therapist whose deep knowledge and study of marital infidelity doesn't seem to have damaged her optimism. In her mid-fifties, she dresses in warm but vibrant colours. In an office crammed with books and artwork, only a pottery jar labelled 'Cognitive Overload' hints that sometimes knowledge can be a burden.

In her professional practice, Brown works with couples

and individuals whose marriages are threatened by affairs. By the time her clients come to her, the affair has usually been discovered and part of what she sees is the rage that betrayed spouses feel at not having noticed what was going on.

'They may have had their suspicions,' says Brown. 'But even in marriages where one spouse has suspicions, how can you ask and have things remain the same? If the other partner is not having an affair, you've created doubt and hostility. If the other partner is having an affair and denies it, now he or she has been rumbled. If the other partner is having an affair and admits it, everything starts to fall apart. So there is no way to ask and have things remain the same.'

That state – of knowing and not knowing – is extremely painful and can last for months or for years. The sheer routine of daily life makes blindness easier, less dramatic, less traumatic.

'So I see people thinking: I should ask. I won't ask. It's self-protection. Many of my clients have grown up in families where no one ever talked about risky topics – there's plenty of polite conversation but nothing meaningful – so they don't know how to have the conversation in the first place. But then they think: if we're talking about it that means it could be real. So they try to make it disappear by not saying anything.'

In Brown's experience, the blindness is on both sides: the unfaithful spouse is blind to the possibility of being found out, refusing to see what the consequences might be and preferring to maintain the illusion that no one will get hurt. This isn't stupidity; it's a genuine desire that the affair and the family can peacefully co-exist. And on the other side, the betrayed spouse resolutely refuses to connect the dots because, as long as they're just dots, nothing is happening, nothing has to change, and love remains.

'I had one case,' Brown recalled, 'where the husband had

had an affair and his wife hadn't guessed. And his wife had got a sexually transmitted disease and had gone to the doctor about it. When she told her husband, he just brushed it off, saying, "You must have got that when you were camping with the kids." So she thought no more about it.

'Ten years later, she's at the hairdresser's and she's reading a magazine article about STDs and she figures it out! And only then did she confront her husband. Now, in that case, there was a double blindness: he was blind to being caught and she was blind to what was going on.'

Most people, according to Brown, do intuit that something is amiss. One reason these marriages are so hard to repair is that the betrayed spouse feels so angry, not just with their partner but with themselves; they feel like they are watching a jigsaw puzzle self-assemble: all the pieces snap together, creating a hideous picture that no one wants to see. Self-esteem, that precious self-worth that has been fed by the illusions that sustain love, is destroyed as the truth emerges.

That we will fight so hard to protect our self-esteem is a universal. It doesn't matter how successful or wealthy people are. They all need to feel that they're good people, even – or especially – when they're bad.

'I knew my actions were wrong but I convinced myself normal rules didn't apply. I thought I could get away with whatever I wanted to.' Even Tiger Woods was wilfully blind when it came to his own marriage.[4]

'Success confers its own blindness,' says Brown. 'Successful people believe they can get away with it. I talked once to a group of men who'd all become millionaires before the age of forty and who'd had affairs. They don't even see the danger! It isn't a love of risk. They think: the wives will never know, so where's the harm? Everything else in their lives has worked out, so they think they have some kind of magic, that their success has meant that they can have everything they want and they're invulnerable. And they were completely blind to the harm that they had done. They just couldn't conceive that, as good men, they'd done something bad.'

Talking with Brown, she feels like a veteran, her consulting room a battlefield where wives and husbands have waged titanic battles to preserve their self-respect. Blindness helps them do that, she says. And where children are involved, adulterous spouses can be especially blind. They convince themselves that kids, of any age, know nothing, notice nothing, that just by dint of being children they couldn't have any insight into the lives of grown-ups. It's a comforting fallacy often bolstered by the kids themselves, who say nothing because they are trying so hard to keep the family together. Everyone colludes in the collective fantasy that the family is fine.

'One couple I've worked with, they're semi-separated,' Brown recalls. 'They had a lot of fights in front of their kids and the husband moved out into an apartment that was above the garage. And they got together for one of the kids' birthdays. But both the husband and the wife said they thought the kids didn't suspect a thing. Well, their kids are thirteen and ten and Dad isn't living at home any more . . .'

Talking to Brown, it's clear that this kind of blindness is so common that it no longer surprises her. But she also thinks that the blindness that accompanies affairs often started very much earlier. One of the many downsides of living in communities where we are always surrounded by people like ourselves is that we experience very little conflict. That means we don't develop the tools we need to manage it and we lack confidence in our ability to do so. We persuade ourselves that the absence of conflict is the same as happiness, but that trade-off leaves us strangely powerless.

'In many cases, affairs start because people are conflict-averse or intimacy-averse. People stay away from stuff that needs to be dealt with; they think that they mustn't ever say anything negative – they don't know how to articulate criticism or doubts in a way that won't feel like an attack. So then when they finally articulate their discomfort, via the affair, it does come out as an attack and provokes more attacks. A lot of this derives from not dealing with emotions, not understanding one's own feelings. It feels easier to be blind than to deal with uncomfortable feelings.' Running throughout Brown's conversation, and the experience she's had in her practice, is a belief that we become blind because we are so afraid of what we might see and what we might feel. Our identity and sense of self-worth depend on the people we love, to the extent that we cling to them even though they do us harm.

'We want our parents to love us and one way to do that is to be what they want us to be,' recalled Louise Miller.

Miller was a client of Brown's, coming to her for advice and therapy after years of an abusive marriage in which she had worked hard not to notice what was going on around her. Miller was so eager to please the people she loved, she says, that she never really dared to question anything.

'I got married in my early twenties – I really didn't want to but I thought that was what you do. I was dating, I was the right age to get married, I got married. Then, in my thirties, I had kids and I thought: I'll have this perfect life according to my parents' thinking. I had a beautiful huge home with a big garden in a nice neighbourhood and I thought: now I will have my nice life. I didn't see *me* until I was forty. All those years I was trying to do what my parents wanted, what my husband wanted. I thought, if they were happy, I'd be happy. But I was just blind to myself!'

So anxious was Louise to secure the approval and love of

her parents and her husband, by sticking to her 'cookie cutter' idea of what happiness and family life should look like, that she was too scared to ask any serious questions about what was happening around her.

'When I was growing up, there was never any alcohol in the house – not even for cooking. So when I met my husband, I had no way of knowing he was an alcoholic. I met him in university, and when he was a little wild, I just thought that was party behaviour and he'd grow out of it. But he never did. And I'd complain but he couldn't stop. Then one day his father said to me, "Do you know you're married to an alcoholic?" I was in my forties! How can you be in a relationship with an alcoholic and never even see it?'

In a desperate attempt to break free from everyone else's expectations for her, Louise had an affair with a colleague at work.

'I never thought anything would happen. I became very depressed and guilty and one night I told my husband. I thought that, once I told him, we could reconnect and fall in love again! And that's when we went to see Emily. And I really hoped she would know the end of the story and everything would be all right. It took me a long time to see that I had choices. And that it was my life.'

As Louise tells me her story, it feels as though layers upon layers of blinders are being removed, one at a time – the love for her parents, the love she had for her husband, the love she has for her children. She had struggled so hard to cling on to these because for years she simply did not believe that she was anybody without them. Emily says how amazed she is at how far Louise has come. But her journey is one she could never have made without daring to confront the truth about herself and her marriage.

Tales of marital blindness are legion, the stuff of high drama and low comedy alike. From Othello to Pierre Bezukhov to *Mad Men*'s Betty Draper, we can identify with characters who won't see the truth, because they let us explore our deepest fears, that we might be wrong about each other or wrong about ourselves. We laugh with relief because it isn't us, and we weep because it so easily could be.

Nowhere is that drama more intense or more threatening than in families damaged by child abuse. Although we are all so conscious of 'stranger danger' and go to great lengths to ensure that our children keep well away from anyone unknown or suspicious, it remains the case that most child abuse occurs within families or involves perpetrators known to the children. According to the NSPCC, fully 16 per cent of children experience sexual abuse before they reach sixteen years old. With numbers like those, you have to wonder: how can it be that, within such a small unit as a family, abuse goes unnoticed?

'In the majority of cases of child abuse, it is family members or friends who are responsible,' says Chris Cloke, head of Child Protection Awareness for the NSPCC. 'It's often very hard to see because there's often a great deal of love – for the family, for the child – which just doesn't want to acknowledge what's going on. Lots of people don't even want to acknowledge that child abuse exists at all – and they'd far prefer to think of stranger danger than of the fact that it mostly occurs within families.'

One of the many people on the front line at the NSPCC is Felicity Wilkinson, who runs the charity's helpline. 'You often find a situation where a mum is in a relationship with a man who is abusing her kids. That is someone she is in love with and the last thing she wants to think about is that they would do that kind of thing. It can take a long time for it to sink in, even where there are certain signs.

'One case that springs to mind is a woman who was saying that she was aware her partner had a conviction from the past for sex abuse. She was trying to convince herself that that didn't matter now because it had all happened such a long time ago, so he must have changed. She was really calling to ask for confirmation – hoping against hope that I would say it was so long ago that she need not worry. She was in love with this man and he was doing a lot for her and looking after her kids. She just didn't want to think that her kids were at risk.'

Wasn't it hard, I asked Felicity, for parents to acknowledge that there might be danger in their own family?

'It is always hard. So hard. When I worked as a social worker for a local authority, the parents always struggled with this. And it was very hard for the parents to acknowledge that their own behaviour might contribute to the problem. They loved their kids and hoped that that was enough. And it's also hard because if they give us, at the NSPCC, information that indicates the child truly is at risk, we are obliged to contact children's services. So they don't want to acknowledge what is going on – and they're afraid to start that whole process.'

'It isn't necessarily that they are unconscious,' says Eliana Gil, 'but that they are unable or unwilling to face up to what is happening.'

Dr Gil works for one of the largest child welfare services in the United States, Childhelp. She has had years of experience watching families make the painful transition from being blind to finally seeing what they so much did not want to see. And she says that there is a pattern to the revelation.

'The way I think about it is this: it is as if someone has been invited to attend something. They turn up, the door is opened and they see it is a surprise birthday party for them. In that moment of shock, they suddenly understand – that's why there was a ribbon on the bed this morning and that's why my brother cancelled dinner tonight and that's why Jane's been acting so strangely. Suddenly all these little pieces of information, which have been stored in memory without meaning, get retrieved in context and have a whole new meaning.

'That is my experience with the mothers. When someone says your child has been abused by the father – suddenly they remember: that's why I found her walking around the room at night and that's why her clothes were in my bedroom . . . All those details, stored without meaning, suddenly acquire meaning.'[5]

Dr Gil works primarily with children who have been abused and their mothers. It is, she says, all too common for mothers to have been aware and yet not aware of what was going on in their own homes.

'That kind of response – of seeing and not seeing – helps to explain how these things go on for such a long time. It doesn't explain why the abuse itself happens in the first place, of course. But it does explain how it can continue for such a long time inside the family. If you maintain an illusion, you don't have to make the hard choices. Life just goes on. But if you accept reality, it forces a huge decision and many people want to avoid that.' According to Dr Gil, it is often several fears together that conspire to keep unwanted knowledge from their minds. If the abusing father is the major breadwinner, fear of losing support and income may suppress knowledge. Fear of shame and social exclusion are powerful forces, too. But underlying all of these threats is a more existential fear, a sense that acknowledging the abuse would destroy everything.

'It's just too dangerous to acknowledge the idea – it's the last thing anyone wants to imagine. Mothers feel that just to ask the question is to question their own reality. And especially mothers who themselves come from unhappy families. They are so idealistic that they want to shield the child. In putting together that illusion and protecting it, they just cannot break through the barrier to explore the possibility that something is wrong.'

The happy family, the happy children are so critical to the mother's sense of her own identity and worth that her doubts have to be quashed.

'For many of the mothers I've worked with, their identity is so tied into the role of being a good mother, or a good wife, that they have very little sense of self. Putting on an identity like a coat becomes very important to them. And they cannot take that coat off; it would leave them too vulnerable. It is like they've invested themselves in this role and they simply cannot afford to challenge their illusion. It is such an invested process. So when it turns out that it was an illusion, they often feel that they have absolutely nothing left.'

For someone navigating such painful issues, Dr Gil is remarkably positive, determined that, out of this family wreckage, real gains can come – but only by recognising what has occurred. She's a passionate believer that, if wilful blindness perpetuates abuse, it is only facing facts that can end it.

'I've been working with a woman who has four children. Her husband was arrested for having a lot of child pornography on his computer and I started working with the mother, and her kids, because they were just in shock when this happened. And at first, the kids seemed okay except that they'd been photographed by him in rather unusual poses.

'As I started working with the mother, helping her to learn how to get along without her husband, other things started to surface. The couple had had no sex for two years, and she thought that was odd but then she figured they were older, maybe it was not a big deal. Then she realised he did have a special relationship with their ten-year-old little girl. And a little part of her was happy for the child – that he had such a strong attachment – but she also started wondering. "I wondered if I should have been concerned" – that was just how she phrased it. "I wondered if I should have been concerned."'

After working with the mother and her children for about nine months, Dr Gil became concerned that the ten-year-old had behaviours compatible with a child who has been abused. So she asked the mother about that.

'And she says, "Well, I guess there was one time I walked in and they were in bed together cuddling and I could see he had an erection." So I asked her if she had talked to him about it and all she said was, "I mentioned it and he denied it so I thought I must have been seeing things."'

For all her experience, even Dr Gil was amazed that so much could have happened and not been seen. Over the next few months, Dr Gil was impressed as the mother gradually developed the courage to put the picture together.

'Gradually things are becoming more clear in her mind but at the time they were just too threatening to consider. Now her eyes are brighter and it is like she has a new sense of herself. But at the time, she couldn't compromise her sense of identity because she couldn't see possibilities for herself. Her daughter paid the price for that, because her mother couldn't see what was in front of her face.'

This is the true cost of blindness: as long as it feels safer to do and say nothing, as long as keeping the peace feels more benign, abuse can continue. Our desire to protect our self-worth can result in others paying a very high price.

Emerging brain science lends a physical reality to the emotional turmoil experienced by the victims of romantic and maternal love alike. A team of neuroscientists at the University of London have spent years studying brain activity in romantic couples and in mothers. They knew that love itself has an evolutionary advantage; we fall in love, mate and look after our children because that is how the species perpetuates itself. But the neuroscientists wanted to understand which areas of the brain are active in response to love and which areas are not.

They found, not so surprisingly, that love activates those areas of the brain associated with reward; the cells that respond to food, drink, money or cocaine respond to love too. That's why it feels so good, to love and to be loved. Moreover, there appears to be some evidence that love may even reduce our fear of death.[6] While it would be inaccurate to conclude that we are addicted to love, it is the case that we need it.[7]

Even more illuminating than the areas activated by love were the areas of the brain that were deactivated. As volunteers lay in fMRI scanners, thinking of their children or their partners, two particular parts of their brains were not engaged. The first was the area responsible for attention, memory and negative emotions; the second was associated with negative emotions and social judgement, the ability to distinguish other people's feelings and intentions. In other words, the chemical processes of our brain that are stimulated by love disable much of our critical thinking about the loved one. Our illusions persist because our brains don't challenge them. Like much neuroscience, this gives a concrete reality to what the poets have always known: love does not judge.

The neuroscience is a helpful reminder that blind love isn't stupidity or ignorance. It is a physical reality of a kind that doesn't distinguish between rich and poor, educated or otherwise. We develop and protect illusions around the people we love because we are made to do so, because we feel our very lives depend on it. What is impressive, though, is that when men and women who have suffered in abusive, unhappy relationships successfully overcome their blindness, and insist on facing the truth, they have surmounted very real, very daunting obstacles.

Such obstacles are even more formidable when they are reinforced by institutional, social and political support. That is what happened in the child-abuse scandals that have ripped through sports organisations around the world. When Larry Nassar was sentenced to forty to 175 years in prison for abusing young American gymnasts, many expressed bewilderment that he could have perpetrated his crimes for so long. How could the girls' parents not have known what was happening, sometimes right in front of them? But Nassar was a hero, ostensibly the gateway to fame and glory, a leader in a competitive sport in a culture that prizes winning highly. The man who promises success to a beloved child: who would wish to question him?

That child abuse has been found endemic in organisations that so loudly espouse virtue and health – not just sports clubs but charities and churches in England, Ireland, Canada, Austria, Australia and the United States – testifies to the insidious power of wilful blindness. Love of tradition, love of parents, love of church all conspired to keep whole communities blind to what they somehow always knew.

'For so long, everyone pretended these things weren't happening. So sad. So ridiculous. If we acknowledge these things, we can address them. But for years, everyone knew. And no one knew. You just couldn't say anything.'

Colm O'Gorman runs Amnesty International in Ireland. He's a powerful force in the land these days, well known and highly respected, organised, efficient and bold. But he wasn't always that way. In the 1970s, growing up in Wexford, he was regularly abused for two and a half years by a local priest, Sean Fortune. O'Gorman was trapped, between his love for his father, his love for his mother and their love of the Church. At the time, he was just a child, with a very fragile sense of identity. When Fortune threatened to tell O'Gorman's father what had happened, the one thing O'Gorman knew was that that could not be allowed to happen.

'Panic raced through me and the world started to spin. I wanted to escape, jump from the car, anything to get away from that awful moment. Anything to prevent what he said he might do. My father . . . it would kill him to know what I'd done, what I was. He would die of shame . . . I knew I could not stay alive if everyone knew, especially if my father knew.'[8]

O'Gorman felt that everything his life depended on would be destroyed if anyone knew what was being done to him. So he kept silent while the abuse continued and for years afterwards. His experience, tragically, was far from unique. The 2005 Ferns Inquiry unearthed one hundred complaints against twenty-one priests in O'Gorman's diocese alone. A year later, the Murphy Report began examining the history of forty-six priests, picked from a sample of 102 against whom complaints had been lodged. Investigations into just those forty-six priests produced allegations from more than 320 children. 'One priest admitted to sexually abusing over 100 children, while another accepted that he had abused on a fortnightly basis during his ministry which lasted for over 25 years,' the report said. 'The total number of documented complaints recorded against those two priests is only just over 70.' Released in 2009, the report found that 'maintenance of secrecy, the avoidance of scandal, the protection of the reputation of the church and the preservation of its assets' were more important than justice for the victims. The report concluded that the vast majority of priests turned a 'blind eye' to abuse, and strongly criticised the Garda – Irish police – for regarding priests as outside their remit; the relationship between Church and police was deemed 'inappropriate'. And that was just in Dublin.

At this level, nothing can quite be a secret. It was,

O'Gorman says, the scandal that everyone knew about but no one would admit. In his own village, people talked about the priests who should be avoided when you were on your own, the ones you shouldn't go to the graveyard with. Likewise, the Garda would, informally, mention that perhaps certain priests shouldn't be left too long with children. Widespread knowledge and widespread blindness co-existed; as O'Gorman puts it, 'They'd tell you but they hadn't told you.' Everyone knew but didn't know.

Eventually, O'Gorman left home and wandered, frequently unemployed and homeless, through the streets of Dublin and London, an outcast who belonged nowhere. It was only many years later that he had the confidence he needed to acknowledge what had been done to him. When he finally confided in his parents, they did not reject him and his life could begin again. He brought a lawsuit against Sean Fortune and he established a helpline for victims of child abuse.

'What silences the child,' says O'Gorman, 'is the fear that the family will be broken up. Family is the only source of love and security that the kid knows. How can he hurt his parents, whom he loves and might also fear? What would he have left? I couldn't prevent what was happening to me and I couldn't escape it, so I just refused to allow it to be true. I would just look at a spot on the ceiling and split myself off from what was happening. In that place, denial kept me sane. I didn't go mad. Finding the spot on the wall meant I wasn't in the room.'

The fact that O'Gorman's wasn't a solitary case, and that abuse was so pervasive, meant that it wasn't only O'Gorman's family that was threatened. Ireland at the time was a highly theocratic culture. The Church ran most of the major institutions and was largely left to do so by the government. Any attack on the Church, therefore, challenged its dominance, threatened its role in the social and political life of the nation.

To dare to question the moral authority of the most powerful institution in the land might make anyone hesitate.

'If one has a strong sense of connection with the Church, then the destruction of that is terrifying,' says O'Gorman. 'It really is unthinkable. Unthinkable. It is a loss of security. It makes you wonder whether any security is real. Suddenly everything is at risk. My acceptability within my institution and by God is because I am acceptable to the faith. If I name all that, accuse all that, do I lose my connection with God? Never mind the power of the institution . . .'

The blind intransigence of the institution has stunned even some of its most faithful adherents. The Pope's envoy to Ireland refused to testify before Irish lawmakers, while none of the bishops who failed to report paedophile priests has been fired. O'Gorman was appropriately daunted.

'Ireland was a country in denial,' says O'Gorman. 'If a whole society is in denial, you are really in trouble – because you believe your survival depends on turning a blind eye to the truth. So the thing that we feared most as a society – that our sense of self would come crashing down – that turned out to be valid.

'But what we didn't question at the time was whether that might be a good thing. We had had a sense of ourselves as a good pure Catholic society, where good exists and always wears a collar. But when we finally understood the cost of that illusion, then we had to let it go. The cost was just so high, the damage so great.'

Sean Fortune, O'Gorman's abuser, committed suicide before his trial concluded. Other priests and bishops retired or disappeared. The Church itself, when it learned of the scale of the abuse, did nothing to protect the victims but moved quickly to protect its assets, taking out insurance policies against the cost of future lawsuits. But some clergy felt let down by their own hierarchy, which left them ignorant and inexperienced in dealing with these cases.

'I knew of the existence of child abuse certainly, but less about recidivism in the offender and the long-term effects in the life of the victim,' one churchman confided to me.

Not surprisingly, he insisted on remaining anonymous. Sitting in the lobby of an elegant Dublin hotel, he would, years ago, have been the centre of attention, a man of power, accustomed to deference. Now our conversation was muted, his presence shrunken, almost furtive. He described to me how rumours would reach him but he never quite knew what to do about them.

'What I still find quite remarkable and almost unbelievable twenty years later is that not a single person among the legal, medical and counselling professions whom I consulted on innumerable occasions advised me either to report an offence to the Gardai or to remove a priest from ministry, except for a very short period of time,' he said. 'I knew that this problem had surfaced in the USA and was being dealt with by numerous US bishops, but their approach offered no great insights into the problem. In fact, they seem to have made all the mistakes that we in Ireland were to make about a decade later. On the home front, we showed a marked reluctance to discuss the problem, hoping, I suppose, that if we didn't discuss it, it would go away.'

That hope – if we don't talk about it, it will go away – persisted for decades. And the Church and police together colluded in keeping it that way. In the end, it was not the Church but the courage of victims like O'Gorman that finally brought priests into court and the clergy's disgrace out into the open. That was the moment when many priests might have sided with the abused, but instead most of them just slunk away. If the problem would not disappear, they would.

Moreover, the Church has continued to protect the identity of abusing clergy, which means they can't and won't be brought to trial. Around the world, the story has repeated itself. It is as though the Church, having been so determinedly blind, wishes to remain so, and would prefer that believers did too. For O'Gorman, this has been their ultimate failure: not to have sided with the truth once it was out there.

'For fear of the worst of ourselves, what we do or people close to us do or institutions do, is we deny the best of ourselves which is our capacity to respond,' O'Gorman says. 'We make ourselves powerless by pretending we don't know.'

As O'Gorman and I discussed the profound impact the scandals have had on the whole of Irish social and political life, I was struck by the sympathy and breadth of his argument. He seemed to be arguing that while the greatest harm was that done to children by priests, further harm still was caused by the Church's moral failure to support their victims. The crisis offered an opportunity for the Church, and its priests, to dig deep and find the best in themselves. But they lacked the vision and courage to do so. Today, the Church has lost the commanding role it once enjoyed across Irish society; people attend mass more out of nostalgia for an ancient ritual than out of faith or respect. A third of the Irish population say they have no trust 'at all' in the Church; the police, the supermarkets and the media enjoy higher levels of public confidence.[9] When I contrast my conversation with O'Gorman and my earlier one with the priest, it is O'Gorman who, despite years of suffering, confusion, poverty and personal vilification, has led the richer life. The priest enjoyed comfort and respect but today is left still embroiled in a battle, between himself and the truth, trying to decide which gets the upper hand.

Some critics might dispute this interpretation, saying the

priest just doesn't care, that his apologies and explanations are just an easy way of making sure he gets to live as he's always lived, without having to change. That is certainly what many said of Albert Speer, Hitler's chief architect and, after 1942, the second most powerful man in the Reich. One of the few of the Nazi elite not to be hanged following the Nuremberg trials, he was outspoken about the criminality of Hitler's regime and determined to accept responsibility for what he had done as a member of the government. In some ways, that decision was Speer's simplest; he believed in collective responsibility. But the hard part for Speer was seeing what it was that he took responsibility for.

'Speer didn't see anything he didn't want to see,' says Gitta Sereny, Speer's biographer. 'I think he would have liked to have that capacity, but he just didn't. Speer was in fact a highly talented man, highly intelligent, but studied obliviousness was his defence. And the defence was there because he somehow knew there was something wrong.'[10]

Sereny saw Speer at Nuremberg but she got to know him when, in 1978, she began a conversation with him – almost an interrogation – that would continue right up until his death in 1981. In her book, *Albert Speer: His Battle with Truth*, she meticulously chronicles Speer's tortuous negotiation with himself, and then with her, as he tries to see, but also wriggle out of seeing, the full horror of what he did as a Nazi. Sereny's is a masterful confrontation, obsessive about detail, challenging Speer's facts and constantly blocking ethical escape routes. What makes their duel so dramatic is that Speer is even more desperate to know the truth than Sereny; she wants to know but he needs to know. The obstacle they both wrestle with is his lifetime of abnegation and blindness. That blindness, according to Sereny, was profoundly motivated by Speer's love for Hitler.

'In the early years, Speer is very hung up on Hitler – and in a very personal way,' she said. 'It's something quite apart from politics. It is more of a father–son feeling. Speer found that difficult to give up; he depended on it. He needed it to feel whole.'[11]

Indeed, when Speer described to Sereny his first meeting with Hitler in 1933, his account comes dangerously close to the purple prose of romantic fiction.

'Can you imagine this,' said Speer. 'Here I was, young, unknown and totally unimportant, and this great man, for whose attention – just for one glance – our whole world competed, said to me, "Come and have lunch." I thought I'd faint.'

Because Speer, an architect, had visited a building site prior to his meeting with Hitler, his jacket was dusty and Hitler loaned him one of his own.

'Can you conceive what I felt?' Speer asked again. 'Here I was, twenty-eight years old, totally insignificant in my own eyes, sitting next to him at lunch, wearing his clothes and elected – at least that day – as virtually his sole conversation partner. I was dizzy with excitement.'[12]

It isn't only Hitler's power that so bedazzled Speer. Hitler saw in the young, mediocre architect far more than Speer saw in himself. Given tremendous commissions for the new Reich, it was clear that Hitler believed him to be talented, important and artistic – all those things Speer longed to be and that his own parents had signally failed to see in him. Hitler, as Speer said later, became his life.[13]

'He saw himself as Hitler's son,' said Sereny. 'All his chances, his opportunities came to him through Hitler. He liked Hitler and he loved Hitler – and it was reciprocated. Hitler really loved Speer and Speer grew to love Hitler.'[14]

Speer's reciprocated love for Hitler, and the political climate around the Führer, was for Speer a deadly combination.

With his own identity so entirely dependent, nothing critical of Hitler could ever be allowed to impinge on Speer's consciousness. He saw pools of blood near one of his building sites. One of the architects in his practice resigned after Kristallnacht. But, says Speer, 'my mind was on other things.'[15] When the evacuation of Jews from Berlin began in 1941, Speer wrote about 'a feeling of unease, a foreboding of dark events', but Sereny challenged him, thinking him evasive. How, she wondered, could he be uneasy if he knew nothing?

'By that time,' Sereny wrote, 'I was very familiar with that sudden sharp look from under those thick black eyebrows when he sensed disbelief. It was not only his look which became both hooded and guarded; his voice on the whole invariably quiet could also suddenly change. "I was blind by choice," he said coldly, "but I was not ignorant."'

In 1942, when Speer was made Minister of Armaments and War Production, blindness and ignorance became increasingly difficult to preserve. Speer was no longer designing rallies and memorials for the thousand-year Reich; now he was in charge of arming Germany and ensuring that the war machine had the labour it needed. In appointing him to this position, Hitler had identified Speer's true genius, which was not as an architect but as a manager and administrator. But just as Speer discovered his true talents, they embroiled him in atrocities. Now he was spending more time with Hitler's inner circle, privy to conversations about the Jews.

'This is when I should have begun to realise what was happening,' Speer said. 'This was the point, I now think, when, had I *wanted* to, I could have detected hints.'

Sereny asked Speer what he would have done if he had known about the Final Solution.

'Don't you know that this is the question I have asked

myself a million times, continuously hoping that I would be able to give myself an answer I could live with?' He rested his head in his hands. 'My answer to myself is always the same,' he said, his voice dark and a little hoarse. 'I would somehow have gone on trying to help that man win his war.'

Speer's moral corruption, Sereny says, 'had its seed in his emotional attachment to Hitler – he likened it to Faust's fatal bargain with Mephistopheles. Achievement and success rooting it ever deeper over the years, he lived – almost addictively – in an increasingly vicious cycle of need and dependence.'[16]

He carefully avoided visiting any labour or concentration camps. His one visit – to Mauthausen – carefully protected him, and other visitors, from anything they might find shocking. But Speer's new role brought him closer and closer to the evil that his ministry perpetrated. In August 1943, he visited Dora, the underground labour camp deep in the Harz Mountains where Wernher von Braun's V-2 rockets were being produced. There, slave labourers worked eighteen hours a day with their bare hands, sleeping in tunnels they had hollowed out, over a thousand prisoners on four levels that stretched for a hundred yards. Without heat, ventilation or water to drink or wash with, the cold and filth and dysentery killed 30,000 men.

'I was entirely unprepared,' Speer told Sereny. 'It was the worst place I have ever seen ... I saw dead men ... they couldn't hide the truth. And those that were alive were skeletons.'[17]

Three months later, the regional Nazi Party leaders and paramilitaries (*Reichsleiter*) were assembled at Posen to learn about the Final Solution in order that they all be implicated. An unresolved debate still rages over whether Speer was still there for Himmler's speech about the extermination of the

Jews. Speer believed he had left before Himmler spoke, but both Sereny and Speer himself doubted his memory. But, whether or not he was actually present for Himmler's speech, he would undoubtedly have learned of its contents.

In January 1944, Speer was losing ground in power struggles with others in Hitler's circle. He also now had unavoidable knowledge of Hitler's genocidal programme. It was too much. Everything on which his identity depended was undermined. Speer's love of Hitler, and Speer's love for the Speer that Hitler had created, became untenable. Studied obliviousness failed and Speer had a breakdown. The bond between them had snapped. When he returned to work three months later, everything had changed.

'Meeting Hitler again was a shock. I stood up as he entered the room. He came up to me very quickly holding out his hand. But even as I stretched out mine, I had an extraordinary sense of unfamiliarity. Of course I hadn't seen him for almost ten weeks, but that wasn't it. It was his face: I looked at it and thought: "My God, how could I have not seen how ugly he is? This broad nose, this sallow skin. Who is this man?"'

The spell was broken. Speer could see the evidence of Hitler's criminality all around. He started secretly to ignore orders, to undermine command, to resist Hitler's scorched-earth plan. When he was arrested and tried, Speer accepted 'co-responsibility' – but not guilt. In prison and after his release, Speer waged a titanic battle with himself, not wanting to believe he was a bad man, but well aware he wasn't stupid either. Like a lover awakening from a dream, he could not quite make sense of what had happened or of what he had become.

'He had loved Hitler, he thought Hitler loved Germany and that was enough,' Sereny told me. 'But once he had seen that his ambitions were wrong, he couldn't feel the same way, about Hitler, about Germany, about himself. Speer's tragedy was that, after Posen and Dora, he really wanted to die. But his will to live was too strong. And so he really spent the rest of his life struggling, trying to become a different man.'

Sereny's account of Speer's life after the war describes an epic struggle between what Speer knew and what he must have known. That debate continues to this day, with some historians still sceptical of what they see as Speer's disingenuousness. Sereny, although she clearly liked Speer, is no apologist for him. She was impressed not by what he had done but by how hard he was finally prepared to work in order to see clearly. She is drawn to his battle because it is so intensely human.

'Not knowing, that's fine. Ignorance is easy. Knowing can be hard but at least it is real, it is the truth. The worst is when you don't want to know – because then it must be something very bad. Otherwise you wouldn't have so much difficulty knowing.' To some degree, Speer's post-war struggle with the truth was Germany's: the desire not to know, coupled with an awareness that confronting the truth was the only way to construct a meaningful future. While he still loved the image of himself that Hitler had constructed, Speer could not become a different man, just as, while it was still in love with the past, Germany could not become a different nation. The pain of that struggle is in all of us, particularly when we are in love and there are truths we don't want to acknowledge. You don't have to be a war criminal to have closets you would prefer not to open.

Nations, institutions, industries, individuals can all be blinded by love, by the need to believe themselves good and worthy and valued. We simply could not function if we believed ourselves to be otherwise. But when we are blind to the flaws and failings of what we love, we become impotent.

As Colm O'Gorman said, we make ourselves powerless when we pretend we don't know. That's the paradox of wilful blindness: we think it will make us safe even as it leaves us defenceless in the face of danger.

3. Dangerous Convictions

> I had to build in faith, against advice.
> That's the only way.
>
> *The Spire*, *William Golding*

It's as easy to fall in love with an idea as with a person. Big ideas are especially alluring. They bring order to the world, give meaning to life. When we join political parties or churches or governments, we find soulmates with the same worldview, the same values, and life feels complete. We may even talk of being 'wedded' to our ideas. Much of our identity is defined by what we believe and we actively seek confirmation of those beliefs. Actually, we go even further: our brain treats differently any information that might challenge our closely held beliefs.

In 2004, a team of cognitive neuroscientists set out to see what this process actually looks like. Drew Westen, at Emory University, was interested in what psychologists call 'motivated reasoning' and what Freud called defence mechanisms: the processes by which people adjust what they know to avoid bad feelings like anxiety and guilt. He theorised that the brain's neural networks would try to satisfy two kinds of constraints: cognitive constraints – we want to put information together in a way that feels rational – and emotional constraints, meaning we want to feel good about the information we take in.

To test his theories, Westen and his team recruited fifteen committed Democrats and fifteen committed Republicans to submit to fMRI scans of their brains while reading political material. As they lay in the scanner, they read pairs of quotes attributed either to President Bush or presidential candidate John Kerry. In each pair, one statement was entirely compatible with the candidate's position, but one statement was contradictory. What Westen wanted to find out was: would the brain treat the contradictions of the preferred candidate in the same way as it would treat the contradictions of a disliked candidate?

What the experiment found was that the partisan participants gave a far rougher ride to the contradictions that came from the candidate they opposed.

'They had no trouble seeing the contradictions for the opposition candidate,' Westen wrote. 'But when confronted with potentially troubling political information, a network of neurons becomes active that produces distress. Not only did the brain manage to shut down distress through faulty reasoning – but it did so quickly. The neural circuits charged with regulation of emotional states seemed to recruit beliefs that eliminated the distress and conflict.'[1]

But, said Westen, the brain didn't stop at eliminating the uncomfortable contradictions. It worked overtime 'to feel good, activating reward circuits that give partisans a jolt of positive reinforcement for their biased "reasoning".'[2]

In Westen's experiment, the reward circuits the brain was using were the same that are activated when a junkie gets a fix. In other words, when we find the thoughts we agree with, or are able to eliminate the ones that make us uncomfortable, we feel that same kind of euphoria and reassurance that addicts feel when reunited with their drug of choice: all is right with the world. At least for a while.

The brain doesn't like conflict and works hard to resolve it. This may be one reason why, when we gather with like-minded people, we are more likely to seek out common ground than areas of difference: quite literally, it feels better. But it also feels rational, even when it isn't. Which means that when we work hard to defend our core beliefs, we risk becoming blind to the evidence that could tell us we're wrong.

In 1942, Alice Stewart had come to Oxford to work as a resident physician at the Radcliffe Infirmary. She was, by all accounts, an outstanding doctor, the youngest woman at the time to enter the Royal College of Physicians. Her colleagues considered her to be a wonderful teacher and an outstanding diagnostician, full of boundless energy, with an appetite for big challenges and hard problems. Doctors were much needed during the war and the fact that, as a mother with two small children, she couldn't be called up for military service made her even more valuable, while her failing marriage meant she was willing and able to go wherever she was needed.

In Oxford, Stewart both treated patients and also led a number of research projects into problematic, puzzling disease patterns. One of them involved trying to figure out why munitions workers filling shells with TNT seemed so susceptible to jaundice and anaemia. In wartime, the factory was staffed by 'the ragtag of the population'[3] which posed the question: were they getting ill because they were vulnerable anyway, or was TNT the culprit? What originally started as a laboratory study soon became a field study: by persuading her healthy medical students to work in the plant and emulate the lives of the factory workers, Alice was able to prove that the diseases were not a consequence of the workers' weaker health but of their exposure to TNT. Subsequent projects – investigating high turnover in labourers using carbon tetrachloride, and another into miners suffering from lung disease – meant that, without having deliberately chosen to do so, Alice found herself working in the field of social medicine and epidemiology. It was an emerging discipline awash with hard problems.

Growing concern about the correlations between disease and poverty led to the creation in 1942 of Oxford's Institute of Social Medicine. Why did poorer people suffer approximately twice the rate of infant mortality, ear, mastoid and respiratory illnesses, ulcers and heart disease and what, in the light of the soon to be formed National Health Service, could be done about it? Stewart was recruited to the institute by one of the founding fathers of epidemiology, John Ryle, and she brought to her work all the indignant energy that was her hallmark.

'Practising medicine without asking these larger questions is like selling groceries across the counter,' she said. 'You go in with an illness; the doctor sells you a pill. It's no more responsible than that. Nobody goes out and asks, "Who didn't come in because he was too sick to come? Why are so many people coming in with this, and so few with that?"'[4] But when Ryle died in 1950, Stewart's progress ground to a halt. Ryle's institute was demoted to the 'Social Medicine Unit' and Stewart lost her mentor and her status.

Abandoned by the Oxford establishment, and left with a tiny salary but no building, no funding and no work, in a field that commanded little respect or kudos, the only way that Alice could make her mark was by identifying – and solving – a hard problem. The burning issues of the day – lung cancer, cardiovascular disease and polio – were crowded. This left just one: leukaemia. Incidence of the disease was on the increase, at a rate that made it look like an epidemic, but the number of patients was still so small that the field was difficult to study using statistics, the traditional tool of epidemiology. Two anomalies caught Alice Stewart's eye. Leukaemia was affecting children aged two to four. That was odd because typically by that age children are healthy: they've survived infancy and haven't yet started school. And the children dying from leukaemia weren't poor: in fact, they came from countries with better medical care and lower overall death rates. How could that be? Stewart decided to interview the mothers of leukaemia victims to see if she could find anything in their lives that might account for this pattern. She didn't know what she was looking for, so her questions began at conception.

'It was a needle-in-a-haystack search,' says Gayle Greene, who first met Alice Stewart in 1992. Even at the age of eighty-six, Stewart was so dazzling that Greene was inspired to write her biography.

'Alice didn't know what she was looking for, so she asked questions about everything: exposure to infection, inoculation, cats, dogs, hens, shop-fried fish and chips, highly coloured drinks, coloured sweets and have you had an x-ray?'[5]

Stewart proposed interviewing all of the mothers of children who had died of leukaemia and other forms of cancer between 1953 and 1955. But she couldn't get mainstream funding for her work. A mere £1,000 was found, from the Lady Tata Memorial Fund for Leukaemia Research, to pay for Alice's pioneering study. With such minimal resources, she had to be inventive. So she designed her questionnaire and took it in person to all the medical officers in 203 county health departments in the country. With characteristic tenacity, she persuaded them to use their own people and local records to answer all the questions on her survey. Her tiny grant was all spent on train fares as she went up and down the country, laden with carbon paper and brown envelopes.

Her study matched 500 leukaemia deaths, plus 500 deaths from other forms of cancer, with 1,000 live children of the same age, sex and region. When the surveys started to come back, the results leapt out. The culprit wasn't the coloured sweets, the pets or even the fish and chips.

'"Yes" was turning up three times for every dead child to one for every live child, for the question: "had you had an obstetric x-ray?" Yes was running three to one. It was a shocker. They were as like as two peas in a pod, the living and the dead. They were alike in all respects except on that one score. And the dose was very small, very brief, a single diagnostic x-ray, a tiny fraction of the radiation exposure considered safe. And it was enough to almost double risk of an early cancer death.'[6]

The recognition that x-raying pregnant mothers increased the chances of childhood cancer was the kind of finding epidemiologists dream of: a hard problem with good data pointing to a clear solution. But, like the thorough scientist she was, when her excitement died down, Stewart questioned her results over and over again and she asked colleagues to check them before she published them. When her article 'Preliminary Communication: Malignant Diseases in Childhood and Diagnostic Irradiation *in utero*' appeared in the *Lancet* in 1956, it caused a stir. The Nobel Prize was mentioned and Alice was asked to repeat her survey in Scotland. Over the next eighteen months, Stewart and her team continued to collect data. Within a three-year period they had traced 80 per cent of all childhood cancer deaths in England between 1953 and 1955. Publishing a full report in the *British Medical Journal* in 1958, they were able to conclude definitively that a foetus exposed to an x-ray was twice as likely to develop cancer within the next ten years as a foetus that had not been exposed.

'We reckoned that a child a week was dying from this practice. We thought that doctors would stop x-raying on the mere suspicion that we were right and we felt that we must hurry to cover all the deaths that occurred in the next ten years, because, once they stopped x-raying, there would be no further cases.'

Alice's fears were unfounded; doctors carried on x-raying pregnant mothers for the next twenty-five years. Not until 1980 did major American medical organisations finally recommend that the practice be abandoned. The place that held out longest was England.

Why did it take so long? How could so many doctors, the world over, have been so blind? Stewart's findings were clear, her data voluminous and, initially, greeted with acclaim. To us now, and to Alice at the time, it seemed obvious that the practice of x-raying pregnant women should stop immediately. What happened?

Many like to lay the blame on a personality clash with fellow epidemiologist, Richard Doll. He had, after all, rushed out a paper refuting Stewart's report; it was a tiny, quick study which he later acknowledged was 'not very good' and whose results he later described as 'unreliable'. But Doll was a dominant figure in the British medical establishment and his voice carried a long way. Alice Stewart's daughter, Anne Marshall, remembered the impact Doll's opposition had on her mother.

'I don't know if Mum was upset by Doll but he certainly made her think again and again. And then she'd settle down and do the work – and she knew she was right. She didn't enjoy a fight but, if she felt strongly about something, she was very good at having one.'[7]

It didn't help that Stewart was an unconventional scientist; she was a divorced mother with two children, at a time when there were few women in science, fewer mothers and when divorce was still not entirely respectable. Looking after her children as a single parent didn't leave Alice much time to network, build alliances or seek out support. Perhaps predictably, many scientists found her abrasive and adversarial. But gender stereotypes alone can't explain why Stewart's findings were overlooked for so long – because they were soon confirmed by a larger study, this time from Harvard University's School of Public Health. Although Brian MacMahon had set out to refute Stewart's findings, he found exactly what she had found: cancer mortality was 40 per cent higher among children whose mothers had been x-rayed. In the early 1960s, one of the largest radiation studies examined 6 million x-ray subjects in New York, Maryland and Minnesota; these confirmed Alice's findings, too. New statistical methods, the advent of computers, all served to make collecting and analysing data easier and more accurate – but all they did, over and over again, was to show that Alice Stewart, with her paper surveys and carbon paper, had been right all along. So why did doctors continue a practice that study after study showed to be so dangerous? How could they be so blind to all the accumulated data?

In part, the dazzle of new technology was to blame. Ever since their discovery in 1895, x-rays had developed an aura of mastery and mystique. They were used as an exquisite and expensive form of portraiture in the 1890s and even used as the ultimate tool for finding a ring that had been mistakenly baked into a cake.[8] Shoe stores boasted of x-ray machines that ensured a perfect fit: 'the salesman, the purchaser and even a purchaser's advisory friend can visually know exactly how well a shoe is fitting, both under pressure and otherwise,' claimed the 1927 patent for the 'shoe fluoroscope'. 'With this apparatus in his shop, a shoe merchant can positively assure his customers that they need never wear ill-fitting boots and shoes . . . parents can visually assure themselves as to whether they are buying shoes for their boys and girls which will not injure and deform the sensitive bone joints.'[9]

With so much investment in it, neither shoe salesmen nor doctors wanted to hear of any risks associated with the new technology. They were wedded to it.

'No one likes to be told they've been doing something wrong all their lives!' That's how Anne Marshall explains the reaction to her mother's findings. 'That's what the radiologists and obstetricians took from Mum's work – that they'd been doing something wrong. There were lots of them and they liked what they were doing and wanted to keep on doing it.'

'Doctors had enthusiasm about radiology that was so enormous that medical centres had invested in all kinds of x-ray equipment,' explains Gayle Greene. 'They didn't like being told that they were not only *not* helping their patients – but they were actually killing them! I think people are very resistant to changing what they know how to do, what they have expertise in and certainly what they have economic investment in.'

But Alice Stewart's survey of childhood cancers did something even more radical and provocative than question standard medical practice or challenge the benefits of new technologies; her findings undermined the prevailing mental model of disease. Threshold theory maintained that, while a large dose of something like radiation would be dangerous, there was always a point – a threshold – beyond which it was safe. But Alice Stewart was arguing that in this case, there was *no* acceptable level of radiation that was safe for foetuses. It wasn't just shoe shops and medical centres; a cornerstone of scientific orthodoxy was under attack.

She had to be wrong. If she was right, too many other assumptions had to be re-examined. What Alice Stewart had provoked in her scientific colleagues was cognitive dissonance: the mental turmoil that is evoked when the mind tries to hold two entirely incompatible views. It could not be true that threshold theory was right – but also that such tiny doses of radiation caused cancers. It could not be true that radiation was both a new wonder tool – that also killed children. It could not be true that doctors cured patients – and made them sick. The dissonance produced by mutually exclusive beliefs is tremendously painful, even unbearable. The easiest way to reduce the pain – the dissonance – is to eliminate one of the beliefs, rendering dissonance consonant. It was easier for scientists to cling to their beliefs: Threshold theory and x-rays both worked; doctors were smart, good, authoritative people. And so Alice Stewart and her findings were sacrificed to preserve the big idea. Dissonance is eliminated when we blind ourselves to contradictory propositions. And we are prepared to pay a very high price to preserve our most cherished ideas.

The theory of cognitive dissonance was initially developed by Leon Festinger around the same time that Alice Stewart was studying childhood cancers. He had developed much of his theory studying the religious millenarian movements of the nineteenth century, but he yearned for a live, contemporary case study to test his ideas. In September 1954, he found his opportunity in a newspaper story.

> PROPHECY FROM PLANET CLARION. CALL TO CITY: FLEE THAT FLOOD. IT'LL SWAMP US ON DEC. 21, OUTER SPACE TELLS SUBORDINATE.

The story described a suburban housewife, Marian Keech, who believed, on the basis of automatic writing, that the Earth would be flooded on 21 December. The fact that the group held such a specific belief about an event destined to occur on a specific date made this a perfect test case for Festinger's research: what would happen when a deeply held belief – a big idea – was disconfirmed by events? That the end of the world was due in months, and not years, made it practical too. When, as Festinger predicted, the flood failed to take place, would Mrs Keech surrender her belief in the light of experience? Festinger's theory suggested that she would continue in her faith but also, crucially, that it would become stronger than ever.

Even more unconventional in his research methods than Alice Stewart, Festinger and a few of his colleagues from the University of Minnesota set out to infiltrate Mrs Keech's community. For two months, they monitored the beliefs and varying levels of commitment among a small group with whom Mrs Keech had shared the automatic writing that she believed came to her via extraterrestrial messengers. Dr Thomas Armstrong, a physician at Eastern Teachers College in Collegeville, and his wife Daisy became Keech's devoted followers and they, in turn, recruited numerous students until there was a core of some eleven devotees.

Mrs Keech's messages described an apocalyptic vision, according to which Lucifer had returned to Earth in disguise and was leading scientists to build ever greater weapons of destruction. Their work would culminate in the earth falling apart and the disruption of the entire solar system. While forces of Light struggled to reclaim humanity, man's only hope was that enough people were open to the light to escape another explosion.

Festinger went out of his way to point out that Keech and the Armstrongs weren't crazy and they weren't psychotic. 'True, Mrs Keech put together a rather unusual combination of ideas – a combination peculiarly well adapted to our contemporary, anxious age,' Festinger wrote. 'But scarcely a single one of her ideas can be said to be unique, novel or lacking in popular support.'[10] There was nothing in her belief system that people haven't believed before – or since.

Central to these beliefs was the prediction Mrs Keech received that the world would end with an enormous flood on 21 December. Only true believers would be saved. 'The Supreme Being is going to clean house by sinking all of the land masses as we know them now and raising the land masses now under the sea. There will be a washing of the world with water. Some will be saved by being taken off the earth in spacecraft.'[11]

The messages were so bizarre and the belief system so open to ridicule that Festinger took pains to document just how serious and how real the group's commitment was. These people were not a bunch of kids pretending. One particularly devout member, Kitty O'Donnell, quit her job, quit school, lived off her small savings and moved into an expensive apartment because she did not expect to need what little remained of her cash. Two members – Fred Burden and Laura Brooks – gave up their college studies; Laura threw away many of her personal possessions. Dr Armstrong was eventually asked to resign his college position; the amount of time he spent talking to students about flying saucers had caused a flurry of parental complaints. But he was not dismayed, considering this merely 'part of the plan'.[12] His wife chose not to bother getting her dishwasher repaired: 'It isn't worth it, because the time is so short now.'[13] And when Mrs Keech received a call from a salesman of cemetery lots, she calmly explained that burial was 'the least of my worries'.[14] However ludicrous the prophecies may seem to us, this group lived their lives in the sincere belief that the flood was imminent.

Mrs Keech and her followers confidently expected flying saucers to transport them to other planets before the cataclysm occurred. Several false alarms, when messages seemed to promise the arrival of spacemen who failed to arrive, tested their faith. But on each occasion, the group either reinterpreted the messages to fit events or blamed themselves for faulty understanding. On the eve of the promised flood, the group spent the day together in 'peaceful idleness', confidently awaiting their rescue. Arthur Bergen, a teenage member of the group, complained that his mother had threatened to call the police if he wasn't home by two o'clock the next morning. 'The believers smilingly assured him that he need not worry – by that time they would all be aboard a saucer.'[15] Warned not to wear metal of any kind, they fastidiously eliminated it from their clothing – zippers, snaps, belt buckles, bra clips – and removed foil from chewing gum, watches from wrists.

The last ten minutes were tense. When one clock said 12.05, a chorus of people pointed out that a slower clock was more accurate. But even when the slower clock confirmed midnight, no one appeared and nothing happened. No flood, no flying saucers. Mrs Keech continued to receive long, confusing messages from 'the Creator' but by 2 a.m. Arthur Bergen had to take a cab home to his mother. By 4.30 a.m., the group was distraught, close to tears and some were beginning to show signs of doubt. How would they handle the disconfirmation of their passionately held beliefs? This was the crux of Festinger's two-month study.

At 4.45 Mrs Keech received a new message. 'Not since the beginning of time upon this Earth has there been such a force of Good and light as now floods this room and that which has been loosed within this room now floods the entire Earth.'[16] The goodness of the group had saved the world from flood.

The group was jubilant: their belief system was intact. But a greater change overcame Mrs Keech. Previously highly reticent, now she was more eager than ever to call the local newspaper and share her good news. Another member of the group insisted the news go further, to the Associated Press; the Creator surely wouldn't want the story to be an exclusive. Despite – or because of – the initial challenge to their belief, their faith now was stronger than ever and the believers more energetic in their proselytising. Evidence had not upset belief. Just as Festinger had hypothesised, disconfirmation had actually made their belief stronger.

And they never lost it. While Mrs Keech eventually left Lake City, she continued to receive automatic messages that she relayed to the faithful. The Armstrongs were as devout as ever, their faith 'boundless and their resistance to disconfirmation sublime'. Of the eleven members of the Lake City group, each of whom had witnessed unequivocal disconfirmation first hand, only two completely gave up their belief in Mrs Keech's writings – and they were the two who had been least committed from the outset.

Festinger's academic account of this episode can't resist some of the humour implicit in it, but the thrust of his argument is deadly serious. What he and subsequent psychologists argued was that we all strive to preserve an image of ourselves as consistent, stable, competent and good. Our most cherished beliefs are a vital and central part of who we are – in our own eyes and the eyes of our friends and colleagues. Anything or anyone who threatens that sense of self produces pain that feels just as dangerous and unpleasant as hunger or thirst. A challenge to our big ideas feels life-threatening. And so we strive mightily to reduce the pain, either by ignoring the evidence that proves we are wrong, or by reinterpreting evidence to support us.

Psychologist Anthony Greenwald called this phenomenon the 'totalitarian ego',[17] which, he said, operates just like a police state: locking away threatening or incompatible ideas, suppressing evidence and rewriting history, all in the service of a central idea or self-image. Marian Keech's followers would reinterpret events to fit their expectations, because not to have done so threatened to destroy their sense of who they were in the world. If doctors and scientists who read Alice Stewart's research believed it, and acted upon it, then they would have had to accept that they had harmed patients. But doctors don't like to think of themselves as sources of harm: they go into medicine to be, and do, good. Scientists embracing Alice's findings would have had at least to question the big idea of threshold theory. But scientists like – and need – big ideas, organising principles; they're what hold the data together, in just the same way that our beliefs and values hold our sense of self together. Acknowledging error, in these areas that are so vital for our self-definition, feels far too costly. Even as late as 1977, the National Council of Radiation Protection argued doctors must have x-rayed only those foetuses that were destined to get cancer. Quite how they could have known which these were, the council never explained. But that scientists should have developed so convoluted an argument illustrates how hard the mind will work to defend its most cherished and defining beliefs.

Festinger argued that, as individuals, we are all highly driven to make sense of the world and of our place in it. And we do so by gathering around us the ideas but also the people who verify our story, so to speak. The work that Drew Westen and other scientists have done more recently has served to illustrate that cognitive dissonance is not just a theory; it has a physical reality in the way that the brain handles information that we like – and the way that it handles the information that causes us distress. The fact that, as we already know, we're drawn to people similar to ourselves merely reinforces this process. Mrs Keech and her followers would have had difficulty maintaining their faith if they had been isolated and alone: confirmation of each other by each other kept their commitment secure. In just the same way, the medical profession stuck together.

Similarly, the bulk of the British political establishment stood together when it came to supporting the invasion of Iraq in 2003. Despite huge and popular protests, and even the resignation from the government of three MPs, Parliament consistently supported motions in favour of invasion. Then leader of the Conservative Party, Iain Duncan Smith argued that 'if we do not face up to Saddam now, then frankly in two to three years, we could find those biological chemical weapons on our doorstep'.[18] But what we chiefly remember, particularly after publication of the Chilcot report in 2016, was the cognitive dissonance of Tony Blair.

Like many politicians before and since, when it came to foreign policy, the cornerstone of Blair's mental model was the appeasement of Hitler in the run-up to the Second World War. That was the parallel he cited in Chicago in 1999, seeking American support for the war in Kosovo. 'This is a just war, based not on any territorial ambitions but on values. We cannot let the evil of ethnic cleansing stand. We must not rest until it is reversed. We have learned twice before in this century that appeasement does not work. If we let an evil dictator range unchallenged, we will have to spill infinitely more blood and treasure to stop him later.'[19]

And that was the parallel Blair deployed again when he urged Parliament to support him in the invasion of Iraq. 'There are glib and sometimes foolish comparisons with the 1930s. I am not suggesting for a moment that anyone here is an appeaser or does not share our revulsion at the regime of Saddam. However, there is one relevant point of analogy. It is that, with history, we know what happened. We can look back and say, "There's the time; that was the moment; that's when we should have acted."'[20]

Far from refining his belief in intervention, the apparent success of the Kosovo war had reinforced it. And it had strengthened Blair's belief in internationalism. 'We live in a world where isolationism has ceased to have a reason to exist ... We are all internationalists now, whether we like it or not ... We cannot turn our backs on conflicts and the violation of human rights within other countries if we want still to be secure. The doctrine of isolationism had been a casualty of a world war, where the United States and others finally realised standing aside was not an option.'

And Blair was an adoring fan of America. 'You are the most powerful country in the world, and the richest. You are a great nation. You have so much to give and to teach the world; and I know you would say, in all modesty, a little to learn from it too. Yet just as with the parable of the individuals and the talents, so those nations which have the power, have the responsibility. We need you engaged. Stay a country, outward-looking, with the vision and imagination that is your nature. And realise that in Britain you have a friend and an ally that will stand with you, work with you, fashion with you the design of a future built on peace and prosperity for all, which is the only dream that makes humanity worth preserving.'[21]

Blair's mental model of the world was every bit as coherent as Mrs Keech's. It was comprised of individual pieces, each one of which, on its own, made sense. His faith in the United States likewise proved as unswerving as hers was to her voices: 'I will be with you whatever', he wrote to George W. Bush before the invasion of Iraq. When his opponents accused Blair of lying – to the public, to Chilcot's Iraq Inquiry – they were missing the point. Blair was blind to any scenario that didn't fit his doctrine. His mental model affirmed what he already believed: appeasement is fatal, intervention is morally right, solidarity with the United States is essential. Disconfirming data – the fact that peaceful options had not been exhausted, that Saddam Hussein did not represent an imminent threat or have weapons of mass destruction, intelligence warnings that the invasion could exacerbate terrorism, the unpreparedness of the military (in both the US and UK) – was repelled by the greater force of Blair's ideology.

And that, of course, is the problem with strong, coherent mental models: they attract confirming data while repelling, marginalising and trivialising disconfirming data. Organising the world for us, mental models make sense of complexity and tell us what to pay attention to. They stop us questioning the core beliefs that allow us to feel good about ourselves and our world. They confirm our sense of ourselves as righteous and good. That's why architects and supporters of Britain's austerity economics see food banks as encouraging signs of Christian generosity rather than as shameful symptoms of a rich country's punitive welfare ideologies.

Economic models work in much the same way: pulling in and integrating the information that fits the model, leaving out what can't be accommodated. The economist and Nobel laureate Paul Krugman, whose reputation for beautiful models has brought him such fame, recognises how incomplete they can be. In perhaps one of the most explosive comments ever made by an economist, he conceded: 'I think there's a pretty good case to be made that the stuff that I stressed in the models is a less important story than the things I left out because I couldn't model them, like spillovers of information and social networks.'[22]

The problem with models, in other words, is that they imply that whatever does not fit into them isn't relevant – when it could be the most relevant information of all. But we treasure our models and personal big ideas, because they help us to make decisions, about what to do with our lives, who to befriend, and what we stand for. A profound and innate part of who we are, they become so deeply entwined in all aspects of our lives that we may forget how profoundly they filter what we see, remember and absorb. And when our ideas are widely shared, they don't attract so much scepticism. We may not even see them as ideology and we don't see their proponents as zealots. They come to seem normal. But appearances can be deceptive.

'Greenspan's wilful blindness was incredible,' says Frank Partnoy. 'He had a highly simplistic view of how markets behaved. He believed in the core of his soul that markets would self-correct and that financial models could forecast risk effectively.' Partnoy doesn't criticise the former chairman of the Federal Reserve Bank lightly or from the lofty perch of someone observing financial shenanigans from a safe distance. He sold derivatives on Wall Street from 1993 to 1995 and knew, first hand, in gritty detail, just how convoluted, disingenuous, obscure and risky they were. He eventually left the industry, utterly disillusioned by how fraudulent it was. But his years on Wall Street had shown him, up close and personal, what the derivatives market was all about. Now professor of law and finance at the University of San Diego, Partnoy has been watching the derivatives market develop ever since he left it. And he's watched with mounting frustration and disbelief as the so-called 'Maestro', Alan Greenspan, failed to do anything about it.

'There was just so much happening in markets that Greenspan didn't understand – because it was inconsistent with his worldview,' says Partnoy. 'It really illustrates the dangers of having a particular fixed view of the world and not being open to evidence that your worldview is wrong until it is too late.'

Greenspan's worldview was significantly developed in his late twenties and early thirties, when he became a devoted acolyte of the American novelist and economic libertarian Ayn Rand. At this time, Greenspan had given up on his career playing bebop with a big touring band and turned to economics. He dropped out of Columbia's PhD programme to form a consulting firm while developing a close personal relationship, and passionate intellectual relationship, with Rand and her fellow Objectivists. Rand's attraction to men remains somewhat mysterious: an adulterous, failed screenwriter who'd emigrated from revolutionary Russia, she seems an unlikely muse for corporate titans and economic gurus. Her understanding of how markets worked derived from the traumatic experience of having lived through the Russian Revolution, in which her family lost everything. But she never trained as an economist, had never run a business and wrote often impenetrable prose that purported to be philosophy. But Greenspan was smitten, springing to Rand's defence when her novel, *Atlas Shrugged*, received a critical notice. Reviewing the book, Greenspan wrote, 'Justice is unrelenting. Creative individuals and undeviating purpose and rationality achieve joy and fulfilment. Parasites who persistently avoid either purpose or reason perish as they should.' Greenspan could not conceive that a book with such properties might have its flaws.

What Greenspan admired in Rand, and which he embraced with evangelical fervour, was the belief that, if he were only liberated from the regulations and constraints imposed by government, man would attain ever greater heights of freedom, creativity and wealth.

'I am opposed,' said Rand, 'to all forms of control. I am for an absolute *laissez-faire* free unregulated economy. I am for the separation of state and economics.'[23]

In Rand's world, those who could do well would be freed from all constraint to express and articulate the full capacity of their talents; they would achieve joy and fulfilment. Those who weren't up to it – parasites – would fail and get out of the way. It's a touchingly romantic idea, as long as you assume that you will be one of the successful ones.

Greenspan wasn't in love with Ayn Rand, but he was in love with her ideas and they framed everything he did. In his autobiography, *The Age of Turbulence*, he describes her as a 'stabilising force' in his life.[24] Identifying himself as a convert, Greenspan was clearly in awe of her, proud when he could 'keep up with her most of the time'. Ayn Rand was right there, standing next to him, when, in 1974, he was sworn in as chairman of Gerald Ford's Council of Economic Advisers. And his ideas hadn't changed a bit when he took over the Federal Reserve in August 1987. The man with a religious belief in the evils of regulation was now in charge of money supply.

'I do have an ideology,' Greenspan told Congress. 'My judgement is that free, competitive markets are by far the unrivalled way to organise economies.'[25]

'He wanted to do whatever he could to deregulate the market,' says Partnoy, who has studied Greenspan's career critically for many years. 'But he was very clever about it. Rather than lobby upfront for the repeal of Glass–Steagall, he pressed for a series of small incremental changes. I think of it as Swiss cheese: put a few holes in, then a few more – and eventually there's no cheese left! He honestly believed that we would all be better off if regulated markets got smaller and smaller, and the deregulated markets got bigger and bigger. That's how you get to the promised land.'

What's so striking, however, is that all the time Greenspan was nibbling away at regulation, the market was being rocked by a whole series of warning tremors that offered strong evidence that its most deregulated sectors – the sector Greenspan was so eager to help grow – threatened to blow everything up.

In 1994, when Greenspan raised interest rates from 3 per cent to 3.25 per cent, the marketplace was full of derivatives that assumed interest rates would stay low. When interest rates rose instead, all hell broke loose. David Askin, one of the most active traders in complex mortgage derivatives, ran a $600 million fund that went up in smoke in a matter of weeks, filing for bankruptcy on 7 April. Five days later, Gibson Greetings, Air Products, Dell Computer Corporation, Mead Corporation and Procter & Gamble admitted to billions of dollars in losses from derivatives, many of which even their internal financiers did not understand. Congressional hearings were held, in which George Soros testified that, 'There are so many of them and some are so esoteric, that the risks involved may not be properly understood even by the most sophisticated investors.'[26]

In May, Greenspan's Federal Reserve Bank raised the interest rate another 0.5 per cent – and there was a bloodbath on Wall Street. Property and casualty insurers lost more than they had paid out on Hurricane Andrew; hedge funds, banks, securities firms and the life insurance industry lost billions. According to Frank Partnoy, virtually every kind of institution, from every sector of the economy, suffered massive losses.

In 1994, Procter & Gamble sued Bankers Trust for the huge losses they'd suffered from derivatives. The prosecution used taped phone calls that demonstrated just how deliberately and knowingly the bankers had misled the firm. For once, there was some chink of light on the 'dark market' of derivatives and what it showed wasn't pretty – and wasn't regulated. At the same time, the financial services firm Kidder, Peabody discovered losses of $350 million. Part of General Electric at the time, under the legendary Jack Welch, it turned out that no one really understood what traders in the firm were up to. The quarter that the losses were reported was the first time in fifty-two quarters that earnings were less than the previous year. But after all this mayhem, the only legislation that emerged actually made life far harder for would-be plaintiffs when Congress restricted securities lawsuits in 1995.

Frank Partnoy has chronicled each of these debacles, from what he calls 'Patient Zero' in 1987 through to Enron in 2001 and the banking crisis twenty years later. 'It was foolish,' he wrote, 'to deregulate markets simply because large institutions instead of individuals were involved. It was a well-established economic principle that markets with large sophistication and information gaps did not function well. The more they carved up markets, the harder it was for anyone to keep tabs on risk.'[27]

Each one of these failures reinforced the same lesson: derivatives were a 'dark market'. No one could see what went on in these deals and, because there was no statutory requirement to report anything, even the parties to the deals often did not know what they had. Instead, the freedom to report nothing meant that not only did the government not really know what was going on – no one did. They were all equally blind.

That this could continue was possible only because so many people subscribed to Greenspan's ideology. The *Financial Times* journalist Gillian Tett compares such blind faith to the medieval Church. 'If this was a religion, Alan Greenspan was the Pope,' says Tett. 'He blessed derivatives. Then you had the high priests up at the altar, passing out blessings in the financial Latin that the congregation don't understand. The Pope is saying it's all miraculous and wonderful and the blessings come in the form of cheap mortgages.'[28]

A few dissenting voices had the temerity to challenge Greenspan and argue that derivatives required oversight. In 1988, Muriel Siebert testified before the Subcommittee on Telecommunications and Finance, in the wake of the 1987 market crash. The major problem with the market, she said, was derivatives. 'Program trades and index arbitrage end up bringing the volatility and rampant speculation of the futures pits to the floor of the Big Board. Futures have become the tail wagging the dog.'

In 1996, Brooksley Born was appointed to head up the Commodity Futures Trading Commission, the regulator uniquely tasked with overseeing the $27 trillion derivatives market. And, after the string of catastrophes in 1994, she was one of the few eager to impose some oversight. But Greenspan was having none of it. When Born's CFTC issued a 'Concept Release' outlining how regulation might work, Greenspan instantly put out a statement condemning it.

'It seemed totally inexplicable to me,' Born recalled later. 'It was as though the other regulators were saying, "We don't want to know."'[29]

Six weeks later, the hedge fund Long-Term Capital Management, which included Greenspan's former deputy at the Fed, David Mullins, became insolvent. The size of the failure threatened the entire US economy.

'Long-Term Capital Management was exactly what I'd been worried about,' Born said. 'No regulators knew it was on the verge of collapse. Why? Because we didn't have any information about the market.'[30]

At last, the LTCM crisis provoked some support in Congress for regulation. But Greenspan once again moved quickly to quash it. 'I know of no set of supervisory actions we can take that can prevent people from making dumb mistakes. I think it is very important for us not to introduce regulation for regulation's sake.'

And Greenspan and his friends won the day: no regulation for over-the-counter derivatives was introduced. They could continue to trade without any capital requirements or rules against manipulation or even fraud. Greenspan's free market was allowed to get bigger and bigger, and Brooksley Born resigned.

Two years later, in 2001, the sixth largest corporation in America, Enron, went bust. Inside an intricate web of malfeasance lay deadly derivatives, tied to the company's stock price, which left its investors with nothing. They weren't all Enron employees; many were small investors, like Mary Pearson, a Latin teacher who testified before Congress after the company failed.

> I am just a pebble in the stream, a little bitty shareholder. I did not lose billions but what I did lose seems like a billion to me. I was going to use my Enron stock as my long-term health care. I was disappointed in the people that I put my trust in years ago. And after a little time passed on, bitterness came into being, and bitterness will eat you alive if you let it. But sometimes at night I do feel real bitter over what I have lost, because it was a big part of my future, and I do not know how I am going to handle the future now. All I can do is hope and pray I do not get sick.[31]

This was not a narrative Greenspan could see. From his perspective, 'creative individuals and undeviating purpose and rationality' went on to 'achieve joy and fulfilment' and the parasites perished. Until, that is, the banking crisis of 2008.

'This was my worst nightmare coming true,' said Brooksley

Born. 'Nobody really knew what was going on in the market. The toxic assets of our biggest banks were in over-the-counter derivatives and caused the economic downturn that made us lose our savings, lose our jobs, lose our homes.'

Just as Rand had wished, the state and economics had been separated; Greenspan had proved true to the big idea of his life, but blind to the realities of it. Even after the biggest financial catastrophe of his lifetime, when Greenspan came to testify to Congress about what had gone wrong, he held fast to his big idea. It wasn't wrong; it was just flawed.

> CHAIRMAN WAXMAN: You had an ideology. 'My judgment is that free, competitive markets are by far the unrivaled way to organize economies. We have tried regulation, none meaningfully worked.' That was your quote. Now our whole economy is paying its price. Do you feel that your ideology pushed you to make decisions that you wish you had not made?
>
> MR GREENSPAN: Well, remember, though, whether or not ideology is a conceptual framework with the way people deal with reality, everyone has one. You have to. To exist, you need an ideology. The question is, whether it exists is accurate or not. What I am saying to you is yes, I found a flaw, I don't know how significant or permanent it is, but I have been very distressed by that fact. I found a flaw in the model that I perceived is the critical functioning structure of how the world works.
>
> CHAIRMAN WAXMAN: In other words, you found that your view of the world, your ideology, was not right, it was not working?

> MR GREENSPAN: Precisely. That's precisely the reason I was shocked, because I had been going for forty years or more with very considerable evidence that it was working exceptionally well.[32]

Just like Tony Blair's evidence to the Chilcot Inquiry, Greenspan's performance was mesmerising drama: a proud, old man wriggling to protect himself from the sharp, hard prongs of fact. Both fought hard to evade the cognitive dissonance implicit in events that would not change shape just to fit into his ideology. Despite failure after failure, neither would deny his big idea. Greenspan could admit a flaw, not that he was wrong. Eerily reminiscent of Mrs Keech, he was prepared only to see that he had got a slight detail wrong. He couldn't see, or wouldn't see, the financial wreckage strewn right across his career, but instead insisted that his big idea worked just fine for forty years. The free-market economist Friedrich von Hayek once said that 'without a theory, the facts are silent'. But for Greenspan and Blair, wedded to their respective models of the world, the facts became invisible.

Of course, neither Blair nor Greenspan acted alone. Both had the support of the powerful – as long as everything went well. You could say both were blind, but both operated within a collective myopia that reinforced their ideology. And neither has recanted. Greenspan conceded only 'a flaw' while Blair, testifying before the Chilcot Inquiry, remained faithful to his doctrine, now justifying the war on the grounds that it had stopped production of weapons of mass destruction in some distant future:

'Don't ask the March 2003 question, but ask the 2010 question. Suppose we backed off? What we now know is that he retained absolutely the intent and intellectual know-how to restart a nuclear and chemical weapons programme when weapons inspectors were out and the sanctions were changed.'

In this, Blair – like Greenspan – thinks like Marian Keech, summoning cognitive contortions in order to retain the old, big idea. Blair certainly remained more faithful to his beliefs than Richard Doll. Eight years before Doll died, his reputation secured by proving the connection between smoking and lung cancer, he did recant, although with the most modest of *mea culpas*. In 1997, he published a paper, 'Risk of childhood cancer from fetal irradiation', in which he quietly announced the death of threshold theory.[33]

'The association between the low dose of ionising radiation received by the foetus *in utero* from diagnostic radiography, particularly in the last trimester of pregnancy, and the subsequent risk of cancer in childhood provides direct evidence against the existence of a threshold dose below which no excess risk arises, and has led to changes in medical practice.'

But by the time Doll changed his mind, millions of pregnant women had been x-rayed.

4. The Limits of Your Mind

On 23 March 2005, Warren Briggs got into his car and set off for work. The commute to the BP refinery in Texas City usually took thirty to forty-five minutes, but today it felt longer. When he got to the plant, just before 6 a.m., he could scarcely remember driving there. Warren had been working twelve-hour shifts, seven days a week, for twenty-nine days in a row. He couldn't remember the last time he'd had time off. He had mixed feelings about his shifts. Twelve hours off meant more time with the kids. But he still wasn't getting much sleep.

He spoke briefly to the departing night-shift operator and then read the logbook to prepare for the start-up. There was just a one-line logbook entry: 'isom brought in some raff to unit, to pack raff with'. That told him more or less nothing, he thought, grumpy as he started to work.

In front of him sat the control board for the ISOM/NDU/AU2 complex: twelve monitors divided into twenty-four screens. Some screens had pages and pages of information behind them; others were pretty simple alarms. Visitors said it looked like something from NASA; Warren wished it was that exciting.

Warren's boss was late and, when he got in, he was busy. He was always busy because he had a pile of paperwork and a bunch of contracting crews to look after. A lot of the men hated contractors, said they were unsafe and cut corners. Warren didn't mind. Those guys needed to feed their families the same as he did. It wasn't their fault BP brought them in with fewer benefits, less pay. There weren't that many jobs around Texas City to choose from.

We're running so thin. That was the phrase everybody used. At first it just meant the pipes were wearing thin, but now the whole place was wearing out. The plant and the people. So much cost-cutting, you could do the form-filling but not the repairs. Warren's supervisor was buried in paperwork and he had two new operators to train. He probably wouldn't be around much today.

With no one to relieve him, Warren ate his lunch at his desk in front of the control board. Some weird pressure spikes caught his attention and he wanted to keep an eye on them. It was boring, lonely work, cooped up in a darkened room. The equipment he was supposed to be controlling stood outside in the Texas sunshine, one small part of the vast refinery. When people first saw it, they'd say it looked like something on the moon, a space-age settlement full of towers and spheres that went on for miles. Warren didn't share their romance. It was just a refinery, making 3 per cent of America's gasoline. That would fuel a lot of cars.

The isomerisation unit Warren looked after boosted octane levels in the gasoline produced at the plant. Flammable hydrocarbons, or raffinate – the 'raff' in the logbook – went into a 170-foot tower to distil and separate gas components. Higher octane meant higher performance and higher prices. That was the name of the game. Starting the unit was always a tricky time, when it would have been nice to have an extra pair of eyes. In the old days, there had been two operators, but cost-cutting changed all that. Then they'd added a third unit – the NDU – and said it was so easy to operate you didn't need an extra person. So instead of two people for two refinery units, now it was just Warren, on his own, looking after all three.

Around 12.40, an alarm went off but Warren still couldn't figure out where the high pressure was coming from. He decided to open a manual chain valve to vent some of the gases to the emergency relief system and to turn off two burners in the furnace. Just after 1 p.m., Warren's boss called in to see how things were going. When Warren mentioned the weird pressure spikes, he suggested opening a bypass valve to the blowdown drum to relieve some of the pressure. What neither of them knew was that the isomerisation tower was too full, fifteen times more than it was meant to be. But Warren's control panel wasn't configured to display flows into and out of the tower on the same screen and nowhere did it calculate total liquid in the tower. Running thin.

An adventure, one of the guys had called it. An adventure? Sure, he said: each morning when I walk into this place, I wonder if today's the day I'm gonna die. That wasn't Warren's idea of an adventure.

At 1.14 p.m., three emergency valves opened in the tower, sending nearly 52,000 gallons of hot, flammable liquid to the blowdown drum. When the liquid overflowed into a process sewer it set off alarms in the control room. But the high-level alarm didn't go off. While Warren sat in front of his twenty-four screens, a geyser of liquid and vapour erupted from the top of the stack, propelling nearly a tanker full of hot gasoline up into the air and then down to the ground like a tall, ungainly fountain. Within ninety seconds the whole unit and all the contractors' trailers were engulfed in a vast flammable vapour cloud. Then a nearby car backfired.[1]

A mile away, Joe Bilancich was negotiating for a new apprentice scheme. He felt one concussion in the room, then another. Everybody moved to the window. Flames and smoke filled their view while pieces of pipe and metal rained down on the ground.

Forty-five minutes from the site, Eva Rowe heard the blast. Both her parents worked at the site; she called them at once. No answer.

Fifteen people died that day at BP's Texas City site, killed by the 'blunt force trauma' of the explosion. Eva Rowe lost both of her parents. At the time, it was one of the worst industrial accidents in American history.

When investigators, lawyers and executives came to unpick the tragedy that occurred at Texas City, everybody talked about blind spots: problems, processes and warnings that everybody could see but somehow managed not to see. Some of the causes were complex and technical, but some were not. What happened to Warren was simple and obvious and not unique to oil refineries. As we know from the banking crisis, companies don't have to kill people to be dangerous.

According to the US Chemical Safety Board, which spent two years investigating the accident, Warren was one of the most rested members of his team. The Night Lead Operator, who had filled the tower from the control room before Warren had come on duty, had worked thirty-three consecutive days, while the Day Lead Operator – who was training two new operators, dealing with contractors, and working to get a replacement part to finish the ISOM turnaround work – had been on duty for thirty-seven consecutive days. In other words, they were all dog-tired. The CSB estimated that Warren was getting 5.5 hours of sleep per night, and therefore was suffering from what they call an accumulated 'sleep debt' of about a month and a half. That didn't just mean that he felt lousy. 'It is common for a person experiencing fatigue to be more rigid in thinking, have greater difficulty responding to changing or abnormal circumstances, and take longer to reason correctly,' said the CSB. Focused attention on one thing, to the exclusion of everything else – often referred to as cognitive fixation or cognitive tunnel vision – is a typical performance effect of fatigue.[2]

Warren and his operators could not see the problem. They were simply too tired. The UK Health and Safety Executive found that subjective levels of fatigue increase with consecutive early shifts (those starting around 6 a.m.). The third day of working an early-morning shift results, it said, in a 30 per cent increase in fatigue, while the fifth consecutive day of working early-morning shifts results in a 60 per cent increase in fatigue, and the seventh consecutive day results in a 75 per cent increase compared to the first day. The study doesn't even contemplate what happens to people's minds when they've been working like this for thirty days non-stop.

Fatigue, overwork, burnout are not unique to the oil and gas industries. On 11 November 2004, the computer games company Electronic Arts was shellshocked to find itself the target of a blogger called 'EA Spouse' who complained with shocking eloquence about the hours EA expected its programmers to work. Addressing herself to then-CEO (now chairman) Larry Probst, the spouse asked: 'You do realise what you're doing to your people, right? And you do realise that they ARE people, with physical limits, emotional lives, and families, right? Voices and talents and senses of humour and all that? That when you keep our husbands and wives and children in the office for ninety hours a week, sending them home exhausted and numb and frustrated with their lives, it's not just them you're hurting, but everyone around them, everyone who loves them? When you make your profit calculations and your cost analyses, you know that a great measure of that cost is being paid in raw human dignity, right?'

Electronic Arts is the world's leading producer of computer games and 2004 had been a good year for the company. *The Sims*, *Lord of the Rings*, *FIFA* and *Medal of Honor* generated record revenues ($3 billion) and record profits ($776 million). The year was particularly noteworthy because technology breakthroughs – faster processors and improved screen resolution – resulted in a boom for handheld game devices. The introduction of Sony's PSP promised even greater opportunity. But writing about the challenges the company faced going into 2005, Probst made no mention of a workforce that was fried, or an engineering team whose turnover ran at nearly 50 per cent.

When EA Spouse's essay, 'EA: The Human Story'[3] came out, it tore through the computer games community like wildfire. 'I was so angry and in such pain, I thought: either I get a response to this or there's something seriously wrong with the world!' Erin Hoffman, the blog's author, recalled. 'It was students and gamers who propelled the thing. Within forty-eight hours, everyone read it. But it was students who were most angry! They dreamed of working in this industry – and were desperately disappointed to learn how awful it was.'

Today, Hoffman is in less pain, but she's still angry. The gist of her complaint then was that EA routinely scheduled engineers to work 85-hour weeks. When her fiancé Lan had interviewed for a job at EA, neither of them was naive. As computer games veterans they knew that, just before a product shipped, most teams went into crunch mode, which involved long hours.

'They asked Lan in one of the interviews: "How do you feel about working long hours?" It's just a part of the games industry – few studios can avoid a crunch as deadlines loom, so we thought nothing of it. When asked for specifics about what "working long hours" meant, the interviewers coughed and glossed on to the next question; now we know why.'

Crunch is only supposed to be the mode of working at the tail end of a project. At EA, the team started by doing eight-hour days, six days a week. But that quickly turned into twelve hours, six days a week and then into eleven hours a day, seven days a week. Crunch wasn't an emergency; it was a standard. Watching what was happening to her fiancé horrified Erin. 'After a certain number of hours, the eyes start to lose focus; after a certain number of weeks with only one day off, fatigue starts to accrue and accumulate exponentially. Bad things happen to one's physical, emotional, and mental health. The team is rapidly beginning to introduce as many flaws as they are removing. The bug rate soared in crunch.'

As the debate inspired by Erin's essay continued, she and her friends became better informed about the iron laws of human productivity. The forty-hour week is there for a reason; it gets the best work from people. The first four hours are the most productive and, as the day wears on, everyone becomes less alert, less focused and prone to more mistakes. In 1908, the first known study by Ernst Abbe,[4] one of the founders of the Zeiss lens laboratory, concluded that *reducing* the working day from nine to eight hours actually *increased* output. Henry Ford, who studied productivity issues obsessively, reached the same conclusion and infuriated his manufacturing colleagues when, in 1926, he had the audacity to introduce a forty-hour working week. Subsequent studies by Foster Wheeler (1968), Procter & Gamble (1980) and the construction industry and many, many more show that, as the days get longer, productivity declines. No study has ever convincingly argued otherwise.[5]

Once you are doing sixty hours a week or more, you don't just get tired, you make mistakes; the time you spend rectifying errors consumes all the extra hours you work. The classic, and comic, example of this was Frank Gilbreth, the efficiency-obsessed father in *Cheaper by the Dozen*. He found he could shave faster if he used two razors – but then he wasted all his saved time covering the cuts with Band-Aids.

In software companies, a lot of developers like working late; they relish the silence that comes when the sales and marketing folk go home. But that means they need to start later too. Otherwise, the extra hours produce only errors. Software bugs or accidental file deletions can have knock-on effects that take much longer to repair than did writing original code. EA's working patterns weren't just inhumane; they were counterproductive.

Then there is the sleep factor. Missing just one night's sleep has a noticeable impact on the brain's ability to function, as Dardo Tomasi and his colleagues at the Brookhaven National Laboratory[6] discovered when they took fourteen healthy, non-smoking right-handed men and made half of them stay awake through the night. In the morning, both rested and groggy subjects were put through a series of tests that involved tracking ten balls on a screen. As they completed the tests, an fMRI scanner took pictures of their brains, to see how the rested brain differed from the one that was deprived of sleep. They found, not so surprisingly, that the sleepier the subjects, the lower their accuracy in the tests. But it was the detail that was most interesting.

What the scientists found was that two key areas of the brain – the parietal lobe and the occipital lobe – were less active in the sleep-deprived participants. The parietal lobe in the brain integrates information from the senses and is also involved in our knowledge of numbers and manipulation of objects. The occipital lobe is involved in visual processing. So both areas are highly involved in processing visual information and numbers. What was Warren looking at on his twenty-four screens? Visual information and numbers. What do computer-game engineers work with all the time? Visual information and numbers. The higher-order brain activity that was most needed in those jobs was the first thing to go.

While the parietal and occipital lobes were less active, the thalamus, on the other hand, was very busy in the sleepy subjects. Scientists hypothesise that it attempts to compensate for the reduced activity in the parietal and occipital lobes. The thalamus sits at the centre of the brain, and is responsible for the regulation of consciousness, sleep and alertness. It was, in other words, working extra hard to stay alert. All the energy you might want to use to concentrate on solving a hard problem is devoted to the challenge of staying awake.

In evolutionary terms, this makes sense. If you're driven to find food, you need to stay awake and search, not contemplate recipes. But now that, for most of us, work isn't primarily about physical endurance, mere wakefulness is not enough. What these and other studies indicate is that, yes, we can work for long periods of time with little sleep – but what we lose, progressively, is the ability to think. 'A tired worker tends to perform like an unskilled worker.'[7] Or you could say: a smart worker starts to work like a mindless one.

Moreover, sleep deprivation starts to starve the brain. There is a reason why we start to eat comfort food – doughnuts, sweets – when we're tired: our brains crave sugar. After twenty-four hours of sleep deprivation, there is an overall reduction of 6 per cent in glucose reaching the brain.[8] But the loss isn't shared equally; the parietal lobe and the prefrontal cortex lose 12–14 per cent of their glucose. And those are the areas we need most for thinking: for distinguishing between ideas, for social control and to be able to tell the difference between good and bad.[9]

Matthew Walker, at the University of California, Berkeley's Center for Human Sleep Science, has demonstrated the profound long-term effects of sleep deprivation: Alzheimer's disease, cancer, diabetes, obesity and poor mental health. But just staying awake for nineteen hours – not necessarily even working – immediately leaves us cognitively as impaired as someone who is drunk. While most companies are eager to enforce anti-alcohol policies and even sometimes to support those trying to kick the habit, it's rare to see the same enlightened view on overwork. Mostly, those who pull all-nighters, or who go from overnight flights straight into meetings, are regarded as heroic – not, as they should be, as dangerous.[10]

Erin's fiancé Lan joined a successful class-action suit against EA's working practices and he left the company. The 'spouse' turned out to be a little premature: they never married and have since split up. Erin sits on the board of the International Games Developers Association (IGDA) but says the industry hasn't learned much: engineers are still too tired to see straight and the executives who manage them are too tired to see the problem.

'EA changed for a while, but only really because one group saw this as an opportunity to get rid of the guys responsible for the crazy hours. So there was a big political bloodbath and a new regime. Everything got better for six months and then it started all again. They're destroying people who should become our top developers! A lot of studios now won't hire EA former employees because they're so burned out; they say there's just too much work involved in rehabbing them.'

Even rested and alert, you may not be able to see what's right in front of you. In one of psychology's most famous and stupefying experiments, Dan Simons made a video at Harvard that set out to test just how much our mind can see when it's busy.

'It started as a lark,' Dan recalled.[11] 'There had been earlier experiments into visual cognition but in all of them the display was so weird that it didn't feel like real life. So I thought: what if we make this whole thing live? This was quite a lot of fun – I'm a big fan of doing fun research. I do the boring stuff too, but the purpose here was to ask: how extreme can you make this and illustrate the point?'

(Before you read further, you might want to try the experiment for yourself at www.theinvisiblegorilla.com.)

Together with Chris Chabris, Simons made a short film of Harvard students moving around and passing basketballs. One team wore white shirts, the other wore black. Simons himself is in the film but you won't recognise him, he says, because back then he had hair. When they finished making the film, Chabris and Simons asked volunteers to watch it and count the number of passes made by players wearing white. Less than a minute later, when the video ended, they asked viewers if they'd seen anything else. About half said no, they'd seen nothing.[12]

What they had missed was a student wearing a full-body gorilla suit who walks into the scene, stops in the middle of the frame, faces the camera, thumps her chest and walks off. She is on screen for approximately nine seconds.

The experiment has been shown repeatedly, around the world, in front of diverse audiences. I first saw it in Dublin, in an audience full of executives. Like them, I was so focused on counting the passes I never saw the gorilla.

Simons was so stunned by the result that he says that, for several years afterwards, he still kept expecting people to spot the gorilla. But results were always the same. In 1999, Simons and his colleagues published an account of the experiment entitled 'Gorillas in our Midst' and in 2004 they won an Ig Nobel Prize for 'achievements that first make people laugh and then make them think'. Simons has since gone on to make an academic career studying how we pay attention.

'We experience far less of our visual world than we think we do. We feel like we are going to take in what's around us. But we don't. We pay attention to what we are told to attend to, or what we're looking for, or what we already know. Top-down factors play a big role. Fashion designers will notice clothes. Engineers will notice mechanics. But what we see is amazingly limited.'

We see what we expect to see, what we're looking for. And we can't see all that much. I asked Simons whether some people saw more than others.

'There is really limited evidence for that. People who are experienced basketball players are slightly better at seeing what's happening in the video – but that's probably because they're more accustomed to watching passes; it isn't so hard for them to read what's going on. You can train yourself to focus on more than one spot. You might improve your eye muscles somewhat. But the limits are pretty fixed. There's a physical and an evolutionary barrier. You can't change the limits of your mind.'

Simons' video is used for all kinds of safety training. 'The airport security people, you know – they can find what they're looking for but they won't find what they're not looking for, no matter how dangerous it is.' Trained baggage screeners are better than Simons' respondents at spotting weapons, but not much: a third of the time, they will fail to spot weapons of any kind.[13]

Simons is often bemused by the relevance different organisations find in his work. 'The video gets talked about a lot in relation to national security forces and why they didn't see terrorists in their midst. My favourite one is a Baptist preacher who was giving a sermon in which he referred to the gorilla and said that's why the Jews didn't spot Jesus for what he was! But it is most commonly used for safety training – in power plants, for example – where people will focus on procedures and not notice anything that isn't part of the procedure.'

The advent of smartphones has merely reinforced Simons' fundamental finding that there is a limit to how much we can notice. You only have to walk down the street towards fellow pedestrians immersed in maps or texts to see just how out of touch they are with their immediate surroundings. After a decade of experiments by himself and others,[14] Simons concludes that we see what we expect to see and are blind to the unexpected. And there are absolute hard limits to how much we can take in at any given time.

'For the human brain,' says Simons, 'attention is a zero-sum game: if we pay more attention to one place, object or event, we *necessarily* pay less attention to others.'

Simons now researches and teaches at the University of Illinois in Urbana-Champaign. On 6 September 2006, a graduate of the university, Matt Wilhelm, was riding his bicycle when Jennifer Stark hit him from behind with her car and killed him. In the subsequent investigation, it turned out that Stark had been downloading ringtones at the time she hit Matt – a tragic reminder of the realities behind Simons' experiments.

'There was a huge debate, when radios were introduced into cars,' says Simons. 'I'm still not sure I buy the argument but I suppose we can tune out a radio. But driving a car while talking on a mobile phone, or texting, is different. They can seem really effortless but they both use your mind's limited attention resources. You can't do it. Your brain can't do it.'

It isn't about the phone – which is why hands-free sets won't help you. It's about the mental resources that are available to you at any one time. In what sounds like another piece of fun research, Frank Drews, an assistant professor of psychology at the University of Utah, divided forty students into three teams.[15] The first team operated a driving simulator; the second team drove on the simulator while talking on mobile phones. The third team got to operate the simulator after drinking enough orange and vodka to take their blood-alcohol limit to 0.08 per cent, the legal limit for driving in the US and UK.

Comparing the three teams yielded surprises. The team using mobile phones had more rear-end collisions and their braking time was slower. The intoxicated participants exhibited a more aggressive driving style, following the vehicle in front more closely and braking with greater force, but they had no accidents. You should not take from this that it is better to drive drunk than while using a mobile phone! What Drews and his colleagues concluded was that the drivers using mobile phones were dangerous because they simply did not have enough attention to devote to their driving.

Shortly after running the experiment, Drews himself experienced the phenomenon first hand when a driver next to him on the highway drifted into his lane, forcing the psychologist on to the shoulder. Both drivers took the next exit and Drews got out of his car, very upset. 'I knocked on his window. He was still on his mobile phone!' Drews recalled. But when he finally stopped talking, the chatty driver had 'no clue' about the disruption he'd caused. He hadn't seen a thing.

Since 2003 the law has prevented the use of handheld phones while driving – and penalties were doubled in 2017. Yet one out of every five drivers say that they check social media while in traffic, with 33 per cent taking photographs or video while at the wheel.[16] Even the RAC considers these statistics to understate the problem. But while both the law and the RAC place huge emphasis on whether the phone is handheld, the heart of the problem isn't really manual. It's the cognitive cost that proves critical. Humans do not have enough mental capacity to do all the things that we think we can do. As attentional load increases, attentional capacity gradually diminishes.[17] One frustrated psychologist has argued that the case for multitasking is on a par with 'urban legend':[18] a stupid story we like the sound of but that is really nonsense. And this is as true of women as for men; the idea that multitasking is women's unique contribution to the workplace is really nothing more than an excuse for getting the underpaid to overwork.

What's particularly important is that the intellectual capacity we appear to lose first may be what we need most: the ability to discriminate, to make good judgements. Remember Warren sitting in front of his twenty-four screens, so tired that he suffered from tunnel vision? He worried about how to get rid of the pressure spikes because he was too tired to contemplate the harder issue: what was causing these spikes to appear in the first place?

The bottleneck[19] that characterises our ability to receive information explains why we cannot intelligently absorb all the information presented to us on TV screens by Sky News, Bloomberg or the BBC News channel. I will sometimes play clips from finance shows to my business school students; they watch as stock prices scroll along the bottom, weather reports or sports scores pile up on the right and, in the small square of remaining screen space, some hapless CEO will be explaining corporate strategy. What, I ask the students after a few minutes, did you recall? A few swots will quote a stock price or two. Then I'll ask them to critique the CEO's strategy – and they all look at me as if I'm crazy: you mean we're supposed to watch all of that *and* think about it? It's impossible. What we can't do while we are watching such a busy array is think, discriminate, make critical judgements.

When we are tired or preoccupied – what psychologists call 'resource-depleted' – we start to economise, to conserve those resources. Higher-order thinking is more expensive. So too is doubt, scepticism, argument. 'Resource depletion specifically disables cognitive elaboration,' wrote Harvard psychologist Daniel Gilbert.[20] 'Not only does doubt seem to be the last to emerge, but it also seems to be the first to disappear.' Because it takes less brainpower to believe than to doubt, we are, when tired or distracted, gullible.[21] Because we are all biased, and biases are quick and effortless, exhaustion tends to make us prefer the information we know and are comfortable with. We're too tired to do the heavier lifting of examining new or contradictory information, so we fall back on our biases, the opinions and the people we already trust.

This higher-order functioning that we lose when overloaded or exhausted is important – and not just in oil refineries. In the late 1990s, I worked for a company, CMGI, that, in the heat of the first internet boom, bought large numbers of companies. Regularly on a Monday morning, I would encounter bleary-eyed executives hung over with exhaustion, having pulled an all-nighter or two in order to complete the latest acquisition. They were fried but triumphant; they were heroes: the deal was done! But I lost count of the number of transactions that were, even at the time, strategically mindless and ultimately wasteful. Why had we bought these businesses? Too much tunnel vision, too little sleep: no one thought – quite literally – to ask: why are we doing this in the first place?

Although CMGI was a remarkable environment to work in, it wasn't – and isn't – unusual for companies to pour vast resources into deals that bring armies of lawyers and bankers into panelled boardrooms to work through the night, completing the latest acquisition. The leading investment banks require long hours and weekend work from any employee who wishes to be considered for partner, or even to be taken seriously. Many leading investment bankers tell me that, however much they hate it, these are the rules of client service. When I point out that they could solve their problem by having more employees, each doing fewer hours, they look abashed by the simplicity of the arithmetic. The truth is, many of the participants love it: the thrill of the deadline, the mountains of documents, the legal, financial and regulatory complexity of the task.[22]

Yet most of these deals achieve worse than nothing. A study by KPMG found that 83 per cent of the mergers and acquisitions they studied didn't boost shareholder value; 53 per cent actually reduced it. Another study, by A.T. Kearney, found that total return to shareholders on 115 global mergers was a *negative* 58 per cent![23] And while business school professors dissect the corpse of each dead deal, it might be wiser to remember the fried executives who signed off on the strategy. Tunnel vision blinds us to the wider consequences of our decisions. It isn't just control-room operators who are dangerous.

Many psychologists have studied these phenomena, often (like Kahneman and Tversky) to understand why we make mistakes, others more tactically to devise guidelines for safer instrument panels. But one of the earliest was Stanley Milgram, who is more famous for his experiments in obedience (see chapter 6). Although Milgram himself was a native of New York City, he was fascinated by the way urbanites behaved. Years ahead of his time, he instinctively appreciated that the city is a system, in much the same way as the body and the brain are systems. In 'The Experience of Living in Cities' he reflected that the very large number of people who live in the city, together with their heterogeneity, meant that 'city life, as we experience it, constitutes a continuous set of encounters with overload, and of resultant adaptations'. He wondered what the effects of living with so many people, so many impressions, so much information might be. 'Overload characteristically deforms daily life on several levels, impinging on role performance, the evolution of social norms, cognitive functioning and the use of facilities.'[24]

A natural, as well as a professional, observer of human life, Milgram noted that the country shopkeeper might engage his customers in conversations whereas the city supermarket cashier barely had time to complete one checkout before starting on the next. 'The urbanite disregards the drunk sick on the street as he purposefully navigates through the crowd,' Milgram argued, not because he was less friendly or warm-hearted, but because city dwellers had learned to manage the demands made on them by a crowded city. They adapted by reducing the amount of information they took in. If a city was a system that yielded more 'inputs' than anyone could handle, inhabitants responded by taking in less. If the city is a system, then Milgram could see that his fellow New Yorkers were managing themselves in just the same way that our brain manages information when assaulted by too much: letting some impressions in and leaving many behind.

Milgram's argument was provocative because he argued that what got lost wasn't random but precise: when people felt overloaded, he said, they restricted their social and moral involvement. 'Overload is made more manageable by limiting the "span of sympathy".' Milgram wasn't out to enrage city lovers the world over. He was concerned that the load-balancing trade-offs weren't just operational; they were moral. If it is hard to doubt when you're tired, it may be even harder to care.

What is true for cities is equally true for large

organisations in which individuals operate under tremendous 'resource depletion'. Propagandists and brainwashers know what managers and corporate leaders choose to forget: the human mind, overloaded and starved of sleep, becomes morally blind. The Forward Institute runs a programme in which the senior executives from government and business are asked to analyse the wilful blindness of their own organisations. What's remarkable about this is that they can all do so – but it is only in the relative quiet and safety of a residential retreat that they find the cognitive capacity such reflection requires. For the most part, the insistent demands of their work specifically precludes such thinking and renders impossible the time required to walk through, step by step, the ethical consequences of hasty, exhausted decision-making. Just how bad this can get was vividly demonstrated at Abu Ghraib.

'Not only did this soldier work half around the clock [from 4 a.m. to 4 p.m.], he did so seven days a week with not a single day off for a full forty days! I can't imagine any job where such a work schedule would not be seen as inhumane.'[25]

The psychologist Philip Zimbardo served as an expert witness for one of the Abu Ghraib reservists, Chip Frederick. Although his sympathies lay more with Joe Darby, who had handed in the shocking photographs of the prison, Zimbardo understood better than anyone the impact that the situational influences of a prison environment could have on young men. In 1971, he had designed and run the Stanford Prison Experiment, in which twenty-four mentally and physically healthy young men endured a prison simulation for six days. Zimbardo's detailed account of the experiment is hair-raising, but it taught him volumes about the ways in which context dramatically transforms behaviour.[26] A landmark in the study of power and environment, the experiment eerily presaged many of the abuses committed at Abu Ghraib by Chip Frederick and his colleagues.

'There is absolutely nothing in his record that I was able to uncover that would predict that Chip Frederick would engage in any form of abusive, sadistic, behaviour,' Zimbardo wrote. 'On the contrary, there is much in his record to suggest that had he not been forced to work and live in such an abnormal situation, he might have been the military's all-American poster soldier on its recruitment ads. He could have been the best of apples in their good barrel.'[27]

Many forces – fear, corruption, inadequate resources, absence of supervision, written procedures, formal policies or guidelines and an absolute lack of training – conspired to erode those all-American qualities. But, as Zimbardo observes, that was just the beginning. Frederick not only did a twelve-hour shift, seven days a week. After working for forty days, he got just one day off, followed by two more solid weeks on. Even when his shifts were over, he wasn't able to leave the prison but went to sleep in a six-by-nine-foot prison cell that was dirty and noisy.

That Frederick was surrounded by colleagues just as ill-trained and just as exhausted meant no one was awake enough to have any moral sensibility left. Of course, other factors contributed to the abuse of prisoners but what is so striking about Zimbardo's analysis is that, at the simplest level, frightened, untrained guards were left with so little cognitive capacity.

Working hours seems such a small issue – but, by the same token, such a small thing to get right. There's a great deal of bravura attached to overwork. For men especially, complaining of tiredness can look and sound weak. And there's no bio-feedback: if you don't eat, you starve; if you overwork a muscle, it hurts. But when we abuse our brains, we can't see or feel the injury. Thinking is a physical activity – subject to the same limitations as any other part of our body – but we don't experience it that way. We might feel lousy but we are blind to what we are losing: the capacity to reason, to judge, to make good and humane decisions, to see consequences.

Nor is that loss a matter of just a few bad days, weeks or even months. One of the longest ever longitudinal studies of the physiological impact of work started in the 1970s under Michael Marmot. Today, that study can track the consequences of long hours and stress across the lifetimes of 10,000 Whitehall civil servants. And the data are eye-opening. Those working fifty-five hours a week or more begin, in their middle years, to suffer cognitive loss: their performance is poorer when tested for vocabulary, reasoning, information-processing, problem-solving, creativity and reaction times. This level of mild cognitive impairment in middle age also predicts earlier dementia and death.[28] Long hours and sleep deprivation wear out our brains until we are too tired to see what we are doing to ourselves.

I've lost count of how many corporations I've worked with that positively boast about the number of all-nighters they pull. Financial services may not be the absolute worst, but it's rare to encounter executives who don't still feel that productivity is associated with the number of hours they work. Most know that the thinking is flawed but blindly conform, out of fear that healthier behaviour might be mistaken for slacking. Nobody wants to be the visibly responsible soul who leaves work while they can still think straight. Client service, many will argue, just requires being always on – but I wonder how thrilled clients would be if they knew just how brain-dead that service was bound to be.

'You can't change the limits of your mind,' says Dan Simons. But we keep trying. Why? Is it the last vestige of a physical model of heroism for which we lack any intellectual justification? If so, then we'd better find that new model fast, before more reputations and lives are ruined. At the very least, as Western democracies struggle to define some kind of regulatory framework that could protect society from future disaster, we could do worse than demand that, after forty hours of work, everybody just goes home.

5. The Ostrich Instruction

Lie to me just a little bit longer
Lie to me until I'm stronger . . .
I'm not ready yet
To accept
The truth.
So lie to me.

from Heartless (Ridley/Bicât)

'Quite often when people come in here, they don't really lie – they just, what shall I say, underestimate the truth. Some deny it. They're all embarrassed. No one ever quite tells the truth.'

John Hawk isn't a priest, he's professor of dermatology at King's College London. When he sees skin that has been sun-damaged, he asks his patients whether they've been sunbathing. 'You get the most extraordinary vehemence from people who've been using sunbeds constantly. They're prepared to shout at me, insisting they are not harmful. There was one lady – we'd been quite friendly – she said, "I use sunbeds all the time and I love it and you aren't going to stop me. I don't want to know!"' Professor Hawk's angry patient isn't alone. Thousands of people don't want to know that tanning is bad for them and that sunbeds can kill them.

Hawk has heard all the arguments. 'You get people saying it boosts their vitamin D levels – but you don't need to boost your vitamin D levels; food and homeostasis will take care of that. Or people saying it produces endorphins and relieves pain. It's all nonsense. What's so sad about these patients is that they do know tanning is bad for you – that's why they're embarrassed – but they choose not to know.'

That refusal runs very deep, even outliving its victim.

'You can go around in circles, asking yourself why this happened,' said Penny Birch, talking about the death of her daughter Hayley. A flight attendant for Virgin Airlines, Hayley loved the sun and used her freedom to travel to maintain a good tan. 'She did enjoy sunbathing and would often top up her tan on rest days between flights,' her mother recalled. 'But she was naturally dark and never overdid it.'[1]

But at the age of twenty-five, Hayley died of skin cancer. By anyone's measure, that is overdoing it. Described as a 'girly girl who always liked to look her best', Hayley was perhaps no different from any of us who want to feel good about ourselves.

Her story was tragic but it wasn't unique. In Britain, someone dies of skin cancer every six hours; it is the third most common cause of cancer.[2] While most people now recognise that overexposure to the sun is unhealthy, the fact remains that most do not protect their skin from the sun's harmful rays.[3]

'I know I shouldn't – but you feel so great, you look slimmer and everybody always says I look so fit,' a tanned mother of three told me on her return from a beach vacation.

Defenders of suntans argue that sunlight feels so good that it's counterintuitive to see it as dangerous. Or that the risks of melanoma are relatively new – linked to the depletion of the ozone layer – and not everyone's caught up yet. But the research shows that, for the most part, we all know how dangerous overexposure to the sun is. And none of those arguments explains one of the most cognitively dissonant industries of the modern age: the tanning salon.

The 'incandescent light bath' was invented by John Harvey Kellogg. A physician and Seventh Day Adventist, Kellogg ran a sanatorium where he attacked a range of ills, using exercise, vegetarianism and sunshine. (His other claim to fame was the invention of granola and corn flakes.) Kellogg was a passionate believer in the moral and physical benefits of sunlight and, at the end of the nineteenth century, sun baths and sun lamps were used for a wide range of therapies. In 1900, Niels Finsen won the Nobel Prize for using sun lamps in the treatment of lupus. As natural suntans became more popular, sun lamps and sunbeds did too, supplementing tans in the winter or 'preparing' the skin prior to summer vacations. The early association of tanning machinery with health has proved very persistent.

'The tanning industry likes to emphasise beneficial health effects from tanning salons, saying things like "Come to our tanning salon and protect yourself against cancer!"' says Mona Saraiya. She is an expert in melanoma at the Center for Disease Control in Atlanta, Georgia. Coolly discussing the latest research, she's at pains to be as objective and fastidious as she can, nevertheless manifesting the scientist's utter bewilderment at irrational human behaviour.

'Or they say sunbeds are good for vitamin D deficiency or seasonal affective disorder. I do wonder why they're legal. They just are unsafe. Unsafe at any level. It is very frustrating. They are producing more and more cancers!'[4]

In their desire to reduce the dissonance they experience, tanning aficionados come up with some peculiar arguments. Surely, consumers argue, tanning salons wouldn't be allowed if they were harmful – would they? The very fact that they are viable, profitable businesses, that home-tanning machines are on sale, is taken as proof that they must be safe – because otherwise they would be prohibited. That is as powerful a form of social validation as it is possible to find. The very existence of tanning salons provides the confirmation salon customers need to overcome conclusive data. They're blind, of course, but what keeps them confirmed in their blindness is the fact that the salons and home-tanning systems flourish.

'It's incredible, the arguments people come up with to perpetuate something that they know, deep down inside, is bad for them,' says Professor Hawk. 'They think a tan shows that they have leisure and wealth and people like to look like they're wealthy with lots of free time. The sad reality is they've become creatures of habit. They don't want to change. So they just pretend they don't know.'

Pliny the Elder is thought to be the earliest naturalist to write about the ostrich. In his *Historia Naturalis* he is rather rude about the bird, decrying its stupidity: 'They imagine, when they have thrust their head and neck into a bush, that the whole of the body is concealed.' Today, natural scientists say that the bird lays its head and neck flat on the ground in an effort to elude its predators. But however you describe ostrich behaviour, the one thing everyone agrees on is that they absolutely do not bury their heads in the sand.

It's a shame, really, because we need ostriches as a metaphor for the way we all behave. Judges certainly need the bird. When they apply the legal concept of wilful blindness in court cases, they are said to be issuing 'the ostrich instruction'. Scientifically accurate or not, we all recognise the human desire at times to prefer ignorance to knowledge, and to deal with conflict and change by imagining it out of existence.

All of us want to bury our heads in the sand when taxes are due, when we have bad habits we know we should change, or when the car starts to make that strange sound. Ignore it and it will go away – that's what we think and hope. It's more than just wishful thinking. In burying our heads in the sand, we are trying to pretend the threat doesn't exist and that we don't have to change. We are also trying hard to avoid conflict: if the threat's not there, I don't have to fight it. A preference for the status quo, combined with an aversion to conflict, compels us to turn a blind eye to problems and conflicts we just don't want to deal with.

So my children walk straight past the laundry basket on the stairs because they don't want to stop what they're doing to attend to it. And I might not chastise them for it because I can't face another fight. And when I ignore the recycling, I'm hoping my husband will get the message – without a fight – that it needs to be put outside. Of course part of this is just laziness, but a big part of it is refusing to see anything that makes us uncomfortable.

An intriguing study in 1965 showed that our eyes focus on what appeals to us, and avoid what does not.[5] In the experiment, a number of people – men and women, students, housewives and secretaries – were asked to look at ten different pictures, some of which were sexual in content. A camera photographed their eye movements and later mapped these on to the pictures, to show the path of the viewer's gaze. Later, each participant was asked what they recalled of the pictures. Not surprisingly, each gave very different accounts of the same picture.

Ten minutes after the experiment, 'Mrs R' could remember six out of the ten pictures. Prompted, she could eventually recall them all but seemed to have difficulty with picture seven.

EXPERIMENTER: It is a man reading, near a nude woman. Do you remember that one?

MRS R: No, I don't remember that one at all.

EXPERIMENTER: Take a moment. A man reading near a nude woman. You don't remember that one at all?

MRS R: I don't remember that one at all.

EXPERIMENTER: A man sat reading a paper.

MRS R: I remember the window.

EXPERIMENTER: And you could see her profile. You could see her breast.

MRS R: Yes. Now I remember. Just the top. The girl's face turned around, no waistline, that man reading the paper, and that's all I saw.

That was all Mrs R recalled because it was practically all she looked at. Photographs of her eye movement show her eyes stuck pretty firmly to the newspaper.

'Miss I', however, had a different experience: 'This is a man reading a newspaper. There's a woman by the table with her naked bosom. I thought it was very humorous because he wasn't looking at her at all.'

And the photographs of Miss I's eye movements confirm that they roved far more widely across the entire picture.

Many psychologists argue about why we behave like this: how could we know where *not* to look without looking first? But nobody denies that we do do this: we studiously avoid seeing, and remembering, those things that may cause us discomfort. In the same way that we tend to gravitate towards people who are like us, our eyes – and our minds – focus on information, objects, ideas that confirm our sense of self.

This phenomenon isn't quite as extreme as the tunnel

vision in the Texas City control room, but it is similar. Both are stress responses. For Mrs R, who is described as timorous and vague, the picture posed a threat of embarrassment and potentially of conflict: why was she being made to look at this picture? For Miss I, an attractive young woman trained in the arts, the picture posed no threat at all.

Fear of change and fear of conflict have the same effect. It isn't just dermatologists who have to deal with patients embarrassed by their own habits. Doctors' offices witness a parade of patients who knew they should have come in earlier, who missed appointments or scans or check-ups. Debt-counselling services too witness the same ostrich-like behaviour.

'We have people who come in with Sainsbury's carrier bags full of unopened letters,' says Andrew Steward. He works at the Citizens Advice Bureau in Bristol. 'I had one gentleman in here. He had been a financial adviser; his job was to manage other people's money! But when he got into trouble, he couldn't bring himself to open the letters from the bank and the credit-card companies. It wasn't until he was facing a court hearing for repossession that he came to us for help. We managed to persuade the court to hold off in this case. But it was striking that this professional man had become completely disempowered by his debt problems. We see this ostrich phenomenon all the time. A kind of inertia sets in. People live with chronic debt for a long time until a trigger event – often something as bad as a visit from the bailiffs or not being able to withdraw cash – drives them to seek help. But they will still go to the wire.'

Every day in the UK, 277 people are declared insolvent or bankrupt; average household debt (not including mortgages) in 2017 ran at around £84,000.[6] Since 2016, the British have become net borrowers – meaning that they spend more than they earn, and UK savings in 2018 were the lowest they had been since 1963.[7] The banking crisis went some way to slowing our addiction to borrowing but it has done little to erase the vast amount of debt that the housing bubble created in the first place.

'People signed up for mortgages that they couldn't afford,' says Steward, 'because they were at the receiving end of a lot of intense selling techniques, salesmen on quotas, leaflets saying, "Congratulations! You have been selected for a special-rate loan." They believed it. People airbrush the terms and conditions. They just don't want to know.

'Very few of them ever worked out their income versus their expenditure. It's a Mr Micawber attitude – if they can squeak by, then everything will be okay. There's a kind of fatal optimism.'

'I think my moment of wilful blindness was when I decided I needed a mortgage holiday,' Paula Daly told me. Although she'd enjoyed a successful career working as a freelance editor for public sector publications and as a consultant in marketing and design, Daly had always felt that she was not making the most of her creative potential. When she began to make good money, she decided to follow her dream and launch the fashion brand Mouse to Minx: Where Burlesque meets Miss Marple. She researched her idea and conducted a successful pilot inside a friend's store. She admits she 'got seduced by retail' and gambled with opening a shop on Bristol's Christmas Steps and living upstairs.

'I knew I'd made a mistake almost the moment I opened the shop. There wasn't enough passing trade. But I just kept going.' When her business loan ran out, she signed up for a mortgage.

'I got what was effectively a hundred per cent at a high-rate mortgage with a firm called Commercial First. When I started to default, Commercial First were completely inflexible and began charging punitive fees for the missed payments – up to £125 per month.'

Eventually the property was repossessed and Daly lived on benefits, with a pile of envelopes that she hasn't opened because she knows they contain demands for money she doesn't have.

Debt counsellors say that this isn't a matter of intelligence or education; sometimes it's the most educated who have been most blind because they believed they knew what they were doing.

'I think people live very close to the wire financially in this country,' says Steward. 'There's no typical debt client – we see everyone, from people with no English to very sophisticated people. They all share the ostrich complex. Once they get into trouble, their horizons narrow. They look to the next month, day, even hours and work out a way of keeping afloat for that long. Many just can't face the fact that the deal they've worked out cannot hold.'

In business circles, this is known as the 'status quo trap'[8]: the preference for everything to stay the same. The gravitational pull of the status quo is strong – it feels easier, less risky, and requires less mental and emotional energy to 'leave well alone'. Nobody likes change because the status quo feels safer, it's familiar, we're used to it. Change feels like redirecting the riverbed: effortful and risky. It's so much easier to imagine that what we don't know won't hurt us.

One reason business executives worry so much about the status quo trap is because inertia exerts an inordinate pull within organisations. Every change carries with it the possibility of conflict, uncertainty, danger. The business environment is dynamic and difficult enough without going to look for trouble.

Nowhere was this more true than in the financial services

industry in the years leading up to the global banking crisis of 2008. Well before that, anyone breathing knew that property prices and mortgage lending were out of control. By August 2006, Nouriel Roubini described the market as being in 'free fall'.[9] At the end of that year, the collapse had such momentum that a far more humble observer, Aaron Krowne, who had no expertise in economics or finance, started his website, Implode-O-Meter, to track the daily demise of sub-prime lenders.[10] That a huge and fundamental part of the American economy was going bust was not hard to see. Nor was it a state secret that all of those loans and mortgages came from – and went back to – banks. So how could banks not have known about their own risk?

To be fair, some did. Goldman Sachs did, J.P. Morgan did. Cantor Fitzgerald, at the beginning of 2007, quietly shrank its mortgage book. But most of the major banks did not. One reason – and there are many – is that they did not see the risk because they did not want to. Any change to the way that risk was evaluated would provoke power struggles.

Pat Lewis discovered this, first hand. An engineer by training, Lewis is a straight-shooting Midwesterner, well liked and highly regarded. His friends and colleagues say he's a 'stand-up guy'. He joined Bear Stearns in 1998, working in Treasury where he eventually became Deputy Treasurer. He thought the traditional ways of assessing risk were inadequate, so he designed a way to measure the risk carried by each business unit, relative to its returns. He hoped that if the risk and return were wildly out of proportion, this would identify risk that had been underestimated. What Lewis sought was a way of shining a light into areas where risks in the firm were greatest. You'd think that would be helpful – but Lewis couldn't get much support.

'So my discussions with the business units would go like

this: "We want to understand the risks in your business." And they'd say, "Why?" And if you said, "Well, it will drive a portion of your compensation and it's another way – besides just net revenue – to evaluate your business," then they'd say, "Any number you have is too high." And if, instead, you said, "Well, we're just curious and want to gain another insight into your business," they'd think you weren't worth the time of day. So what do you do?'[11]

Lewis is a long-distance runner; he didn't give up easily. For three full years, he plugged away at the project, building a mathematical model that could give ongoing visibility into the risk in each business unit relative to the capital it employed. Finally, when it was sufficiently well honed, Lewis and his boss Sam Molinaro presented a simplified version of their model to their CEO, Jimmy Cayne. He dismissed it as just too complicated.

'The CEO didn't understand it so he didn't want it used internally. It was too political. I was too old to do something useless so I quit doing it. Nobody else wanted to take it on.'

Cayne didn't reject Lewis' risk-based capital-allocation project just because it was complicated. He understood it well enough to know that, if it worked, the project threatened to produce huge amounts of change and conflict within a highly political organisation: people might lose money, they might lose bonuses, they might lose status.

Lacking the courage to confront that conflict, Cayne's decision to cleave to outmoded, inadequate models of risk left his bank structurally blind, without the capacity to see what it was doing. Bankers at Bear Stearns (who loved risking other people's money) were as averse to examining their own risk as dear old 'Mrs R' was to looking at the naked breast.

At the time that Bear Stearns collapsed, Pat Lewis was already interviewing; he moved to become managing director at Cantor Fitzgerald, with no nostalgia for the frustrating inertia of his old employer. 'At Bear,' Pat Lewis recalls, 'you'd have threats of anarchy and people quitting if anyone interfered in a business unit. No one wanted to be the instigator of that. The surest way to get fired was to be a troublemaker.'

The only 'trouble' Pat made, of course, was to try to get a clear view of the business. And he was unusual in being prepared to put up with quite a lot of resistance to do so. But most of us don't persevere as Pat did; most of us stay silent, and silence is the language of inertia. In a groundbreaking study, two Stern School of Business professors studied what they call 'employee silence': the unwillingness of employees to articulate or discuss problems they see around them. Elizabeth Morrison and Frances Milliken challenge all the clichés of academic life: they're neither stuffy, nor pedantic, but find rich material in everyday working lives.

'There was a new initiative coming in the department and a big meeting to discuss it,' Morrison recalled. 'And everyone was talking about it and how awful it was.'

'It inspired a lot of bad feeling and talk and a lot of anxiety,' Milliken added.

'And then we got to the meeting and the subject came up – and nobody said a word! Silence. Nothing. *Nada.* No one raised a word of complaint. Just sailed on through. And that's when we thought: that was interesting. I wonder if that happens everywhere?'

They designed a study to try to understand silence in organisations, and what they found was pretty shocking. Interviewing a cross-section of executives, fully 85 per cent said that they had, at some point, felt unable to raise an issue or concern with their boss. Only 51 per cent said that they felt truly comfortable raising issues or spotlighting problems and a mere 15 per cent said that they had never felt unable to express themselves openly.[12]

'When there are holes in the research process, we generally don't say anything to the directors of the projects,' said one respondent working for a not-for-profit organisation.

'I raised a concern about some policies,' replied another, 'and was told to shut up and that I was becoming a troublemaker. This made me go into detached mode, making me a "yes man".'

One particularly compelling interviewee tells of a co-worker in financial services who was being phased out, he felt unfairly.

'I felt it was a moral imperative to act,' he recalled. 'But in the end, I did nothing.'

The recurrent theme in Milliken and Morrison's research is that people stay silent at work – bury their heads in the sand – because they don't want to provoke conflict, be (or be labelled) troublemakers. They may not like the status quo but, in their silence, they maintain it, believing (but also ensuring) the status quo can't be shifted.

When I replicated Morrison and Milliken's study with European employees, the results overall were roughly the same. What stood out, however, was the reason respondents gave for their silence. Whereas American executives were silent for fear of being branded troublemakers, their UK and European counterparts felt that speaking up would be futile; nothing would change. I'm not quite sure which is worse – fear or futility – but both mean that huge amounts of insight, awareness and knowledge are lost daily in organisations around the world.

Reading these studies is a tremendously sad experience: dozens of smart, engaged, moral individuals who have, on some level, given up. They don't believe that they can change the status quo, and so they've surrendered to it. What's so awful about this is that their decision to turn a blind eye in turn renders their bosses blind. How can the boss see what the employees won't show them? The only consequence of their silence is that the blind lead the blind.

What's also very sad about this research is that it rings so true. Even as I'm writing this, I sit on the board of an organisation that has stopped in its tracks because it cannot face a single, mission-critical problem. Each board member will talk about it in private; it never comes up in meetings. Nobody can face the fight. And so the entire organisation drifts on, consuming time and resources but making no progress. For this business, the recession came as a marvellous distraction, helping everyone studiously to debate its consequences, rather than to address the old, festering sore no one wants to touch. Many board members say they don't want to raise the issue because they don't know how to solve it. But as long as it remains invisible, it is guaranteed to remain insoluble. That is the hidden cost of ostrich behaviour: whether your head is in the sand or just lying prone along the ground, you're in no position to defend yourself. You cannot fix a problem that everyone refuses to acknowledge.

In 2001, I had to fire an executive who had been working for me. I can't remember all of the details but I recall vividly what happened next. Several employees came up to say how glad they were that he was gone. But the reason came as news to me. They were glad to get rid of a sexual harasser. I had had no idea. We worked in a large open-plan office, I could see almost everyone all the time. I had never noticed a thing. I could have known and should have known; for that wilful blindness I was responsible. But why hadn't I been told?

Nobody knowing me would ever imagine I'd condone

sexual harassment. But when I asked why no one had come to tell me what was going on, the answers were complex. Loyal colleagues could see I had a huge amount on my plate; they didn't want to add to my concerns. They loved the company and didn't want to destabilise it. They weren't sure how other colleagues might feel and feared provoking divisiveness in what was a pretty harmonious organisation. Nobody wanted to be the harbinger of conflict. Just as Morrison and Milliken were doing their research, it was played out live, in my office.

'The law on sexual harassment is clear,' Meriel Schindler told me. A lawyer in a large London law firm, she advises clients on these issues regularly. The Equality Act 2010 states clearly that it is illegal to behave in a way that violates another's dignity, creates an intimidating, hostile, degrading, humiliating or offensive environment. It is also illegal to engage in unwanted sexual conduct or to treat a colleague less favourably because their sexual advances have been rebuffed.

'Generally speaking, people understand that there are laws and that something that happened to them may be unlawful,' Schindler said. 'But many people, especially junior people, rarely feel they have the clout or confidence to stand their ground – and HR may advise them, even help them, to move on. It's very rare to have the wrongdoer leave. Actually to bring a claim requires a claimant who is quite fierce.'

Ferocity is rare when women often have experienced harassment, in some form, for so much of their lives. Like UV rays, it can seem harmless while its impact is insidious.

'It starts with little things when you're at school,' one undergraduate told me. 'The wolf-whistling which your teachers tell you to ignore. *Your teachers!* Then you're at a gig and the guys crowd around you and touch you up and you can't move and you can't really stop them. At uni, guys rush past you, arms open, brushing your breasts. Guys flash you as you're walking home at night. And each one of these things is so small and pathetic you feel you can't make a fuss. So you learn to avoid those situations.

'You know why we drink shots? Because you down them in one: that means you don't leave your drink long enough for anyone to drop something into it. We all learn this. It's why sometimes when we dance, we keep our drinks in our hands – though even that's dangerous 'cause you're not watching your drink the whole time.

'And all this stuff: you tell yourself it doesn't really matter but what that just means is that *you* don't really matter. Or that you are the problem. That you're less than, less than important, less than human. And by the time you're thinking that: there is no way you are going to be the person to stand up and say there's a problem. Why would you? You don't count.'

What others might see as minor offences grind away at dignity and self-respect, leaving victims defenceless. They know that being agreeable, cheerful, easy to work with, is what everybody wants from them. When I've spoken with doctors, lawyers, academics, engineers, actors, technicians, flight crew, administrators, politicians and financiers, they all say the same thing: we don't want the fight, we don't want to be type-cast as complainers, as difficult, brittle, bitches. Merely to defend their right to a safe workplace makes them feel dangerously out of line. And having seen few, if any, cases resolved in the victim's favour, they conclude that there's no point raising an issue that they won't win. Fear *and* futility perpetuate abuse.

In industries like entertainment and financial services, sexual harassment has long been an open secret. It's clear that many, many people in Hollywood saw Harvey Weinstein as a predator for years; a few victims talked to each other but nobody else did a thing. In the early days of the internet, the online venture Digital Entertainment Network was identified as harbouring, even operating as a cover for, a paedophile ring, bringing very young hopefuls to Hollywood with promises of fame and riches. John Connolly, who investigated the company, called it an 'industrial home for the blind' because investors like Microsoft, Dell, David Geffen, Michael Huffington and Bryan Singer so studiously turned a blind eye to minors naked in hot tubs. Only as the company approached its public offering in 1999 did the first public accusations and an FBI investigation shut it down. But many of those involved continue to work in Hollywood to this day.[13]

To suggest that the victims' silence, in this context, is compliance adds insult to injury. What the #MeToo movement revealed was that sexual harassment has been pervasive and constant. Two in five women, and one in five men, in the UK say they have experienced unwanted sexual behaviour at work.[14] It's worse still for those in vulnerable positions – on zero-hours contracts, self-employed, in internships or very junior positions – with 43 per cent reporting experiences of some form of sexual harassment at work. Hotel housekeepers, for example, rarely complain about guests exposing themselves or masturbating in front of them for fear of losing the jobs and pay they need to support their families. When I asked the cleaner in my London hotel room about her experience, she said this was a persistent problem and it was why she always tried to prop the door open as she worked. Why wouldn't she complain to her management? 'Because I'm a nobody.'

Although the #MeToo and #TimesUp movements promise that this can change, it will be some time before we know whether it has proved tenacious enough to overcome the profound reluctance that victims feel to discuss harassment and that managers demonstrate to confront it. I've spoken to doctors, teachers, professors, politicians who, despite their professional standing and success, still don't know what to do or how to react. Must they sacrifice their status and hard-won success by speaking out? So powerful is their desire not to be cast in the role of victim that they leave themselves and their junior colleagues unprotected. They can't be blind but some would still like to be.

In 2017, as the #MeToo movement gained momentum, famous names seemed to lose their positions with incredible speed. This made me wonder: how could major organisations safely fire senior figureheads so quickly? The departures followed allegations far faster than any investigations would have allowed. How could so much happen so fast?

'Dossiers,' an American lawyer confided to me. 'We had the dossiers. All along. When your business depends on a famous name, you need to know what they're doing. They're an investment – that means they might also be a risk. It is your business to monitor your risks. You turn a blind eye until the problem is made visible – and then you're ready.'

My confidante didn't and couldn't speak with authority about every case but she had, she insisted, seen enough to know. Nobody would willingly sacrifice a superstar or a high performer until they had to.

The management doesn't want to know; many of the victims themselves would rather not know. Being made to feel 'less than' is as effective a silencer as the deep desire for dignity and respect. The one thing that those experiencing sexual harassment do *not* want is to be characterised as victims for the rest of their lives. 'Nobody wants to be the buzzkill,' is how Lindsey Reynolds phrased it. She and many of her co-workers at John Besh restaurants in the United States described being 'sexually harassed and verbally assaulted almost every day', assailed by 'vulgar and offensive comments, aggressive unwelcomed touching and sexual advances, condoned and sometimes even encouraged by managers and supervisors'. Much of this occurred in public places and was far from invisible.[15] But being cast as 'buzzkill' was so intimidating that, for years, Reynolds and her co-workers kept their mouths shut. As role model, they recalled Anita Hill, the US attorney and academic whose complaint of sexual harassment against Supreme Court nominee Clarence Thomas had led to her character assassination and his appointment. Nobody watching her public excoriation would have been tempted to follow in such footsteps.

Being stereotyped as a victim is nobody's lifetime ambition. It silences so many who have just cause and motive to defend themselves, their friends and colleagues. The passionate desire to salvage scraps of dignity and self-respect from the humiliation that is sexual harassment turns a victim's anger against themselves and loses the name of action. The tragedy is that, in trying to avoid public victimhood, the price paid is silent, invisible, private victimhood: the sense that one isn't worthy of protection, dignity or respect.

Today, nobody can claim not to know about sexual harassment, nor are there any extenuating excuses for the organisational failure to expunge it. But I continue to be amazed by the apathy with which the subject is addressed. 'I hope the movie stars don't just move on to the next big thing,' was how one consultant articulated his concern to me. He readily acknowledged harassment in his own profession, but his statement implied that it was up to celebrities – not up to him, not up to us – to act on what we now cannot fail to see. If wilful blindness makes a sound, I heard it in that sentence.

Libby, Montana, is a long way from everywhere. Sixty-five miles south of Canada, a seven-hour drive from the capital, Helena. The nearest big city is Spokane, Washington – and that's a good three-and-a-half-hour drive away. But as you cross the border from Idaho, coming into Montana, the countryside becomes breathtakingly beautiful. Rising out of icy lakes, the Cabinet Mountains scream into the sky, clad in dense pine forest. This is the America of legend: big skies, bold landscapes and raw.

It says everything about the people of Libby that, when you reach the town, it doesn't feel remote. Only around 2,500 people live here, but they've made it a place that you want to be. The Libby welcome is warm and proud. They aren't glad to see you because they lack for company; they're glad to see you're lucky enough to share their town. The hotel guide says that Libby's assets 'include clean water, clean air, beautiful scenery and close access to nature's playground', but I'd say its assets are its people.

Stoical is the word most people use when talking about Libby. Because, while it's beautiful, it's also a tough place to live. Until the 1920s, most of the men worked in logging. Dangerous work, and seasonal, logging was a hard way to support a family. So when vermiculite was discovered in the mountains, things picked up. Year-round employment, some of it indoors. Gayla Benefield still remembers the day her father, Perley, got a job there, because it was her birthday.

'My father had been out of work prior to 1954,' Gayla recalled. 'He had had a rough year and things were tough and suddenly he came home – it was September 17, 1954 – and said he had a birthday present for me: he had a job!'

Gayla looks like she belongs in the mountains. With the blondest hair and palest complexion, her Norwegian heritage is obvious. She belongs here and knows it. Her parents moved to Libby when she was two and, after a string of disappointing jobs, the mine was a godsend. Perley loved his work, loved the men, and the sense of doing something important. But most important of all was the chance to earn a regular wage,

Social Security and a pension. Starting off as a sweeper in the dry mill, he hoped he'd move on up to driving one of the big trucks. But for now, Perley had found a secure future for himself and his family.

The Universal Zonolite Company produced raw materials for housing insulation, concrete, wallboard, roofing, even soil conditioner. There seemed no end to the usefulness of the material. Ninety per cent of the country's supply came from Libby and was shipped all over America. Even though it only employed about a hundred men, it felt like an important business, helping America to grow. And working there had its privileges: in 1959, Perley boasted that the company was such a great employer they were giving everyone free x-ray check-ups.

'Dad was just so thrilled at work,' Gayla remembered. 'All the guys loved working at the mine; it was like a fraternity up there. Dad loved operating equipment and he worked his way to the top of the mountain, grading the roads. In winter, we hoped for snow because that would mean he'd get paid double time.'

What he didn't know, because no one told him, was that concerns about the safety of the mine had started three years earlier, when an engineer from the state health department, Benjamin Wake, had conducted a hygiene study measuring air quality in the mine. It was dusty: so thick with dust that the filters in his vacuum pumps kept getting clogged. And it wasn't, as the men had been told, just 'nuisance dust'.

'The asbestos in the air is of considerable toxicity,' he wrote. 'Inhalation of asbestos dust must be expected sooner or later to produce pulmonary fibrosis.'[16]

Although the toxicity of asbestos wasn't definitively established until 1964, Wake already knew that pulmonary asbestosis 'is a progressive disease with a bad prognosis'. He returned to the mine in 1958, 1960 and 1962, each time making recommendations for repairs to the ventilation systems and working conditions that might protect the workers. But levels of asbestos continued to rise, and the workforce increased to 150 men. Nobody told any of them what they were breathing or how dangerous it was; even though state authorities were monitoring the mine, they weren't sharing their findings with anyone but the company's senior management. But the company x-rays – that great free gift Perley boasted of – bore out Wake's prognosis: of the 130 workers x-rayed, 82 already showed signs of lung disease. But neither the men, nor their doctors, were told anything.

In 1961, Gayla married Gary Svenson. He was serving in the military but, when he came home, he went to work at the mine, too. But, unlike Perley, he hated it.

'Gayla's dad got me a job there when I came out of the service. I didn't like it, I didn't like the dust. You'd put the ore in sacks, thump them on the ground – the stuff went up your nose. We were given respirators, but nobody used them because they got all clogged up in fifteen minutes.'

Gary lasted only four months at the mine, before leaving to go into a car dealership.

But that same year, W.R. Grace, a large American corporation traded on the New York Stock Exchange, bought the mine and production really took off. By now, the medical establishment and Grace knew that asbestos was toxic. Libby's vermiculite went all over the country. Monokote, the company's fireproofing spray, was used everywhere, even at landmark sites like the World Trade Center, where it was applied to steel support beams. The world's leading authority on asbestos estimated at the time (1969) that not one man spraying it would be alive in twenty years.[17] But no one in Libby knew that. A 1969 test showed that 24,000 pounds of dust came out of the large stack at the dry mill daily, with asbestos levels as high as 20–40 per cent. The Libby mine had several stacks and production continued to increase.

But Perley's joy in his work did not. In 1964, he went to the doctor and was told he had a heart condition, and should find some lighter work at the mine. He was only fifty-two but the management found him some easier jobs and, on the days his chest pains were worse, all his friends at the mine pitched in to help him out.

Gayla told me, 'He said: "I'm so lucky they let me work with this heart condition." He really felt so grateful. Guys would help Dad up the steps and carry his kit; they helped him all the way because he couldn't walk and step up two steps. What he wanted most of all was to be able to stay for twenty years so he could get his pension. But from 1968 onwards, he just got chest pains so bad, he got more and more ill, then he got pneumonia and started missing work.'

In 1969, the mine manager, Earl Lovick, conducted a study of his employees. With statistical precision, he noted that 'although 17 per cent of our 1 to 5 years' service group have or are suspect of lung disease, there is a marked rise (45 per cent) beginning with the 11th year of service, climbing to 92 per cent in the 21 to 25 years' service group'.

By now, Perley had been working at the mine for fifteen years. In 1971, Earl Lovick stopped smoking and had an operation to have pleural plaque removed from his lungs. But the men under him continued working at the mine, with no idea of what they were handling or how dangerous it was. At the age of fifty-nine, just five days before he was due to receive his pension, Perley died. And Gayla began to think something was wrong.

'What tipped me off was the tragic way the man died and the way the company never sent a card. I started investigating and started talking to my friends' fathers and there was another man who was forty-nine when he died. I thought perhaps Grace didn't know what was going on. And I didn't really know what it was – I didn't know it was asbestos.'

By this time, Gayla had a job reading meters for the power company. She'd spend the daytime going from house to house, talking to people, meeting everyone. And what struck her was how many men were at home, sitting on the back porch, using oxygen tanks. The more she talked to people, the more she learned how Grace was paying them off, making private settlements that no one could disclose. All the men had worked at the mine.

'Then my mom got sick. She'd gone to talk to an attorney about Dad's case and he heard Mom cough and asked to see her medical records. He called her back and said she had classic asbestosis. She had been going to hospital for years here and the doctors that had been treating her for pneumonia knew what it was, and not one of them ever told her.

'And then I remembered once, when Dad was still alive, Mom broke her leg and was in hospital for two weeks and I think the doctor took two x-rays for her leg and nine for her chest! Grace had an underground study going on, examining chest x-rays to understand the progression of the disease. But here's the thing: she never worked at the mine!'

Margaret had never worked at the mine, but it didn't matter. Each day, when Perley had come home from work and hugged his wife, he was covered in dust. He tracked dust all the way through the family home. There was dust in the family car. You didn't have to work with vermiculite to be contaminated by it. There was dust all over town. Everyone was at risk.

In 1990 Grace closed the mine. A fall in demand for its product, coupled with increasing and ongoing liabilities, meant the business was no longer viable. But it didn't mean that Grace's involvement in the town was over. They knew – had known for decades – that the legacy of their ownership would be many years of responsibility for their former employees and their families.

Gayla's mother had received an out-of-court settlement from W.R. Grace for $100,000, of which she ultimately received just $67,000. Adding up the medicine receipts alone, Gayla found it cost her mother over a million dollars to die.

'She'd be fine in the mornings but by noon her lungs would be full. It was horrific because she would curse Dad, curse the company,' Gayla recalls. 'At this time her own mother was ninety-nine and getting a hip replacement – and here was my mom scarcely able to breathe. Her own brother is still alive *today*, doing ballroom dancing. This is the way our family is. We just don't quit.'

Gayla certainly didn't quit. She talked to everyone she knew – which was pretty much everybody in town. Many of them had also made private settlements with Grace that they weren't allowed to discuss. Asbestosis and mesothelioma riddled Libby and W.R. Grace had known about it ever since they bought the mine.

Just before her mother died in 1996, Gayla got her permission to sue W.R. Grace for her mother's death. Margaret Benefield hoped she'd manage to make her daughter rich and Gayla says that, in a way, she did. But it wasn't money she was after.

'Of course they tried so hard to stop me. Made offers of three hundred, four hundred, five hundred thousand dollars. But it always had to be secret and that isn't what I wanted. I wanted it to be public. I wanted everyone to know what was going on in this town. And I wanted to be able to talk about it.

'The last offer they made me was $605,000 and a letter

of apology. I asked if I could publish the settlement on the internet and they said no, so I said no. I had to have a guilty verdict. The jury came back with an award of $250,000 – but I got that guilty verdict. But you know, the local press was never there. No press at all. Just a tiny blurb in the paper. We were suing a Fortune 500 company and it was the only time there'd been a guilty verdict for secondary exposure leading to wrongful death. And it didn't make the news.'

Full of rage at what Grace had done to her family and to her community, Gayla would talk to anyone who would listen. But mostly they wouldn't listen. Local media, she's convinced, were intimidated by Grace. So too were most local politicians. Everywhere she looked, Gayla saw people dying slow, agonising and expensive deaths – and nobody wanted to know.

But in 1999, she struck lucky. Andrew Schneider, an investigative journalist from out of town – Seattle – came to Libby, researching a feature about the 1872 General Mining Act. He ran into Gayla and, with some knowledge of W.R. Grace's malfeasance in the past, he paid attention to her story. When the *Seattle Post-Intelligencer* published his front-page story, all hell broke loose.

> First it killed some miners. Then it killed wives and children, slipping into their homes on the dusty clothing of hardworking men. Now the mine is closed but in Libby the killing goes on. W.R. Grace knew, from the time it bought the mine in 1963, why the people in Libby were dying. But for the thirty years it owned the mine, the company did not stop it. Neither did the governments. Not the town of Libby, not Lincoln County. Not the state of Montana, not federal mining, health and environmental agencies, not anyone else charged with protecting the public health.[18]

The Environmental Protection Agency was called in for what would ultimately become the largest Superfund clean-up site in American history.

As Gayla had uncovered W.R. Grace's knowledge of the town's contamination, she'd discovered shocking information: not just secret x-rays but secret autopsies, doctors keeping quiet and state authorities burying information. But nothing was more disturbing than Gayla's discovery that so many of her friends and neighbours did not want to know what she had uncovered. 'People would cross the street when they saw me coming,' she recalled. 'They shunned me as though I had something contagious. People said I was crazy or that the lawyers were giving me kickbacks – and these would be people whose own family members were dragging around oxygen tanks!

'One line of defence was, people would say: if the doctors thought there was something wrong, they'd tell us. But they took the secret x-rays and didn't tell anyone! The mayor said: "I know it's really bad but what can we do?" I had visions of the town jumping on the bandwagon and fixing it but instead people said nothing. They just buried their heads in the sand.'

Gayla was angry and frustrated when townspeople fought against Superfund status, and fought against getting an asbestos clinic established. She was trying to bring help, know-how and money to the town – but the town didn't want to know.

'The businessmen and townspeople were all making money from the miners! I don't understand why one didn't stand up and say: enough is enough. But they didn't. That this community would let people die – it was just incredible to me.'

Though they were now divorced, Gayla and Gary Svenson were still friends and he listened to her. 'It divided the town. People didn't want to believe it. There was real hatred between those who liked the company and those who were sick. To this day there are workers who still believe that W.R. Grace did nothing wrong. They were paid a wage to do a job and made a living for them and they are satisfied with that.'

Even among her own family, Gayla encountered opposition. 'My brother-in-law used to brag about how much money he was making – said he could buy himself a new pair of lungs. And this was after my mom and my dad had died of the disease. He died a horrible death in six months.' His sons and wife were subsequently diagnosed with asbestosis.

'We had old loggers who would say, "I could go out in the woods and die tomorrow." But I'd say to them: that tree wouldn't come back and kill your children and wife! We even had people who made bumper stickers saying, "And no I don't have asbestosis!" No one had the courage to confront me face to face, they just muttered and didn't help. They just wanted to deny the whole thing.'

'I went along with that whole "it's not that bad" attitude for quite a while,' admits Leroy Thom. He's now one of Gayla's strongest allies. 'I had a friend who was on oxygen but, you know, he seemed to get along just fine – we used to go bowling together. And then, just suddenly, he just died. It really made me think: maybe I haven't appraised this as I should.'

Leroy worked at the mine for sixteen years. Today, though he's been diagnosed with asbestosis, he runs a machine shop and devotes a lot of his energies to the town's Center for Asbestos Related Diseases. He's affable and laid-back but he says himself that he's been on a steep and emotional learning curve.

'There was a lot of opposition to the clinic, and some people used to come in the back door. They didn't want to be seen coming in! But the good thing is that people trust it – especially people who have the disease. On the other side, though, is the fact that people are like ostriches – they don't want to acknowledge that the clinic even exists, because it proves that the disease is here. It divided our community. Still today, even among some of the workers, they will say things like: you're not missing an arm!'

Gayla isn't the kind of person to be daunted by opposition, even the silent intransigence that she has encountered for years in Libby. Staunch support from old friends and neighbours helped her persevere in getting all the bad news out in the open. Finally, in 2000, the EPA and the Agency for Toxic Substances and Disease Registry agreed to screen all former Grace workers, their family members and anyone who had lived in Libby for at least six months up to 1990. They were expecting about 2,000 people; over 6,000 turned up. Then they extended the screening to anyone who had lived or worked in Libby. One of Gayla's oldest friends and staunchest allies, Les Skramstad, had already been diagnosed with asbestosis; so had his wife Norita and his son Brent. He knew first hand how everyone in the town felt.

'It was like waiting for your draft notice during the war,' said Les. 'It was like going out to the mailbox – that long walk – hoping that the long white envelope from the government wasn't there.'

In December 2000, when the ATSDR released 'Mortality from asbestosis in Libby, Montana', it showed that the death rate in Libby from asbestosis was forty times higher than in the rest of the state and eighty times greater than anywhere else in America.

By now, Gayla was getting hate mail; it just made her more relentless. What kept her going was the belief that the wives and children of the miners could be, must be helped – by decent compensation and good healthcare. Inspired by the wish that the next generation wouldn't have to suffer as her own parents had, she hoped fervently that, the more the town knew, the more it could do for its children. That dedication received a stunning blow when she discovered that Libby's school was contaminated.

'Grace had tested the running track at Plummer School in 1983 and found that the runners were stirring up dangerous levels of asbestos. Underneath the bleachers was completely contaminated – and that is where the kids play during the game. The skating rink – where kids played in the summer when it wasn't frozen – had vermiculite tailings at its base. That is the angriest I have ever been! Angry at the town, angry at the town fathers who knew the material had been dumped there. The principal of that school loved kids – he had retired – but you'd think he'd have stepped forward to say: perhaps you should just look at the school. But he hadn't said a word! The story had broken wide open in 1999 and here we were, it was 2002, and nobody had said a thing! And for three solid years, those kids were exposed. My grandkids' first day of latency was their first day of kindergarten.'

That same summer, Gayla and her second husband were both diagnosed with lung abnormalities. Neither of them had ever worked in the mine.

As the years have gone by, the EPA has continued to find vermiculite all over Libby and to try to clean it up. In June 2009, the federal government finally declared Libby the site of a public-health emergency. An earlier attempt in 2002 had been thwarted by the previous administration's Office of Management and Budget.

Today, if you go to the centre of Libby and stop for coffee, you can sit and watch as EPA trucks drive up and down the roads, removing contaminated topsoil or bringing in fresh topsoil for Libby gardens. But, to this day, not everyone has participated in the clean-up; some still don't want to know. So what does it mean if your garden is cleaned up – but your neighbours refuse to have theirs done? The EPA can't stop the wind blowing.

'There are still plenty of people who blame me for bringing this up,' says Gayla. She's at home now, mostly retired from her activism that brought help and the EPA and the clinic to the town. 'People would just have got sick and died but business would have gone on as usual. Kids would still be at risk of contamination when they played at school! But I wanted people to have everything that my parents didn't have. I didn't want them to just go home and die – die broke. I thought it was better to look this thing in the face than just pretend it wasn't there.'

How does she explain the ostrich-like behaviour of so many people in the town? With the mine closed, no jobs were at risk – what could they hope to gain by ignoring the health crisis all around them?

'I think,' she starts, accustomed to having answers. She stops. 'I think,' she starts again, and stops. 'Maybe they thought that if you didn't talk about it, if you didn't look at it, it would go away. They didn't want a fight. It's the emperor's new clothes: if we say it's fine, maybe it is fine.'

People who've lived in Libby a long time all comment on the stoicism of its people. They don't whine and they don't want to think of themselves as victims. What Gayla understood was that they were victims of W.R. Grace when it came to lung disease, but they'd be victims of their own blindness if they did nothing about it.

The story of Libby is an epic tragedy and it's important to remember that at its heart is W.R. Grace, a corporation that knowingly put its employees in danger and then concealed that danger from them. It tracked the rates and risk of asbestosis, mesothelioma and other lung abnormalities without any of its victims knowing their condition. And, in 2001, Grace declared bankruptcy as a way out of mounting, apparently endless, litigation. On one level, the people of Libby refused to see what was happening around them because it simply beggared belief that a publicly traded American business could be so cavalier with the lives of its employees and their families and get away with it. But what makes the story doubly tragic is that, once the facts were known, still so many of its victims refused to see what had happened to them.

When Gayla Benefield's mother gave her permission to sue W.R. Grace, she hoped the case would make her daughter rich. The wealth that Gayla gained was in learning how powerful she was, in discovering how smart and well informed she could make herself, and in articulating her powerful passion for making Libby a stronger, healthier community. She was hungry for change and unafraid of conflict. It was only her determination, over a period of twenty-five years, that finally allowed everyone to see what had happened and how it could be different.

Pliny would have been proud of her. For although we can blame him for first creating the inaccurate image of the ostrich with its head in the sand, we can't blame him for being one. In AD 79, Mount Vesuvius erupted, covering and then preserving the city of Pompeii. While most people ran away from Vesuvius, Pliny went straight into the danger zone to look, learn and rescue survivors. He died in the attempt. But in his honour, the most violent volcanic eruptions (such as Krakatoa) are called Ultra-Plinian in honour of the man who preferred knowledge to ignorance.

6. Just Following Orders

In September 2004, the wreck of HMS *Victoria* was discovered off the coast of Tripoli. With its prow buried in the sand, it stood perfectly vertical, like a skyscraper. The 10,000-ton iron-plated leviathan served as the burial ground for 358 British sailors who had died in one of the most bizarre blunders in naval history.

At the time of the disaster, Sir George Tryon was sixty-one and at the height of his powers; vice-admiral in the Royal Navy, he looked every inch the Victorian gentleman. Standing six foot tall, with long sideburns, beard and moustache, it wasn't only his position as commander-in-chief of the Mediterranean fleet that gave him authority. From the time that he'd joined the navy as a cadet, aged sixteen, Tryon had enjoyed a brilliant and unimpeded career. He had served all over the world, was highly regarded, well connected and, by all accounts, affable, energetic, deeply knowledgeable, and praised for his humanity, insight and love of a prank. Contemporary portraits suggest someone rather intimidating, though it is hard now to know whether that was a feature of personality or of rank.

What is clear is that Tryon was far from the Victorian archetype his picture suggests. He thought long and deeply about the traditions of the Royal Navy and sought to restore the verve and initiative for which it had once been famous.

Under Admiral Nelson, Tryon believed, men had been inspired with a mission and entrusted to make their own decisions in the heat of battle; only that way could commanders react with the flexibility and spontaneity that intense naval warfare demanded. Just obeying orders was dangerous because too much about war at sea was unpredictable. The very fact that Nelson's own death in 1805 at the Battle of Trafalgar had not compromised Britain's victory was testament to the independent initiative Nelson had inculcated into his navy. It was that spirit Tryon longed to recapture.

Although he may not have labelled them as such, Tryon knew that his officers were capable of being ostriches – conflict-averse and eager for a friction-free career. He took the unusual step of encouraging greater openness by specifically asking all of them to tell him about any risk or threat to the British fleet that might not come to his attention in the normal course of business. He insisted that the safety of the ship and its men should always come first: mere obedience was not enough. In an age of deference and intimidation, he worked hard to inspire in his men a sense of autonomy and independence sufficient for the most threatening and unforeseeable of naval encounters. In today's terms, you might say that he preferred an open-door policy to micromanagement. His was a controversial, even radical, position; many of his contemporaries clung to the practice of sending highly detailed instructions, signalled through flags, which could be long-winded, slow and hard to see in the smoke and clutter of war. For Tryon this issue wasn't theoretical but a matter of life and death. On occasion he could be deliberately uncommunicative, believing this was the best way for his men to learn how to think for themselves in unpredictable circumstances.

June 1893 found Tryon on manoeuvres, commanding HMS *Victoria*, heading a column of six ships; his deputy,

Rear-Admiral Markham, headed a second, parallel column of five ships. Orders stated that each column was to turn 180 degrees to change direction. But each ship needed at least 730 metres to turn and there wasn't space enough between them for both columns to complete their turn without colliding. With orders so ambiguous and dangerous, Markham hesitated; surely the intention was not to turn the ships into each other's paths. When no action ensued, Tryon sent a signal saying, in effect: 'What are you waiting for?' This public rebuke stung Markham into action; it is said that, right up to the last minute, he hoped his orders would be changed. But he did as he was told.

The orders were not rescinded or changed. Inevitably, the two vast battleships collided, causing the largest peacetime loss of life in the history of the Royal Navy. HMS *Victoria* capsized in just thirteen minutes, taking Sir George with it. His last words, apparently, were, 'It's all my fault.' How could two battleships and two experienced seamen be so blind? A court martial was never able fully to explain the incident to everyone's satisfaction. Tryon, of course, was not there to explain or defend himself; Markham did survive and was both blamed and exonerated for following orders: 'Admiral Markham might have refused to perform the revolution ordered, and the *Victoria* might have been saved,' wrote two admirals at the time. 'Admiral Markham, however, would have been tried by court martial, and no one would have sympathised with him as it would not have been realised that he had averted a catastrophe. Unconditional obedience is, in brief, the only principle on which those in service must act.'

Parodied in the Ealing comedy *Kind Hearts and Coronets* (in which Alec Guinness plays a Tryon-like figure gleefully crashing his ships), what today might strike us as absurd, to the Victorians was tragedy; certainly Tryon would have regarded it as such. For it was precisely Markham's failure to seize the initiative and *not* blindly obey which could be seen as the heart of the problem. Everything Tryon had believed in was proved by the accident – but, at the same time, his foolish death discredited everything he stood for. Whether for comedy or tragedy, the event is chiefly remembered for revealing the tension and difficulties inherent in following orders.

Such blind obedience is not, of course, the exclusive province of military men. Hierarchies, and the system of behaviours that they require, proliferate in nature and in man-made organisations. For humans, there is an evolutionary advantage in hierarchies: a disciplined group can achieve more than a chaotic crowd. Within the group, defined roles and status can ensure internal harmony, while disobedience threatens conflict and friction. The disciplined, peaceful organisation is better able to defend itself and co-ordinate its interests than a confused, argumentative group that agrees on nothing. The traditional argument in favour of hierarchies and obedience has been that of the social contract: it is worth sacrificing some degree of individuality in order to ensure the safety and privileges achieved by a group.

Psychologists understand that this social contract is more than utilitarian. Much of human happiness lies in our being able to contribute to a purpose larger than ourselves – but few people can achieve that sense of greater purpose alone. We need other people to help build our art galleries or ballparks, to make scientific breakthroughs and to solve our most challenging problems. So we surrender some autonomy to the authority of the larger purpose and, in doing so, we become responsible *to* it. This may not feel like a radical shift – indeed, we may not even be conscious of making it. But how we act and what we see is profoundly altered when we obey.

The great psychologist of obedience was Stanley Milgram,

the social scientist who was so thoughtful about the overload of city life. Haunted by accounts of the Holocaust, Milgram sought to understand whether and why individuals obey authorities even when the task is morally repugnant, there is no reward for doing it and there is no punishment for disobedience. Using today's jargon, he would have asked: is obedience hardwired?

He did so in the 1960s by running a famous series of eighteen experiments, each of which were permutations of the first. A volunteer was invited into Milgram's basement lab at Yale and told that he (or she) was involved in an experiment to gauge whether or not punishment was effective in learning. The volunteer – or 'Teacher' – was to read word pairs to the 'Learner', who was, in reality, an actor. The Learner had to indicate which word pairs went together. If the Learner made an error, the Teacher had to administer an electric shock. Each shock would be progressively stronger, starting with 15 volts and progressing to 450 volts: a lethal dose. The Learner would simulate pain so that the Teacher would believe the electric shocks to be real. What Milgram wanted to know was: how far would the volunteer Teacher comply with a series of instructions that come increasingly into conflict with their conscience? Would the Teachers continue to deliver the shocks, even though they were clearly causing pain and even, perhaps, death? Since there was no punishment for quitting – and no reward for continuing – how far would volunteers go before refusing to obey?

Because the experiment has become so famous, it's important to reiterate a number of critical points about it that have been forgotten or misunderstood. The experiment was not about violence or aggression; what Milgram sought to test was obedience to authority. Participants were not being explicitly violent – though the distance between the Teacher and

Learner would become germane. Nor was there any incentive for the Teacher to continue with the experiment. Each volunteer was paid $4 plus travel expenses for their participation, regardless of how long they stuck with it. It was central to the experiment that it was 'coloured by a cooperative mood'[1] conducted without any fear or threat of any kind. Any volunteer could stop, or leave, at any moment. The authority present was a well-mannered scientist in a white coat: not a boss or a bully, not a troop commander, merely an ostensibly objective observer trying to do research, which the volunteer was assisting.

Before setting out to conduct his experiments, Milgram asked three groups – psychiatrists, college students and middle-class adults – how they expected the volunteers to behave. 'They predict that virtually all subjects will refuse to obey the experimenter; only a pathological fringe, not exceeding one or two per cent, was expected to proceed to the end of the shockboard.'[2]

Although an academic experiment in a college setting, the experiment was 'vivid, intense and real' for all of the participants, and what Milgram discovered shocked and troubled him so much that it was ten years before he published a complete account of his work.[3] Sixty-five per cent of the volunteers obeyed fully. 'Of the 40 subjects, 26 obeyed the orders of the experimenter to the end, proceeding to punish the victim until they reached the most potent shock available on the generator. After the 450-volt shock was administered three times, the experimenter called a halt to the session.' What Milgram found wasn't aggression, for he observed 'there is no anger, vindictiveness or hatred in those who shocked the victim. Men do become angry; they do act hatefully and explode in rage against others. But not here. Something far more dangerous is revealed: the capacity for man to abandon his humanity, indeed the inevitability that he does so, as he merges his unique personality into larger institutional structures.'[4]

Many permutations of the experiment followed.[5] Some of Milgram's colleagues found his results so surprising that they attempted versions of their own. One of these addressed the criticism that Milgram's situation depended too much on the performance skills of an actor. Perhaps its outcome could be explained by the fact that the actor had not really been very convincing and therefore the volunteers had intuited that they were doing no real harm; it just wasn't real enough. To test that critique, Charles Sheridan and Richard King enlisted thirteen male and thirteen female students to participate in a similar experiment where, instead of an actor simulating pain, a cute fluffy puppy was used.[6] In this version, the level of shock was exaggerated on the display cabinet but real (albeit lower) shocks were administered to the dog. 'The first of the three actual voltage levels produced foot flexion and occasional barks, the second level produced running and vocalisation, and the final level resulted in continuous barking and howling.' There was no danger of bad acting spoiling the reality of this experiment.

Other conditions remained the same: there was no sanction or punishment for disobedience and the team adopted Milgram's script to ensure a like-for-like comparison. Like Milgram too, this team had asked a classroom of male and female students (not participants) what they expected the outcome to be. Everyone anticipated high levels of disobedience. Sheridan and King were also interested to find out whether there was a significant difference in responses from men and women, hypothesising that 'women would be less willing than men to inflict harm on a cute puppy'.

Once again, they were wrong. Levels of obedience obtained

from the male volunteers were close to those obtained by Milgram in the original experiment. But, without exception, 100 per cent of the female volunteers 'complied with instructions to shock the puppy all the way to the end of the scale'.

Milgram's experiment has been repeated often, and in many countries. (Milgram himself had hoped to repeat them in Germany but his early death prevented him from doing so.) The highest rates of full obedience were found in South Africa and Austria; the lowest in Australia and Spain.[7] In particular, in one version of the experiment (Experiment 5) that featured scheduled and scripted protests from the Learner, the obedience rate went from 70 per cent to 82.5 per cent; howls of protest did not cause participants to doubt their actions.[8] And the passage of time has not produced different behaviours. In 2008, Michael Portillo repeated the experiment for a BBC television programme. He misunderstood the experiment (he was using it to make an argument about aggression) but the results were virtually identical to Milgram's. In March 2010, French television producers seemed to think that recreating Milgram's experiments would make a fine game show;[9] their motives may have been different (and Milgram would have hated the use to which his work was put) but their results were the same: most participants went all the way.

Milgram struggled long and hard to understand his own, highly disturbing, findings. And he concluded that when we are part of a group, or an organisation, we change our focus.

> Although [he wrote] a person acting under authority performs actions that seem to violate standards of conscience, it would not be true to say that he loses his moral sense. Instead, it acquires *a radically different focus* [my italics]. His moral concern now shifts to a consideration of how well he is living up to the expectations that the authority has of

> him. In wartime, a soldier does not ask whether it is good or bad to bomb a hamlet; he does not experience shame or guilt in the destruction of a village: rather he feels pride or shame depending on how well he has performed the mission assigned to him.[10]

That shift of focus is fundamental. It makes us blind both to the alternatives we have to obedience (every one of Milgram's participants was free to stop) and it blinds us to our individual moral responsibility for our actions. We focus so intently on the order that we are blind to everything else. When we obey orders, our concern to be a good soldier, to do a good job, means that we no longer see that we have a choice or that we are morally responsible for it. Rear-Admiral Markham felt that he had to obey Tryon's orders and, when he did, it was the order and not Markham that was deemed responsible for the deaths that ensued.

Another way of thinking about this is that when we agree to submit to authority in order to pursue a larger good, we exchange an individual self (with responsibility for our conscience) for a social self that is responsible to the whole. The most traditional way of portraying this is that the individual self lives at home and the social self goes to work. But if you think of yourself on your own and then in a party, you recognise the same person but in different roles with different manners, styles and connections. The individual self is an actor, responsible and autonomous; the social self is an agent, working with and on behalf of others. Same people, different roles, different focus.

Milgram concluded that this shift of focus wasn't a personal failing and the problem of obedience wasn't wholly psychological. It was a necessary and inevitable aspect of belonging to a group. When the individual is working alone, conscience is brought into play. But when working within a hierarchy, authority replaces it. This is inevitable, because otherwise the hierarchy just doesn't work: too many consciences and the advantage of being in a group disappears. Conscience, it seems, doesn't scale but gives way to authority. This might explain the tragically poor decisions followed by firefighters called to tackle the fire in Grenfell Tower. Initially, residents of the tower were told to stay put and firefighters were given the instruction that inhabitants were not to be evacuated.

'It looked like a film, people were shouting and screaming, they were panicking and wanting people to help,' the fireman Daniel Egan later recalled. 'My first thoughts were that we needed to get everybody out. I could hear the roar of the tower. It was obvious.'

It was obvious yet the 'stay put' order wasn't rescinded until 2.47 a.m. The fire brigade had been called at 12.54. Egan told the subsequent inquiry that he had not expressed his opinion to senior officers because he assumed they had the fire under control.[11]

It may even be that the more committed we are to the moral purpose of an organisation, the more obedient we become; obedience is read as a sign of commitment. In Ohio, a group of psychiatrists decided to find out whether nurses would obey doctors, even when the doctors' orders clearly endangered the lives of their patients. What is so interesting about this study is that it involves a highly conscientious group of individuals working in a hierarchical organisation. When asked, nurses are quite clear that their primary concern must be for patients; that is typically what has brought them into their profession in the first place. So they bring a high degree of commitment and enthusiasm not just to the tasks of their work but to the purpose of their work. But this, it turns out, doesn't protect them from the dilemma of obedience.

In the study, twenty-two nurses – twelve from a municipal hospital and ten from a private hospital – were instructed to administer an obviously excessive dose of medicine. The drug itself was unauthorised, which is to say it wasn't on the ward stock list and hadn't been cleared for use. The doctor ordering the drug would do so on the telephone and would be a physician whom the nurse did not know. (The drug itself, of course, was a placebo so that the patients were never in any danger.) Rather like Milgram, the Ohio team also canvassed thirty-three graduate and student nurses, asking them what they would do in these circumstances. Thirty-one said that they would not give the medication.

But, in the experiment, it turned out that twenty-one of the twenty-two participating nurses were prepared to administer the drug. Moreover, they expressed no real resistance to the order and did not appear to experience any internal conflict or even any conscious awareness that there might be a problem. Only one refusenik felt any hostility to the doctor ordering the wrong drug. The rest merely felt somewhat tetchy or confused. 'Insofar as the nurse is concerned,' wrote the Ohio team, 'the psychological problems involved in a situation such as the one under discussion are operating to a considerable extent *below the threshold of consciousness* [my italics].'[12] What most surprised the team that conducted the experiment was not that the nurses obeyed, but that their obedience had rendered them so entirely blind to their primary duty of care for the patient that they could see no conflict at all.

The Ohio nurses had just one test, one chance to disobey. But in Milgram's original experiment the volunteers had multiple moments when they could have refused. However, the fact that they were operating a sliding scale – from 15 volts to 450 volts – may, in fact, have helped them to obey. There was never a single moment at which the delivery of the shock suddenly seemed absolutely wrong. Instead, applying lethal shocks was something the volunteers learned to do only by making baby steps along the way.

'There was never a moment when it seemed so bad that you had to stop.' That comment comes not from one of Milgram's volunteers but from Walt Pavlo, a mid-level executive at MCI. Unlike a hospital, the long-distance phone company didn't have a high moral purpose that instilled commitment and obedience. What it did have was a highly competitive culture and big rewards for employees who played the game. But most of all, says Pavlo, it was full of people who wanted to be good employees.

'When I started out, I was thirty, eager and ambitious. Everything was going right. I had a new job, a great family, and MCI was a big go-ahead company, full of smart young people just like me. I was psyched.'

Now in his fifties, Pavlo is a softly spoken but intense conversationalist. If you didn't know his background, his seriousness might worry you; it is as though he's still puzzling over a problem he just can't resolve. His mind is restless and, even if he's talking about old times, he's still looking for new insights. As we sat together in a Washington DC hotel, we must have looked like any two executives having a business meeting. But this conversation was different because Pavlo is a convicted white-collar criminal.

'My boss, Ralph McCumber, had been a navy commander, had served in Vietnam. He had a kind of military bearing: very neat, very methodical. And you just knew he was tough. I don't know how you knew, you just knew.'

Pavlo's job was to make sure that the outstanding amounts owed by the long-distance carriers to MCI got paid. He was really just a debt collector but excitement around the new, entrepreneurial company and around the newly deregulated industry made him feel bigger and more important than that. And highly dedicated.

'I'd get up at four-thirty every morning, get to work about five-thirty. I'd have a meeting with McCumber around seven-thirty to go through problem accounts. It took me about three months to become McCumber's first lieutenant.'

There was much about MCI's operations that Pavlo didn't understand: how they let their customers run up such huge debts, why they took on customers delivering trashy products like sex chat and psychics, and why they paid commission on sales to customers who didn't pay up. But Pavlo was the new boy and he trusted the business would eventually make sense. In the meantime, he was most concerned to make a good impression. So when McCumber came and told him about a forthcoming RIF, Pavlo felt anxious.

'What's a RIF?' he asked.

'Reduction in Force,' McCumber explained. 'We fire people in the fall to save a few months' salary, then rehire in January. It's an annual ritual around here so MCI can make its year-end earnings numbers and clear out the dead wood.'[13]

Pavlo's assignment, three months into his job, was to fire one of the bookkeeping clerks, Eslene. She was fiftyish and suffered from vertigo but, he was told, she had to go. From Pavlo's perspective, he had to be the bad guy to a nice old lady who needed her job for the health benefits. And he did as he'd been ordered.

'Cheer up,' Eslene told him as she left. 'You're going to be a great manager.'

Pavlo felt like an executioner but he didn't leave. He was being a good employee and a good provider to his family. A few months later, Pavlo and McCumber came up with the idea of getting delinquent customers to sign promissory notes – legally binding promises by clients to pay back what they owed. Since they represented obligations to MCI, they could be counted as assets and the company's bad debt disappeared. Pavlo knew it was a fudge but it seemed to work, so he kept doing what he was told.

'Of course there was never a direct order to cook the books,' Pavlo explained to me. 'Instead it was just a kind of wilful neglect. No one would ever ask how the debt disappeared. So since nobody told you to stop, you kept going. The only order we had was just: make the debt vanish. Don't bring me problems, bring me solutions. Nobody wanted to look into the detail.

'The other thing about it was: nobody seemed to get hurt. The company did fine. The shareholders were doing great. The customers were still running their sleazy businesses. Where was the harm? You couldn't see any. What you could see was the reward: promotions, swanky hotels, nice resorts. So you just look away. You do what you're told and you don't look too close.'

After two years, Pavlo started smoking, something he'd despised in the past. Turning a blind eye to the mess that he couldn't clear up – a mess that, in fact, he was exacerbating – was a horrific, cognitively dissonant experience. The good guy and the bad deeds just couldn't co-exist. The way he dealt with it was to anaesthetise himself.

'I hated myself. And I hated my customers. And I hated the company. Because, in my mind at the time, I thought: they're making me do this. MCI is making me smoke and drink and write these notes. It's not me, it's them. And how do you go back? I went into that company with such high ideals and, after a while, I couldn't figure out how to get out.'

Twenty years later, and after serving a two-year jail sentence, Pavlo is still in pain, trying to reconcile in his own mind how he could have done things that he knows were wrong. He's devoted years of his life to teaching college and business school students how he went wrong, hoping he can help them recognise the traps he fell into. The problem, he says, is not that you are asked to do one big, bad deed; it is that there are so many tiny steps along the way that there is never a moment when it's simple to say 'no'.

'I don't consider myself a bad person. I know right from wrong. But I could rationalise some very irrational behaviour that now appals me. Why did I think that this was right? I was doing my job. I did what I'd been told to do.'

Pavlo moved, by baby steps, from doing things that felt bad to committing acts that were illegal. His is a rare experience, though the phenomenal cost of white-collar crime – estimated at 2 per cent of all business revenues – suggests that it may be less rare than we would like to imagine. But in most cases, obedience is not about doing something knowingly illegal. It may be as simple as following orders that – like Pavlo's promissory notes – just don't make a lot of sense.

That, at first, following these orders didn't seem a big deal – not a resigning matter – is more important than might appear. Each unpunished infraction implies approval. At Facebook, a number of data breaches occurred before Cambridge Analytica's and experiments that exploited user data were conducted without users' permission. But as long as no one protested or banned such initiatives, what about them looked wrong? At Enron, the way that Sherron Watkins put it was: serial killers start with cats. Minor irregularities, unpunished, signalled that the organisation wouldn't be vigilant about accuracy or ethics. Watkins was the first person to raise serious concerns about Enron's suspect accounting methods, just weeks before the company collapsed. But the sixth largest corporation in American didn't start out corrupt; it had become that way by letting minor infractions slide. When you've done

one thing that you really should know is wrong, and you're not punished for it – indeed, like Pavlo you may be rewarded for it – then the next infraction is easier. And the next. Follow one bad order and you'll follow another.

Pavlo's pain was personal but his predicament is more pervasive than you might expect: loyal, dedicated employees who cut corners, run risks not because they're greedy or cruel but because they're desperate to be seen to be doing a great job. When, in its hot pursuit of growth, Wells Fargo (ostensibly one of the better, more conservative US banks) decided that each of its customers should have eight of its products – 'Going for Gr-Eight' – most employees recognised the goal was at best overambitious, at worst stupid. Across the industry, customers typically buy three or four products from their bank, not twice that. Unable to hit these targets the right way, sales executives found the means to hit them anyway: largely through creating 3 million accounts for customers who had never asked for or agreed to them. A year later, it emerged that bank employees had been issuing unwanted insurance policies too.

In London, Kweku Adoboli fell into the same trap. A black Ghanaian, educated at a Quaker boarding school in Yorkshire, he had taken the school motto for his own: *Non Sibi Sed Omnibus* – not for self but for all. Choirboy, head boy, he was eager, hardworking and utterly dedicated to the institutions that encouraged him. After a successful internship, he was grateful to be given opportunities to work for UBS in Stockholm and Hong Kong before moving to the bank's trading floor in the City. To be so warmly endorsed by what looked and felt like the throbbing heart of the British establishment inspired in Adoboli unquestioning commitment.

After Northern Rock collapsed and the global banking crisis gathered momentum, most of the senior management at

UBS left. With just thirty months' trading experience between them, Adoboli and a new supervisor were asked to manage a trading book with over $50 billion in assets: roughly the same size as the GDP of Ghana. To do the job well meant managing risks in funding, credit, foreign exchanges, hedging, dividends, short borrow and other products. You had to understand intricate details of regulatory differences across regions, the rules for every provider and how to trade every single asset class. Not surprisingly, Adoboli was out of his depth, fast.

'There were many occasions when I would pluck up the courage, yet again, to report to one of my senior traders that we had lost a few million dollars the previous day because of one type or another of structural problem in the book,' Adoboli told me. '"What can we do to fix this?" we would ask. The answer, invariably, would be: "You are the experts on this, you need to find a way to make it work."'

Desperate to please his bosses, Adoboli used the bank's money for unauthorised trades, entered false information to cover his tracks and exceeded the daily trading limit assigned to each employee. He was, he said, trying to be helpful. And as long as he was making the bank appear healthy, nobody looked and nobody seemed to care.

'There were moments when people asked how we were managing to do what we did! But they just got told to leave us alone to get on with it. And you do; you allow it to persist because you're a good soldier. You collude in an abusive system but you think you're being loyal! I was being courted by other banks but I kept saying: I can't leave UBS. I felt I had to stay; they depended on me!'

Adoboli felt out of his depth, but he didn't think he could do anything about that without being disloyal. So he did what he was told to do. Three years later, he found himself in a corner again. Believing that the market was due to crash, he wanted to start selling to protect his clients. But he was told not to.

'The bank's research team had put out a 147-page long piece explaining why the markets were going to be rising over the coming summer. This, of course, is an inherent bias in investment banks because rising markets beget higher commissions and profits. I came under pressure from increasingly senior people to toe the line.'

Once again, he did as he was told. 'Tired, confused, and having become what I now understand to be "resource depleted", I capitulated. We began trading in expectation that the markets would rally. This was on July 1st. Tragically July 1st marked the beginning of a sell-off of up to 40 per cent in some of the markets we had positions in. And having lost clarity of mind, we made a series of increasingly desperate decisions to try and resolve the escalating loss. Like frogs in a boiling pan we just couldn't see how bad things were getting.'

When he could no longer conceal losses amounting to $2 billion, Adoboli was fired. The good soldier, choirboy, head boy was arrested, tried and sentenced to seven years in prison. Several members of the jury wept as the verdict was announced.

Kweku Adoboli and Walt Pavlo sadly are not alone. They share many characteristics: slightly on the outside, eager to be inside; enormously dedicated to, and trusting of, their institutions; prepared to go to almost any length for approval, achievement and success. It isn't about the money; it's about being seen to be reliable. And when, later on, they emerge from a frenzy of overwork and overwhelm, they are dazed, as though coming out of a trance in which all they saw or thought about was what their bosses wanted. And in that mono-focus, they lost all sight of who they were or what they, as individuals, might have believed in for themselves.

They don't at all abjure responsibility for their actions but seem, even after all these years, baffled and confused as to where their true selves went during the time that they were so focused on what their leaders and their organisations wanted.

'Losing my sense of self,' Adoboli told me, 'meant sacrificing all that I hold dear: it meant losing my idealism and hope; it meant losing my desire to help build communities and be part of a family; it meant losing my self-belief that I could make a change and make a difference to the lives of others.'

That Adoboli carried a significant mortgage won't have helped. The credit frenzy of the early 2000s created what may have been the most compliant workforce in history. With much to lose by asking hard questions and (apparently) much to gain by obedience, it was the rare organisation where challenge and dissent could be discerned. That phenomenon has been perpetuated by the rise of zero-hours contracts and the precariat: a segment of the population utterly but precariously dependent on the whim of bosses and markets. No boss can expect heightened vigilance or creativity when stepping out of line – even to help the organisation – risks losing everything. So it isn't just the desperate workers who are precarious; the entire organisation lays itself open to risk and irrelevance by ensuring nobody will feel safe enough to question or speak out. Scrutiny, creativity and reflection are inevitable casualties when your ability to feed or house your children is constantly on the line.

Obedience poses a huge problem for large corporations. In 1998, when BP bought Amoco, John Browne, CEO of the new combined company, ordered a 25 per cent cut in fixed cash costs across all refineries. The order was made regardless of the condition of each site. And so, over the next three years, the management responsible for the Texas City site reviewed everything: maintenance, service agreements, personnel, equipment testing and tools. Everything was cut, down, it was said, to the number of pencils.

The 25 per cent cut was not a target, it was a 'directive' and the cadre of managers responsible for Texas City implemented it. They did so despite their knowledge that, under Amoco's ownership, the plant had been run down, and despite repeated warnings about the site's safety. An internal 2002 BP PowerPoint presentation says: 'If we do not achieve a significant improvement [in] safety performance at the Texas City refinery, one of our co-workers or a contract employee will be killed.'[14] A graph illustrating fatalities in the past twenty years powerfully illustrates the point. A further report showed the poor state of the infrastructure, citing high rates of absenteeism and a large backlog of overdue inspections. The following year, a safety report says that 'the "checkbook mentality" blame and status culture still exists throughout most of the Texas City site and this limits health, safety, environmental and general performance. Budget and HSE priorities are not aligned.'

Cost-cutting, personnel reductions and cutbacks on training put everyone at Texas City under increasing pressure. Between 1994 and 2004, the site experienced eight blowdown drum incidents, of which only three were investigated. In 2004 alone, three major incidents caused three fatalities.[15] Yet, that same year, prior to a meeting to discuss cuts, one manager sent the following email:

> Which bit of 25% don't you understand? We are going to be wasting our time on Monday discussing this topic unless you come prepared to commit to a 25% cut. I have much more interesting things to do with my time than getting up at 3am to travel to Chicago for a non-productive meeting![16]

The order that came from London to cut costs was followed clearly and effectively – even in the face of repeated warnings that the infrastructure was not safe and that, as one report put it, 'we have cut routine budgets to the point where we are not doing the routine maintenance essential to keeping units up. We cut 10%, cut 10%, cut 10% . . . without regard for risk.'[17] When consultants working at Texas City asked executives whether they felt there were any safety problems not being addressed, those in high management positions answered 'I am not aware of any'. They had been instructed to cut costs and that's what they focused on.

Just as no one told Wells Fargo salespeople to open fake accounts and nobody instructed Pavlo or Adoboli to cook the books, no one at BP headquarters in London said: 'Make the cuts, we don't care if people die.' Of course they didn't. But the effect of their directives was to block out other considerations. When employees at BP were surveyed on corporate priorities, they cited number one as making money and number two as costs and budgets. And even though managers on site knew there were safety problems, were grief-stricken by accidents and honestly anxious about how to make the refinery safer, they turned a blind eye to the problems and obeyed. By the same token, the contractors who were told to cut the budget for cladding Grenfell Tower didn't foresee the fatal and tragic consequences of their obedience.

That, of course, is the problem with targets, and managing by objectives. Implicitly they communicate the same message as Pavlo's boss: we don't care *how* the target is achieved, as long as it is achieved. Such is the power of obedience that other considerations (ethics, legality, safety) become invisible to social beings who want to make a contribution. When the inexperienced jailers at Abu Ghraib were told to 'soften up' prisoners, they were not told how to do so, they were not informed as to the usefulness of their work. They simply did as they were told. That their cruelty elicited not a single valuable piece of military intelligence was not relevant: they followed orders that eliminated other concerns.[18]

Hierarchies and obedience persist even in the face of extraordinary danger. A National Transportation Safety Board review of thirty-seven aeroplane accidents concluded that up to a quarter of all plane crashes are caused by 'destructive obedience' inside the cockpit.[19] In a study eerily reminiscent of Sir George Tryon and the HMS *Victoria* disaster, many flight-crew errors were attributed to accepting the authority of the captain even when he was getting things wrong. Commercial aeroplane pilots typically enjoy tremendous authority: they have three to four times more experience than their first officers; many have come from the military and they are not accustomed to being questioned. Only the pilot in command has explicit authority to deviate from rules in an emergency. As a consequence, it feels very difficult to challenge them. The NTSB study, which analysed cockpit communications captured on flight recorders prior to crashes, found that 25 per cent of all accidents could have been prevented if the pilot had been challenged when making an error.

Obedience is so strong that it can even blind us to our own self-interest. The classic example of that extreme is the kamikaze pilot or the suicide bomber, for whom obedience to a cause is powerful enough to overrule the instinct of survival. Those cases are always cited as being culturally determined – by the Japanese love of their emperor or by religious extremism. But in far tamer, academic experiments, in which volunteers have been ordered to harm not an anonymous 'Learner' but themselves, the same results have been found.[20] Volunteers will more readily self-harm than disobey.

Corporations rarely agonise over the problem of obedience

but the military has done so for centuries. From a legal perspective, military law states that a soldier must obey orders unless that order is manifestly illegal. If the order is illegal, then the superior who issued it is held responsible. But any doubts that a soldier may have about the legality of the order should be resolved in favour of obedience. (Intriguingly, the same rules of conduct apply to lawyers too.[21]) We may tend to think of the military as having a culture of blind obedience, but that is far from the case. One of the few of Milgram's volunteers who did *not* obey was, he said, inspired by his military training in which he was taught that he had a right to refuse illegal orders.

The Nuremberg trials that followed the Second World War did not allow obedience as an excuse because the prisoners being tried there were the superior officers and also were high-ranking political officials. In more recent times, the charters establishing international tribunals relating to war crimes in the former Yugoslavia and in Rwanda have not allowed obedience as an excuse. Only in the former Communist bloc and some parts of the Third World does following orders provide any kind of legal protection.[22]

'When we are training young officers, we talk about duty, roles, responsibility but we never talk about obedience,' says Ian Stewart. He teaches at the Royal Military Academy at Sandhurst. Why, I wondered, didn't they talk about obedience there?

'Despite what some of our friends outside the organisation sometimes seem to think,' said Stewart, 'obedience to us sounds blind, going through the motions without thinking, without thinking yourself into the situation. That's really not a good idea, especially now. If you act like a cog in a wheel, you become very predictable – and then it is very easy to work against you.'

In 2017, the British Army published its Leadership Code. The words 'obey', 'obedience' and 'orders' do not appear in it. Instead, the emphasis is on 'mission command': the mutual trust between leaders and those they lead, all of whom, it insists, must do as they would be done by. General Sir Nick Carter, Chief of the General Staff when the code was produced, argues that shared understanding and trust is a fundamental bulwark against blind obedience.

'We distinguish between drill and manoeuvre. If you look at orchestrated movements, like the Horse Guards on parade, that is a drill. It is predictable, rehearsable, and doesn't call for immediate, individual decision-making. Manoeuvres are where you need solid decision-making and that's where the philosophy of mission command comes in. It requires that you establish mutual trust and common understanding with your team. If you believe they have the capability to have their potential unlocked, you can be open-minded in instructions you give them. But if mutual trust and common understanding aren't in place, you have to rely on obedience and order. If you don't know them, you don't know if you can trust them. So mission command is a fundamental element of leadership.'[23]

'There's a process of socialisation going on at Sandhurst, or at West Point,' Ian Stewart said. 'This is almost theatrical on a grand scale. We bring them here for a year – volunteers, who come willingly, with a spring in their step. We are inculcating values and beliefs and the way of being, in a military sense. It isn't obedience; it is about becoming one with the organisation. It's what, in business, you might call authenticity. We like to think that we are in the job of encouraging authentic leaders so that their own values and the values of organisation are aligned.'

In an environment where peer pressure is immense, and

a desire to conform inherent, how can the military teach its young officers to think for themselves, to deal with orders that may be quite uncomfortable?

'We are very good at exercises and role play,' says Stewart. 'So we intentionally put them in situations where they are supposed to feel uncomfortable. Military training is about making automatic a codified ethical way of behaving. Under pressure, little sleep – that's how our exercises work. Ten days with maybe three, four hours sleep a night, being assessed, people on their case, threats changing all the time. Last week – we had an exercise set around a mosque and an order to search the mosque. The men on the course decided that wasn't the right thing to do, that there was another way to deal with the situation that would not inflame it. That's the kind of thing we want them to think about. While it isn't Helmand, it is as close as dammit as we can make it. We will do exercises like that over and over again to the point where we hope that, when it is real, that second nature kicks in. That is what military training is about.

'The lesson they're supposed to learn is: if you feel too uncomfortable, don't do what you think you are supposed to do. The more choice-making we give people, the more engagement and efficiency they show. If you just get people to press a button, we can't expect them to be thoughtful. An immoral order should never be followed; that ethical dimension must be part of who we are. But I'm not claiming we always get it right one hundred per cent of the time.'

The hard part is being able to recognise what constitutes an immoral or illegal order. While all soldiers are provided with legal support if they refuse to follow an order that they believe is illegal, in fact the ambiguity of much conflict means that no one can be confident their decision will be sanctioned. Most soldiers aren't trained lawyers and, despite all the exercises, confusion over responsibility persists. But at least Stewart is exploring it with his students. It's a conversation that rarely occurs within business environments, where many executives fondly imagine that military command-and-control would make their lives easier.

'I had this conversation once at business school,' Fred Krawchuk recalled. A lieutenant-colonel in the US Army, when we spoke, he had just arrived in Kabul, in the midst of Operation Moshtarak. As you might expect of someone working in a highly volatile context, he thinks about obedience very carefully.

'I was the only one at business school who was a military officer on active duty. We were discussing leadership and someone said: "For you, Fred, leadership is easy. You give orders and people follow." It is not that easy. If people don't respect you, don't trust you, there are lots of ways to get blown off without "disregarding orders". It isn't black and white.'

Before going to Afghanistan, Lieutenant-Colonel Krawchuk served as a Special Forces officer assigned to the US Pacific Command in Hawaii, where he was responsible for communications, security and development strategies in Asia. This meant working with host nations, local populations, non-governmental organisations and local governments to build infrastructure – water, medical care, education – in highly unstable conditions. It doesn't, he says, lend itself to quick or simple solutions.

'Obedience is too simple. In a highly complex situation, like this one, anything too simple doesn't work. And it is a misservice to sit back and wait to be told what to do. Of course you do as you're told but there is something else about moral courage, about standing up for what is right. It might mean you assume some risk and write a position paper or schedule a briefing to help solve some of these difficult problems we're facing right now. You don't just wait to be told what to do. When do you pick the fight? How far do you take your ideas? As someone who believes we need comprehensive answers to complex situations, I think we need more than just people doing what they're told or waiting to be told. My experience is there is a lot more struggle with that than with illegal orders.'

What Krawchuk is struggling with is not obedience itself, but its side effect, which is blindness. When all you do is obey, you become blind: not seeing consequences or alternatives or possibilities. I'm haunted by that email from the harried BP executive: 'Which bit of 25% don't you understand?' It sounds so desperate, frightened of consequences if the order to make cuts isn't obeyed. Under these conditions, the independent thought Krawchuk values simply isn't possible. The industrial style of managements, with its full bureaucratic panoply of job descriptions, targets and KPIs, instils focus – but at the expense of a personal integrity and accountability. When the Home Office decreed a hostile environment for immigrants, the policy was swiftly translated into numbers. Just hit the numbers. The numbers, of course, made it easier to forget the human cost that the numbers represented. And even after it transpired that the targets had wrecked the lives of many fully entitled to live in Britain, still those responsible didn't think to question the policy.

'What happened unfortunately during those years and has continued is that we had an unhealthy obsession with numbers,' former cabinet minister Sayeeda Warsi later acknowledged. 'We were wedded to unrealistic targets ... and what we ended up with was, I think, the unintended consequences of the policy we are now implementing.'[24]

As long as I hit my targets, does it matter how? Does it matter what they actually mean? If the sales team needs eight accounts per customer, who cares how it happens or whether it's wrong? If the building's on fire and I'm not a fire marshal, it isn't my job to call 999.

What Milgram's experiments demonstrate is that, however much we think we won't obey, for the most part we do. It is a default behaviour, at least in part because its opposite – reflection, independent thinking – is much more effortful. Obedience is another kind of shortcut, in which we trust someone else's thinking above our own. It's easy and simple, especially when we're tired, distracted and don't want a fight. And so it both amplifies and articulates all those other forces that make us blind.

The military has had to grapple with the full spectrum of obedience, from Nelsonian initiative to the unquestioning following of orders. More than a few tragedies – from the sinking of HMS *Victoria* to My Lai and Abu Ghraib – have forced them to reflect on the considerable intellectual challenge that obedience presents. This has made them all wary of the power that obedience confers, a wariness that it would behove corporate executives to consider. Dealing daily in life and death, the military knows the costs of its mistakes are high and irretrievable. But Fred Krawchuk's story about being at business school is telling: his business colleagues seemed to envy what they imagine to be the military model of obedience – just do as you're told – unaware that it's dangerous and out of date.

General Sir Nick Carter's philosophy of mission command is quite different from obedience; its advantage is the high level of trust which allows soldiers to make on-the-spot decisions miles from central command. But the shared understanding on which it depends requires long-term commitment. A highly precarious workforce, comprised of casual labourers who may not even know one another, never mind their boss, who worry about paying rent and feeding their children, won't be able to work this way. That means obedience will take over, which explains how, one cold January night, hospital security publicly dumped a sick, disoriented woman onto the snowy Baltimore streets, wearing just a hospital gown and socks. The danger of vulnerable workers is that they are likely to do exactly as they're told, right or wrong.

That the military doesn't regard blind obedience as an admirable goal should give any executive pause. Blaming a few 'bad apples' is the opposite of leadership: taking responsibility for leadership is central to its meaning. When business and political leaders wonder why they have lost public trust and respect, they could consider how far their own command-and-control systems, their obsession with goals and targets, keeping a firm, heavy heel on the neck of economic and financial growth, have created the conditions in which laws are broken, lives destroyed and the social contract shredded. Most of the gravest mistakes in both the business and the political world are perpetrated by eager executives, keen to please, hungry for reward and convinced that blind obedience is their only path to success. Who is more wilfully blind: the executives who believe this, or the leaders who motivate them to do so?

7. The Cult of Cultures

No snowflake in an avalanche ever feels responsible.

Stanislaw Jerzy Lec

Walt Pavlo didn't stop at writing promissory notes. As bad debts at MCI ballooned, he found himself spending more and more time with crooks and charlatans.

'Everywhere you looked,' Pavlo recalled, 'everybody was on the make and on the take. At MCI, sales sneaked deadbeats onto the network. Finance wrote worthless promissory notes. Accounting hid MCI's past-due balances. The customers on MCI's network were ripping off MCI and I was covering them up on behalf of the company.'[1]

Everybody Pavlo spent time with seemed to be ripping people off. One of the most colourful, and the most dangerous, was Harold Mann, who dreamed one day of running a vast, vertically integrated porn empire. He owed MCI money, of course – that's how he and Pavlo met – but he also owed about $600,000 to a smaller company called TNI. But TNI also owed MCI $2 million. One day, bubbling with enthusiasm, Mann came to Pavlo with an idea. Mann would take over collecting TNI's debt, but the money he collected wouldn't go to MCI. Pavlo and Mann would keep it for themselves and Pavlo could cover the traces with another promissory note. As Mann pointed out, Pavlo was surrounded by cheats; he was the only one who hadn't yet figured out how to make money at it. Till now. If he couldn't beat them, why not join them?

Pavlo couldn't resist the temptation. 'I also thought: I've been on the road, chasing these deadbeats for years and what do I have to show for it? No time with my family. Everybody else is getting rich – and I'm taking home a lousy salary. When I could be . . .'

Four years after he'd joined MCI, Pavlo was sitting with his wife on a Cayman Island beach, smoking Cohiba cigars and thinking that life had never been sweeter. He'd finally made it.

At MCI, Pavlo had learned to obey orders, even when they were repugnant – like firing the clerk – or stupid – like issuing promissory notes. Spending most of his time with cheats and fraudsters, he had learned to conform – to them. They ripped the company off; so would he. They operated without concern for anyone but themselves, and so could he. Despite a moral upbringing and a nagging sense that he was doing the wrong thing, Pavlo conformed to the crooks around him. At the time, he said, it was like he lost sight of everything he was and everything he stood for.

Stanley Milgram distinguished clearly between obedience and conformity. Whereas obedience involves complying with the orders of a formal authority, conformity is the action of someone who 'adopts the habits, routines and language of his peers, who have no special right to direct his behaviour'.[2] Milgram knew what he was talking about; he had been a student of Solomon Asch, the great American psychologist of conformity who in the 1950s had conducted a series of experiments that demonstrated just how readily individuals will conform to a group.

In his experiments,[3] Asch assembled college students for a simple test: shown a single, vertical, black line of a certain length, they needed to identify which of three separate lines matched it in length. All but one of the students had been told beforehand to choose an obviously 'wrong' line. The other, isolated, student gave his opinion last. In nearly 40 per cent of the cases, the isolated student chose the obviously wrong answer. Repeated trials of the experiment showed that only a small minority – 8 per cent – can be counted on always to conform and only about a third can be counted on never to conform, but the vast majority of us – 58 per cent – will, under certain conditions, conform.[4] Under social pressure, most of us would simply rather be wrong than alone.

The distinguishing feature of conformity is that it is implicit and it feels voluntary; after all, no one is telling us to choose the wrong line and there is no legitimate or formal reason to do so. Just as we prefer to spend time with people like ourselves, so we like to fit in. When we find that we don't fit in, we can change the people or change ourselves. Conforming is the choice – sometimes conscious, sometimes not – to change ourselves.

Since Asch, a great deal of work has been done trying to discover whether some people are more likely to conform than others, whether there is a 'conforming personality'. Not surprisingly, it's been found that people are more likely to conform to those of higher status than to mere peers – we'd rather conform to models of success.[5] Minority group members are likely to conform when they are the sole member of their minority. Unlike in Asch's study, when the experiment was repeated at the University of Oregon in 1979, men were found to be more likely to conform than women. Perhaps most interestingly, those who conformed were more likely to believe in external factors, such as luck, chance or fate; those who believed that they alone had control over their lives were less likely to choose the wrong line. But, just as when Asch conducted his original experiment, when those conforming were shown their error, they all responded with astonishment: 'Oh, God, I must be blind! What's the matter with me . . .'[6]

Every organisation and industry has a culture: the accretion of norms, rules and behaviours that define it. Culture provides immense strength: a shared sense of mission and how it is to be accomplished, an environment of camaraderie, reciprocity and shared understanding. Companies with healthy cultures don't need to spell out rules in detail because everyone knows that how work is done matters as much as what gets done. But strong cultures can have downsides: they may be exclusive, arrogant, macho or cut off from the society that they serve, as is routinely the critique of financial services and high tech. Organisations or industries with extremely steep hierarchies may deify those at the top, making them invulnerable to challenge or criticism; culture is what teaches everyone else to fall into line. That criticism is routinely levelled at healthcare systems around the world.

'I was delighted when I got the job in Bristol,' Steve Bolsin recalled, 'especially because Bristol had a reputation for not appointing people from outside; they tended to make appointments from within their own ranks. They seemed to have a dislike of outsiders or at least didn't take them on very well.'

Despite that reputation, Bolsin, an anaesthetist, moved to Bristol in September 1988 and at first enjoyed the new city and the new job. He was particularly interested in paediatric cardiac surgery; that Bristol did quite a lot of it was one of the hospital's attractions. But quite quickly he became concerned.

'I remember from early on that operations seemed to take a long time to complete. I'd come home late, then go back to the ICU to do a ward round on a sick child who'd spent most of the day in theatre. My wife Maggie would ask: is this what it is supposed to be like? Where I'd been working before – at the Brompton – we would finish these operations around three or four in the afternoon. But at Bristol, we'd be finishing at seven or eight.'

That the operations were taking so long meant that they were more dangerous for the children. During the procedures – usually to correct congenital heart defects – the heart has to stop beating. So cold solutions are put into the heart to stop it beating; that way patients shouldn't need oxygen for about forty minutes, during which time the operation would be done.

'If you take any longer,' said Bolsin, 'the survival of the heart cells is at risk. And if it takes very much longer, heart cells would start to die and the child would not survive or else would be very sick for a very long time afterwards. So time was critical and expertise was important. And the fact that these operations were taking so long was a big worry.'

Bolsin figured out that the operations were so slow for two reasons. Some of the surgeons hadn't been trained formally in this type of surgery and each operation was a huge opportunity – but also a huge challenge – to do everything right in time. In paediatric cardiac surgery, there's no such thing as a routine case; congenital abnormalities are all slightly different and surgeons without tremendous experience might not have the understanding to deal with subtle changes. That one reason might apply to any hospital. But the second reason was unique. 'As far as the surgeon, Mr Wisheart, was concerned, there was a real issue of technical competence.'

Bolsin tried to figure out how to tackle the problem without a full-frontal attack on Wisheart, who was, at the time, both medical director and chair of the hospital medical committee. This meant that he was, for a number of years, one (if not two) of the 'Three Wise Men', a system designed to respond to concerns about fellow doctors in the NHS.

'In 1991 we had some mixed audit meetings – meaning there were cardiologists, surgeons and anaesthetists there – where we discussed the hole-in-the-heart operation. The surgeons recognised that our mortality rate was higher than for the rest of the country. And they thought the thing to do was to improve the case management – improve the way we prepped the kids for operation, improve the ICU. They were looking everywhere except where they needed to!'

Bolsin collected data on the operations, showing that Bristol's mortality rate was 27 per cent – compared to 5–8 per cent for the country as a whole. So Bolsin called more meetings, trying to get to the bottom of the problem. But when he circulated the meeting minutes, in which he described paediatric cardiac surgery 'reaching crisis proportions', he was told: 'these minutes will not be circulated, this is not how we do things, I do not want you keeping minutes again'.[7] Part of the problem, he discovered, was the ancient tribalism of doctors.

'There were a lot of structural changes going on within the NHS at the time and a big debate within Bristol about whether anaesthesiology should be part of surgery or part of support services. Of course we didn't want either! And it was certainly well known that surgeons don't like being told what to do by anaesthetists. On several occasions, it was mentioned to me that anaesthesia doesn't want to raise its profile too much because we were already under fire, with people trying to pick it off. So there was a lot of jockeying for position. That warfare and tribalism was a feature of what was happening.'

From 1989 to 1992, Bolsin amassed data – not itself an easy task as cross-disciplinary audits weren't customary and incurred a fair degree of defensiveness. As the subsequent Kennedy Report said, 'they [the hospital] were actively collecting and discussing data. They were quick, however, to deny any adverse inferences drawn from the data, by resort to plausible justifications such as case mix. To some, this could be seen as wilful blindness; to others, a justifiable reaction in the context of difficult procedures with low numbers performed under less than ideal circumstances.'[8] Bolsin also continued to ask everyone he could think of to help him tackle the problem. Many of his senior colleagues assured him that the matter would be raised with Mr Wisheart or with the trust's CEO, Mr Rylance, but none of those attempts succeeded in achieving any open discussion. Most of Bolsin's senior colleagues felt that they should just be trusted to get on with things.

Bolsin became so frustrated that he suggested to his fellow anaesthetists that they simply stop giving anaesthetics. After all, he reasoned, no anaesthetics would mean no operations. But his colleagues wouldn't hear of it; the department was getting too much flak. If it caused more trouble, it might just get lumped in under surgery – and no one wanted that.

Bolsin continued to search for allies anywhere he could. By 1991, mortality rates at Bristol were twice the national average. In 1992, Bolsin discussed some of his data with Phil Hammond, a GP who (unbeknownst to Bolsin) wrote for *Private Eye*. The appearance of Hammond's articles in the *Eye* led to a flurry of questions and meetings but no action. By 1994, a new paediatric cardiac surgeon had been appointed and, on 6 January 1995, he approached Wisheart, asking that he not carry out an operation on an eighteen-month-old boy, Joshua Loveday. Claiming that this was the first he had heard about any concerns over these operations, Wisheart persisted and the child died.

'Wisheart . . . never accepted that he should stop doing paediatric cardiac surgery,' says Bolsin. 'He was incredibly stubborn, more stubborn than you can ever imagine.'

Everyone in the hospital knew. When Bolsin, frustrated and demoralised, tried to change jobs, he soon realised that everyone in the NHS was aware of what was going on in Bristol. Cardiff medics wanted their own paediatric cardiac unit because Welsh doctors didn't want to send their children to Bristol. Across the country, everyone knew Wisheart was a dangerous doctor. But nobody was prepared to do a thing to stop him.

'My wife Maggie was working as a nurse in the hospital,' Bolsin recalled. 'She worked in the emergency room and she was often seeing surgeons. One day, she saw the cardiothoracic registrar come down and she covered her name badge and went over to chat to him. And she asked him, "What's going on in the cardiac unit? What's all the fuss about paediatric cardiac surgery?" And he said, "Everyone knows Wisheart can't operate but all the trouble is just being stirred up by someone who has it in for him." She said, "But you said he can't operate!" And the registrar looked at her and said: "I know that. But I'll tell you what: you don't shop your colleagues." Then Maggie uncovered her badge and he looked really embarrassed – but he'd given the game away. You can kill children in large numbers but don't shop your colleagues.' This was conformity beyond Asch's wildest nightmares.

Frustrated, ostracised and convinced his reputation as a troublemaker would prevent him getting any other appointment within the NHS, Bolsin emigrated to Australia. A new cardiac surgeon was appointed to Bristol and the problem might have remained invisible but for Bolsin's decision first to contribute to a Channel 4 documentary, *Broken Hearts*, about the hospital and, finally, to report Wisheart to the General Medical Council.

'The GMC rather half-heartedly said to me, "We will have to tell the people you're complaining about." I said I could deal with that. They really didn't want to investigate, but they had to. I remember being told by their investigator, an old Met Police investigator who came out here to interview me: "You realise you are the only doctor who ever complained?" I had no idea! It's absolutely incredible and tells you everything about hierarchies in medicine. They just didn't want to see what might be true.'

The Kennedy Report referred to a 'cardiac club', but in fact the club at Bristol extended well beyond the cardiologists and cardiac surgeons. Many doctors, managers, clinicians and nurses had known what was going on for years. And while the exact number of children who would not otherwise have died can never be known for sure, the report puts that number at thirty to thirty-five infants. The cost of conforming to this club was very high.

The series of scandals that have hit the NHS over the last six years (Furness General, Cardiff University, Royal Glamorgan, Morecambe Bay, Gosport, Tayside, Mid Staffordshire) have displayed similar patterns to those Kennedy uncovered in Bristol. Poor patient care is never hidden from view; it occurs out in the open where it can be seen, even filmed, by many. Those lower down the pecking order become distraught and may attempt to raise concerns. But members of the club turn a blind eye.

It's easy, and perhaps comforting, to look at people like Pavlo or the Bristol doctors, to condemn them and imagine that they're utterly different from us. But the powerful desire to belong, to which they succumbed, isn't a criminal urge but a human one. There is a physical reality to the pain that we feel when we are excluded. Uncomfortable feelings of social exclusion and physical pain arise, in part, from the same regions of the brain; and the same neurochemicals that regulate physical pain control the psychological pain of social loss, too. When we form and validate our social relationships, this stimulates the production of opioids that make us feel great. (When relationships dissolve, likewise, opioids aren't produced and we feel awful.) As the pioneering psychopharmacologist Jaak Panksepp put it: 'social affect and social bonding are in some fundamental neurochemical sense opioid addictions'.[9] In other words, our desire to seek social connections with others comes from chemical rewards as well as social ones.[10]

We can all remember how this feels from schooldays: the fun of being part of a clique, the misery of being left out. However independent we may be (or want to be) we know that we can achieve little alone; to be excluded is to be both lonely and impotent. But when we gang together in like-minded groups, we become more effective, learn shortcuts and feel ourselves validated. Conformity is compelling because much of our sense of life's meaning depends on other people. Pavlo felt foolish when he didn't have any of the measures of success valued by the people around him; he felt great when he could join their club. Even though he was fully aware that what he was doing was wrong, his need to belong blinded him to alternatives and consequences. And so our sense of leading a meaningful life hinges crucially on being included.

Cyberball is mostly known as a 1980s arcade game, first released by Atari and maintained, to this day, for lovers of retro video games. Multiple players, each on a separate computer console, can throw a ball back and forth. But there's another version, refined by psychologists, with the aim of simulating social exclusion. Using this software, you can pit volunteers against each other or against pre-programmed players who will behave as you need them to. So you can play this *Cyberball* with lots of players or, as in one experiment, with just one real participant who, after a brief period of inclusion, is slowly but surely ostracised. This experiment wasn't designed to prepare students for college life or medicine; it was designed to measure how 121 individuals respond when they're not part of the game.[11]

In the experiment, after the experience of ostracism, the volunteers took a test, the Kunzendorf No Meaning Scale, which assesses the extent to which life is viewed as meaningless (e.g. 'Life is a cruel joke' or 'I don't care if I live or die'). As you might expect, the excluded players were more likely to feel their lives to be meaningless. A similar experiment, but with real people delivering positive or negative feedback, showed similar results: those who were rejected not only found less value in life; they also felt no desire even to search for new meaning. The experience of exclusion left them feeling hopeless and demotivated.

The Florida State University team that conducted these studies devised several more, but they all led to the same conclusion: ostracism makes individuals feel they lack purpose, have less control over their lives, are less good moral beings and lack self-worth. Those secondary-school cliques aren't just adolescent anomalies: human beings hate being left out. We conform because to do so seems to give our life meaning. This is so fundamental a part of our evolutionary make-up that it is strong enough to make us give the wrong answers to questions, as in Asch's line experiments, and strong enough to make us disregard moral lessons absorbed since childhood. The carrot of belonging and the stick of exclusion are powerful enough to blind us to the consequences of our actions.

Assimilation into the cultural norms of an organisation is a profound experience. It isn't always as colourful as Walt Pavlo's but it invariably leaves a deep imprint. Of course, the first step of conformity is taken by the choice to enter a particular profession or organisation: those that are chosen are selected and, importantly, self-selected to fit in. In medicine, academics studying incoming students found that young medical students were unlikely, if they saw something unethical, to blow the whistle. But what was more striking was that, after three years of medical training and ethics classes, they were even *less* likely to rock the boat. In other words, these students came in as conformists – and ended even more so.[12]

'By the time you are at med school you are pre-selected as someone likely to be intimidated by hierarchy,' says Steve Bolsin. 'By end of training – in four years – 97 per cent will not rock the boat. It's recognised in research from the US, Germany, UK, all over the world. It is called the hidden curriculum of medicine.[13] We know that mistakes are a huge problem in medicine – in the US, they're estimated to cost between seventeen and twenty-nine billion dollars a year. "I want to be in the right group" is a very important part of it. I don't want to be seen not supporting my peer group. Everybody wants to be part of the in-group.'

When, in April 2017, consultant surgeon Ian Stuart Paterson was convicted on seventeen counts of wounding, through unnecessary breast operations, most attention focused on the degree to which patients described him as being 'like God' and even recommended him to their friends. But his operations weren't conducted in secret; he operated in Heart of England NHS Trust and a private healthcare provider, Spire. He'd already been suspended from Good Hope hospital near Birmingham, and both patients and GPs had complained about him. Nevertheless, he was allowed to perform hundreds of unnecessary, dangerous operations for nearly twenty years. The hidden curriculum was hard at work.

Even non-conformers are susceptible to the rewards of conformity. Although in its early days the computing industry was populated by an eclectic blend of artists, musicians, scientists and iconoclasts, eagerly inventing an ecosystem that they believed would dislodge cultural monoliths, in time Silicon Valley has become a cultural monolith of its own. Its celebration of immature young men hellbent on making their names and fortunes is pronounced enough to be the butt of jokes and sitcoms. But that doesn't mean it's a funny place to live or to work.

'I came into this industry,' Ted Corden told me, 'because I was just dazzled by the way that programmers thought, the way that one thing led to another to another – until you were in some weird place you'd never imagined before. I'd always liked gadgets; I had a really early computer and this just seemed to be the place where the most exciting, out-there stuff was happening.'[14]

Corden worked in computing, made a lot of money, much of which he then contributed to a venture capital firm. I met him when I was running my first software company in the US in the 1990s. He stood out for being articulate, thoughtful, imaginative. Sure, he wanted to make money – and did – but he always seemed to be about a lot more than that.

'When I joined the firm, I made a few early investments that paid off well,' he remembered. He was being modest. He'd invested in some of the biggest, earliest internet companies and been successful beyond any expectation. 'I made enough money that, for the first time in my life, I felt comfortable, safe, like my life was taken care of. And that meant I could relax a little, live a little.'

Corden's idea of living a little wasn't wild: it meant leaving the office in time to pick up his kids from school. Or staying home if one of them was sick. Sometimes his wife would swing by to take him out for lunch. His was scarcely exotic behaviour. But it drew attention.

'One day the head of the firm asked me if I'd go to the east coast overnight. A deal meeting the firm couldn't miss. I said no: it was the night of my son's school play. He looked at me like that was some kind of joke. Then he got pretty heavy: is this some kind of joke? Do you think we're running a retirement home here? He was astonishingly unpleasant – I couldn't repeat some of the things he said. Anyway, suffice to say – I missed the play, I got on the plane. I went to the meeting.'

The deal took days to close. Back at the office, everyone welcomed him like a hero. Only now, looking back, does he see what was really going on. The whole episode had been a test: was he one of the guys? Would he sacrifice family to the firm?

As the internet bubble expanded, so did the tests. Long trips. Long nights. Big glitzy launch parties with rock stars in penthouse suites. Girls. Boys. Drugs. He says now that he wasn't really part of it – but he didn't stay away.

'Now I look back on it, I can see we were all big swinging dicks. It's what we called ourselves and it's who we became. We hated everybody. We were smarter than everybody, tougher than everybody. We could out-work, out-screw, out-smoke, out-buy anybody and anything in the universe.'

But hadn't he been the home-loving, uxorious father of two? Ruefully he acknowledged, 'Yeah, I had been. I was. But . . .' There was a long pause. 'I got scared. We had this stance: biggest, fastest, smartest. Limos. Private jets. But I was scared that maybe I wasn't that good, maybe I wasn't all that smart. When I hung out with the guys – all the fear went away. I mean, it was kinda fun.' There isn't a hint of fun in his voice as he says this.

But this kind of fun was easy to join because all of Corden's colleagues were male. If he had wanted to do something else, he'd have found little social support. At the time, fewer than

5 per cent of venture capital partners were female; by 2016 the number had reached just 7 per cent. The macho culture of Silicon Valley was in its infancy, entirely unchallenged, and the not-so-hidden curriculum here was: boys will be boys. My own software business was one of a group of some forty companies; for all but one year, I was the sole female CEO. At our 'summits' when all the CEOs gathered, a favoured pastime after dinner and a lot of drinking was to race rental cars around the hotel parking lot. That was inevitably when I retired to bed with a book.

High tech has always been a boys' club, remarkable for the degree to which it venerates its pioneers as much for being obnoxious as for being original. Famous for screaming at employees and mistreating his first wife and child, Steve Jobs is the patron saint of Silicon Valley, providing the perfect alibi for assholes. I've lost count of the number of aspirants who've argued seriously that genius and abusive behaviour are necessary bedfellows, that being 'nice' and being brilliant are incompatible. You won't change the world by following the rules, so the rules don't apply; anyone following them must be a loser. The adolescent misogyny of *The Social Network*'s Mark Zuckerberg made crass sexism a hallmark of entrepreneurial promise. A culture's heroes send the clearest of signals about what matters and what it takes to be included, and the heroes of Silicon Valley, whatever their hidden depths, were more famous for gross insensitivity and extreme wealth than for any strategic acuity. That they have become so rich and so famous entices more like-minded males to join in. Such caricatures establish the norms by which ambitious, immature young men are measured and measure themselves.

Zuckerberg's oft-quoted mantra 'Move Fast and Break Things' isn't very different from the Corden generation's 'Go Big or Stay Home' and the pull of conformity is exacerbated by the overheated competitiveness of the high-tech market. In Silicon Valley, where everyone is competing for investment, scale, talent and wealth, the bifurcation between winners and losers is extreme – and nobody wants to be a loser. Instead, a fierce vortex of ambition and speed sucks in and dizzies those drawn to its promise and drama.

'It was so heady!' Corden remembers. 'The speed of it, the excitement – the sheer exhaustion of it! Drinking from a fire hose, that was the phrase. We *never* went home. Working across time zones, thinking: any day now – an IPO, millions, billions. We all kind of lost our minds.' In Corden's case, losing his mind meant a separation from his wife and kids, losing touch with friends, never having time to think. When the dot-com bubble burst in 2001, it came as a relief. He couldn't understand how he'd become such an asshole.

'A shuddering halt, like stepping off a fairground ride. When I had time to decompress, there were things I remembered that made me shudder, still make me shudder. Was that me? How? My wife said it was nearly two years before – as she put it – I came back to myself. I've never done a lot of drugs but this was coming down from a really incredible high. Or low . . .'

Corden went to work at an investment bank and tried to use the new job to reset his life. School plays were back on the calendar, as was dinner with his wife. Until one Monday in May, he came into work to find a card on his desk. It was a Mother's Day card, signed by his male colleagues with a smattering of insult and innuendo. He quit. He knew himself well enough by now, he said; if he stayed, he'd end up conforming.

The sexism of Silicon Valley – poor pay and promotion for women, sexual harassment, stereotyping, legendary lewd humour – doesn't surprise Corden. He claims that his generation wasn't as dangerous as the industry he observes today; he was just building out e-commerce sites, he argues, nothing as complex or potentially as dangerous as artificial intelligence or disrupting democracies. When I suggest this sounds like special pleading, he readily concedes that it is probably as much fun to be part of the in-crowd today as it was when he was young. But the risks of wilful blindness now – absence of debate, polarised, binary thinking and a lack of perspective – are greater.

Ted Corden and Walt Pavlo both describe the experience of conformity as one of being almost literally carried away: as though they had somehow become separated from, blind to, their conscious rational selves. In fact, what happens when any of us conform turns out to be physiologically interesting. Asch's conformity experiments have puzzled psychologists and neuroscientists for years, but now the development of fMRI technology allows them to study the brain at the point that it conforms.

In 2005, neuroscientist Gregory Berns and a team of researchers at Emory University placed thirty-two 'normal, right-handed volunteers' into an fMRI brain scanner and asked them to compare not lines, but three-dimensional objects.[15] In one version of the experiment, they had to decide by themselves which two objects were the same. In another, they decided after knowing what their fellow participants had decided. And in a third version, they cast their vote after knowing what a computer had decided. What the scientists sought to discover wasn't whether the volunteers would conform; they knew by now how likely it was that they would. Instead, they wanted to know what kind of brain activity was involved. If, in the act of conforming, activity in the prefrontal cortex was dominant, this would indicate that conformity was the result of conscious decision-making. But if activity centred in the occipital and parietal regions of the brain, then that would suggest that conformity was an act of perception – that social influence had altered what the volunteer *saw*.

The three-dimensional test was harder than Asch's and so the participants made more mistakes, even without any external input. But they conformed at the same rates. And when they did so, there was *no* activity in the prefrontal cortex – that is, no conscious decision was being made. In other words, knowing what the group saw *changed* what the participants saw; they became blind to the differences. They weren't thinking for themselves.

The scientists concluded that the areas of the brain responsible for perception are altered by social influences. What we see depends on what others see. That was a remarkable enough finding. But several other insights emerged from this experiment. Knowledge of the group's decision seemed to reduce the mental load on the volunteers; less thinking took place when they knew what the others thought. A good match could stop thinking because it felt right. So instead of the group benefiting from the collective wisdom of many, in fact what it got was reduced thoughtfulness from each one.

When asked in a debriefing questionnaire how they explained their conforming errors, the participants had no sense of having conformed; they believed that they had all reached the same decision purely serendipitously. They may have thought that they'd made a free choice where in fact they had not. Just as Asch and Milgram had surmised, the conforming decision was not experienced, not felt at all, but was entirely implicit.

Furthermore, in the rarer examples of a participant taking an independent stand against the crowd, something else happened: the amygdala, the area of the brain that governs emotions, became highly active. Something tantamount to distress seemed to take place. Independence, it seems, comes at a high cost.[16]

Berns' findings have all kinds of interesting applications, from the profound to the trivial. Studying teenage taste in popular music, the same researchers found that a big determinant is anxiety about not matching the taste of the in-crowd. The same may be applied to all kinds of fads and tastes: did you read *Fifty Shades of Grey* because you wanted to – or because you worried about being left out of the conversation? Did you join Facebook after a careful consideration of its privacy policies or just because all your friends had already joined? How far did clients who invested with Bernard Madoff do so because they carefully considered their options or because they wanted to belong to the same club? How often in life are we really just going along for the ride?

Of course, we all assimilate to a degree – society would cease to function if we did not. But one of the biggest risks of conformity, according to the psychologist Irving Janis, is that our sense of belonging blinds us to dangers and encourages greater risk-taking. He cited the example of Picher, a mining town in Oklahoma, which was, at one time, the largest producer of lead and zinc in the world. But the mines were so extensive that some of them ran underneath the town. In February 1950, some 200 residents were told to evacuate because of the imminent danger of a cave-in. But the city fathers just laughed; one attended a Lions Club meeting wearing a parachute, just to show how silly the rumours were. Unfortunately, the other inhabitants in Picher followed his lead, costing some of the men and their families their lives when the town collapsed days later.

Janis was working in the 1970s, well before the advent of fMRI scanners. But he hypothesised that lack of vigilance and excessive risk-taking are a form of 'group derangement', and he argued that this type of behaviour could be found in any kind of group. Most famously, he outlined his hypothesis in detailed studies of military disasters: the Bay of Pigs, the Korean War, Pearl Harbor and the escalation of the Vietnam War. Well before the neuroscience was available to support his theory, Janis believed that, in a group, the pressure to maintain a consensus results in less thinking. Members don't look for information to confirm or disconfirm. 'Selective bias is shown in the way the group reacts to factual information, mass media, experts and outside critics. They spend little time deliberating the obstacles to the plan and therefore fail to work out contingency plans.' And he concluded by summarising a groupthink 'law' which is the central irony that lies at the heart of all corporate cultures: 'The more amiability and esprit de corps among the members of a policy-making in-group, the greater is the danger that independent critical thinking will be replaced by groupthink, which is likely to result in *irrational and dehumanising* [my italics] actions directed against out-groups.'[17] The downside of the cosy feeling of togetherness is that everyone is less vigilant and more vulnerable to bad and dangerous decisions.

Groups subject to groupthink typically imagine themselves invulnerable, like the Picher city fathers and the young men (and CEOs) of Silicon Valley. They rationalise warnings out of existence and believe passionately in the moral superiority of their group. Enemies and outsiders tend to be demonised: women just 'don't get' or can't do technology, arts graduates are too 'fuzzy'. Dissent is rare and difficult because self-censorship expunges it and because consensus and unity are deemed the ultimate good. In most organisations, the good team player is implicitly defined as the person who goes along, not the one who asks hard questions. I've even heard boards discuss how, and why, they are invulnerable to groupthink, oblivious to the irony inherent in their confidence. In fact, of course, being a truly good team player involves having the confidence to dissent – but that is rarely what's meant by this trite accolade.

Serving on the Bear Stearns board of directors, Henry Bienen, the president of Northwestern University, learned just how prized board unanimity can be. Completing an annual questionnaire about the board's effectiveness, he opined that some meetings seemed somewhat perfunctory, short on discussion and debate. He was subsequently subjected to what he called a 'woodshed' discussion when he was roundly chastised by Jimmy Cayne, the same CEO who had rejected Pat Lewis' risk-assessment model. Bienen quickly saw that criticism was not welcome and he was not invited to stand for re-election when his term expired.[18]

Just before the UK bank HBOS was taken over, I chaired a panel in the City of London about board governance. Taking part was Dennis Stevenson, then chairman of HBOS. We were all pretty amazed when he turned up at all – everyone knew the bank teetered on the edge of collapse. But he did more than turn up; he eulogised the outstanding board he chaired, citing as evidence the fact that, even in this crisis, 'we are as one'. He seemed oblivious to the notion that the unity of his board may have been a contributory factor to the bank's mess in the first place.

Conformity is a huge challenge to good governance. Having sat on boards of private companies and non-profits, I've watched with alarm as dissent is stage-managed out of existence. Enough pre-work (and often rehearsal) before the board meeting gets everyone aligned; a good meeting is deemed a harmonious, not a contentious one. When it comes to remuneration committees, this is even more pronounced. 'They always put me on the RemCo,' one non-executive director boasted to me, 'because they know I'll support their pay rises and bonuses.' You won't appear on any honours list if you aren't deemed 'reliable' and even quangos (which are supposed to be at arm's length from government) find their less pliable candidates marginalised. Although democracy depends on independent thinking, it's hard to find governments that foster or tolerate it.

As horrifying as many of the revelations around Uber and Harvey Weinstein have been, as striking has been the reluctance of investors and board members to withdraw support. Despite a string of scandals at Uber – hiking prices at times of natural disasters, drivers assaulting passengers, sexist comments by CEO Travis Kalanick, sexist ads promising to pair customers with 'hot chick' drivers, film of Kalanick fighting with an Uber driver, accounting errors that led to drivers being underpaid, sourcing confidential medical records about an Uber customer who claimed she had been raped, Susan Fowler's blogpost about known sexual harassment at the company and a data breach that 57 million Uber users were not told about – no directors of the company have stood down. Eventually they were persuaded to fire Kalanick but all appear to have been blind to their responsibility – and they kept him on the board. Similarly, despite a trail of settlements and claims of sexual misconduct by Harvey Weinstein while running Miramax, the owner of the company, Disney, now faces accusations in a lawsuit that it 'knew, should have known or was wilfully blind'. Boards have become social status symbols and nobody wants to risk being booted out of the club.

But the concentric circles of conformity and groupthink can ripple wider still. Individuals influence each other, reducing thought. Groups influence other groups, pushing each other into positions of greater extremism. In a competitive marketplace, the moral dislocation that Pavlo and Corden experienced can spread, like a contagion, crossing borders, engulfing global institutions and economies. That's what happened in the banking crisis which became an economic crisis and has produced a democratic crisis.

In California, Florida and most of the northeastern states, house prices appreciated at an average rate of 10 per cent in the years 2001–6. Because, during that same time, Alan Greenspan at the Federal Reserve was bringing interest rates down to record lows (reaching 1 per cent by 2003) you didn't need to be a great mathematician to understand that you would get a higher rate of return on your house than on your savings account. So home ownership ballooned, reaching an all-time high of 69.2 per cent in 2006. But many of these new purchases weren't really homes; they were investments.

'I started buying houses because, well, that's what everyone was doing!' Looking somewhat abashed, Deborah Laird still struggles in her effort to capture how she felt just a few years earlier. A high-school science teacher with a pension, she'd never been an active investor. Deborah wasn't greedy; she had always lived modestly and remains rather proud of her thrifty lifestyle. But, in 2003, that changed.

'All you ever heard was how much money people were making, selling houses, buying houses. I'd lived in the same house for fifteen years; I started to feel stupid! I reasoned with myself that it wasn't like I was actively helping anybody by staying out of the market. So I decided to trade up.'

Laird sold her Boston apartment and bought herself a house. She was surprised by how much money she'd made. And it had been so easy.

'The mortgage was simple. Finding properties wasn't hard. And after teaching physics all day, it was fun to have something else to talk about in the staff room. Everyone was doing it.'

By 2006, Laird wasn't just a science teacher any more; now she was a landlord, with three apartments and two houses. This made her part of a club. Everyone she knew was buying flats and houses. 'And then I had a cancer scare. It wasn't a big deal – I mean, now I can see it wasn't a big deal. But at the time, my God, I was scared. And I just stopped everything. I mean – it's not like I needed another house! And between appointments and scans and teaching and looking after all the properties, I was just burned out. And the money seemed so stupid – if I was going to die next year, what would it bring me? So I stopped.'

Her home today is comfortable but not ostentatious. It's decorated mostly with pictures of nephews and nieces; the sofas are dotted with cushions she embroidered herself. It's not the headquarters of a property tycoon. But Laird feels she had a lucky escape.

'Looking back, I feel like I went kind of mad. It was like: property was the hot thing and I was doing the hot thing and everyone was doing the hot thing and we were all in it together. And I have never been someone who ever cared about that stuff before! Now I think my cancer was a kind of warning, or a blessing. Because if it hadn't come along – I might never have stopped. And where would I be now?'

Halfway across the country, in Plano, Texas, Laird's conformity to her peers was amplified at the corporate headquarters of Countrywide, the company that had supplied mortgages for Deborah Laird's tiny property empire. There, Catherine Clark was aggressively recruited to help build the business even faster. With deep experience at a senior level in large corporations, Clark had an exemplary résumé and high moral standards. What had enticed her to Countrywide was its entrepreneurial energy and ostensible appetite for change.

'They told me they wanted my experience of different

corporate cultures in other places I'd worked. But once I got there – they just wanted me to conform. There was no real liking for new people. Everyone talked about the "Countrywide way" and that's what you were supposed to stick to. It meant that newcomers were all frustrated – we were just shut down.'

The company needed her to bring in more senior executives, to deepen the talent pool and diversity of the team. But, once again, she was frustrated.

'I found an African American from Bank of America – perfect for the position. And my boss says, "Why would we consider him? He would be hard to understand." (In other words: he's not like us.) There was another potential candidate from WaMu. He was very well qualified but he was gay.'

What shocked Clark most was the lack of dissent within the organisation. 'Where I'd worked before, my most trusted advisers would argue with me. No one was afraid of conflict. People would scream at each other – and then, the next day, they'd be playing golf together. It wasn't that it was a culture of screamers either; it's just that dissenting voices were okay.

'But at Countrywide, in meetings, there was no dissent. There were lots of whispers afterwards, but no argument in the meetings. In the Consumer Markets Division, Joe was known for his tirades. You would be called to his office, he'd scream and yell at you with his door open so everyone could see. So everyone got the message: toe the line or else.'

Clark started as an outsider and left because she felt she couldn't accomplish anything. The overwhelming conformity of the aggressive sales culture, however, was part of the appeal to many who stayed.

'I love this business!' says Pamela Vincent, who stayed with Countrywide until it merged with Bank of America. 'Housing is an important American value. There is something worthwhile in what we do, helping someone buy their first home. And I love the sales culture; there's a lot of celebration, a lot of deadlines, a lot of ups and downs and it's exciting because this is where the money is made. Each month you start from zero and you can see the money made producing loans.'

Vincent still doesn't think anyone did anything wrong. She defends NINA loans (available to those with no income and no assets) as 'great for the self-employed'. And, anyway, Countrywide didn't start the crisis; they just followed the market's lead.

'At Countrywide, we weren't the first to do sub-prime mortgages but we did start applying sub-prime practices because we continued to see housing appreciation. The bedroom ATM! The house goes up – why not take a new mortgage? These kinds of loans can be very valuable in the hands of a very astute home-owner who is economically savvy. My former brother-in-law put four girls through college, just refinancing his house. Lots of people did that. Appreciation was thought to cover all ills.'

But didn't she think that, some day, market appreciation of properties would have to stop – or at least slow down?

'Well, no one else thought they would. And it's like Chuck Prince at Citigroup said: you had to keep dancing. Why wouldn't you? It was fine as long as everyone else kept doing it, too!' That infamous quote from the CEO of Citigroup perfectly describes how conformity works in the marketplace: everything's fine as long as no one dissents, bucks the trend, or fails.

'There was endless wilful blindness,' says Michael Sarnoff, chief credit officer at a large Midwest bank. 'The entire food chain from borrower to lender to securitiser to auditor to rating agency to end investor. They all went along for years, they all got sucked in and conformed to perpetuate the madness.'

Sarnoff worked in the mortgage industry for twenty years. His vantage point allowed him to see the chain reaction, in which all the participants conformed to the same errors.

'In 2003, I think we hit an all-time high in terms of volume. The sub-prime lenders were multiplying and everyone knew the loans were just stupid: loaning to people with terrible credit, no income, occupancy fraud, income fraud – but nobody cared because appreciation was taking place. Then they all started throwing wood on the fire in the form of additional lending so you could lend to anybody, to a dead person! The amount of crime in the mortgage industry was just incredible.'

Theoretically, the market was hugely diversified: a plethora of borrowers, lenders, securitisers, auditors and rating agencies competing with each other was supposed to spread risk and generate a wide range of products and business models. But competition between the participants was so fierce that instead they all copied each other. The drive to compete created more and more uniformity. It wasn't just that everyone was working from the same assumptions; they all used the same software.

'Desktop Underwriter is software that has about one hundred fields and you put the data in and it produces either an approval or a caution,' says Sarnoff. 'You can't close a loan with a caution. So it's really the industry standard – everybody uses it – so everybody was judging the same people the same way. The software was written by employees at Freddie Mac and Fannie Mae; they were right there at the table and, because they're such a force in creating standards in the marketplace, they just perpetuated it.'

That so much of the market was fraudulent perturbed Sarnoff and he'd complain to anyone who would listen. But even so, and despite his seniority and expertise, he couldn't change the game. In order to compete, he needed to be able to attract and retain a sales force. And no salesperson would stay working for him if they didn't have the same chance to earn the huge commissions their peers were making. So even at his own bank, Sarnoff sometimes had to turn a blind eye to the absurdity of NINA loans and the proliferation of fraud.

Nevertheless, he remains especially critical of the ratings agencies that were asked to grade the debt that was packaged up into mortgage-backed securities.

'Moody's and Standard & Poor's were manipulating the data to keep securities going through, making them appear larger or more secure than they were. I knew people who'd rate a security and, by the time the paperwork got through, all the data had been changed and falsified. The real problem was that since the seller paid for the rating, they didn't mind incompetent audit teams or falsified results, as long as they got their AAA ratings. I have friends on audit teams who'd see their final results changed. I wouldn't do it, but many did. Everyone was in on it. But it really was: if you can't beat 'em, join 'em.'

And of course by the time the packaged securities reached Wall Street, there were plenty of traders to sell them.

'Insane consumers, greedy lenders, loan officers who'd do anything to get information through the system, poor underwriters who were no more than box checkers, a cheap labour force, Fannie Mae and Freddie Mac and a president who pressured them to increase home ownership, biased rating agencies, securitisers, and all the stupid investors who bought CDOs and CDOs squared,' says Michael Sarnoff. 'All equally blind. All greedy. There was just a horrible deterioration in the moral fabric of people. And a lot of wishful thinking. But the structure of the global industry means no one feels responsible.'

Sarnoff says the crisis was like watching a plague sweep through a town as, slowly but surely, each part of the industry succumbed to the same disease. This was conformity on an epic scale, as institution after institution caved in to the same thinking: if you can't beat 'em, join 'em; if we don't do it, someone else will; toe the line or else; you have to keep dancing. What he saw was wilful blindness amplified: we may all know it's wrong, but if I won't see it, then you won't see it and they won't see it. We may not have seen collaborative, collusive conformity on such a scale since the totalitarian regimes of the 1930s. At the start, however, there were no dictators; there was only the market. And the central challenge of the episode is the revelation that the more competitive the market became, the more it became uniform and the more conformist its leaders became. Risk was concentrated, not diffused. What Pavlo and Corden and Sarnoff saw on a personal level turned out to be true on a global scale: the more competitive a society becomes, the greater is the compulsion to conform, no matter how repulsive the norm becomes.

'This has been the greatest privilege of my life to serve as vice president to a president who is keeping his word to the American people.' That's how Vice President Pence kicked off a Trump cabinet meeting in June 2017, establishing the formula for praise and adulation for the president that every other member proceeded to emulate – or top.

'This group has the exact right message and is being responded, response is fabulous around the country.'

'Mr President, I am privileged to be here. Deeply honoured to be here. And I want to thank you for keeping your commitment to the American workers.'

'Thank you, Mr President. It's a new day at the United Nations. We now have a very strong voice. People know what the United States is for, they know what we're against and they see us leading across the board.'

The premise of working in teams is the premise of democracy: that a broad cross-section of different kinds of people, bringing a range of experiences, beliefs and expertise, will make better decisions for all of those whom they serve. Footage showing the craven conformity of Trump's cabinet, its preference for sycophancy over dissent, broadcasts a humiliating display of wilful blindness. But such groupthink wasn't exclusive to the cabinet; of the 122 conservative intellectuals who signed the 2 March 2016 'Never Trump' letter (which argued that the candidate was too inconsistent, unprincipled, reckless, inflammatory, undemocratic and dishonest to serve as head of state) roughly half fell in line behind the president in under a year.

Janis' great insight – that being part of the group increases risk-taking – has never been more relevant or urgent. Individually we might pause and think before sending a suggestive text to a subordinate, before hiding a data breach, before buying a house we can't afford or before supporting a president we have described as 'fundamentally dishonest'. But when everybody's doing it, we feel safe, at exactly the moment when the stakes make it more dangerous.

What none of the experiments or the neuroscience or the biochemistry can tell us about conformity is how bad it feels when it goes wrong. Because in choosing to stick with the crowd, we steadily blind ourselves – to alternatives, to bad news, to doubt, to the individual values that we thought defined us – until we find ourselves dazed, confused and in the dark, wondering what happened.

8. Complicit

BLUMENTHAL: Doesn't that term of service conflict with the FTC [Federal Trade Commission] order that Facebook was under at that very time that this term of service was, in fact, provided to Facebook. And you'll note that the FTC order specifically requires Facebook to protect privacy. Isn't there a conflict there?

ZUCKERBERG: Senator, it certainly appears that we should have been aware that this app developer submitted a term that was in conflict with the rules of the platform.

BLUMENTHAL: Well, what happened here was, in effect, wilful blindness. It was heedless and reckless, which, in fact, amounted to a violation of the FTC consent decree.

Senate Committee on the Judiciary, Senate Committee on Commerce, Science, and Transportation, 10 April 2018[1]

In January 2001, Walt Pavlo pleaded guilty to wire fraud and money-laundering and was sentenced to two years in prison. It might as well have been twenty, for he had lost everything: his job, his wife, his family, most of all his sense of himself. To this day, you can read the anguish on his face as he struggles to reclaim the good man he always thought he was. He's neat, well dressed, attentive, punctual, and these things matter to him disproportionately; every detail signals whether he's still on track. He has to convince a tough jury: himself. And he still isn't sure of the verdict.

When he got out of prison, Pavlo contacted Frank Abagnale, the famous fraudster whose life story was the subject of Spielberg's film, *Catch Me If You Can*. Abagnale advised him to start talking to people about his experience. If you stick at it, Abagnale advised, you can be successful, but you have to have the right message. Pavlo took this advice and started teaching business school students how easy it is to go wrong. He would give up to eight talks a day for a single fee. Punctilious about not making too much money, he didn't want to profit from his crime.

One day, he was giving a talk in South Dakota.

'It was very cold outside. I was talking to a bunch of sophomores and I smelled smoke. But I kept on with my talk. Ten minutes later, smoke started rolling in through the air vents. We evacuated the building. About ten minutes later, it turned out it was no big deal – just someone burning pizza boxes. But when we all came back in, I asked, "How many of you smelled smoke and said nothing?" Everyone giggled and raised their hand. "How come no one said anything?" Some said they didn't want to look stupid; others said they weren't sure it was smoke. But that is how it is in business. You smell the smoke. You know there's something wrong and you think: maybe it's just me, maybe I'm wrong – and you don't do anything. By the time there's a fire in the building, it's too late.'

Although he didn't know it, Pavlo had witnessed an accidental re-enactment of a famous experiment conducted in 1968 by two young psychologists, Bibb Latané and John

Darley, in which they placed one, two or three volunteers in a room and asked them to fill in a questionnaire. As they did so, the room slowly began to fill with smoke. The two psychologists wanted to know under which conditions the volunteers would be most likely to do something about the smoke: were you more likely to respond to an emergency when alone or with confederates?[2]

Their results were shocking. One person alone would, within two minutes, do something about the smoke: look for its source, check its temperature, go and get help. But when there were two people in the room, only one out of ten reported the smoke. The rest stayed, doggedly filling out their questionnaires while coughing and rubbing their eyes. And when there were three people in the room – which the psychologists theorised should produce three times the response rate of one person – only one in twenty-four people reported the smoke within the first four minutes, even though, by then, they could scarcely see.[3]

Darley and Latané coined the phrase 'bystander effect' to describe what they'd discovered. Their interest in the phenomenon had been sparked by the murder of a young New Yorker, Kitty Genovese, who was stabbed to death in the middle of a street in New York City. At the time, it was thought that up to thirty-eight people had witnessed the attack, which lasted more than half an hour, yet not one had so much as phoned the police. Preachers, news commentators and politicians instantly pontificated about callous New Yorkers and inner-city anomie, but Darley and Latané were sceptical. Was it just New Yorkers who were especially venal – or would anyone respond passively to an emergency? Which, if any, of us was so superior?

Their very first experiment isolated volunteers in booths and led them to believe that they overheard someone having an epileptic seizure. In cases in which the volunteers thought that they alone knew what was happening, 85 per cent reported the incident. But where the volunteers believed that others elsewhere would also know about the seizure, only a third did anything about it. What the experiment indicated was that the more people witness an emergency, the fewer will intervene. Collectively, we become blind to events that, alone, we see readily.

In that first experiment, the witnesses knew others shared their knowledge, but they were isolated from one another because Latané and Darley wanted to rule out conformity as one of the explanations for the behaviour. Just knowing that other people were aware of the problem – even without knowing whether anyone had actually taken steps to address it – was enough to prevent any form of intervention. Once you put people together in a group, as in the smoke-filled room, bystander behaviour might be exacerbated by conformity but it clearly was not determined by it.

Their results provoked a flurry of variations, in which men and women, black and white, young and old, were witness to all kinds of emergencies: robberies, faints, asthma attacks, screams, falls, crashes and electric shocks.[4] They all confirmed the original thesis: the more people that witness an event, the less likely it is that any will respond to it. Even just thinking about other people reduces levels of altruism.

Unlike in the US, English law recognises the importance of bystanders and attempts to formulate a response to them. The legal doctrine known as 'joint enterprise' says that bystanders can find themselves convicted of murder, even where there is no evidence as to who inflicted the fatal blow. It was most famously used in 1952 to convict Derek Bentley, whose words 'let him have it' preceded the death of a police officer. More recently, four men were convicted of murder in the case of sixteen-year-old Tyrone Clarke, who was stabbed to death by a gang of up to thirty youths. Even though it wasn't clear who had struck the fatal blow, all four who could be identified were regarded as guilty.[5]

But the law doesn't change behaviour and new headlines keep confirming Darley and Latané's findings. The advent of mobile phones should have made reporting incidents faster and easier, but they haven't influenced our willingness to do so. In 2005, a young woman described trying to help a fellow passenger on a London bus, after he'd been stabbed. Not only, she said, did most people melt away; she herself had done nothing when hearing cries for help from the upper deck.[6]

In the spate of tragic deaths of young children like Tiffany Wright and Khyra Ishaq, both of whom starved to death, the press has been quick to blame social services. But what is so striking in these cases is that the children were seen by neighbours and bystanders who did nothing. In the case of Khyra Ishaq, a neighbour witnessed the little girl eating bread off a bird table because she was so underfed. Screams and cries of 'let me out' had reportedly been heard coming from Khyra's house, where a neighbour said she once saw the little girl whimpering in the back garden before her death, dressed just in her underwear. But cultural norms – don't be a nosy parker sticking your nose in where it isn't wanted – meant that Khyra died seen, but not seen. When Tiffany Wright died, Alan Jones of the Safeguarding Children Board pointed out that family friends and neighbours were more aware of what was going on than the authorities, but this provided the starving child with no help or protection at all. And when David Askew, a 64-year-old man with learning difficulties, was bullied to death after years of abuse, blame fell on the local council for failing to rehouse him – even though his neighbours, who had witnessed his torment for years, had done nothing to prevent such cruelty. These crimes needed no CCTV cameras to be noticed; they were seen by a broad community of bystanders.

There is no reason to conclude that these witnesses were exceptionally venal individuals. That's what Latané and Darley's work had proved. We are all likely to behave this way. Just as we think we won't obey Milgram's instructor, so we do not believe that we would be passive onlookers. But the evidence is against us. What the bystander effect demonstrates is the tremendous tension between our social selves and our individual selves. Left on our own, we mostly do the right thing. But in a group, our moral selves and our social selves come into conflict, which is painful. The non-intervening subjects of Darley and Latané's experiments had not, they said, actively decided against intervention. Rather they were frozen in a state of indecision and conflict about whether and how to intervene. Looking for a way out of that discomfort, they choose the easier path, a kind of moral shortcut.

One of the initial explanations for bystander behaviour was ambiguity: it can be hard to know quite what's happening or what response is most appropriate. But perhaps too we are ambiguous about our own role within the event. We hope that the situation isn't so dire that it needs our intervention. Perhaps it will pass or we've just misinterpreted it. Responding could provoke conflict and we don't like conflict. Conformity comes into this, too: I sure would look like an idiot if I rushed to help and it turned out to be nothing. Our fear of embarrassment is the tip of that iceberg that is the ancient fear of exclusion and it turns out to be astonishingly potent. We are more likely to intervene where we are the sole witness; once there are other witnesses, we become anxious about being judged by the group.

Most common experiences of bystander behaviour are

trivial, or feel that way. You may hear a young employee being mocked by her peers for her dress sense. You don't intervene because the gossip doesn't matter to you. But harm is being done because being mocked at work is professionally damaging. So we may think of intervening, but most of us talk ourselves out it. We are all bystanders to something: homelessness, poverty, harassment, cruelty, sadness. Our most frequent exposure to bystander apathy occurs at work, where we see (or think we see) colleagues indulging in abusive, unsafe or illegal activity. We don't want to be the ones to complain, we don't want to seem superior and, anyway, we might be wrong. Where this concerns clothing, it might not matter much. But where it involves vulnerable people, it can be highly dangerous. This emerges powerfully in a study of nurses who regularly observed a colleague, Annie, cruelly abusing patients.

'She had a really negative effect on patients, especially the elderly ones or those who were long-stay,' one of the nurses, Sean, recalled. 'Making a big deal about getting them a bedpan or helping them to the bathroom during the night meant a lot of them would stop taking anything to drink from late afternoon to ensure they didn't need the bathroom during the night . . . and yet dehydration is a big problem with elderly patients. And we had a number of patients who suffered a long, painful night because she had been really abrupt with them when they'd first asked for something for the pain, and they were too scared to ask again.'[7]

Annie was the talk of the hospital; everyone – even those on other wards – knew she was a terrible nurse. But no one did anything. Some said she was intimidating: 'When drunks were admitted to the ward, she never had any trouble from them. If even a big, drunk, aggressive guy gets the vibe that he should behave himself or else, you can imagine how easily the rest of us were intimidated by her.' They were afraid that if they did say anything, and nothing happened, working with her would only get worse. Others blamed themselves, hoping they could figure out how better to work with Annie.

'At first, I thought of this as my problem,' Sean admitted. 'I was pretty new and I'm not the most assertive of people.'

Some nurses made excuses for her, explaining what a hard life she had had, while others tried to focus on her redeeming qualities: she was good in a crisis. All the nurses tried to avoid working with her and they all talked about her. Like all workplace gossip, the fact that everyone knows what is going on turns out to be part of the problem. Talking about the problem feels like action – but it isn't.

'Knowing that colleagues were concerned and keeping an eye on her made me feel a bit better about it for quite a while,' recalled another nurse, Mandy. 'It was only gradually that it dawned on me that nothing had actually changed: she was no better; in fact, she was probably getting worse.'

Responsibility for Annie was being diffused: since everyone knew about it, in theory everyone was responsible for it – which means that they all wanted someone else to act. But by remaining passive, the nurses *reduced* the likelihood that anybody would bring about a positive resolution.

Diffusion of responsibility explains much behaviour that otherwise appears inexplicable. If everyone knows, then someone, surely, will do something. Who is that someone? Someone else, not me. Tulip Siddiq is now a Labour MP but when she began work in Westminster as a parliamentary aide, one of the first things she learned was that sexual harassment was rampant. Everyone warned her about it – but nobody did anything to curtail it.

'Right after I started, people said, "Don't go in a lift with him." "If you are working late, avoid this guy." "This guy once slapped me on the bum." "This guy at a conference invited me back to his hotel,"' she said. 'It was the culture. It was very much accepted and you were just warned. You knew which male MPs to avoid, which sounds terrible, but everyone knew.'[8]

It isn't just women who are at risk when working in Westminster. One sixth-former, Louis, described to the *Financial Times* his work experience with a Conservative MP. 'Even as a seventeen-year-old, it was blindingly obvious how this man used his power, influence, the prestige of Parliament and the clear power imbalance in a deeply inappropriate way.' The MP he worked for was well known for 'alcohol problems, habitual groping and inappropriate behaviour towards younger men' yet other employees – men and women – covered up for him. 'They saw covering for and essentially ignoring his behaviour as part and parcel of their job. In retrospect, silence is complicity.'[9]

In November 2017, the Members and Peers Association, MAPSA, found that 53 per cent of their members had 'experienced, witnessed or heard of bullying/harassment during their time of employment' but only 21 per cent had reported anything. Of those who did, 84 per cent reported that their complaint was never resolved. All of those hearing, knowing of the complaints were bystanders. They may have written the Equality Act which outlaws such behaviour; they just weren't going to live by it.

Whose job was it? 'Crazy, crazy Westminster' was how the practice was shrugged off. MPs act, essentially, as independent employers of their staff. They have power, autonomy, influence – not just in Parliament but across their party. So nobody thinks it their job to protect party workers from rape, harassment, bullying. At the start of 2018, after a rash of complaints and horror stories, an official HR service for MPs' staff was set up on an interim basis – but it wasn't established to deal with complaints, only to proffer advice. A cross-party group of MPs and staff intend that the parliamentary commissioner for standards should be given new powers to suspend MPs found to have harassed staff but, as of summer 2018, no date is in place to vote on the initiative. Nor is there any provision for whistleblowers or witnesses who see something untoward.

What is so remarkable here is that these complex manoeuvres are byzantine responses to something that should be so straightforward; the enforcement of laws in Parliament passed by Parliament in 2010. Everyone pays lip service to the law while colluding in lawmakers' own non-observance. Numerous accounts of assault and rape, a private WhatsApp group and a 'spreadsheet of shame' naming MPs accused of harassment testify to the pervasiveness of sexual aggression that has characterised the British Parliament for as long as anyone can remember. More remarkable still is the number of female MPs and peers who know what goes on because they have experienced harassment themselves – but still do nothing. As one Labour baroness commented, 'We have allowed this to happen. We are perpetrators of this.'

Knowledge confers responsibility but when everyone knows, who is responsible? It's the easiest thing in the world to assume that it is someone else: someone smarter, more powerful, more senior, more articulate, bolder, older: anyone as long as it isn't me. And when, as in Parliament, there is nobody to go to – no HR department, no ombudsman – sheer ambiguity leaches accountability out of the system. Where everyone could be responsible, nobody is.

Excuses proliferate. I've heard one female MP argue that the House of Commons is an ancient institution and that it will take time for its traditions (those of harassment and assault) to change. History offers no such alibi for Silicon

Valley; it is supposed to be our future. At Tesla, women described the ethics hotline – ostensibly a safe place to report harassment – which appeared to neither be staffed nor respond to reports. At Uber, when engineer Susan Fowler complained of harassment, she was simply told to find a job in a different group – or put up with the offence. Even HR leaders didn't think it was their job to intervene. When her blogpost about her experience there went viral – with its deceptively quiet title 'Reflecting on One Very, Very Strange Year at Uber' – this was Melinda Gates' response:

'Obviously I'm outraged, but what I'm not is shocked. The only people who didn't know what was happening in Silicon Valley were the ones trying very hard not to see what was right in front of them. I don't think there's a woman who has worked in tech who hasn't experienced some form of bias or sexual harassment somewhere along the way – myself included.'[10]

At the beginning of 2018, as the dust seemed to settle after the frenzy of the #MeToo movement, I asked many male executives how it had impacted their organisations. Not one of them could tell me. Did they acknowledge that, statistically, unless they worked alone, it was implausible that they worked in companies where sexual harassment was absent? Reluctantly they recognised that their organisations could not safely claim to be immune. Everybody was horrified by what #MeToo had revealed – but just as talk can feel like action, sympathetic support had become a surrogate for change. Nobody could describe what, if anything, had improved. They assumed, hoped, imagined but did not know what had happened in the places where they worked. Had they asked? Well, presumably somebody, somewhere would do that. But not them. They themselves had done nothing.

It's become clear that such harassment isn't confined to

any specific industry or kind of organisation: for-profits, not-for-profits, NGOs, seekers after profit, seekers after truth, all have fielded armies of bystanders. And they aren't all faceless bureaucrats. One medical consultant described her experience of sexual harassment by an NHS colleague as her husband, also a physician, sat listening, both merely hopeful of change.

At a pinch, you might explain this behaviour by the unease that all sexual issues provoke. Sexual harassment is always painful: to experience, to talk about, to hear about. But the same bystander blindness pertains to practical business issues that lack all such emotive power.

'The safety procedures we had in the plant would let a grossly unsafe vehicle out of the plant and into the hands of the public,' Bill McAleer told me. He was a General Motors lifer, proud of his company and the wonderful career that it had provided him. But when aggressive cost-cutting became the norm, he grew increasingly concerned about the quality of GM's products.

'I'm talking about gas leaks, suspension failure, brake failures, steering wheels coming off: everything that can happen to a car. That called into question the entire manufacturing procedure at General Motors that had been cut viciously for over five or six years.'[11]

McAleer became increasingly alarmed by what he saw and wrote to the board with his concerns. He never got a reply. Over time, the company had developed a culture in which bystander behaviour was the norm. GM's CEO, Mary Barra, described what she called 'the GM nod', which was 'when everyone nods in agreement to a proposed plan of action but then leaves the room with no intention to follow through ... The nod is an empty gesture.'[12] As prevalent was what came to be called 'the GM salute: a crossing of the arms and pointing outwards towards others, indicating that the responsibility belongs to someone else, not me . . . No single person bore responsibility or was individually accountable.'

The GM nods and salutes ensured that, when problems were raised in the relevant committees, nothing would be done about them. Employees frequently omitted to take notes at critical safety meetings because they believed that GM's lawyers would not want any documentation about problems. But they wouldn't be called problems, because employees had been urged to 'write smart: don't use judgemental adjectives and speculation'. Executives were given a number of words to avoid, with suggested replacements. 'Problem = issue. Condition = matter. Defect = does not perform to design.' And they were told, in what the memo's author described as an attempt at humour, 'not to use phrases such as "Kevorkianesque", "tomb-like", "maniacal" or "rolling sarcophagus".'

But the ignition switch problems *were* problems. Fatal problems. Over 30 million cars eventually had to be recalled, but by then, by GM's estimate, 124 people had been killed by cars with serious and very real defects. Artificial language and gestures could blind the company to danger for only so long before their theatre was revealed for the make-believe it really was.

In 1997, Enron's mining and metals team had staged a holiday skit of *The Wizard of Oz*. Sherron Watkins played the Wicked Witch and the Wizard was played by Jere Overdyke in a scarlet satin pimp suit, pretending to be CFO Andy Fastow.[13] Everyone could read the subtext: just as the wizard is a fraud, so the company's financial wizardry was nothing more than smoke and mirrors. The audience laughed knowingly – every one of them a bystander. They may have felt themselves merely passive witnesses to a crime too big for them to stop – but the reality was that, with every crooked contract, Enron employees validated and perpetuated their crooked corporation. The crucial point about bystanders is that they have potential influence, and their choice not to use it means that they morph into perpetrators. A neutral stance isn't possible. The collapse of the sixth largest corporation in America wasn't achieved by a few bad guys but by thousands of bystanders.

That everyone was well paid, that they all liked each other and had so much in common, that many were exhausted by long hours and global travel, all helped to secure their collusion. But what moral clarity they might have had was also severely confused by the intense ambiguity of their environment. Orientation videos and TV ads for Enron specifically celebrated the 'defiant and the visionary'. CEO Skilling and Chairman Lay deliberately set out to build a vast company that operated with the freedom and latitude of entrepreneurial start-ups. They actively poured scorn on rules and regulations and encouraged competitive risk-taking, to 'move fast and break things'. At the same time, they were spending a fortune lobbying Washington to get any inconvenient regulation abolished. Today, it is impossible to hear and read about Enron's culture without thinking of Uber, Facebook and much of the rest of Silicon Valley.

Bystander behaviour need not always involve a crime. Indeed, in business it's often more obvious in the failure to adapt and innovate in response to new competitors or technologies. Classically, this is taught as the blindness of buggy-whip manufacturers to the rise of the automobile, or the myopia of American car manufacturers to the emerging excellence of Toyota and Nissan. The cases are legion but teaching the stories of these industrial train crashes never seems to reduce their number.

In 1999, the advent of the internet and the rise of digital

music had all of the record labels dazed and confused. Why were kids stealing their music? How could they be stopped? Although the music business was the closest thing to organised crime I'd ever witnessed, you could feel their pain. Nobody wanted to pay for music any more – anything you wanted could be found for free online somewhere. Of course, the record companies didn't do nothing. They dabbled in a few internet initiatives but were too venal to make good partners for anyone. They invested heavily in lobbying, hoping that they could stop the future happening. But whatever they tried to do, it was always too late.

Even if you weren't in the music business, this was easy to see. And it didn't take a gigantic leap of the imagination to see that what was happening in music was just a glimpse of the future for the movie industry. But it hadn't happened to them yet. Broadband penetration in the late 1990s was still under 50 per cent in the US. Even though, theoretically, you could download a movie, in practice nobody had the patience to do it down phone lines. But the music business presaged the looming disaster lying in wait for the film and network businesses.

That's what it looked like to me when I approached the studios with a proposal that was, in essence, a precursor of iTunes. Wouldn't it make sense to seize the initiative and learn about online distribution and consumption now, rather than wait to have it owned by someone else? At the time, I ran an online media business called iCAST. Well connected and extravagantly well funded, we had a lot of meetings in Hollywood; even if people didn't like or understand all of our ideas, they wanted our money. I remember in particular one meeting with an army of executives from Disney, many of whom are still in place to this day. We laid out the threat, as we saw it, and proposed a number of ways we could work together to seize the initiative. I didn't recognise it at the time, but in this meeting we witnessed the full panoply of bystander behaviour. They all saw what was happening in the music business. They understood that the same crisis awaited their business. But no one was willing to take the risk of intervening. The market, they said, was ambiguous; no one knew for certain how digital entertainment would develop. And whose responsibility was it to take the first step? Corporate politics meant that doing nothing would always be safer than recommending a bold course of action. Besides, the executives asked, if the strategic risk were real, wouldn't some of the other studios be doing something about it? If they weren't, why should Disney? Nobody in the room – though they were all proudly very senior – felt quite senior enough to take a decision. I remember sitting there thinking: in the 1980s, the TV companies were dubbed the 'three blind mice' because of their failure to take the advent of cable seriously. Now the film studios and networks were producing the remake.

You only have to mention the words 'wilful blindness' to hear the same story about any industry: how beverage companies ignored vitamin drinks, packaged-goods businesses didn't think about all the waste they produced or where it went; pharmaceutical companies studiously ignored off-label prescribing or opioid abuse, while gun manufacturers pretend a secondary market (selling to kids and criminals) has nothing to do with them. The knowledge is there, spoken or unspoken, but the so-called leadership does nothing. And this isn't just because these are older, more traditional industries. When, in 1995, Netscape – producer of the world's first mainstream internet browser – went public, Microsoft, the world's largest and most important software company, had nothing to compete with it. CEO Bill Gates felt compelled to write a long memo to the entire workforce, explaining that the internet would one day become a big deal. Of the tens of thousands of tech-savvy people working for Microsoft, did nobody notice the advent of the internet? Of course not; but most just behaved as though it wasn't there. Just as Google missed social networking and the biggest hotel companies in the world ignored Airbnb. Everybody saw these innovations – but nobody seemed to think it was their job to do anything about them.

These are classic business stories, because it is so human and so common for innovation to fail not through the lack of ideas but through lack of courage. Speaking up about challenging ideas, new business models and threatening technologies requires a level of bravery, reflection and articulacy most people feel they lack. Business leaders may claim that innovation is what they want but they're often paralysed into inaction by hoping and assuming that someone else, somewhere, will take the risk. Perhaps the crunch will come after they've retired. They may see a crisis looming but, like the experiment participants, would rather continue earnestly to complete their questionnaires than get up and acknowledge that the room is full of smoke and they can no longer see. Just like the witnesses to a crime, once someone does intervene, bystanders are left feeling anxious and uncomfortable, dimly aware that they missed their moment.

Nobody really knows if bystander behaviours are innate or learned, but they certainly start young. Most children witness bullying at school, by teachers or peers or both, and feel uncomfortably grateful not to be the victim. They may even learn, as my son did, the invaluable life lesson of how to stay off a bully's radar screen. But a salient characteristic of all bullying is that it craves an audience that most kids, acting as bystanders, provide.

In recent years, America's Department of Justice and the

police have become very interested in bullying, calling it the most under-reported safety problem on American school campuses.[14] Two-thirds of school-shooting perpetrators (for which the shooters were still alive to report) had previously been bullied; that they occur at all may, in some part, be attributed to the rage and frustration felt by the victim, for whom all bystanders are colluders. Similarly, studies of teen-age suicides often uncover a history of bullying, usually at school where it is visible and known about but never acted on.

Bystanders aren't neutral, but play a crucial role in bullying. Despite many campaigns, and the requirement that all UK schools have an anti-bullying policy, a national survey into bullying in 2016 showed that 50 per cent of schoolchildren said that they had been bullied, of whom 19 per cent had been bullied every day.[15] In many instances, student bystanders act as 'reinforcers', providing an encouraging audience, while others merely protect the bully by their failure to intervene. Both validate the bully by their very presence. Only 10–20 per cent of witnesses ever provide any real help. Perhaps most disappointing of all is the police observation that bullying is little reported because children follow adult examples.

'It is at school that children learn to be bystanders,' says Ervin Staub.

Staub has devoted his life to the study of good and evil. He is a Holocaust survivor and his work on genocide and mass violence has led him to work in Rwanda, Burundi and the Congo, as well as New Orleans and Los Angeles. His interest in bullying derives from his observation that all mass violence requires, and is inflamed by, bystanders. It's for that reason that he conducted a lengthy study of bullying in schools, which is where, he believes, the behaviour starts.

'Sadly, teachers don't intervene often. It turns out that some teachers think kids should take care of their own business.

So they don't do anything. But this is problematic because, as adults, we should provide kids with guidance. When we are passive, that sends a message that there's no need to act.'

Teachers and parents often won't intervene because they think the children need to learn to deal with the problem themselves. But the kids take the wrong message, learning instead to do what the adults do: nothing. And then that message gets amplified.

'I very much believe that bystanders give perpetrators and bullies a message that what they are doing is accepted. It tends to make them believe that they are supported.'

I've seen this for myself, at my children's school. When female students complained about harassment from nearby builders and decorators, it was their teacher who told them to do nothing, not to respond. The young women were left confused and angry: was this really their lesson for life?

In Massachusetts, Staub has begun to develop a curriculum to teach kids how better to respond when they see bullying. Its goal, he says, is to create a sympathetic but unaccepting attitude to bullies.

'We try to help the students understand the impact on kids who are bullied; kids don't process that necessarily. And we train them to engage. They don't have to do it alone, just turn to a friend and say: "Hey, we need to do something here, we have to stop this." We also try to get them to turn towards and support the victim because the passivity of bystanders makes victims feel there is no sympathy for them. You know, it often takes very, very little to stop a bully; people just don't realise the power that they have.'

Staub wants people to learn that they can intervene and that they can (and must) do so safely – because that is the only way effectively to prevent violence. Much of his teaching has spread; in London, many young people have learned that when they see an individual bullied and harassed by racists, their most effective response can be to engage the intended victim in conversation. The balance of power shifts once isolation stops.

'I have done work in Rwanda for many years now and one of the things we do there is try to help people understand the influences that lead to violence, what are the social conditions and psychological changes that people undergo. By providing this kind of information, I believe it is less likely that people close their eyes. They know what to look for. Things that normally go under your radar, when you know what you are looking for, those things are likely to connect, to click in. You think: I have to pay attention to this; this matters.

'One of my strong positions is that in the case of mass violence, we must act early. It is easier to act earlier – before ideologies and positions have developed and intensified. It's just the same in individual situations, even if you're not thinking about ideology, just thinking of a bully. Once they're a little way down the road, they're in a position where if they stop in response to someone, they lose face. So it's easier to intervene before they have too much to lose.

'The same is true in other group situations. We tend to think: this is a small thing, it's not big enough to worry about it. But by the time it is big enough to worry about, it is too late. Mass violence evolves progressively, always with small steps like excluding people, creating offices that serve discrimination. When no one does anything about those changes, that sends a sign: a sign that they can go further. I'll give you an example: Goebbels. After the Evian Conference in 1938, when the community of nations gathered in Switzerland to talk about taking in Jewish refugees from Germany, no one wanted to take them in. Goebbels wrote in his diary: "They would like to do what we are doing but they don't have the courage." He took the message that if, at the first step, no one would stop him, then he could keep going.'

Today, over forty years since he collaborated on the bystander experiments, John Darley works within the leafy enclave of Princeton. He's since moved on to do important work that explores how large organisations, and the people in them, become corrupt. In many ways, he has not strayed so far from his original, groundbreaking work. The greatest evil, he argues, always requires large numbers of participants who contribute by their failure to intervene.

Darley was born into psychology. As a teenager, he remembers his father helping Leon Festinger with logistics when he infiltrated the cognitive dissonance of Marian Keech and her flying saucer devotees. He is still curious about the social and organisational structures that reinforce the darker aspects of human behaviour, and particularly intrigued by the way that morality impinges on thinking only intermittently.

'The moral mind is not our default mind,' he says. 'In a very competitive environment, where you're under a lot of stress, a lot of cognitive load, you won't necessarily even see that there is a moral consideration at all. Most corruption, I think, starts with an intuitive act, not a deliberate one. Is this a System 1/System 2 error? I wonder.'

Darley is referring to the work of his colleague Daniel Kahneman, who argues that we operate two modes of thinking that he calls System 1 – which is intuitive, associative, very fast and born of habit – and System 2, which is more deliberative, analytical, slow and hard work. System 2 is what we use when solving difficult maths problems, but one of its other purposes is to monitor System 1 for errors.

'Many decisions made intuitively are reasonable,' Darley continues. 'But the problem is that sometimes they are not.

And the reasoning system monitoring – System 2 – is intermittent and lax. That's the problem: no alarm goes off. So you sell mortgages to people who can't afford them but you're in a competitive environment, under a lot of pressure to perform, so you don't monitor the morality of your actions. And, of course, as soon as that mortgage is securitised, you're not responsible for it so you don't care if the owner defaults. Responsibility has been diffused. From your perspective, System 1 worked just fine. I think if you look at how all of this plays out, you see that in conditions of high stress – from competitive environments, compensation structures or just company politics – the high stress tends to distance moral reflection.'

Darley has written extensively about the degree to which corruption on a wide scale, and evil on a wide scale, require large numbers of participants and bystanders. Corporate meltdowns, like Enron, Arthur Andersen, Lehman Brothers, Carillion, require the work of thousands of people, all failing to see the moral implications of their work. And you can't have historic catastrophes, like genocides, unless millions of individuals have taken, in effect, the same moral shortcut, driven by fear and uncertainty to focus on what's easy.

'Under conditions of high stress,' Darley continues to gnaw on the problem, 'you may still have inklings, suspicions. But you may inhabit an environment that valorises blindness, so you don't look. Who or what is it you are blind to? In the end, I think it's you. You become blind to yourself. To your better self.'

In 1938, the residents of Mauthausen were feeling optimistic. Their quarry was once again being used, as massive rebuilding in Germany and Austria brought new business to the town. In nearby Linz, great plans were progressing: a new bridge, town hall, art museum, party headquarters and two monuments, one commemorating the *Anschluss* and one commemorating the composer, Anton Bruckner. The economy was looking up too because the building of a new concentration camp created jobs and new business for suppliers and craftsmen.

When prisoners began to arrive in August, the SS tried hard to keep the population at a distance. But the camp was in full view, and ordinary life had to continue. Inevitably that meant that the brutal treatment of prisoners was witnessed by many bystanders. One was a farmer, Eleanore Gusenbauer, who didn't like what she saw.[16] So she wrote to complain:

> In the Concentration Camp Mauthausen at the work site in Vienna Ditch inmates are being shot repeatedly; those badly struck live for yet some time, and so remain lying next to the dead for hours and even half a day long. My property lies upon an elevation next to the Vienna Ditch and one is often an unwilling witness to such outrages.
>
> I am anyway sickly and such a sight makes such a demand on my nerves that in the long run I cannot bear this.
>
> I request that it be arranged that such inhuman deeds be discontinued, or else be done where one does not have to see it.

9. Out of Sight, Out of Mind

St James's Square is one of London's most elegant addresses. A short stroll from Buckingham Palace, it is lined with fine, tall Georgian buildings embracing a quiet, shady park square. Prohibitive parking charges prevent it from being too crammed with cars, while the refined inconvenience of its layout stops taxis using it as a rat run. Just off Pall Mall, it's in the heart of gentlemen's clubland. The fine sweeping staircases and high marble halls of the Naval and Military Club suppress the acoustic, while deep armchairs envelop hushed conversations. The Dukes of Norfolk and of Cleveland have kept family houses in the square since the eighteenth century, just two of the seven dukes and seven earls in residence. A few doors down is Chatham House, home of the Royal Institute of International Affairs, and scene of many a high-level confidential briefing on world politics. The 'Chatham House Rule' is a byword for frank but confidential conversations that don't leave the building. At one time, the elegant terraced house was home to the Earl of Lovelace and his wife, Ada, daughter of Lord Byron and an early computing pioneer. For the young couple, the square was the perfect London residence: exclusive, close to the heart of power. Next door is the London Library, the world's largest private lending library, founded by Thomas Carlyle. Thackeray was its first auditor, Dickens, George Eliot, Kipling, Shaw,

Henry James and T.S. Eliot among its members. Its Piranesi staircases bind together a maze of buildings packed with over a million volumes. St James's Square is picture-book London: intimidating as an oyster on the outside, seething and expensive within.

It's a long way from the sulphur-scented streets of Texas City. But St James's Square is also the headquarters of BP. It's here that Lord Browne of Madingley issued his order for cost-cutting and here too that the Group Chief Executive of Refining and Marketing, John Manzoni, ensured that it was implemented. If you look at an organisation chart for BP, you'll see Browne at the top and Manzoni immediately underneath. From there, it's about seven layers of management down to the guys operating the Texas City refinery. Seven layers, 4,800 miles, a six-hour time difference and a cultural chasm between the two locations.

Like many multinational corporations, it's impossible to put the whole org chart on a page because nothing is simple. The Business Unit Leader (BUL) is responsible for the refinery, but alongside him works an HSSE (health, safety, security, environment) manager and a process-safety manager; they're responsible for numerous sites, so, on any given day, they could be in Texas City – or somewhere else. Towards the bottom of the pyramid, it gets particularly hairy, with Tier 1, Tier 2, Tier 3 and Tier 4 managers, each with accountability of various kinds. It got complicated, not just because there were so many titles, acronyms and responsibilities, but because the people kept changing: five plant managers alone, between the years 2001 and 2003.[1]

Additional organisational change occurred in 2003 and 2004, when BP issued its 'Management Framework'. The BP South Houston complex was dissolved, the director became the refinery Business Unit Leader, and the process-safety department became part of the new HSSE department with a new manager.

The impact of these organisational changes on process safety was summed up by consultants studying the refinery just weeks before the explosion. 'We have never seen an organisation with such a history of leadership changes over such a short period of time. Even if the rapid turnover of senior leadership were the norm elsewhere in the BP system, it seems to have a particularly strong effect at Texas City. Between the BP/Amoco mergers, then the BP turnover coupled with the difficulties of governance of an integrated site . . . there has been little organisational stability.'[2]

Instability, of course, meant a lot of people moving up – and out. No aspiring manager wanted to stay in Texas City. Why, the site wasn't even in Houston, America's oil capital, but a half-hour congested drive on the Galveston freeway. High-flyers might do a stint but they'd soon be on their way – wasn't that the fun of working for a global business? The managers could move, and did – frequently. Everyone else, the guys 'closest to the valve', stayed put; where else were they going to go?

The men running the isomerisation unit reported to bosses on site who reported to a regional vice president, Pat Gower in Illinois, who reported to a group vice president, Mike Hoffman, who reported back to Manzoni in leafy St James's Square. And Manzoni's job wasn't simple either.

'I have ultimate accountability for several of the businesses inside BP,' Manzoni explained in his deposition, taken after the explosion at Texas City. 'It's the refining business. There is a retail business. There is a lubricants business. There is a marketing business. There is [a] chemicals business. If I were to give you a sense of that, these are very diverse businesses. In language and in companies that you may be more familiar with, it's a bit like putting Coors, Whirlpool, GAP, General Motors all together and running those businesses all together.'

With so much on his plate, detail was never going to be at the heart of his working day. Asked about the Texas City 'assets', Manzoni was unapologetic. 'It would be very unusual,' he said, 'for me to look at individual assets.' The year that Manzoni became Group CEO, Texas City had been described as 'in complete decline'. In 2003, an audit claimed that the 'condition of the infrastructure and assets is poor at the Texas City refinery'. In July 2004, Manzoni finally paid a visit to this, the largest refinery in his portfolio. But, according to his deposition, he still had no inkling that anything was wrong.

Q: And you are telling me no one told you about the problems that existed at the plant during that visit?

A: Actually, I left the plant with a sense that programs were being put in place and that – and there was something called the 1000-day program.

Q: Have you ever talked to any superintendents?

A: I have done it in the past. I can't remember whether I did on that visit in Texas City.

Q: Did you ever talk to a guy named Ray Hawkins?

A: No.

Q: If he – if you had spoken to him and he told you, 'Do you know what? My day-to-day activity is nothing more than crisis management, eventually something is going to fall off the plate,' what would that tell you?

A: There is a problem.

But of course, no one told Manzoni – they knew about him, but they rarely saw him. No one at the refinery had the kind of relationship that would make them seek him out to tell him the truth. Just that year, the site had already seen $30 million of damage due to a ruptured furnace pipe, and two months after Manzoni's visit, two workers died opening a pipe flange. But apparently Manzoni didn't notice this either.

> I am not sure I was made aware of compliance issues or gaps in operations. You know, we obviously focus on continuous improvement in all aspects of our business but I am not sure that I was specifically made aware of any gap. I believe nobody knew the level of risk at Texas City because, if they had known, I have absolutely no doubt we would have taken different and substantively different actions.

Manzoni's argument is intriguing because he's using a logical shortcut: assuming that there could not have been a problem because, if there had been, someone somewhere would have taken action. Since no one took action, the problem could not have existed. But the deposition reveals all the details Manzoni never saw: the impact of budget cuts, the absence of updated fire equipment, deferred maintenance, cut safety training. It rehearses the sequence of reports, audits, consultants' reports, surveys and warnings that all drew attention to safety issues at the plant. But all of it, it seems, passed Manzoni by.

> Q: Tell me why the plant wasn't shut down to fix these problems before this explosion occurred.
>
> A: I can't tell you actually because I wasn't aware of the problems before the explosion occurred.[3]

Throughout his deposition, what is so surprising is the frankness with which Manzoni demonstrates his own blindness. Not only did he not know what was going on, he doesn't appear to think that there was anything to know. He is so vague in his deposition that his critics might just conclude he's lying, but I don't think he is: the very fact that he is so brazenly unconcerned by his own ignorance makes him weirdly credible. Although he acknowledges the gravity of fifteen deaths, he seems at a loss to understand why he should be involved. He has no real understanding of Texas City, is unprepared but also strangely relaxed, annoyed only that everyone insists on digging up history when what he really wants is to fix the problem now he can finally see it.

What comes out loud and clear in his testimony is the unbridgeable gulf between Manzoni, the élite, educated British executive, and the men close to the valve whose issues can neither be heard nor seen. Watching Manzoni, it's tempting to ask the question: where was he? And the answer would be: a very, very long way away. Separated by miles, by background, by culture, by status. Even the deposition was conducted in Chicago, a long way from everything, and everyone, that mattered in the case.

In 2007, Lord Browne resigned from BP, for a host of reasons, not least of which was the damage done to BP's reputation and stock price by the Texas City accident. Between 2005 and 2008, as other oil companies saw their stock prices rise by 30–40 per cent, BP went through prolonged losses and only modest gains. This provoked a great deal of soul-searching within BP as it struggled, under new CEO Tony Hayward, to reorganise the business. The company chastised itself for 'poor listening' and for its celebration of complexity as a virtue (they considered it a competitive defence) rather than a problem. Attempts were made to reduce the organisational chaos of the company, by keeping executives in their jobs for longer, rewarding crisis prevention over heroic crisis management and by ostensibly simplifying corporate structures. It became famous for the fervour with which safety was addressed inside its offices, with much attention paid to posture, repetitive stress injuries and loose cables; executives, at least, were safe.

By the end of 2009, the company leadership was feeling confident again, its share price rising and it was nearly ready to start talking publicly about how profoundly it had changed. But leaders were cautious. After all, it wasn't as though Texas City was over. At the end of the many lawsuits that had followed that explosion, BP had reached a plea bargain with the US Justice Department, in which the corporation paid a $50 million fine to avoid criminal charges for violations of the Clean Air Act related to the fatal explosions. But that deal was contingent on BP fulfilling its settlement agreement with the Occupational Safety and Health Administration (OSHA), something it hadn't done. Instead, in every year that followed the refinery explosion, another worker died on the job at Texas City and, by October 2009, the corporation still faced 439 outstanding safety violations at Texas City alone. Less than six months later, the Deepwater Horizon oil rig exploded and then sank, leaving the largest offshore oil spill in US history. When, after weeks of trying and failing to contain the disaster, CEO Hayward complained that he wanted his life back, the distance between St James's Square and the Gulf of Mexico yawned wider than ever.

One of the arguments put forward to support globalisation is that, because we have the technology to connect everyone, business can and must expand across the globe. We don't need to be in the same room together any more. Between the internet, video conferencing, email, mobile phones and social networks, distance doesn't matter. What's so painfully obvious in BP's case is that none of this technology bridges the gulf. Distance does matter. Manzoni couldn't see the 80,000 people who worked for him; he had no relationship with most of them. He didn't ever see their working conditions and, perhaps worst of all, he didn't see that *not* seeing might pose a problem. When, in the midst of the Deepwater Horizon crisis, Tony Hayward said he wanted his life back, he seemed utterly impervious to the oil-rig workers who would never get their lives back or the fisheries workers who had lost their livelihoods for ever. As for pensioners whose savings might have been invested in the company – well they were completely invisible.

Technology can maintain relationships but it won't build them. Conference calls, with teams of executives huddled around speakerphones, fail to convey personality, mood and nuance. You may start to develop a rapport with the person who speaks most – or take an instant dislike to them. But you'll never know why. Nor will you perceive the silent critic scowling a thousand miles away. Video conferencing distracts all its participants, who spend too much time worrying about their hair and whether they're looking fat, uncomfortable at seeing themselves on screen. The nervous small talk about the weather – it's snowing there? It's hot and sunny here – anxiously reflects the vast differences that the technology attempts to mask.

Physical distance isn't easily bridged, no matter how refined the technology. Instead, we delude ourselves that, because so many words are exchanged – email, notes and reports – somehow a great deal of communication must have taken place. But that requires, in the first instance, that the words be read, that they are understood and that the recipient knows enough to read with discernment and empathy. What's tragically obvious in Manzoni's deposition is that he has no idea who is working for him or what they are worried about. It's extremely hard to communicate well with people you don't really know, whose concerns you cannot see.

Communication technologies have developed exponentially since Milgram did his obedience experiments, but there's one version of those experiments that has become more relevant than ever. In the original experiment, the victim could not be seen or heard and 65 per cent of obedient subjects delivered shocks to the maximum limit. In that version, one of the subjects commented, 'It's funny how you really begin to forget that there's a guy out there. For a long time, I just concentrated on pressing the switches and reading the words.'[4] But in a second version, the victim was in the same room as the subject, sitting just a few feet away. That proximity reduced the number of fully compliant subjects to 40 per cent. And when the subjects were made to touch their victims' hands, placing them on a shock plate, human contact meant that only 30 per cent finished the course. With the victim sitting in the same room, establishing eye contact and eventually physical contact, everything changes. It is so much easier to be blind to the consequences of your actions when you do not have to see them play out.

Similarly, John Darley conducted a variation on his bystander-effect experiments, when he placed some pairs of participants in a room face to face, and others sitting back to back. After four minutes, they heard the sounds of an accident: a workman apparently fell to the floor, groaned and exclaimed, 'Oh my leg!' Eighty per cent of those working face to face responded to the accident; only 20 per cent of those sitting back to back did so. Relationships – real, face-to-face relationships – change our behaviour.[5]

Physical distance changes how we think and feel about each

other; the existential distance implicit in hierarchies works the same way. It's harder to care about, or even consider as human, the individual who resides a long way up, or down, the org chart. Placing people within a hierarchy changes how others see them; it may even change how they come to regard themselves. I've known some companies where individuals would introduce themselves by name, followed by their position in the pecking order: 'I'm James; I'm a Band 6' or 'I'm Sarah, I'm a senior vice president' as though their status defined them as much as their names.

What hierarchy does to identity, bureaucracy does to work: turn it into an objective process of standardised transactions whose measurements and data require as little humanity as possible. The intent is to facilitate the smooth running of highly complicated organisations; it may also be to try to ensure some level of objectivity and fairness across people and tasks along long chains of commands. But the outcome can be pernicious: compelling attention to status and targets, independent of social meaning. Much management derives its mental model from manufacturing, with each action defined and measurable. But the risk of managing people like machines along an assembly line is that they come to act like machines too.

In September 2007, Bella Bailey was admitted into hospital suffering from a hiatus hernia and breathing difficulties. She left the ward for an endoscopy and, when the procedure was concluded, a porter brought her back and left her sitting in a chair. Her daughter's niece was visiting that day and she repeatedly asked that Bella's oxygen be reconnected. A health-care assistant kept reassuring her that a nurse would be along in a moment – but the nurse never came. Eventually Bella was transferred back into bed but not before being dropped. When her daughter Julie came to the hospital, she was so aghast at what she saw that she determined never to leave her mother alone in the hospital; she and family members stayed with Bella until she died there. What they saw during that time horrified them: patients screaming for nurses, neglected, bullied, abandoned in a hospital that was dirty, chaotic and under-staffed.[6]

Julie didn't abandon her mother even after death. She campaigned tirelessly to draw attention to the multiple failings of the Mid Staffordshire NHS Foundation Trust. Two inquiries, one in 2009 and another, led by Robert Francis in 2012/13, uncovered a bureaucracy with all the hallmarks of wilful blindness.

Medicine is notorious for its steep hierarchies, with godlike CEOs and consultants stretching all the way down to outsourced cleaners on zero-hours contracts. But this hierarchy was woven into a bureaucratic tangle of authorities: not just the Department of Health in Whitehall, but Strategic Health Authorities (SHAs) and Regional Health Authorities, the Commission for Health Improvement (CHI) the Care Quality Commission (CQC), the PCTs, GPs and MPs, along with many Royal Colleges. In theory, the key to managing such complexity lies in data. But Mid Staffordshire was drowning in data – to the point where much management debate seems to have been about numbers, not patient outcomes. When the hospital lost its three stars (supposed to indicate quality of care) and fell to zero, that failure was attributed not to poor care but to poor record-keeping. So egregious was the demand for reporting that it was as though generating data was the central mission of the hospital. The Francis Report called this 'a culture focused on doing the system's business – not that of the patients'.[7] When the Healthcare Commission reported that the hospital didn't fulfil its requirements in children's services, the hospital explained that insufficient data had been provided – and undertook to improve its data collection. Above all, hospital leadership focused on its overriding goal: to achieve trust status, which would give management more autonomy and be a marker of success and status within the NHS. But whether a hospital was granted trust status depended primarily on its finances and governance; patient care didn't really come into it. Overwhelmed by a blizzard of data, some meaningful and some not, the board kept its eyes on the goal.

'While it is clear,' the Francis Report concluded, 'that in spite of the warning signs, the wider system did not react to the constant flow of information signalling cause for concern, those with the most clear and close responsibility for ensuring that a safe and good standard of care was provided to patients in Stafford, namely the Board and other leaders within the Trust, failed to appreciate the enormity of what was happening, reacted too slowly, if at all, to some matters of concern of which they were aware and downplayed the significance of others. The Trust's culture was one of self promotion rather than critical analysis and openness. This can be seen from the way the Trust approached its FT (Foundation Trust) application, its approach to high Hospital Standardised Mortality Ratios (HSMRs) and its inaccurate self declaration of its own performance. It took false assurance from good news, and yet tolerated or sought to explain away bad news.'[8]

Consultants, said Francis, manifested 'professional disengagement' and the management had no 'culture of listening' to patients. 'The Trust was operating in an environment in which its leadership was expected to focus on financial issues, and there is little doubt that this is what it did. Sadly, it paid insufficient attention to the risks in relation to the quality of service delivery this entailed.' Meanwhile, the alphabet soup of overseers and regulators assumed that what they didn't know was known by others – so they didn't bother to communicate with each other. The consequence, said Francis, was that no effective consideration was given to the effects of cost savings and staff cuts on patient safety and quality.

Meanwhile, far away in Whitehall, generic national standards were being formulated, handed down from on high to consultants and managers who might or might not pay attention. The consequence: 'there was often a disconnect between the policy decisions being made and their practical implementation'.[9]

It is estimated that between 400 and 1,200 patients died from the substandard care they received at Mid Staffordshire hospital. It is entirely possible that everyone working there imagined themselves to be doing a good job: putting in long hours, trying to hit targets and stay on budget, blind to the full human impact of their actions. When you slice and dice work into discrete, defined units, or diffuse it across multiple organisations that don't talk to each other, you don't need incompetent or venal people to produce a bad outcome; conditions are already in place for a moral disaster.

'No one knows the true scale of child sexual exploitation (CSE) in Rotherham over the years. Our conservative estimate is that approximately 1,400 children were sexually exploited over the full Inquiry period, from 1997 to 2013. They were raped by multiple perpetrators, trafficked to other towns and cities, in the north of England, abducted, beaten and intimidated. There were examples of children who had been doused in petrol and threatened with being set alight, threatened with guns, made to witness brutally violent rapes and threatened they would be next if they told anyone. Girls as young as 11 were raped by large numbers of perpetrators.'[10]

Alexis Jay's introduction to her inquiry into child sexual

exploitation in Rotherham is designed to shock. She had seen how far a vast, attenuated network of civil servants, doctors, teachers, social workers, taxi companies, council members and police had become blind to the human horror of what was happening in their town; she didn't want her readers to follow in those footsteps. What she had uncovered persuaded her that the fact there were so many people involved ensured that responsibility had become diffuse: 'an issue,' as Jay put it, 'that belongs to everybody but effectively belongs to nobody'.

The scandal of Rotherham derived and was supported by the baroque interplay of hierarchical and bureaucratic authorities, each determined to defend and protect its own. Children were marginalised and forgotten. Targets drove behaviour, as, of course, they were intended to do. They kept everyone tightly focused on their immediate job, their individual tasks. Which allowed everyone to lose sight of the meaning of what played out right in front of them. By the early 2000s, school heads were reporting that girls were being taken away from school gates at lunchtime to give oral sex to men in the lunch break – but when the Director of Education raised concerns with the police, she was shown a map.

'A map of the North of England was overlaid with various crime networks including "Drugs", "Guns" and "Murder". She was told that the Police was only interested in putting resources into catching "the ring leaders" who perpetrated these crimes. She was told that if they were caught, her local problems would cease.'[11]

Taxi drivers were a key part of the system that allowed child sexual exploitation to flourish. Jay's investigation encountered reports of girls being raped, beaten and forced to perform sexual acts, all in taxis where they were serially abused or trafficked to other towns. Licensing of taxi drivers is the responsibility of the local authority – and yet it was the council itself that regularly contracted these taxi drivers to transport some of the region's most vulnerable children. Crucial connections between the council, the police and the licensing authorities appear to have been non-existent, with each doing what each, individually, considered to be their job.[12]

At a time of austerity, when each authority felt under severe threat, the interaction of so many different groups provoked turf warfare; everyone fought to protect their jobs or department. The police didn't want to spend their resources on problems that weren't among their own targets; they'd gain nothing from it. Those operating independently of managerialism could see what was going on – they just couldn't get any attention from those immersed in task lists. An innovative but non-statutory youth project called Risky Business operated at street level and, according to Alex Jay, 'they were constantly at odds both with the police and with social services in attempting to get something done. They themselves hadn't any statutory powers to act but were the people face to face with the children in danger; everyone else was quite a long way away.' Yet Risky Business, the least powerful organisation with the closest insight, was resented.

'There was a great deal of tension between that part of the service and the children's social care side,' Alexis Jay told me. 'It appeared that when they achieved some success, there was a degree of jealousy, a sense that they were treading on the turf of other professionals where they had no right to do so. The social services seemed to think that they had ownership of the whole of child protection and these were amateurs coming in with their own concerns about child protection, which the children's social care side seemed to view as very much exaggerated.'[13]

Measurement by target militated against truth-telling;

instead, every statutory group had a vested interest in making the problem disappear. So when, in 2005, the police carried out an audit, they proposed that the large number of girls be removed from monitoring. Risky Business challenged the recommendation but children's social care supported the police and references to all the girls simply vanished.

Reluctant to accept the level at which children were being sexually exploited, the children's social care managers found ways to reduce evidence – in one case, insisting that nothing could be reported if it had not been witnessed first hand. Such an ad hoc rule made it virtually impossible to present any evidence at all.

Not surprisingly, it was hard to recruit qualified staff to work in this environment; at one point the job vacancy rate was as high as 43 per cent. From 2005 to 2008, children's services were in the midst of being reorganised into seven localities with two managers each. It was a huge distraction, with some managers lacking experience in social work or child protection. More people were at least now working in the same space – but with no agreed line-management arrangements.[14] In the years 2009 to 2014, five different people held the position of director of safeguarding and the appointee in 2010 had seven managers in her first year.[15]

But bureaucracy cranked on. Throughout the period, inspections, monitoring visits and reviews continued apace: fully sixteen reports were issued in fifteen years. These reports and audits all required vast amounts of work and meetings, with overstretched employees racing around to complete the latest paperwork. Everyone was very busy.

'From a very early stage,' Jay told me, 'the board that preceded the Safeguarding Children Boards was producing vast numbers of plans and protocols, many of which seemed quite decent. But nobody checked whether they were being implemented or if they were any good!'

Most reports are full of commendation; work seems 'promising' and 'moving in the right direction'. Meetings multiply, process abounds, the paperwork is getting better, targets are being hit – and everyone is finding ways *not* to include the scale or scope of the living, breathing, abused problem. As striking as the number of reports, however, is the proliferation of jargon, of bureaucratese that masks the human nature of the problem everyone fails to deal with. None of the reports writes about a child, the experience of a child being serially abused. Instead, there are references to case numbers, to risk scores. The most human the language ever becomes is found in references to 'Child S', who was murdered.

'I have a strong personal commitment to describing the absolute horror of the experiences these children had – and not protecting anybody from it,' Jay insisted to me. She knows all the arguments that such language is designed to avoid identifying or labelling a child, but believes that its effect is to hide the true harm being done to the most vulnerable. 'When I asked children in these circumstances, they said to me, "We want people to know what happened, how terrible it was, and we need to be believed!" And you will not get that if it all comes wrapped up in professional jargon.'

The complex system that evolved to tackle the exploitation of children in Rotherham was riddled with bureaucracy, hierarchy, turf warfare, ideology, process and measurement. The more ornate the system became, the harder it was to see through all the administration into the heart of obscenity. Putting a letter and a number against an individual child – the initial signifying a name, the number representing how greatly they were at risk of being abused – turned the work of many well-intentioned individuals into a machine for processing nameless victims. In that process, both the victims and those who imagined they were helping were themselves transformed into cogs, parts of a manufacturing process whose ultimate products were the reports that were opaque. The sheer distance, from one part of the system to another, from the powerless to the powerful, became too long and tangled to show anything meaningful or human. Rotherham is perhaps the apotheosis of managerialism: the belief that work is done best when sliced, diced and measured. Its advocates maintain that objectifying labour puts a healthy distance – or objectivity – between the worker and the work, making both more efficient. But that distance is exactly what blinds everyone to the consequences of their actions.

This is, of course, why some leaders genuinely prefer distance; they believe that they could not do their jobs if they were immersed in the messy, human detail of the mission. Hierarchy protects them; distance yields protective objectivity, ostensibly. Britain's General Haig, who presided over the slaughter of a whole generation of young men in the First World War, could not bear to visit a military hospital. One of his subordinates, on first visiting the battlefront, is reported to have burst into tears, crying, 'Good God, did we really send men to fight in that?[16] Haig preferred to watch the numbers. Albert Speer was always very careful not to visit the labour camps he oversaw – or, on the one occasion he visited Mauthausen, to stick firmly to the guided tour that shielded him from reality. Even Eichmann and Himmler became physically ill when confronted with the consequences of their decisions.[17] In Iraq, Brigadier General Janis Karpinski was responsible for sixteen prisons – 17,950 inmates – spread across a country slightly smaller than France. Although Abu Ghraib, with 6,000 prisoners, was the largest, she didn't spend a lot of time there. And the only interrogation she witnessed was one that she was invited to see. Like all the other senior officers, she never visited at night when the abuses occurred. The argument for distance is that eliminating proximity clarifies the mind and facilitates more objective decision-making. It can also blind you to details that you'd prefer not to see.

Structural blindness was built into the way that BP did business, not because its leaders wanted to be blind but because, to be competitive, Browne believed the business had to be big, it had to be a 'super major'. Built through aggressive mergers and acquisitions around the world, it was inevitably spread across continents, time zones and cultures. The company was well aware of the problem; it's why so many surveys and processes were put in place to attempt to hold everything together. But bureaucracy, however elaborate, didn't fix the problem. Manzoni and his boss, Lord Browne, were both blind to the routine risks being run at Texas City in part because they weren't familiar enough with the site or the people to care about them. They were abstractions, numbers, profit generators and cost centres, leaving decision-makers not objective but blind. But it wasn't just geography that left them so dangerously out of the loop. It was also power.

Power imposes distance between those who have it and those who do not. The powerful are quite often unaware of this, the best struggle against it, but the distance is always there. Power circumscribes whether you're spending most of your time in elegant London clubs or at the Grand Prize Barbeque on Texas City's Palmer Highway. Power determines whether you are talking to chief executives or superintendents. Power decides whether you fly in the splendid isolation of a private jet or first class instead of in economy, next to the young mother who needs help with her restless child. Power lets you, like the Google founders, arrive at meetings via paraglider, not stuck in San Francisco traffic. The legendary commute of Lehman Brothers' CEO, Richard Fuld – limo to heliport, helicopter into Manhattan, limo to office and private lift into the office – kept him fully ensconced in a physical bubble weak signals could not penetrate. But while such luxuries may seem attractive, they come at a cost: isolation. The bubble of power seals off bad news, inconvenient details, hostile opinions and messy realities, leaving you free to inhale the rarefied air of pure abstraction. It is another risky by-product of inequality that those at the top, with the most power, make decisions without contact with those at the bottom who will be most impacted by them. Like the cave dwellers of Plato's parable, the powerful see only shadows of reality flickering on their walls, grateful to be so comfortably protected from external realities. The rough gives way to the smooth in a frictionless ascent.

Moreover, recent research into power shows that the powerful appraise information differently. In one experiment, participants were subjected to personality appraisals that evaluated the need for dominance. Those who scored higher were put into a separate group from those who scored lower and both groups were then asked to evaluate students for internships. While the powerful did not completely ignore information that challenged stereotypes, they still gave it less attention. Dominant people, it appears, use snap judgements and conform to received wisdom more than do the less dominant. Those who need power, and those who have it, think differently and with greater confidence. The stereotypes they fall back on can be counteracted – but doing so requires a great deal of motivation and cognitive effort. Power does corrupt, and more insidiously than even the powerful appreciate.[18]

Frances Milliken, one of the academics responsible for work on organisational silence, did a marvellous study comparing how those in power communicate differently from those who lack power. She found that, like the rich, the powerful are different from other people. Confronted by risky situations, they are more likely to expect positive outcomes. They're so optimistic at least in part because they have – or think they have – the power needed to overcome most adversity. That psychological distance between themselves and others means that they don't think as concretely as other people – they lack the material – and so inevitably they have to think in far more abstract terms. But what is frightening about Milliken's study is that the combination of power, optimism and abstract thinking makes powerful people more certain. The more cut-off they are from others, the more confident they are that they are right.[19]

Just to add a little spice to what might otherwise have seemed a rather dry linguistic inventory, Milliken chose to focus it on the response of officials during Hurricane Katrina, which killed more than 1,200 people in 2005. Milliken and her team collected a vast array of public statements by officials during the disaster and analysed the language of each piece according to the amount of power held by its speaker. It must have been a lugubrious process but the conclusions feel real. Sure enough, she found that federal officials – those with the most power and who didn't live in New Orleans – were very much less troubled by events, more optimistic that the crisis would be effectively dealt with, and far less prone to doubt. Psychologically this becomes self-reinforcing: the less they knew, the less curious and concerned they became.

The poster child for this conclusion, of course, must be Michael Brown, the director of the Federal Emergency Management Agency (FEMA). Although Milliken is wonderfully discreet and doesn't shape her argument around his pronouncements, he was a walking demonstration of her contention. On the day that the hurricane first hit landfall in Louisiana, Brown seemed relaxed, reminding emergency-services personnel 'not to respond to hurricane impact areas unless dispatched by state, local authorities'.

Two days later, he received an email from a FEMA colleague: 'Hotels are kicking people out, thousands gathering in the streets with no food or water. Hundreds are still being rescued from homes. We are out of food and running out of water at the dome.'[20] But Brown, despite the detail he received, didn't seem worried as he responded: 'Thanks for update. Anything specific I need to do or tweak?'

Four days later, he told ABC's Ted Koppel that he had been unaware that 20–25,000 refugees were stranded at the city's convention centre without food or water.

> BROWN: We first learned of the convention center – we being the federal government – today.
>
> KOPPEL: Don't you guys watch television? Don't you guys listen to the radio? Our reporters have been reporting about it for more than just today.
>
> BROWN: We learned about it factually today that that was what existed. When we first learned about it, my first instinction [sic] instinct was: Get somebody in there, give me truth on the ground, let me know because if it is true, we've got to help those people.
>
> KOPPEL: But here we are, five days after the storm hit, and you are talking about what is going to happen in the next couple of days.
>
> BROWN: I just want to say to the American public that they do need to understand exactly how catastrophic this disaster is. And they do need to know that we are going to have every available

> resource to do everything that we can. We're going to take care of these victims. We are going to make it right. We are going to make certain that the devastation that has been reaped [sic] upon these people is taken care of and that we get their lives back in order.[21]

Brown's responses are so remote, so confident and so extraordinarily abstract. There are no individuals, no fear or hunger in his response. There are only abstract 'victims' whose lives someone somewhere is going to get back in order. Koppel's responses, while polite, finally exploded with disbelief – and real detail.

> KOPPEL: Mr Brown, some of these people are dead. They are beyond your help. Some of these people have died because they needed insulin and they couldn't get it . . . You say you were surprised so many people didn't make it out. It's no surprise to anyone that you had at least 100,000 people in the city of New Orleans who are dirt poor, who don't have cars, who don't have access to public transportation, who don't have any way of getting out of the city simply because somebody says, 'You know there's a force-five storm coming? You ought to get out.' If you didn't have the buses there to get them out, why should it be a surprise to you that they stayed?

It's hard, in reading these exchanges, not to be reminded of the bureaucratic conversations that took place in Rotherham or the cost discussions around Grenfell Tower: powerful people thinking only in abstract, not about people, their children and their lives, but only, with increased confidence, about numbers.

The distance imposed by geography and implicit in power is reinforced by the structures within which work gets done. It's been that way ever since 1776, the year Adam Smith published *The Wealth of Nations* and extolled the glories of the division of labour. While it might take one man a day to make a single pin (or ten pins if he were skilled), he explained, ten men could produce 48,000 by each taking on a separate part of the work. (Today, Smith's observation is commemorated on the twenty-pound note.) As most manufacture became a good deal more complex, and more lucrative, than pins, the idea became embedded in industry. Of the 30,000 components in a modern car, for example, each one may contain thirty sub-components that have passed through fifteen countries in the course of its production. A Land Rover Discovery will receive power steering and fuel injection from Germany, coolant hoses and exhaust manifolds from Hungary, front lighting from France and shock absorbers from Poland. For BMW to produce a Mini (which, despite its size, still contains 3,600 to 4,000 parts) requires that the cast of the crankshaft be made in France, shipped to BMW's plant in the Cotswolds where it is drilled and milled into shape, after which it is shipped to Munich to be inserted into the engine that is returned to England for placement in the car which may be returned to France to be sold. Such attenuated processes have multiple aims: to reduce costs, to use the most specialised labour, to provide employment and take advantage of currency hedging and tax breaks. Division of labour has become central to our concept of work: governments, for-profit, non-profit, service and commodity businesses all seek to use specialised talent to deliver faster, better, cheaper results. As Adam Smith argued, with greater specialisation comes greater efficiency and productivity.

But in an established corporation like BP, that meant that the cost-cutters didn't know much about safety. Why should they? It wasn't their department. They had – or claimed to have – very little insight into the consequences of mandated savings; that wasn't their job. Manzoni lacked refining experience and, according to his executive assistant, Lord Browne showed 'no passion, no curiosity, no interest' in safety.[22] In theory, there were plenty of other people to look after those details, but the company's internal inquiry shows a concatenation of poor communication between them all.

The division of labour isn't designed to keep corporations blind but that is often its effect. The people who manufacture cars aren't the people who repair them or service them. That means they don't see the problems inherent in their design unless a special effort is made to show it to them. Software engineers who write code aren't the same as the ones who fix bugs who also aren't the customer-service representatives you call when the program crashes your machine. Companies are now organised in ways that routinely facilitate departments becoming structurally blind to one another.

Not only are some companies blind to the dangers of their ornate systems; some even trumpet their complexity as a new-fangled form of both emancipation *and* efficiency. At Facebook, advertisers can place their own ads, which means that they feel completely in control of their highly customised campaigns (freedom!) and Facebook doesn't have to pay people to do the work that makes the company money (efficiency!). That also means that campaigns might be illegal, as some were found to be in 2016. Because advertisers can choose the audiences they wish to reach, it was possible for them to exclude African Americans, Asian Americans and Hispanics from housing ads. This can be illegal, as the 1968 Fair Housing Act prohibits house ads from discriminating on the basis of 'color, religion, sex, handicap, familial status, or national origin'. But the ads were approved in fifteen minutes.[23]

As so often seems the case, Facebook executives reacted as though startled and amazed to discover what goes on inside their company. First it defended its advertising options, then it changed them, insisting that if they learned of anything else discriminatory, of course they'd rush to act. What was extraordinary then, but has come to seem predictable now, is that the company felt so comfortable with its own blindness. Corporate policy seemed to be: we don't really know what goes on here but if any of it is bad, sure we'd like to know.[24]

Which was pretty much the company's response to the revelation that, during the 2016 US presidential campaign, thousands of dollars of advertising had been placed by Internet Research Agency, a Russian troll farm known to engage in propaganda.[25] Apparently nobody in the company had noticed – that's what happens when you automate advertising – but once again the company seemed grateful that somebody else had. Though the business made over $25 billion from advertising, they were blind to where that money came from.

From its earliest days, the internet pioneers were evangelical about giving away power. In contrast with hierarchical business where power rested with élites – newspaper editors controlled journalism, publishing houses selected authors, record labels chose musicians and film studios made movie stars – the internet promised to liberate buried, invisible talent. Theirs was an exhilarating vision and much of it, at least early on, represented a sincere passion for diversity, transparency and openness. But as the business of the web developed and it became clear that there were fortunes to be made there, scale became the goal: 'Go Big or Stay Home', as one corporate mantra put it. And what cheaper way to go big than to outsource all the work to the users? (Nobody ever seemed so keen on outsourcing profits.)

The wilful blindness implicit in outsourcing reached a new level when Facebook invited developers to build apps that exploited its user data. Psychologist Aleksandr Kogan's personality quiz app took advantage not only of the data about users who had installed it; Kogan also received the dataset of every friendship formed in 2011 in every country in the world at the national aggregate level.[26] What happened to the data? Facebook would apparently never have known had not reporters found out that it was passed to Cambridge Analytica. How did that firm use the Facebook data? Facebook was blind to that too. Had trusting users agreed to their personal information being used to target ads in the 2016 US presidential campaign? And where is the data now?

It may never now be possible to know whether, in fact, this diffusion of data made an impact on the US election results; all we can know is that either Facebook did know and didn't care (which the company is unlikely to admit) or simply had no idea what, in fact, was going on. The more the saga unfolded, the more questions emerged, the more blind the company appeared to be. This is ironic because its entire business model appears to depend on the wilful blindness of its users, as the company has steadily expanded the amount of data it sucks from them.[27] Perhaps executives were too busy moving fast and breaking things to notice who was breaking what. But Facebook's routine defence – we didn't know but we're fixing it now – continues to reveal that, however much it might (or might not) know about its consumers, it is wilfully blind to its own operations – and to the consequences of its own technology. You could argue that its business model is predicated on systemic blindness: it is cheaper to respond to what other people see than for the company to look. The claim that these companies are merely platforms conveniently obscures responsibility.

Structural blindness assumes a physical reality with the development of outsourcing. Corporations, eager to reduce fixed costs and overheads, suddenly realised that they didn't have to employ all the talent they needed. If they could buy it in, then they could eliminate swathes of management while retaining, or even increasing, negotiating power. The markets loved the idea because it looked as though huge areas of expense and exposure were eliminated from balance sheets permanently. Entrepreneurs, from Uber and Deliveroo drivers to the subcontractors for Carillion, leapt at the idea because it meant that, instead of working for dreary monolithic organisations, they could set up their own businesses and be masters of their own destiny in a competitive marketplace. At least that was the idea.

In reality, the disaggregation of work has made it harder than ever to connect all of the pieces; you need huge swathes of management to oversee outsourcing, competitive bidding, partnerships and contractors. What used to be departments are now outside firms but someone still needs to get them all to work well together. But, once you outsource or subcontract work, it loses its visibility while the company loses expertise. Nobody should be surprised by this; that lesson has been well understood for thirty years.

When he came to investigate the *Challenger* space shuttle disaster, this is exactly what the great physicist and iconoclast Richard Feynman discovered. As an outsider, he had little concern for the hierarchies within NASA; in telling the story, he revels in his contempt for rank and deference. Focused as a cat on a rat as he chases down every conceivable source of information, truthfulness and insight, he delights in crashing through barriers and filling in gaps. He eventually, and triumphantly, figures out that a major cause of the disaster was the O-rings, which, in the extremely low temperatures to which they were subjected, must have cracked. But the O-rings, of course, weren't made by NASA. They were made by Morton Thiokol, an aerospace company that used plastic specially made by the Parker Seal Company. NASA was based at the Kennedy Space Center in Georgia but also at the Marshall Space Flight Center in Huntsville, Alabama; Morton Thiokol was based in Brigham, Utah, and Parker Seal in Lexington, Kentucky.

When the Morton Thiokol team became concerned about the low temperatures forecast for launch, they did their best to relay their concerns. But the engineers couldn't raise a red flag until they got support from their management. As sub-contractors, they had little leverage; after all, NASA was their customer. Nevertheless, two meetings were called to address concerns. Given the geography, of course, these had to be conference calls and, given the number of people involved, not everyone could attend, or attend both calls. NASA was under political pressure to launch; Morton Thiokol was under commercial pressure and could never have had the power to stop the launch. In the inquiries which followed the disaster, the sheer difficulty in understanding what had happened aptly reflected the endemic nature of the problem: a director from Morton Thiokol had to turn up – uninvited – at one of Feynman's meetings in order to be able to share what he knew.[28]

It has been argued that the *Challenger* was a uniquely complex project that took place long ago before we had sophisticated tools for managing such elaborate endeavours. That may be true but it isn't reassuring. Outsourcing need not even be complex to fail.

In 2009, SIGG, the Swiss makers of trendy aluminium water bottles, discovered that outsourcing their manufacture didn't give them the control their high-end brand needed. SIGG's chic products had developed a substantial following from conscientious consumers worried about the bisphenol-A found in many hard plastics. BPA has been linked to diabetes, heart disease, premature puberty in girls and lower sperm counts in men. The claim that the SIGG bottles didn't pose this hazard was important to their consumers, who wanted a permanent water bottle to reduce waste (good for the environment) and one that was free of BPA (good for the drinker). But, in fact, SIGG did not manufacture the lining of their bottles; a third party did. And that third party did not tell SIGG what materials they were using.[29] When it transpired that there was, after all, some small amount of BPA in the liner, the company was publicly trashed by its customers and the CEO lost his job. The company had been manufacturing blind.

It's hard to imagine a product much simpler than the SIGG water bottle; its example should give any energetic outsourcer pause. On a grander scale falls the epic collapse of Carillion, the conglomerate that promised to relieve the UK government of the complexity and management of building and running schools, hospitals, motorways, railways and even some aspects of the British Museum. The government outsourced to Carillion and Carillion subcontracted out much of that work to yet others further down the chain. The orthodoxy that sees private firms as always more efficient and cheaper than the public sector meant that Carillion had to win contracts on razor-thin margins. Unforeseen problems – like the discovery of asbestos at the Royal Liverpool University Hospital – made projects financially even more risky. The aggregation of many such projects made the entire business unsustainable. But the attenuated chain of relationships meant that the government didn't see what it didn't wish to see, while senior management devolved projects and cost-cutting to subcontractors who were rarely shown the whole picture. The original idea was that risk was outsourced; the reality turned out to be that knowledge, expertise and insight were pushed down the line. Once you outsource critical functions, you may be blind to how the work gets done. The cynical will conclude that that is precisely what outsourcing is for.

It's sobering to recognise that outsourcing has become so embedded in Western economies, that there are no areas in which it is not considered. We outsource our wars now, through private security firms, and much of our policing: in the US and the UK, the number of private guards is now more than twice the number of public police officers.[30] Services, once deemed social, are now so elaborately distributed across contractors and subcontractors that it becomes difficult to measure or manage the consequences when a firm like Carillion fails.

Everyone who's ever worked in an organisation knows how intensely difficult it can be to prevent silos, to find people who are intellectually able and politically prepared to connect the dots. As Alexis Jay discovered, tracing the knotty skein of jealous relationships between agencies in Rotherham, it takes effort, commitment and mistakes to overcome the sheer difficulty people have working with each other, negotiating the complex interface between their personal ambitions and organisational goals. But the silos take on a substantial reality when we are talking about separate institutions – be they companies or organisations – with different mandates, goals, power bases and agendas. When John Snow, US Secretary of the Treasury between 2003 and 2006, testified before

Congress on the role of financial regulators in the 2008 financial crisis, he explained how part of the problem was that he couldn't even see the problem.

> Nowhere in our financial regulatory system is there anyone with full accountability and full 360-degree view on risk and leverage. I remember in 2005, sensing that there were developments in the debt markets, the sub-prime and the mortgage markets that needed to be better understood. I took what was deemed to be a fairly extraordinary step and called in all of the substantive regulators of the mortgage market. I asked them to give their considered views on a sub-prime crisis. But I wanted to get their view. But no one of them had that view. They had pieces of the puzzle. It's like the blind man and the elephant. They are all touching a piece of it, but they don't know what the big picture is.[31]

If he had difficulty peering through a structural morass of regulation, how much more difficult was the challenge of gaining a holistic view of the market itself? The division of labour, institutionalised into different organisations, had taken the once simplistic task of buying a home and blown it into so many different transactions that, apparently, no one could put the pieces together any more. That was the conclusion the London School of Economics drew when asked by the Queen why no one saw the banking crisis coming. 'The difficulty was seeing the risk to the system as a whole rather than to any specific financial instrument or loan. Risk calculations were most often confined to slices of financial activity, using some of the best mathematical minds in our country and abroad. But they frequently lost sight of the bigger picture.'[32]

At least Snow knew who to summon and government was

expected to exercise oversight. Today, in the United States, identifying who has authoritative insight into critical subjects is hard to do. In 1996, on the grounds that 'a gun is not a disease', Congress slashed the budget for the Centers for Disease Control by the exact amount used for gun-related public health research; at a stroke, the research stopped. In July 2015, the US House of Representatives rejected an amendment that might have allowed it to resume.[33] This makes it hard to find authoritative data with which to understand the rate and pace at which gun deaths increase or decrease. And gaining insight into patterns of any disease has become harder since, in 2017, the Trump administration prohibited the CDC from using particular words: vulnerable, diversity, entitlement, transgender, foetus, evidence-based and science-based. Whatever one's views on such subjects, stopping research and discussion is a certain recipe for blind government.

Such overt acts of prohibition seek to blind us to what needs to be known. But notwithstanding such bans, understanding the big picture, as Snow sought to do, has become more difficult. The combination of global economic activity with pervasive communication technologies has turned what was, in Adam Smith's day, a complicated system into a complex one. The differences are profound. Complex systems aren't like pin manufacture: predictable and repeatable. They may repeat themselves occasionally – but you won't know where or when until it happens. That means they still need to be but can't ever be wholly understood or explained by expertise. It also means that they aren't susceptible to efficiency; if you don't quite know how a system behaves, then taking away margin for error can be fatal. The shift from complicated to complex has been gradual and subtle and remains difficult for even the most well-intentioned to appreciate. But managing our new complexity as though it remained merely complicated is a form of wilful blindness that would rather sentimentalise the past than understand the present. Anachronistic management systems that trust to hierarchy, bureaucracy, efficiency, targets and incentives now reinforce the silos and turf wars that isolate information from relevance and people from people.

We don't see things that are too far away, that are too distant from our own experience, too separate from our own concerns, or simply too complex to assemble into a single diagram. But we also don't see things that are too far away in time. The past, and the lessons it could teach us, recedes from view unless we find ways to memorialise it and keep it present, within our lines of sight. After a raft of redundancies, most banks now contain few employees with any memory of what led to the crash of 2008. US banks lost 400,000 jobs between 2007 and 2012, leading one Morgan Stanley banker to fear the memory loss. 'Fifteen years from now, will management come to work every day with sufficient scarring or not?'[34]

In Libby, Montana, Gayla Benefield and Gary Svenson used to make wooden crosses every year, each one painted with the name of a victim of asbestosis. Some in the town complained; they didn't want their loved ones' names used in a campaign. So Gary built a pergola down by the river and intends to raise money by selling small medallions, each engraved with the name of one of those lost to the dust of the vermiculite plant. That way, he says, people can choose to have their kin memorialised or not. He wants the town to remember, and visitors to the town to learn, what happened there. But already another, bigger, pergola has been set up next to his, as though to make sure his doesn't get all the attention.

As for BP, Manzoni is now back in London, running the

British Civil Service. When he talks publicly about his time at Texas City, he tears up and recalls the lessons he says he's learned. But he hasn't gone back. One man left there still carries with him a searing memory of the explosion. Dave Senko supervised the contractors who were killed but he was at another site on the day of the accident. Today, his hands shake as he talks about the friends he lost. Many of them had wanted to quit the project, he says, because they didn't feel safe working at the site. Senko had persuaded them to stay. He misses these men and carries them on his conscience. BP, he told me, wouldn't allow a memorial to them on the site; they weren't BP employees, just subcontractors. So he waged a one-man campaign to get a memorial at the contracting firm's offices. They eventually gave in.

'What is on the memorial?' I asked him.

He was too upset to speak. I waited. Silence. Then he handed me his phone; on it was a picture of a small stone slab. All it says is: 'March 23, 2005'. No names. No description. After he'd pestered his company a little more, Dave was able to add a light and a small pear tree. He goes there some evenings to check it's still there and that the light still works. One time, the security guard came over and asked him to move. He was outraged and said they could call the police if they wanted to. He wasn't moving.

'Remembering is important,' he said. 'It matters. If you can't see these things, they'll just keep happening.'

Why do we build institutions and corporations so large and so complex that we can't see how they work? In part, it's because we can. Human hubris makes us believe that if we can imagine something, we can build it; and if we build it, we will understand it. We are delighted with our own ingenuity and intelligence; it gives us a sense of mastery and power which can be entirely illusory. Like Daedalus, we build labyrinths of such cunning complexity that we cannot find our own way out. We become blind to the blindness these complex structures necessarily confer. So we forget all about it.

10. DE-MORALISING WORK

Events and ideas enjoy a curious relationship. Sometimes they seem to develop in lockstep, like Rousseau and the coming of the French Revolution. At other times, ideas emerge as a critique of prevailing social moods, just as Romantic idealisation of sentiment grew out of the Industrial Revolution. That contentious relationship is analogous to what happened at the turn of the century when so much public energy suddenly centred on money. As the Western world experienced a financial bonanza, with global markets reaching new highs daily and consumers avid for each new avenue of expenditure, along came a bunch of psychologists and economists with a challenging message: money doesn't make people happy.

What? In the middle of a consumer explosion, when £5,000 handbags flew out of stores and people bought homes whose garages were larger than their former houses had been, how could it be that money didn't make us happy. But that's what positive psychologists like Martin Seligman and economists like Richard Layard have been saying. And to prove it, they showed that, despite increases in GDP, overall life satisfaction hasn't gone up. And the richest countries weren't the happiest.

As it's emerged, the data, and its corollaries, have caused a big stir, as they should have. After all, if GDP growth doesn't make people happy, why are all Western economies still pursuing it so ferociously? Is happiness itself a more meaningful goal? If it is, then how should it be measured – and, if money won't increase it, what will? As the questions have mounted, a lot of thinking has stalled. Hmmm. If money wasn't going to make people happier, how should a government, or political movement, measure success?

In companies, the money/happiness debate is a bit of a conundrum, too. Some CEOs thought they saw a light at the end of the tunnel: did this mean they didn't have to pay their employees so much? Not surprisingly, nobody was volunteering to take pay cuts on the grounds that they thought it would make them feel better. Could it mean that shareholders wouldn't be so insistent on growth or dividends? If there were any shareholders who thought they would be happier with less, they have been a silent minority.

The reason the argument stalls is simple. Just because money can't make people happy doesn't mean that we aren't motivated by it. We are. In a 1953 experiment, patients were asked to hang on horizontal bars for as long as they could; most could take it for about forty-five seconds. When subjected to the power of suggestion and even, in some cases, hypnosis, they could stretch to about seventy-five seconds. But when offered a five-dollar bill (which today would be worth about £20) the patients managed to hang from the bars for 110 seconds. Anything that allows you to increase your performance by 150 per cent is pretty motivating.[1]

Nor was that some weird anomaly of 1950s America. More recent studies have shown that the mere idea of money can make people persevere more and work longer.[2] Another study showed that money changes what we remember. In that experiment, volunteers were shown a selection of images, each accompanied by a price. Remembering one picture was worth five dollars; remembering another was worth merely ten cents. Testing their subjects the next day, they found that their participants were far more likely to remember the high-price scenes.[3] Much of this motivation may not even be conscious; humans tend to adapt the degree of effort they expend according to the magnitude of reward they expect.[4]

Serious students of human motivation like Daniel Pink argue that money may make us work harder but it doesn't make us work smarter. Citing experiments conducted by Dan Ariely, he argues that money inhibits creativity and problem-solving, the kind of higher-order thinking on which developed economies depend.[5] The problem is that knowing money doesn't make us smarter may not make us smart enough to eschew it.

We want money for a very good reason: it makes us feel better. A fascinating series of experiments by a team of Chinese and American researchers put volunteers through their paces in a *Cyberball* game in which they were slowly but surely socially excluded, with the result that they registered distress. But then, in their distressed condition, they were made to count money and their mood lifted. As a control, some were asked to count paper, just to ensure that it wasn't the repetitive task of counting that had the ameliorative effect. Paper, it turned out, wasn't an analgesic, but money was. Simply counting the money made people feel stronger.

What held true for psychic pain turned out to be true for physical pain also. Students submerged their hands in very hot water: 43°C (109.4°F) for ninety seconds, 50°C (122°F) for thirty seconds and then again 43°C for a minute. The pain they experienced was lower after counting money than after counting paper. And while it might be tempting to dismiss the results as indicative of loan-depleted American students obsessed with cash, the students who volunteered for the experiment were Chinese, rewarded by nothing more than course credits for their participation.[6]

Money does influence us and it does make us feel better. That's why companies pay overtime and bonuses. It may not, in and of itself, make us absolutely happy – but, just like cigarettes and chocolate, our wants are not confined to what's good for us. The pleasure of money is often short-lived of course – because it's insatiable. There are always newer, bigger, flashier, sweeter products to consume, so the things we buy with money rarely satisfy as fully as they promise. Psychologists call this the hedonic treadmill: the more we consume, the more we want. But we stay on the treadmill as steadfastly as on our phones, hooked on the pleasures that, at least initially, make us feel so good.

What all this has shown is that money may be the richest area ever discovered for the study of unintended consequences. From which it should follow, but rarely does, that managers and compensation committees need to be tremendously thoughtful when deciding how to apply such a powerful, even irrational, motivator. Because money has a more complex influence on people than just making them work longer.

'Money certainly changes the way you think,' says David Ring. He's an internationally renowned orthopaedic surgeon at one of the top hospitals in the United States. Ring's tall, handsome and, for the most part, silent – except when he starts talking about his work, which is when he really comes alive. He loves what he does, but doesn't love the role that money plays in medicine.

'Doctors who own stakes in testing labs order more tests; I've experienced that, first hand. Colleagues working in surgical centres that they own – they take the money, the government pays the facility fee and they get some of that money. Now if you're doing that kind of case, the way to make money out of that is to spend less. So if you're working at your own surgical centre, you will treat a fracture with pins. Then the same doctors will go to treat the same kind of case but this time they're in a hospital, so they'll use an expensive plate. They will tell you that with a straight face. They bypass questionable ethics. Some of it is conscious and some of it I'm sure they just don't see.'

Could that mean, I asked him, that money might influence a diagnosis?

'Change diagnosis? I think so. The minute you see dollar signs in your patient's eyes, it changes how you think. You have to learn not to look at their insurance – get as far down the diagnostic path as you can before you know their income. It's impossible not to be swayed by the profit motive. I'm an academician and devoted to things that don't earn money but I watch people come in on my path and gradually get off of it. First, they just want to do well in their practice, just to be good surgeons. After a few years, they start to realise that what they do determines how much money they make and they start to learn a new game. The old game was: diagnose well, communicate well, do the surgery well. The new game becomes: make money. They don't really see the game change, they're blind to it. But it changes.

'Arthroscopy for arthritis, that's a classic example. You definitely don't cure osteoarthritis with arthroscopy. There was one brave guy in a Veterans Administration hospital in Texas who did a pilot study comparing knee arthroscopy with washing the knee and with cleaning the knee out. All three treatments were equally effective! But there's a lot of money in arthroscopy. So the response of American orthopaedic surgeons was very defensive. It is a wilful blindness – you bypass curiosity and scientific knowledge and concern for your patient and go straight for profit motive and preserve your position.'

Ring is a vocal critic of the role that money plays in medicine. But that doesn't mean that he feels himself to be immune to its influence.

'You could say that I'm really high-minded because I'll fly to Sheffield to teach or do research in my free time – but I still get caught up. You can see the temptation, especially in Massachusetts where there is only one good payer – workers' comp. It is devilishly good. You can make so much out of one case. So I can make a lot of money – ten times what I can make from Medicare or an HMO [health maintenance organisation]. It is so tempting; with just a few workers' comp patients, you've made your year's income in a month. If this is the going rate, why should I be the sucker?'

It would be easy enough to dismiss Ring's insights as merely indicative of the American medical system which, notwithstanding Obama's reforms, often lacks the sense of social purpose and service that characterise the NHS at its best. But you don't have to spend very long talking to British doctors before one theme becomes very clear: one reason the NHS hierarchy is so powerful is because consultants have the power (or influence) to allocate private work, and time for private practice. Aspiring doctors don't want to rock the boat because that's one way to ensure such lucrative work never comes your way. The transformation of GPs' surgeries into small (or not-so-small) businesses has, similarly, threatened to drain some of the social impulse out of the service. At the same time, cosmetic surgeons, weight-loss nutritionists, homeopaths and teeth-whitening dentists have embraced a market outlook with a fervour Ring might find daunting.

What is striking about Ring's perspective is not just that

he's so forthright but that, unlike most of us, he is highly conscious of the influence that money has on him, as well as on his colleagues. Money is not making these doctors less motivated; they're as motivated as ever – maybe even more so. What money changes is their behaviour.

In a series of experiments carried out in 2007, participants got to play Monopoly (or were forced to, depending on your view of the game). Some came away with £3,000 of play money, some with £125 and some with none. They were then taken across the lab, ostensibly to another room for another experiment. But on their way, they encountered a woman who spilled a box of pencils. The volunteers who had made the most money from the Monopoly game turned out to be the least helpful, picking up the fewest pencils. In another version of the experiment, volunteers encountered a colleague who seemed to be highly confused about a task. The participants who were not thinking about money spent 120 per cent more time helping their colleague than those who had money on their minds.[7]

Then the researchers wondered whether they were just asking for a form of social interaction of a kind that the money-primed participants weren't very good at. So they designed an opportunity to do something that was easy and money-related: donate to the University Student Fund. But the participants who had been reminded of money donated only 39 per cent of their payment (on average) to the Student Fund. Their peers, who were not so conscious of money, donated 67 per cent.

The volunteers who had money uppermost in their minds weren't entirely without values, however. When they were given difficult or impossible tasks to perform, they worked 48 per cent longer before asking for any help. They persevered – but they persevered alone. What the researchers concluded was that, while money was great at motivating individual effort, it carried with it significant negative social side effects. In the conflict that we all experience – between our interest in ourselves and our concern for others – money appears to motivate only our interest in ourselves, making us selfish and self-centred.

A further set of experiments confirmed this insight. When reminded of money – by screensavers, posters or watercolours – participants put greater physical distance between themselves and others. Given the choice, they were also more likely to want to work alone and to prefer solo leisure activities. Small reminders of money produced large changes in behaviour, making people less social, less connected to others. They were more motivated than ever, but more isolated, less helpful and less concerned for their fellow man.[8] They became socially disengaged. Over time, the researchers concluded, the mere presence of money elicits a market-pricing orientation towards the world. Money makes people feel self-sufficient, which also means they don't need or care about others; it's everyone for themselves.

Subsequent studies have added nuance and subtlety to this raw finding: the study of economics provokes more positive attitudes to greed among its students, and economics professors are less likely than those from other disciplines to donate to charity. Just thinking about money can make people act towards others with less empathy and compassion.[9] It may, by implication, make people care less.

Nowhere have the consequences of focusing on money been as stark as at Grenfell Tower. Choices weren't centred on safety or even on human beings, but only on money: 'We need good costs for Cllr Feilding-Mellen and the planner tomorrow at 8.45am!'[10] Life-saving sprinklers might have been installed but nobody was thinking about the people in the building, whom they didn't know and would never meet. Money crowded out the human element in decisions.

Perhaps few of us make life-or-death decisions like those at Grenfell Tower. Perhaps few of us make decisions about large sums; that doesn't insulate us from the dehumanising influence of money in our working lives. Performance-related pay, performance bonuses and all kinds of incentive plans are designed to elicit harder work and perseverance from the workforce. But the unintended social consequences of such plans can be perverse and extreme.

'Every branch office had its own incentive scheme,' Paul Moore told me. Between 2002 and 2005, Moore was head of Group Regulatory Risk at HBOS, the largest mortgage lender in the UK. 'I remember one in particular: every Saturday, once the office closed for the day, the sales staff would all get together. And the sales advisers who'd beaten their targets, they got cash. But if you'd failed to beat your target, you were given a cabbage. Cash or cabbage, in public, every Saturday.'

The ritual humiliation of employees was just one aspect of the company culture that alarmed Moore. To him, it signified that money had obliterated all other motives within HBOS, even concern for employees' respect for each other, and for their customers. 'When we were doing a review,' Moore said, 'one woman in Scunthorpe told me: "We hit our targets but we have never hit our sales targets ethically." What she meant by that was that the pressure to hit targets was so great that they were all anybody thought about. So there was a culture of bullying in HBOS, focused on sales numbers. I don't think people had started that way; it's what working for the company turned them into. The management just didn't think carefully enough: if you demand a sales increase of ten per cent, and then only allow a cost increase of three per cent, then you are going to get some highly improper sales and some very anti-social behaviour. And that's what happened.'

Moore's job was to look for all aspects within a company's processes, procedures and balance sheet that exposed it to risks. That meant, inevitably, spending a great deal of time poring over balance sheets. But, for Moore, the greatest exposure didn't lie in the numbers. It lay in the people, the culture and their incentives. What he came to see within the firm was that the management – the CEO and his executive teams – were so driven by earnings (and their own compensation, which derived from earnings) that they couldn't, and wouldn't, see the impact that the company's culture had on individual morality or the wider society that the company served.

When he shared his insights with the CEO, Moore was fired. He was later vindicated when, in September 2008, the bank collapsed. Testifying to the parliamentary select committee six months later, his rage was still palpable.

> Anyone whose eyes were not blinded by money, power and pride, who really looked carefully, knew there was something wrong: that economic growth based almost solely on excessive consumer spending, which was based on excessive consumer credit, which was based on massively increasing property prices which were caused by the very same excessively easy credit could only ultimately lead to disaster. But sadly, no one wanted or felt able to speak up for fear of stepping out of line with the rest of the lemmings who were busy organizing themselves to run over the edge of the cliff behind the pied piper CEOs and executive teams that were all being paid so much to play that tune and take them in that direction.[11]

A subsequent survey of 563 risk managers undertaken by Moore, in conjunction with Cranfield School of Management, cited culture and remuneration practices as two of the chief causes of the banking failure. These most hard-nosed and numerate of analysts didn't think regulation or economic models were chiefly at fault, and they were entirely dismissive of the idea that banks had failed due to 'global circumstances beyond anyone's control'.[12] What went wrong, they thought, was the culture: people's attitudes to money. Pursuit of profits had effectively displaced concern for people. 'A constitution for knaves may produce knaves' is how one economist described what happens when money becomes the chief motivator.[13]

Of course we all want to earn a living but the moral fading that accompanies financial incentives may be more profound than anyone is quite willing to acknowledge. When companies overpay, as firms like Enron did and many banks and Silicon Valley businesses still do, in effect they are saying: Look at the money, don't look at anything else. And employees often absorb exactly that message. 'I reckon that for the first ten years, all I'll focus on is the money,' one young engineer told me. 'Then I'll start to think about my family.' Even before he had joined his firm, he expected to have to leave all other considerations behind – and was prepared to do so. I have met many men and women just like him.

The trade-off between social and financial motivations and the sense that one works against the other is intuitively understood; surely this is what lies behind the public outrage surrounding executive bonuses. It is not just envy, or fury at the increasing gap between rich and poor, but an implicit understanding that the more money an individual earns, the less engaged he, or she, becomes in the general welfare of the nation. If I earn £10 million a year, I need not concern myself with the condition of NHS hospitals or my local school, the mental-health issues confronted by my workforce or the lack of employment available to young people – because I can buy my way out of any of these predicaments should I encounter them for myself. Given enough money, I can be an island. I might even come to believe that there is no such thing as society because I no longer feel dependent on society to get what I want. The overpaid may not feel it, but one consequence of their compensation is that they become disengaged from the rest of us. It's an interesting thought that high rates of pay might become indicators of low levels of social engagement.

One of the first people to identify the strange and often unintended consequences of money was the social scientist Richard Titmuss. Born in 1907 to a Bedfordshire farmer, his family moved to London where, at the age of fourteen, Titmuss went to work in his father's transport business. When his father died a few years later, he moved to an insurance firm; now the family's major breadwinner, a serious salary and a permanent position were crucial. Working in insurance taught Titmuss a great deal, about how people lived, moved, worked or lost their jobs. He had boundless energy and deep curiosity about how the world worked. Why did people behave as they did? Why was there so much inequality?

Self-taught and highly motivated, Titmuss eventually left the dusty world of insurance to work on social policy; by the time the Second World War was over, he was well known and highly regarded. Despite never having attended a university, Titmuss became professor in social administration at the London School of Economics. He was, demonstrably, a man who knew a lot about motivation.

Much of Titmuss' academic work informed the post-war development of the welfare state and the creation of the National Health Service. To all intents and purposes, he was a good, old-fashioned policy wonk: embroiled in the minutiae of social legislation and politics, a man who never really lost his passion for statistics. And then, three years before he died, he published a book that blew up the world of economics. *The Gift Relationship* argued that money didn't always motivate people; in fact, paying people could undermine their moral motivation. Using the example of blood donation, Titmuss showed that paying donors made them less willing, not more willing, to donate blood and it increased chances that the blood supply would be contaminated when donors were paid. The book caused a sensation worldwide because it dared to challenge the two fundamental tenets of modern economics: first, that individuals make rational economic decisions; and second, that individuals are motivated only by self-interest. If people did less when offered more – what could that mean for economics?

Titmuss died before he could follow up his argument, but his book, and the questions he posed, continued to infiltrate and disrupt economic thinking. The idea that we make economic decisions rationally came under a lot of fire, with an army of behavioural economists demonstrating that biases and shortcuts interfere with rational decision-making. And evidence mounted that money and behaviour might have a more complicated relationship than was allowed for in the popular economic models of the time.

One of the most interesting studies came out of Switzerland, where two economists wanted to test their theory (derived from Titmuss' work) that, far from enhancing our motivation, money might destroy it.[14] In 1993, they visited two communities in central Switzerland designated as potential sites for nuclear waste storage, and asked 305 residents whether they would be willing for the storage facility to be located in their neighbourhood. More than half of their respondents (50.8

per cent) said that, if asked, they would vote in favour of having the facility in their community. This wasn't because they were enthusiastic about nuclear waste: nearly 40 per cent believed there was a chance of a serious accident and nearly 80 per cent believed that many local residents would suffer long-term effects from it. But they thought, if the storage facility was necessary, it might as well be in their area. In other words, their sense of a common, social good overcame their individual reservations.

What was most interesting, however, was what happened when the two economists offered to pay residents to house the nuclear waste store. The amount offered wasn't trivial: between $2,175 and $6,525 per individual per year – near or above the community's median monthly income. But now the level of acceptance *halved*. The two economists tried raising the amount of compensation offered to see if that could influence their respondents. Only *one* person who declined the first offer was prepared to accept anything higher and only 4.9 per cent said that the amount of the compensation mattered. You might have thought that, with two reasons to support the project, commitment would be higher. After all, now the Swiss residents could do good *and* make money. But that isn't the way it worked. Just as in the lab experiments, the mere prospect of money reduced people's sense of connectedness to the community.

Nor was this some weird Swiss peculiarity. An experiment in Nevada reported similar findings: pay diminished the respondents' sense of commitment to one another. Subsequent studies reinforced these findings.[15] When there was no penalty for lateness when collecting their children from a childcare centre, parents were rarely late. But once they were fined for being late, the possibility of losing money didn't make them more punctual – it made them less so. Nor could their previous punctuality be revived; when penalties were abandoned, parents still didn't care as much about being on time. What had started as a social relationship had been reduced irrevocably once money was introduced.

What these group studies showed was just what the lab experiments with individuals had gleaned: money blinds us to our social relationships, creating a sense of self-sufficiency that discourages co-operation and mutual support. Thinking about money can make people forget that they are human.[16]

Nobody yet quite understands why money works the way that it does. Economists have speculated that motivation may work in ways similar to cognitive load.[17] Just as there is a hard limit to how much we can focus on at one moment, perhaps we can be motivated by only one perspective at a time. When we care about people, we care less about money, and when we care about money, we care less about people. Our moral capacity becomes as limited as our cognitive capacity is. That most business environments discourage any expression of emotion blinds us to how aberrant, and anti-social, such lifeless behaviour can be.

We're at the raw edge of brain science here. A number of fMRI experiments have attempted to understand what happens when the brain makes a moral choice. Some have looked at the brain as it decides between two conflicting options; others have tried to see the difference between a utilitarian decision (do I take the bus or the train?) and a moral decision (should I lie?).[18] The findings are unclear. Certainly moral choices occupy a great deal of brain capacity, and they seem to employ autobiographical memories (which implies empathy) and social awareness. But no one knows how to trace motivation, at least not yet. It seems to sit on the cusp between brain and mind in a relationship that is endlessly fascinating but still obscure.

Empirically, however, we do know that one incentive – money – seems to crowd out our more social motivations. Since the mere presence of money evokes a market-pricing orientation, people become commodities and every commodity has a price. That is one reason why the use of money to enforce social behaviours is, and feels, so inappropriate and doomed. The idea that you can keep couples together by offering them tax incentives is, in effect, to use an anti-social tool to enforce pro-social behaviour. Proposals to engage parents in their children's school conduct by issuing fines for non-attendance of parent–teacher meetings follow the same pattern. You can't commoditise relationships and then expect people to care more; it's like trying to accelerate by pumping the brakes.

Knowing that economic incentives diminish our concern for others, we ought to deploy them with tremendous delicacy. But most firms don't. Instead, they're used like sledgehammers in the delicate china shop of human motivations. When economic incentives are over-weighted, they send a signal that it is money, and money alone, that matters. Complex remuneration packages – the infamous Long Term Incentive Plans – encourage bankers to spend hours thinking about their financial relationship to their institution, at a time when the human consequences of their decisions should be more important. The financial incentives that appeal to self-interest may fail in ways companies don't expect because they undermine the moral values that you need people to bring with them to work. As David Ring said, money changes the way you think – and it changes the way you think about everything. But most companies remain blind to how profoundly, and pervasively, this impacts the way that people do their jobs.

The social disengagement induced by money would explain why, when senior managers at Countrywide would gather to look at the company three years out, they could have such extraordinary discussions.

'A lot of us on the operations side and risk-management side would have meetings which led to a discussion of sub-prime mortgages,' Catherine Clark recalled. 'The sales people got such high commissions, they wouldn't stop. We kept asking: what happens in three years' time? And the only answer we ever got came from the guy in charge of all the back-office servicing: he said the technology infrastructure would not keep up with all the foreclosures.'

What is so memorable about the scene Clark paints is that there aren't any real people in it. There are just sales – and a looming IT problem. Nobody can see that the IT problem represents thousands of families losing their homes. By the same token, when we learn how many investors identified the looming failure of the banking industry, what's remarkable is not that these bright individuals had such foresight – but that their chief thought was they could cash in on it.[19]

At a time when BP was so focused on cost-cutting, mergers and acquisitions, it's perhaps not surprising that market thinking predominated. In 2002, the company was on a very aggressive growth path, about to deliver one of the strongest financial performances in its history. That's when members of the Health and Safety Team got together to run a course. Part of the training involved an analysis of the decision whether to place contractors at Texas City in temporary trailers, permanent trailers or permanent buildings. But that isn't how they chose to think about the cost-benefit analysis. Instead, a PowerPoint presentation shows an analogy with the Three Little Pigs. Each trailer option is designated a straw house, stick house or brick house – with, for good measure, a fourth option which is a blast-resistant house. This is BP's cost-benefit analysis of the three little pigs:

Frequency: the big bad wolf blows with a frequency of once per piggy lifetime.

Consequence: if the wolf blows down the house, the piggy is gobbled.

Maximum justifiable spend (MJS): a piggy considers it's worth $1,000 to save its bacon.

1.0 piggy lifetime × $1,000/piggy life = $1,000

Which type house should the piggy build?[20]

In making their decision about what kind of trailer to build, the BP executives had to calculate the value of a life ($1,000), the number of people in a trailer, the cost of a trailer and the likelihood of a fatal accident in which a 'piggy' might be killed, or 'gobbled'. You have to ask how this analogy helped them towards a moral decision. I hope somebody was appalled but I can imagine a fair amount of laughter as the metaphor was teased out. It isn't clear from the presentation whether this was a training exercise, a decision process or both. What is clear is that human beings weren't under consideration. The Texas City contractors were animals, with a market value. And they were, ultimately, allowed to work and die in houses of straw.

It would be wrong to believe that BP was unusual in thinking this way. Academic research suggests that when more people think about money and frame their choices specifically as business decisions, the more likely they are to act unethically; mere exposure to the concept of money elicits unethical behaviours. Outside of the world of lab experiments, we can see this happen: Ford, when it calculated the costs of reinforcing the Pinto's rear end, as compared to the cost of lost lives; A.H. Robins, when it chose not to recall the contraceptive Dalkon Shield; W.R. Grace, when it chose bankruptcy as a means of shaking off the dust of Libby, Montana; Mid Staffordshire hospital, when it focused on achieving trust status over concern for patients; Rotherham council, as it prioritised austerity over the safety of young girls. When the decision was made not to install sprinklers in Grenfell Tower, did anyone actually cost out the cash value of lost lives – or was money so much more salient than human lives? When executives of Carillion diverted funds from the company's pension fund, they stared at spreadsheets that did nothing to articulate the grief of employees left bereft at the end of their working lives. When the Archbishop of Dublin, Kevin McNamara, took out insurance against claims resulting from priests abusing children, what was he doing but placing market concerns over social ones? He could have removed accused priests from their ministries and tried to get them help; he might have launched a thorough investigation, imposed a child-protection policy or alerted other bishops – but he turned a blind eye to people and focused instead on protecting the Church's assets. In treating people as less important than things, work becomes both demoralised and demoralising and we become blind to the moral content of our decisions.

Money and wilful blindness make us act in ways incompatible with what we believe our ethics to be, and often even with our own self-interest. Driven by our desire to see ourselves as good, we value money because it appears to be the external proof that we are good – and much of society reads it just the same way. So the problem with money isn't fundamentally about greed, although it can be comforting to think so. The problem with money is that we live in societies in which mutual support and co-operation is essential, but money erodes the relationships we need to lead productive, fulfilling and genuinely happy lives. When money becomes the dominant motivator, it doesn't co-operate with, or amplify, our relationships; it disengages us from them. The further removed we become from our neighbours, the more siloed in our self-sufficiency, the easier it is to treat people as things, to turn a blind eye to the human costs of toxic cultures and to make immoral decisions.

This isn't caused by money alone. All the other organisational forces of wilful blindness – obedience, conformity, bystander effects, distance and division of labour – combine to obscure the moral, human face of work. Money keeps us very busy, often too busy, to see clearly and work thoughtfully. It keeps us silent too, fearful lest debate or criticism jeopardise salaries. Money reinforces and often appears to reward those core, self-identifying beliefs that blind us to alternatives and to argument. You could say that if we are just obeying orders, fitting in, diffusing responsibility for people who are a long way away and, anyway, maybe not our concern at all – then money is the final incentive to keep looking away. The fact that money tends to be addictive – the more we have, the more we feel we need – merely ensures that the cycle is rewarded and perpetuated. To paraphrase Burke, all that evil needs to flourish is for good people to see nothing – and get paid for it.

No one visiting Stanford University could fail to be impressed by its sheer scale or its wealth. Spread over twelve square miles, it's ten times larger than Vatican City and the vast avenues of palms leading to fountains and Spanish courtyards are reminiscent more of Renaissance papal power play than 21st-century cutting-edge research. Such lavish public buildings feel brash in their confidence, but their rooms harbour perpetrators of doubt and scepticism. At the heart of the campus, ensconced in an unremarkable lino-floored, book-lined room, sits Albert 'Al' Bandura. In many respects, Bandura is the grand old man of psychology: its most cited living author, the father of social-learning theory and one of the first people to argue that children's behaviour derived not just from reward and punishment but from what they observed around them. That this seems such an obvious thought to us nowadays is testimony to how profound Bandura's impact has been on our thinking. The very phrase 'role model' would scarcely exist without him.

Much of Bandura's work has so seeped into public consciousness that we are barely aware that it is there, and his work has attracted scores of awards, honours and distinctions. At the age of ninety-two, this hasn't stopped him working, nor has it rendered him complacent. For all his eminence, he's an engaging and accessible man whose mild manner belies a tenacious mind. And one of the issues he has wrestled with for years is the process by which individuals lose sight of morality in their need to preserve their sense of self-worth.

'People are highly driven to do things that build self-worth; you can't transgress and think of yourself as bad. You need to protect your sense of yourself as good. And so people transform harmful practices into worthy ones, by coming up with social justification, by distancing themselves with euphemisms, by ignoring the long-term consequences of their actions.'

One of the most prominent ways in which people justify their harmful practices is by using arguments about money to obscure moral and social issues. Because we can't and won't acknowledge that some of our choices are socially and morally harmful, we distance ourselves from them by claiming they're necessary for wealth creation. Nowhere is this more dangerous, he argues, than in our attitudes to the environment and population growth. The easiest way for those who resist calls to curb population growth, and who oppose environmental controls, is to represent themselves as the good guys because they just want to make everyone better-off and don't want to put the economy at risk.

'To defend their positions, they can't say, "Sure, we're the bad guys and we want to rape and pillage the planet,"' Bandura told me. 'They have to vindicate harmful practices that take such a heavy toll on the environment and the quality of human life – they have to make out that what's harmful is, in fact, good. And one way they do that is to use the notion of nature as, in fact, an economic commodity. So they see nature in terms of its market value rather than its inherent value.' That's why, Bandura argues, those who claim to love nature can also support, for example, drilling for oil in Alaska. They can't see themselves as destroyers, so they position themselves as the rational liberators of natural wealth. In this vein, Bandura quotes Newt Gingrich: 'To get the best ecosystem for our buck, we should use decentralised and entrepreneurial strategies.'[21] Similarly, when Donald Trump signed an executive order in April 2018 requiring the Interior Department to reconsider President Obama's ban on offshore drilling, he positioned himself as liberating the nation from his predecessor's act of deprivation: the ban, he said, 'deprives our country of potentially thousands and thousands of jobs and billions of dollars in wealth'. It is, says Bandura, the economic justification that makes the environmentally damaging decision possible. Seeing nature as just a source of money blinds such decision-makers to the moral consequences of their decisions.

Bandura has spent a lifetime dissecting the moral disengagement required for the perpetration of criminal and inhuman acts, a journey that has taken him from the tobacco industry, the gun lobby, the television business to the multiple industries implicated in environmental degradation. He has a deep understanding of the forces at work that encourage employees to be blind to their collusion in these processes. But nothing enrages him more than the economic justifications used to defend continued population growth.

'I went to a conference in Germany,' Bandura recalled, 'where a young African woman spoke about the tremendous difference that birth control and health education had had on her community. The fact that she and her peers now had control over the number of children that they conceived and raised had transformed their lives. And she spoke of this very eloquently. And there, in that audience of well-heeled Europeans, rich Westerners, *she was booed!*'

When he recovered from his shock, Bandura analysed what was going on in the minds of the audience. What drove them, he reasoned, was their recognition that Western birth rates won't pay for the pension requirements of the elderly; if the West doesn't produce more children, it can't sustain the wealth needed to look after parents when they retire. Therefore, even though consumption and environmental degradation are clearly linked, the needs of the market trump the needs of the planet.

Nor was this a purely Western phenomenon. The need for money effectively positions infants as money-making machines.

> In some countries [Bandura writes], the pressure on women to boost their childbearing includes punitive threats as well. The former prime minister of Japan, Yoshiro Mori, suggested that women who bore no children should be barred from receiving pensions, saying, 'It is truly strange

> to say we have to use tax money to take care of women who don't even give birth once, who grow old living their lives selfishly and singing the praises of freedom.' In this campaign for more babies, childbearing is reduced to a means for economic growth.[22]

In this mindset, children are nothing more than money-makers in the eyes of politicians merely crunching the numbers, blind to the moral, environmental or humanitarian consequences of their policies. Market thinking has obliterated moral thinking on a grand scale.

So persuasive (and pervasive) has the economic argument in favour of population growth become, says Bandura, that all of the major NGOs have had to stand aside from it. Fear of alienating donors, criticism from the progressive left and disparagement by conservative vested interests claiming that overpopulation is a 'myth' served as further incentives to cast off the rising global population as a factor in environmental degradation. Population growth vanished from the agendas of mainstream environmental organisations that previously regarded escalating numbers as a major environmental threat. Greenpeace announced that population 'is not an issue for us'. Friends of the Earth declared that 'it is unhelpful to enter into a debate about numbers'. The fear of losing money disabled those very organisations best placed to understand the ultimate consequences of thinking only about money.

What money does, Bandura argues, is allow us to disengage from the moral and social effects of our decisions. As long as we can frame everything as an economic argument, we don't have to confront the social or moral consequences of our decisions. That economics has become such a dominant, if not the prevalent, mindset for evaluating social and political choices has been one of the defining characteristics of our age. Numbers look objective, a neutral language with which to communicate contentious ideas. But of course what they are, how they're defined, is far from objective. It's just that the numerals blind us to the thinking behind them. As long as the numbers work, we feel absolved of the harder, more inchoate ethical choices that face us nonetheless. We appear to have gone from having a market economy to being a market society (if that isn't an oxymoron) and it's an interesting thought that our obsession with economics has just been one long sustained phase of displacement activity.

Money is just one of the forces that blind us to information and issues which we could pay attention to – but don't. It exacerbates and often rewards all the other drivers of wilful blindness: our preference for the familiar, our love for individuals and for big ideas, a love of busyness and our dislike of conflict and change, the human instinct to obey and conform and our skill at displacing and diffusing responsibility. All of these operate and collaborate with varying intensities at different moments in our lives. The common denominator is that they all make us protect our sense of self-worth, reducing dissonance and conferring a sense of security, however illusory. In some ways, they all act like money: making us feel good at first, with consequences we don't see. We wouldn't be so blind if our blindness didn't deliver rewards: the benefit of comfort and ease.

But in failing to confront the greatest challenge of our age – climate change – all the forces of wilful blindness come together, like synchronised swimmers in a spectacular water ballet. We live with people like ourselves, and sharing consumption habits blinds us to their cost. Like the unwitting spouse of an alcoholic, we know there's something amiss but we don't want to acknowledge that the lifestyles we love are killing us. The dissonance produced by reading about our environmental impact on the one hand, and living as we do, is resolved by minor alterations in what we buy or eat, but very few significant social shifts. Sometimes we get so anxious we consume more. We keep too busy to confront our worries, a kind of wild displacement activity with schedules that don't allow us to be as green as we'd like. The gravitational pull of the status quo exerts its influence and global conferences end when no one has the stomach for the levels of conflict they engender. In our own countries, no politician shows the nerve for the political battles real change would require.

We know that the world is unlikely to limit temperature increase to 2 or even 1.5 degrees C but still we're obedient consumers; we might change if we were told to, but we're not. So we conform to the consumption patterns we see around us and all become bystanders, hoping someone else somewhere will intervene. Our governments and corporations grow too complex to communicate with themselves or to change and we are left just where we do not want to be, where our only temporary consolation is cash.

This is wilful blindness on a spectacular scale and it could leave us abject with despair, were it not that, all around us, are individuals who aren't blind. That they can and do see more, and act on what they see, offers a possibility that we can be wilfully sighted too.

11. Cassandra

Oedipus: I cannot leave the truth unknown.

The Theban Plays, Sophocles

'I wasn't surprised. I'd been saying for months that something like this was bound to happen. It was so obvious. You push these boys too far, what's in their heads is so awful and so violent. Of course you're going to have problems with violence.'

On 5 November 2009, Nidal Malik Hasan shot and killed fourteen people on Fort Hood military base. Cynthia Thomas was deeply upset but she was not surprised by what had happened. Earlier that year, she had started the Under the Hood coffee house to offer soldiers a refuge from the base, a place to hang out where they could find comfort and, if they wanted it, psychological, psychiatric and legal help.

'This stuff happens, on a smaller scale, all the time: soldiers killing someone or stabbings, shootings. All the time. People don't understand. We can have two weeks and there will be three, four, five violent incidents. And people don't see them. The violence. Everything is just all the time. A soldier snapping and doing this is not surprising. People don't want to see it, they don't want to hear about it. But it's here. It will go on happening.'

Cynthia Thomas is a Cassandra. In ancient Greek mythology, Cassandra was royalty: the daughter of King Priam and Queen Hecuba. Besotted by her beauty, Apollo fell in love with her and gave her the gift of prophecy. But when she spurned him, he retaliated by adding to her gift the fate that no one would believe her. So the Trojans ignored her when she warned them not to bring in the great wooden horse left by the Greeks. And it was Cassandra who warned Agamemnon of Clytemnestra's murderous rage on his return from the war. She must have known she was doomed to die then too, because that was her unique talent: to see what others did not.

The savage irony of Cassandra is that, as we read her prophecies, we know that they are true, but no one else does. As such, she is one of the first characters in literature to offer readers that invaluable plot device: superior knowledge. Believing Cassandra, when everyone else derides her, we see simultaneously two contradictory points of view. We learn that any situation can contain truths that we may not be able to see but that are, nonetheless, visible. And she teaches us that often it is the despised who know most.

But Cassandra captivates our imagination also because she embodies that baffled rage that we all feel when no one else can see what we see. The epitome of frustration, because Cassandra is doomed always to be right she shows us that the truth is knowable but won't necessarily set us free.

The world is full of Cassandras, individuals whose fate it is to see what others can't, who are not blind but feel compelled to shout their awkward, provocative truths. That's why, after any industrial or organisational failure, individuals inevitably surface who saw the crisis coming, warned about it and were mocked or ignored. In Libby, Montana, Gayla Benefield was a classic Cassandra when she insisted that there was something wrong with her town. But when you meet Gayla, she has none of the wild eyes or inspired fury of the classic portrayals of Cassandra; there is nothing physically that marks her out as a rebel or nonconformist, but she seems, from an early age, to have seen things that others did not.

'In high school, I remember our teacher wanted us to have silhouettes, taken behind a sheet. And there was just something about it that made me uneasy. I didn't know why it wasn't right but I knew it wasn't.' Gayla paused for a moment, reaching for the facts, trying to make sure she captures an accurate memory. Then she laughed. 'Maybe it was just that I wasn't going to take off my false boobs! Whatever it was, I led the walkout.'

Taking a stand seems to have become something Gayla did easily. She felt comfortable being different, even when it meant being pilloried or left out.

'I took mechanical drawing in high school – no girl ever had done that at our school, but I didn't know why. I remember: I was sat in a far corner away from the boys! My grandfather was a Russian immigrant who ended up in eastern Montana. He taught me not to fight the system – but always to question it. He was the best American you could ever find. He was always trying to find a better way to do things. I never danced to a different drummer but I questioned. I've never been a blind follower. I've always questioned.'

Cassandras are often also whistleblowers, determined not just to see what others see, but to act upon it, trying to alter fate. Both acknowledge what others won't see because they are questioners, driven to ask: What is really happening? Does it have to be that way? Am I missing something? Is there some other explanation or solution? They're driven, dedicated, often quite obsessive truth-seekers – even (or sometimes especially) when no one agrees with them. But that is almost the only generalisation you can make about these extremely and wilfully sighted people.

The world contains millions of Cassandras, in all walks of life and all different. Academics have struggled to find identifying qualities they all have in common, but to no avail. It used to be thought that whistleblowers were more likely to be women because, as newcomers to most institutions, they didn't have the same stake in the status quo. It was a nice theory but turned out not to be true.[1] There doesn't seem to be any correlation between age or years of service, and neither pay nor education level turn out to be good predictors either. Religion doesn't seem to play a definitive role; while all Cassandras have a pronounced sense of right and wrong, as many derive their morality from history or personal experience as from any formal faith. And, despite the fact that these troublesome truth-tellers are sometimes thrown into jail or sent for psychiatric assessments, there seems to be no evidence that, as a group, they are crazy.

What we do know is that society needs people like Cynthia Thomas and Gayla Benefield: individuals willing to ask awkward questions, trace tricky connections and challenge embedded assumptions. Because while it's impossible to quantify the economic cost of wilful blindness, it's even harder to measure the full extent of white-collar crime and corruption. In the United States, in 2000, the Ethics Resource Center found that a third of public and private employees had personally observed misconduct. A far higher percentage – 80 per cent – of directors of internal auditing said they had observed wrongdoing by their organisations. And when Harry Markopolos testified before Congress about the Madoff fraud, he argued that 'white collar criminals cause far more economic harm to this nation than armed robbers, drug dealers, car thieves and other assorted miscreants put together.

These fraudsters steal approximately five per cent of business revenues annually, dwarfing the economic losses due to violent crime, yet not nearly enough federal law enforcement resources are devoted to catching them.'[2]

In the United States, vast amounts of federal legislation have been introduced to try to protect whistleblowers. The first of these, in 1912, protected federal employees who wished to offer information to Congress, and much subsequent legislation has been focused on ensuring that government employees in particular are protected. The No Fear Act (2002), the Sarbanes-Oxley Act (2002) and the Whistleblower Protection Act (1989) seek to protect employees from retaliation and the loss of their jobs, while the False Claims Act sought to elicit help from ordinary citizens against contracting fraud. In recognition, after the Madoff scandal, that the Securities Exchange Commission needed whistleblowers to police the market, these laws offer a percentage of the settlement to the whistleblower; to date, the Justice Department has recovered more than $20 billion.

UK legislation around whistleblowing is similarly complex. The Public Interest Disclosure Act (PIDA) of 1998 provides a legal framework to protect individuals who report malpractice, and it covers all employees except the self-employed and members of the intelligence services. In 2007, PIDA was updated and addressed anyone bringing forward information that suggested that a crime, miscarriage of justice or damage to the environment had occurred or was likely to occur. The number of cases brought has risen steeply, from 157 in the year the act became law to 1,761 in 2009. Employees have logged 9,000 claims alleging victimisation but, of these, 70 per cent were withdrawn without a public hearing, and of the remainder only 22 per cent were won. PIDA has generally been seen as lacking effectiveness because it offers remedies only after whistleblowers have suffered – generally by losing their jobs. It is too hard, too slow and too little. In 2013, the Enterprise and Regulatory Reform Act promised whistleblowers protection from bullying, harassment and retaliation, but also introduced a ragbag of financial infrastructure that did little to reassure whistleblowers operating in the public interest. EU directives have sought to protect those exposing sweetheart tax deals, but while all of these initiatives seek to encourage truth-telling, they generally fall far short of guaranteeing sincere whistleblowers real safety.

The organisation PROTECT (originally called Public Concern at Work) runs an adviser helpline for whistleblowers. It was founded in 1993 in the aftermath of the sinking of the *Herald of Free Enterprise*, the Clapham rail crash and the collapse of BCCI. Every one of these events had revealed that staff had been aware of dangers but had not felt able to raise the matter internally, or to pursue it if their concern was not taken seriously. Since the introduction of the act, PROTECT has been the first port of call for many whistleblowers who, in the majority of cases, have attempted to raise their concerns but found that they were either ignored or victimised. The organisation does the majority of its work with the NHS and financial services. In both, CEO Francesca West observes small changes at a glacial pace.

'Financial services are under a lot of pressure to ensure that the Senior Managers Regime is working,' West told me. The Senior Managers Regime attempts to make senior executives personally and individually liable for mistakes and failures. 'It is too soon to see if it is effective; it all needs more time to embed. But we have seen one case where a whistleblower came forward and the bank would never have known what was happening otherwise. In that case, a senior manager did get his hand slapped and the very idea that you could chastise such a senior individual may show progress. But the huge complexity of the industry and the regulatory system (the FCA and PRA) doesn't help.'[3]

In the case of the NHS, real momentum behind supporting whistleblowers was driven by the Francis Report, commissioned after the scandal of Mid Staffordshire NHS Trust. Robert Francis QC finally laid to rest the age-old management response to whistleblowers: that they can be ignored because they are usually disgruntled employees. Such an excuse was dangerous and wrong not just because the balance of risk on their part is so great, but because even if they were disgruntled, it did not automatically follow that their complaints were incorrect or unimportant. Francis further argued that the NHS needed to develop a culture in which every employee understood and used their freedom to speak up; how else could management know what was going on?

The recommendation could not have come soon enough. Of all the industries and organisations I have studied, I have never encountered one as vindictive, abusive or harrowing as the NHS in its treatment of staff who wish to raise concerns. Bullied, mocked, ostracised, their motives questioned and their professionalism doubted, the many NHS workers who have striven to solve problems by talking about them routinely received punishment, not rewards. A vast body of evidence – 600 individuals, 43 organisations and 19,500 staff survey respondents – convinced Francis to argue for guardians in every NHS organisation and the creation of a National Guardian's Office.[4] The guardians were supposed to be people to whom anyone in a hospital or trust could go with concerns. It didn't get off to a great start, with its first leader stepping down after just two months – for the simple reason that the job was impossible. It was supposed to be part-time, running concurrently with her role as chief nurse at Guy's and

St Thomas' NHS Foundation Trust. Since she was replaced, in the first half of 2017, 2,735 cases were raised, of which 923 concerned patient safety and 1,143 bullying and harassment. Most came from nurses.

PROTECT's Francesca West is wary. 'You can see some trusts have gone in with clear buy-in from the top, given people good protected time, with the right people and the right seniority for people to raise concerns and for concerns to be followed up,' she told me. 'That means that the good trusts got better, but my concern would be that I don't see what is in place to catch the bottom hangers. I don't see what the Guardian's Office is doing to stop the next Mid Staffs. The National Guardian's Office has no statutory powers. And the Freedom to Speak Up Guardians are often too junior, with no budget, no protected official role.'

Suspicion of whistleblowers, and their motives, is pervasive. Yet what whistleblowers demonstrate, time and again, is that the greatest harms are perpetrated not in private but in public – and not alone but by large numbers of people with many witnesses and bystanders. Cassandras and whistleblowers stand in that crowd, see what is happening, but somehow find within themselves the courage or the need to speak out. Far from being suspect troublemakers, they are typically the most loyal, dedicated workers to be found.

Most start as optimists, not nonconformists but true believers. Typically, they are neither disgruntled nor disappointed; they're not innately rebels but are compelled to speak out when they see organisations or people they love taking the wrong course. When the anaesthetist Stephen Bolsin started investigating the poor success rate in paediatric cardiac surgery, his aim was simply to improve it.

'I was new to Bristol. I expected to raise my family there. And I thought: let's make this a centre of excellence. If there's something we can improve, let's do it. If there's something we're doing wrong, we can fix it!'

Similarly, Bill McAleer, who had spent his entire working life at General Motors, loved the company that had changed his life for the better. What drove him to speak out was loyalty.

'I was a poor boy in Georgia and started on the line at GM and they paid to get me a degree in philosophy and a graduate degree, and they moved me up and I became an executive and I travelled all over the world and I saw GM make enormous changes in people's lives,' he told me. 'It really was an excellent company, I was quite proud of it.[5]

'There was nobody talking up for GM at the time that these events occurred. There were just people speaking up for themselves and nobody was looking after the shop! Being a whistleblower I don't think anybody who ever did it took it lightly.'

After leaving Uber, Susan Fowler was very careful to distance herself from the company before writing the blog about its culture of sexual harassment. She didn't want to attack her industry or Silicon Valley in general. What she wanted to do was make both better, just as, at HBOS, Paul Moore saw himself as an honest broker, the guy to keep everyone safe.

'I thought I was there to do some good,' Moore told me. 'It was a bit of a mission – integrity and financial services meant a lot to me. I think that came from a mixture of what my parents taught me and what you might call what you're given from Him upstairs. I always believed that I was a representative of the customer and the shareholder and those who could not see and understand all the detail that I could see.'

When Sherron Watkins wrote to Enron CEO Ken Lay, she thought he would welcome her questions and appreciate that, far from trying to wreck the company, she was trying to save it.

'I'd been so loyal!' Watkins recalled. 'I thought his first response would just be to want to get to the truth, to know what was going on in his company! It was the sense that, if you tell the captain the ship is sinking, he is going to man the lifeboats.'[6]

The letter that Watkins wrote, detailing accounting problems she could not resolve and risks she believed Lay did not know about, did not go to the press; she wrote to Lay as the person she believed was most likely to fix the problems she'd identified. And Watkins never went public. Only after the company had collapsed did investigators find her letter.

'I thought good would prevail, that we'd unwind some deals, restate earnings, that they'd be grateful to me for identifying the problems. I only found out later that Lay almost instantly took legal advice about whether he could fire me!'

When Harry Markopolos first started examining Bernard Madoff's investment strategies, it wasn't with a view to discovering criminality. The last thing on his mind was identifying systemic failures in the financial system or the Securities Exchange Commission; he wanted to succeed within them. As Markopolos explored Madoff's business, he hoped to copy him, not bring him down.

In many instances like this, what enables Cassandras to see what others don't is a tremendous eye for detail. Markopolos says that thousands of hours of doing maths by hand is what prepared him for the moment that he saw Madoff's numbers.

'I knew immediately that the numbers made no sense. I just knew it. Numbers exist in relationship, and after you've studied as many of them as I had it was clear something was out of whack. As I continued examining the numbers, the problems with them began popping out as clearly as a red wagon in a field of snow. Anyone who understood the match of the market would have seen these problems immediately.'[7]

Like many Cassandras, Markopolos didn't allow distance or theory to obscure the nitty-gritty of what he saw. But when he provided the SEC with all of that detail, no one there had the skill, training, patience or experience to understand what they were looking at. 'The magnitude of this Ponzi scheme,' Markopolos wrote, 'is matched only by the wilful blindness of the SEC to investigate Madoff.'

For many Cassandras, God is indeed in the detail. They don't wrap themselves up in dogma, but relish facts and arguments. In just the same way that Alice Stewart immersed herself in all the domestic detail that might explain childhood cancers, Cassandras typically like getting down to the bare bones of otherwise abstract problems.

That's what James Hansen did, in the late 1970s. Having completed his PhD, writing on the atmosphere of Venus, he was a geek, not a dissident, buried in his data and oblivious to the student riots that surrounded him. Soon Earth's atmosphere became more captivating than Venus's, as he grappled with the detail of chlorofluorocarbons and the ozone layer. One of his key interests, he wrote, was 'radiative transfer in planetary atmospheres, especially interpreting remote sounding of the earth's atmosphere and surface from satellites'. In 1981, he published a paper predicting that the following decade would be unusually warm, and the decade after that warmer still. He was right, and he kept being right, but his work was full of detail and caveats, identifying areas of ignorance and uncertainty that would constitute a lifetime's work.[8] His work didn't begin with ideology. He started with detail and merely kept following where the data led him.

It's also what Daniel Ellsberg did. He was perhaps predisposed to be sceptical of authority; at the age of fifteen, Ellsberg lost his mother and sister when his father fell asleep while driving. 'I think it did probably leave an impression on me: that someone you loved and respected could fall asleep at the wheel and they needed to be watched. The car crash alerted me to the possibility that the world can change in a flash for the worse.'

It was detail not dogma that turned him against the Vietnam War. Ellsberg had been in favour of the war – even to the degree that he had broken up with his girlfriend who opposed it. After working for Robert McNamara at the Defense Department, Ellsberg insisted on going to Vietnam and seeing for himself, first hand, what the reality of government policy was. On his return, he read the 7,000 pages of the Pentagon Papers and learned in detail of the many times the public had been misled by administrations that pursued the war, promising success to the public even as they knew it could not be won. It was the detail of those documents, coupled with his own experience, that made him risk 115 years in jail for sharing what he'd found out. And it is in the detail of further papers he read concerning the United States nuclear strategy that made him, at the age now of eighty-seven a whistleblower again, revealing government plans for, and true consequences of, a nuclear war.

Detail, evidence, research drove Sheila Bair too when, in 2006, she was appointed to head the Federal Deposit Insurance Corporation – the government insurance company that guarantees some 800,000 American banks. Bair had been worried for some time about the amount of debt that banks were carrying. She had watched the growth of sub-prime mortgages with alarm and now she wanted to find out what was really going on. What she did was simple: she bought a database of sub-prime loans and studied it, something any federal regulator could have done.

'We just couldn't believe what we were seeing. Really steep

payment shock loans and sub-primes . . . Very little income documentation, really high prepayment penalties."[9]

Without the beguiling fog of ideology, and with the gruesome details right in front of her – data about real people buying real loans for real houses – she was in no doubt about what was going on around her. In March 2007, she issued a cease and desist notice to shut down one of the sub-prime offenders, Fremont Investment & Loan.

From an entirely different vantage point, Aaron Krowne gained the same insight. Krowne wasn't a financier, far from it. He was a computer science and maths graduate working as a software developer. Fascinated by economics since the dotcom bubble, he was just a keen, smart observer who liked asking himself questions about what he saw around him.

'I have a strong moral sense from my father and I learned you collect the data, form a hypothesis and try to confirm or disprove the hypothesis. You don't impose your views on *a priori* findings; you present what you find even if it isn't what you want. Because it is important for all our lives and the wellbeing of society. I just felt a need to say something and speak up.'

What gave Krowne something to speak up about was his experience in 2005 when he tried to buy a home.

'I was in a situation where I had to leave the apartment I was in or buy it. The owner wanted to sell, so I looked at the buy-versus-rent fundamentals and made a chart of the price for that kind of unit over ten to twenty years. And it spiked up just like a bubble! Everyone was saying – you have to buy! But I said: Look at the fundamentals. I'd have had to get an exotic loan to come out ahead monthly and I just didn't feel comfortable after such a rapid run-up. So I declined and had to move.'

Towards the end of 2006, Krowne noticed a lot of

sub-prime lenders going under. He thought that the bubble he'd spotted was about to pop so he launched a little website to ask hard questions about what was going on, why, and who was responsible.

'It started as just a single page, with seven or eight lenders on it. I called it Implode-O-Meter for a little humour, the whole thing was so ridiculous. I posted it on some economic blogs I frequented and it caught on. Traffic steadily increased and it got picked up actively by newsletters and a few months later by Bloomberg TV and CNBC. By March 2007, it was pretty well ensconced as the biggest site for the mortgage industry itself, with everyone sending in tips and information.'

The site was fed by the industry it reported on, so Krowne was getting live, first-hand, unmediated information from hundreds of sources across the industry. What his site demonstrated was that the knowledge was out there.

'Ninety-nine per cent of the information that we got – tips from people in the companies – proved correct. People out there knew what was going on in their organisations. We'd get a lot of vociferous denials from management – but the angrier they got about leaks, the more true the leaks turned out to be. There were very few instances where the problem was a disgruntled employee making things up. We did all we could to verify the information, at risk to ourselves, but the information we got was usually very honest. There is a phenomenon where whistleblowing is almost always accurate. Otherwise why take the risk?'

Krowne wasn't a banking insider or a policy wonk or even an economist. He was just a guy on the ground who looked around and asked himself questions about what he heard and saw. Being an outsider may have been an advantage, giving him a less biased perspective. Most Cassandras feel like outsiders, either by accident of birth, or life, or by dint of what they see, which sets them irrevocably apart.

Heather Brooke grew up in two different places – the US and the UK, where she went to an 'absolutely terrible' school in the Wirral. When her parents divorced, she returned to the States, where she trained to be a journalist. It was there, she said, that she developed her expectations of government.

'I picked up a different attitude to the sense of entitlement people have about their leaders,' she told me. 'Americans expect to be able to find out where their taxes are going; they expect to be able to influence their local school boards. It is considered their right to get involved.'

She moved back to the UK in 1997 and found much that she relished.

'I found British people to be less blind to the world. In the US, I find that American people have total ignorance or a lack of curiosity about the world and they also have a lot of ignorance and confidence that what they are doing is right. They haven't considered other options. I have more debates here than in the US. Americans will skirt controversy where UK people are willing to get into an argument; they enjoy playing devil's advocate.'

But what Brooke did not like was the British political system, its tradition of deference and its absence of citizens' rights.

'People here are kept in their place and trying to make a change is considered rude, brash. Lobby journalists in particular have a lot to lose. They're mostly first-class people who've finagled their way into the heart of power. They're made to know that it is a privilege for them to be let in; they have no confidence you can challenge authority and still get stories – any information you're given is a gift, not a statutory right. That's how Britain runs. That leads to a lot of consensus because everyone wants to agree, not be the odd person out causing trouble. I was an outsider anyway and didn't do things that way. It just wasn't the way that I thought about power.'

Brooke began to write her first book, *Your Right to Know*, which looked at what new rights the Freedom of Information Act (2000) might bring when it came into force in 2005. Since it was taking so long to implement, she'd assumed that it would bring massive procedural changes – but when she started making enquiries, it seemed that no one was doing much to prepare. This made her suspicious, so she tested the waters by asking about MPs' expenses.

'I asked about expenses just because, when I'd been a reporter in Washington state in 1992, I had asked for a politician's expenses and that had been a big story there, so I thought I'd do the same here. But there, I'd got the information in a day! Here, the result was totally different. What they published in October 2004 was just one number – they'd just added everything up! It was a meaningless number and you couldn't tell if it was legitimate or if they'd just made it up. So I kept asking and they kept refusing and I thought that was very questionable – so I kept on.'

Brooke was well on her way to breaking one of the major political scandals of her generation but that wasn't her prime motivation. What she really wanted was to change the way that people looked at their government.

'My motivation is a very American one, it's about civic responsibility: this is my government and I have a right to know. But it also went beyond that. I was asking these questions not as a journalist but as a campaigner. I wanted to be able to do the kind of journalism that *didn't* incur favours. I didn't want to have to owe favours and get to see reports because I'd schmoozed people. I think that's quite corrupt.

What I was trying to do was to change the way journalists work here.'

But the *Daily Telegraph* ended up getting the big scoop on MPs' expenses the old-fashioned way: they just wrote a cheque. That meant that they owned the data, but what Brookes had wanted was for it to be in the public domain. For one newspaper to buy the data achieved nothing. She'd wanted all of us, as citizens, to have the right to know where our money was going and why. Brookes was thrilled by the uproar the information produced but profoundly disappointed that her more fundamental campaign – to change the relationship between people and politics – hadn't been understood.

'In the old days, the *Sunday Times* put investment into the Insight team and they were willing to challenge the authorities. And with expenses, I had done that, too. But nobody else had done anything! They put in a few Freedom of Information requests but they never followed them up. They never used the law to change the system. They took "no" for an answer. But they hadn't served the higher purpose of journalism, which is to challenge authority and reveal inconvenient truths.'

Challenging authority in the interests of truth is what all Cassandras do. This makes them awkward, annoying and difficult. Such qualities are often used in attempts to discredit them and to isolate them, but it is those same qualities that drive them to persevere.

'My father was a bizarre character,' Paul Moore recalls. He's careful not to say that he is like his father, but he clearly thinks that they had a lot in common.

'He had a massive sense of integrity and won an open scholarship to Oxford when he was sixteen and a half. He was an extraordinary personality – incredible integrity, thinking out of the box. He was never in the box. I guess there's quite a lot of him in me.'

Even before he was fired, Moore's position at HBOS had been contentious because he insisted on challenging and questioning CEO James Crosby's authority and strategy.

'Crosby fired me because he didn't like me as a person and he didn't like the challenges I raised to his strategies: stack 'em high and sell 'em cheap. He didn't like that I said this carried enormous risk and they needed to reconsider it. He really didn't brook any challenge to his authority and he didn't like the fact that I was always asking, was always going to be asking, difficult questions because that was my job.'

'When my relatives heard I was working at a bank, they thought I was going to be a teller!' Frank Partnoy laughs now at what he considers, nevertheless, to have been a significant advantage when he became a Wall Street investment banker.

'I grew up in Kansas and didn't have the built-in blinders that someone with more pedigree might have. My parents didn't go to Harvard or Yale. And maybe to me the stakes seemed lower. To many people, once you're at Morgan Stanley and have climbed the mountain, the idea of leaving it behind is unthinkable. For me, it wasn't such a big deal.'

In *F.I.A.S.C.O.*, Partnoy unsparingly chronicles his growing enthusiasm and then disgust with the trading world he moved in. Not being from that world helped him to see what kind of world it was – and what the costs of conformity would entail.

'Everyone I knew who had been an investment banker for a few years, including me, was an asshole. The fact that we were the richest assholes in the world didn't change the fact that we were assholes. I had known this deep down since I first began working on Wall Street. Now, for some reason, it bothered me.' Partnoy left and wrote first about his own experiences and then, in *Infectious Greed*, about the rampant explosion not in derivatives but in financial disasters caused by derivatives.

He predicted that there would be more, and this was early, in 2003. (In 2002 he had also tried to explain to Congress that Enron had collapsed not because of a few bad men but because of derivatives, but no one really paid attention then either.) In 2006 he was back in Washington, warning about the structural problems inherent in credit-ratings agencies like Moody's. And then in 2013, with Jesse Eisinger, he wrote an explosive analysis of Wells Fargo.[10] Apart from having a strong stomach for unpopular positions, why could he see what others did not?

'I am the sort of person who wakes up every morning, I wipe the slate clean and everything is up for grabs and I am constantly questioning everything. I think also there's something about my educational experience at Yale Law School. Those three years are so focused on questioning everything; that's what Yale Law School is by design – an institution whose constituents are trying to make the world a better place all the time. It seems to generate a lot of people who don't wear blinders and try to keep them off, almost religiously.'

Partnoy left banking to work in academia, a world, he says, where prestige, intellectual respect, is the equivalent of a bonus. You can't use prestige, he says; you can't spend it. It just makes you happy. But he's not only a professor; as well as academic papers, he also writes popular books about finance and history and he testifies before Congress. He is never exclusively wedded to one mindset, but always travelling between perspectives. It's what political theorist Hannah Arendt called 'thinking without a bannister'.

'Even within my profession, I think people climbing the ladder are constrained. So you have to make sacrifices not to be constrained. For me, freeing myself from those constraints is what gives me happiness and gives me freedom. When you are a teenager, or in college, you're always re-examining your life. But when most people graduate, they stop doing that and I wonder why. Is it that it gets too draining to keep questioning your life?'

This highly unconstrained travel, between points of view, is hard work and it can be risky, not just because it can take you off well-established career paths, but because it provokes questions that, as a Cambridge professor once sternly reminded me, 'one is not invited to ask'. Questions that one is not invited to ask make everyone uncomfortable, not least because they don't easily lend themselves to prepared answers. But in the intersection between perspectives, real insight can be gleaned.

For Deborah Layton, what ultimately turned her into a Cassandra was her sense of history. Layton's own background, she says, pulled her in two directions: she was both a great conformist and also a rebel.

'I'm the youngest of four kids – my siblings are ten, eight, seven years older than me. So as I grew up, I was very used to looking up to others and abiding by their rules. When they'd grown up, I was stuck at home with ancient parents. I started to rebel and get attention by doing silly things – climbing the tallest tree, smoking, not turning up at school. So needing acceptance, that made me a good follower – but being a bit of a rebel saved me.'

Layton was one of the few survivors after the Reverend Jim Jones led 918 of his followers to commit suicide at the Peoples Temple in Guyana. Layton had been an outstanding follower – life at a Yorkshire boarding school, she says, had equipped her to fit in and shut up – but throughout the seven years that she belonged to the Temple, there was never a time she didn't notice when things weren't quite what they purported to be.

'I never spoke up in the Peoples Temple. I was scared to

death all the time. But I watched and I worked hard to look more loyal than anyone else because I figured if he trusted me more than others I'd have more freedom not to be watched so closely. There was always this little voice saying: "Get out! Get out!" And, of course most of the time I didn't get out because I was so scared. But there were other things too. Like one day, I'd been smoking secretly and Jim called me over and I thought he could read my thoughts. But he didn't ask me anything and I realised: he doesn't know everything. I held on to that for many years. And then, after I'd been made financial secretary, I knew how much money we had. So I couldn't understand, when we got to Guyana, why we had to live in such awful poverty. It just didn't make sense.'

Small incongruities kept Layton puzzled and puzzling. But what ultimately got her to escape from Guyana was a sense that she was watching history repeat itself.

'My mother had been born in Germany and my father used to tell us about her life there – the concert musicians who'd played in her home, which had been an elegant Bauhaus building. They'd had an art collection from Hamburg, fabulous paintings and a wonderful Klimt sculpture. We had an etching of Albert Einstein that he'd signed – and all of this made me realise how much my mother missed Germany. You could feel the loss, the loss of a whole life, a whole culture. In our basement there was a suitcase with canned goods – they were emergency rations. So it was already in my mind that bad things could happen and you had to be prepared.'

When Jim Jones started preaching about the enemies that the Temple faced and began to practise mass suicide drills, Layton felt an overwhelming sense of *déjà vu*.

'When Jim talked about apocalyptic events, I think to a lot of people they were just unimaginable, but they sounded real to me because, in our family, apocalyptic events did happen.

Since my childhood I'd known that these things were real. I knew that thousands of people, of families, could die – and it wasn't just some abstract history lesson. It was what happened to people like me. It was exactly what happened to people like me. I knew that, if I didn't get out, I would certainly die.'

Layton did escape and tried to warn government officials of the very real danger that threatened the Jonestown population. None of them grasped the reality or the urgency of what she was saying and action came too late.

'What disturbs me now is that Jonestown isn't even in the history books. No one knows about it any more. But there are still cults. Enron was a cult. America has been cultified, and being an individual and standing proud doesn't happen much. When I got back to California, I went to work for a stock brokerage. And I realised there were men on the trading floor who'd get million-dollar bonuses and they'd take getting yelled at and abused because they had so much at stake – spectacular homes and kids in private schools. And they couldn't stand up and say "no" because they had to keep these jobs.

'All of us cross these lines of not speaking up on our own behalf. It's true of marriages too; people think it could never happen to me. It happens in abusive relationships – you think you love him so you don't speak out. To take true notice will change your life. But it definitely puts you on the outside. It's just the way you see things.'

Although ensconced inside an establishment newspaper – the *Financial Times* – Gillian Tett is, in her own way, an outsider too: a pretty, slight, blonde woman working in structured finance. That she has a gentle lisp and a PhD in anthropology definitely set her apart from mainly male, macho bankers. In 2006, when she and her team became seriously alarmed by what they saw in structured finance, they tried to point out the dangers. It was, she says, a lonely endeavour, too boring and technical, too much nitty-gritty, and bad news to boot. But she credits some of her insight not to her outsider perspective but to her training as a social anthropologist.

'Anthropology is a brilliant background for looking at finance,' she said. 'You're trained to look at how societies or cultures operate holistically, so you look at how all the bits move together. And most people in the City don't do that. They are so specialised, so busy, that they just look at their own little silos. One of the reasons we got into the mess we are in is because everyone failed to ask hard questions: Why are credit cards so cheap? Why can I get such a big mortgage? The silence suited everyone! Who had incentives to see? No one. What was missing in banking was the wider perspective, the context. But that didn't happen in finance. It wasn't in anybody's interest to look further.'

That absence of holistic thought, Tett believes, allows us all to become narrow and deep. Buried deep at the bottom of our riverbeds, we are blind to connections and dependencies. We see only what we know and like and are lulled into a sense of mastery by our isolation from challenge. That feels comfortable, of course, until different perspectives bring unwanted and unwonted challenges.

'One of the most powerful people in the US government at the time stood up on the podium at Davos and waved my article, the article that predicted the problems at Northern Rock, as an example of scaremongering.'[11]

The fragmentation of the banking world, together with its sheer complexity, she argues, encouraged financiers to regard banking as its own world, distant and detached from the rest of society. This became very clear when she was summoned one day to Canary Wharf, which is, she was at pains to point out, an island.

'So I was called to Canary Wharf by this banker who said:

"I don't know why you keep saying CDOs and structured finance are opaque and murky. It's all on Bloomberg terminals; it's right there." But what, I asked him, what about the people who don't have Bloomberg terminals? He looked at me as if to say: there are people out there without Bloomberg terminals – and we're supposed to care about them? He had just retreated to his Bloomberg cyber village.' The chain that linked a synthetic CDO of ABS, say, with a 'real' person was so convoluted it was almost impossible for anybody to fit that into a single cognitive map.[12]

Being able to draw a cognitive map requires travelling well outside our immediate knowledge and safety. It means meeting people not like ourselves, in industries and neighbourhoods far from our own and, when we're there, having the confidence and curiosity to keep asking questions. Robert Shiller, the Yale economist who so famously warned about the property bubble and impending financial collapse, says that his work is deeply informed by his wife, who is not an economist at all, but a clinical psychologist. Drawing our cognitive map calls on a breadth of experience – either from different disciplines or different life experiences.

At first sight, there's nothing remotely unconventional about Roy Spence. He's enjoyed a highly successful career running a Texas advertising agency whose clients have been some of the business greats: Sam Walton of Wal-Mart, Herb Kelleher of Southwest Airlines. He also worked on presidential campaigns with Bill Clinton, with whom he's been friends since the 1970s. Spence's company does what all ad companies do and Roy is like successful executives you meet everywhere: handsome, energetic, polite, punctilious. Just an ad guy, you might think.

But Roy was one of the few people to turn down business with Enron. And he seems to be one of those people who can tap into the *zeitgeist* and see things that others don't. Was it being in Texas, when the rest of the ad world is based in New York, that gave him his particular take on events?

'It helps,' he agreed. 'It helps that if you come home from Manhattan with your head stuffed full of nonsense, everyone here will tell you.'

But much more important, he felt, was his experience growing up with his sister, Susan, who was born with spina bifida.

'When I used to push my sister to school, I thought I was crippled. If you come from a place that is vulnerable to start with, it's out in the open: we have something different going on here. That changes who you are and how you look at things. When you're out there, you see yourself being looked at and you become the watcher, too. You start to see how other people see. And the vulnerability of other people, too.'

He stopped for a second, remembering his sister.

'People thought my sister was different. Well, she was: she could never walk. But people couldn't see beyond that. You saw how blind they were. And it makes you think: if they're missing so much about me and about her, what am I missing about them?'

The image of the young Texan boy pushing his sister to school, scrutinising faces while trying to imagine the thoughts behind them, is striking: simultaneously, he sees through his own eyes, his sister's eyes and the eyes of those watching him. The dialogue he has with himself about those different perspectives is one definition of thought.

What Roy describes is akin to empathy but goes far beyond it. He doesn't see through the eyes of power, but through the eyes of the vulnerable. This perspective is typical of Cassandras and whistleblowers.

'There was one difficult moment when we were in Bristol

and our daughter Natasha was about five or six,' Steve Bolsin recalls. At the time, he was encountering a lot of resistance to the questions he kept asking about the failure rate of Bristol's paediatric cardiac surgery.

'And one night Maggie and I were discussing this – what to do about Bristol? – and Natasha came downstairs in her nightgown holding her teddy and asked what we were arguing about.

'Maggie said: "Too many kids are dying and Dad doesn't know what to do." She just looked at me and said: "You have to stop them killing the children." It was quite obvious to a five-year-old that it was thoroughly reprehensible behaviour. It was so bloody obvious! It is not morally acceptable to experiment on little children. You should be looking at the individuals the system is supposed to serve, instead of seeing the whole thing as just a power game.'

It is in the nature of the power game that it blinds its players to the powerless. But the game changes entirely when that perspective alters.

'I am married to a soldier,' says Cynthia Thomas. 'But you shut your feelings down in the military to survive. They all choose to bury their heads in the sand because it is easier that way. It is drilled into your head that you have to be supportive. And you believe that the military will take care of them if something happens. So you are in this bubble where you can't really see what's going on.'

For years, Thomas says, she lived in that bubble. She took it for granted that the military would look after her husband and their family, that nothing would go wrong, that they were okay. And she was surrounded by other wives and families who did exactly the same thing. But then, as the Iraq War wore on, she started to see events from a very different perspective, the perspective of powerlessness.

'Tim was wounded in 2005 and came back on life support. In 2007, he was redeployed even though he was not supposed to be. He had brain injuries, fractures on his pelvis. His doctor said: he won't be able to save himself if gets shot at. But they didn't care, they redeployed him anyway. And then my stepson called and said he was joining the marines. The bubble popped. I thought – oh my God, after everything that happened, these wars are going to be endless and our kids will be fighting them. That moment, I thought: if I don't do something or try to, this will go on for ever. And I was upset but I finally did something, I opened up to human beings.'

Seeing life through the eyes of young vulnerable men, in a world where most mass media only charts the progress of the powerful, showed Thomas a world of suffering she had been blind to. Thomas' mantra now is that, in war, there are no unwounded soldiers – and she has opened her coffee house to tend to all of the wounded. Anyone can come in, regardless of political opinion. It was her openness to them that allowed her to see how dangerous life was becoming for the soldiers of Fort Hood. The soldiers aren't getting the help they need, she says, because once diagnosed with post-traumatic stress disorder (PTSD) they aren't supposed to be redeployed.

'There's real pressure here not to diagnose it. We have soldiers on fifteen medications and they have an adjustment disorder, a mood disorder, you can call it anything but PTSD because they know if they have PTSD they can get a medical discharge and the government would have to pay them for being disabled and that's a lot of money. The military is a business; if your employee can't do his job, you get rid of him. So you just have this tension building, boys needing help and everyone refusing to see they need help.'[13]

At first, it was hard for Thomas to find a site for her coffee house; just having that physical presence would raise issues that most of the town preferred to overlook. Killeen, close to Fort Hood, is a tightly knit military community; many fear getting in trouble with command; everyone hopes that trouble will pass them by. But Thomas sees what others won't because she looks with the eyes of the most vulnerable.

'Just looking around this community and seeing the cost of the war, it is so hard on a daily basis. Walking around on post and looking at really young faces – eighteen, nineteen – they're babies! Oh my God, they don't grasp the severity of it. Nobody understands. You can't describe it. We have boys coming back so young and their lives are ruined. No one knows the cost of war. They don't want to think about it. They'd have to look in the mirror and say: this is what we did.'

Cassandras all believe that if you can overcome wilful blindness, and force people to see what is happening, that that alone will bring change. They're prepared for conflict because they see it as a necessary step towards change. But, in some cases, they recognise that the facts alone won't prove powerful enough. You need the influence of public opinion.

'To be honest, I am the sort of person if I have something to say I will say it,' says Margaret Haywood. To her, this is a statement of fact that she can do nothing to alter. 'I'm not purposefully hurtful but I am quite an upfront person. Safeguarding vulnerable adults is very important to me, and doing nothing was never really an option. I had to do something about it to put things right.'

A qualified nurse, Haywood first worked for the BBC's *Panorama* when she supplied back-up support to an unqualified carer going undercover to investigate how easy it was to get a job. The experience had given her a taste of how powerful such programmes can be and when *Panorama* asked her to go undercover herself, she had no qualms.

'We were acting on complaints that we'd received after

that first show went out. We knew there was a problem and we knew the only way to deal with it was to go and take a look. I applied for jobs using my own qualifications; it was all above board and the first six hospitals were fine. And then as soon as I stepped on to the ward, I knew there were problems.'

At the Royal Sussex County Hospital in Brighton, Haywood found patients without care plans, with blank medical charts, left in bed most of the day without dignity or attention. One elderly woman waited over two hours for a commode; others were left afraid, ignored and without pain relief. There was, she said, no continuity of care; patients were screaming in pain, left in their own dirt and left alone to die.

'Fluid charts were not maintained so you had no way of knowing what the patients had had to eat or drink. It was absolutely awful. I went to the ward manager and her response to me was: it was more about financial constraints. I understand money but we are talking basic human needs – filling a chart in, giving medication! It doesn't take money, just time management from nurse or carer. That is what spurred me on. The fact as well that the sister on the ward was more concerned about financial implications – that worried me even more.'

Secretly she filmed many of the horrors that she witnessed. She felt she owed it to her patients and their relatives (many of whom had complained to no avail) to let the world see what was going on inside the hospital.

'Sometimes things can take too long,' Haywood explained to me. 'I knew it was controversial what I did but I reported my concerns and I tried to go through all the proper channels and nothing was taken on board. It all took such a long time and those people were at risk of further harm. What happened to me was a drop in the ocean compared to what was happening to the poor patients.'

Her empathy with her patients cost her dear. After a four-year inquiry, the Nursing and Midwifery Council's fitness-to-practise panel struck her off the nursing register. It was their toughest possible sanction, imposed, they said, because she had violated her patients' right to privacy. The public outcry was immediate and vociferous – not least because the BBC had, before the broadcast, gone to great lengths to secure the agreement of every patient's relatives, many of whom were as eager as Haywood to have the hospital's abuse revealed. Over 40,000 people signed petitions supporting her and, five months later, the High Court overturned the judgement on appeal.

'Well, of course I was delighted. Not just with the decision but with all the nurses who'd backed me. Nowadays, when I'm teaching and do a session on whistleblowing, I say: you have to live with your decision. If you do nothing, you might be keeping a vulnerable person at risk of further harm. You have to be able to sleep at night. Imagine that patient is your granddad or grandmother – would you like someone to do something about it? However hard it is, you can't lose empathy for the people around you. You have to see through their eyes. If you're blind to them, what are you doing there? To me, they are what the job is all about.'

After Hurricane Katrina, Maria Garzino felt that same commitment when she saw the people of New Orleans on television. 'The looks on their faces: that hopelessness thing,' Garzino recalled. A member of the Army Corps of Engineers, she had recently come back from Iraq and what she saw on the news coverage seemed horribly familiar.

'You look at the faces of individuals and they know they have a good chance of being dead very soon. And they're pleading for help that should be there. And you realise: it isn't coming. It didn't come. The failure was something beyond an inadequate response. It was a break in trust. When someone doesn't do their best, your trust is gone. How do you restore it? I volunteered to go down to New Orleans in any capacity because I wanted people to understand that the Army Corps cared deeply. All I could guarantee was that I would do my best. That's the only way you can restore trust.' Garzino was experienced in emergency work and she loved it. After begging and conniving to be sent to New Orleans, she was made pump team installation leader, assigned to install new pumps that were supposed to protect the city for the next fifty years.

'Pretty quickly I realised something was wrong. Working with contractors on emergency work is very fast-paced so you need a relationship of trust. The first things that are said are: this is [a] twenty-four-seven project; we are going to help each other, that's the deal. Failure isn't an option. Forthright disclosure is essential; you have to be direct and honest. But I was noticing that contractors didn't want to say anything; they were hiding things and it was hard to get information.'

Garzino kept pressing for the information she needed and hoping for the best. But she didn't understand how the firm MWI had got the contract for pumps that appeared to be ill-suited to their task.

'My problem is: this seems to be good-old-boy network, we tell you what we need to know. This is not a good candidate for partner of the year. Delivery dates were short. We have only a few months to get the pumps in place. NOAA (the National Oceanographic and Atmospheric Association) is predicting three or four storms that year that could hit the area, so we have to get this done. Then the schedules slipped. That was unacceptable.'

As Garzino relayed the detail of her story to me, she struggled to stay calm. Her frustration with a firm that didn't seem to care about deadlines or quality or the life-and-death nature of the job distresses her to this day.

'We started testing and the pumping systems fell apart each time we turned them on. Very concerned is an understatement. When you turn these pumps on, they blow their guts out – in very different ways. The head people would bypass me and call New Orleans and get lesser requirements. So they tried to reduce specification. Well – why even bother testing? It was so ridiculous, they never made it through testing. The final test was laughable – they just did away with testing the pump assembly and said, "Hopefully they will hold together long enough."'

Garzino finally cracked when she heard the people of New Orleans being assured that the pumps would keep them safe. She knew no such guarantee could be made. Being very careful to follow the chain of command fastidiously, in 2006 she began to press for a process of review. When she couldn't get any satisfaction, in 2007 she went to the Office of Special Counsel (the part of the Department of Justice charged with investigating whistleblower complaints by federal employees). The OSC insisted the Inspector General of the Department of Defense investigate her concerns. While that report upheld many of her complaints, it nonetheless concluded there had been no serious violations. But Garzino would not be deterred and submitted highly detailed counterarguments. She was emotional about her campaign, but she knew it was the nitty-gritty engineering detail that proved her argument.

'Two a.m. I'm replying to emails. I have a twelve-foot-tall pile of documents on my desk. If you paid me for the work I did on this,' Garzino recalled ruefully, 'I could retire right now. Every night. Every weekend. If you realise you won't give up, then you must do the best job you can.'

The Inspector General was told to look again, but again came back saying the pumps were safe. In an unprecedented move, the OSC then decided to appoint an independent engineering expert to analyse all the available information. His report entirely vindicated the years of Garzino's effort, finding that the pumps installed in New Orleans did not protect the city adequately and that the Army Corps of Engineers could have saved $430 million in replacement costs by buying proven equipment.

'Everything I said was affirmed; it was the greatest day of my four years in this thing. It absolutely justified the pain.'

Pitting herself against the Army Corps, against a powerful contracting firm, made for a long and frightening battle. Why, I kept wondering, hadn't she given up? A passionate love of engineering (coupled with a hatred for bad engineering) was part of the answer. So too was a determination to finish what she had begun and a serious commitment to public trust. But key to Garzino's determination was her sense that someone had to stand up for the people of New Orleans, who had already been so badly let down.

'There was a day we drove down to where the pumps were going to be installed. I remember there was a lot of debris around, they were changing the road to allow heavy construction traffic to get through. They raised the body of an eight-year-old girl. And no one would look. No one wanted to acknowledge what had just happened. But that is what needs to be at the forefront of your mind! Let's talk about this! But they couldn't even look that in the eye. People don't want to look at a really bad thing. One reason this stuff is allowed to happen is because people don't want to look at it and acknowledge it. There were a whole lot of people there that day but no one talked about it.'

Garzino was highly motivated to act because the human cost of error was visceral; she could not *not* see it. The capacity to see the wider, human cost of blindness is tremendously motivating and comes up in almost all whistleblower testimony. The empathy isn't intellectual or abstract, it's personal. It is far easier, sometimes, to fight on behalf of others than purely for oneself. Nowhere was that motivation more evident or more powerful than in the explosive arrival of #MeToo.

Ashley Judd, the first movie star to go on the record about Harvey Weinstein's sexual harassment, was just twenty-nine years old when the producer tried to persuade her to give him a massage. She must have had her suspicions, as she decided to order cereal for breakfast, on the grounds that it would arrive quickly and she could leave. Weinstein asked if he could give her a massage, a shoulder rub, would she watch him showering?

'I said no, a lot of ways, a lot of times, and he always came back at me with some new ask,' Ms Judd said. 'It was all this bargaining, this coercive bargaining.'[14]

To get out of the room, she told Weinstein that she would have to win an Oscar in one of his movies if he wanted to touch her. But what she did next mattered most: she told her father, then her mother, then her friends what had happened. She learned that Weinstein's behaviour was an open secret. And, when the *New York Times* asked her to go on the record with her account of the meeting, she agreed. What her testimony, and that of others, did was to reveal a pattern of harassment and abuse. The power of the stories was in that pattern: they were too similar to be independent fabrications. However steep the hierarchy of power might have been – and in a casualised industry like Hollywood, it is very steep indeed – networks proved more powerful still. As more and more women spoke up, many said they were motivated by concern for their children, for the less powerful people in their lives, for those without the presence or fame to gain support and protection.

Networks are not only powerful mechanisms for sharing

information; they are also vital ways to protect it. The women of #MeToo protected each other by their sheer number – but there was a historic precedent, when newspapers across the United States chose to publish the *Washington Post*'s exposure of the Pentagon Papers. The challenge then was the same as the challenge now: are you going to come after *all* of us? In their global collaboration, the newspapers behind the Panama Papers and Paradise Papers found the same power.

What Cassandras and whistleblowers show us is that the forces that enable wilful blindness can be overcome. That this can happen feels heroic but is rarely experienced as heroism in real life. Men like Steve Bolsin and Joe Darby, women like Margaret Haywood, Ashley Judd and Gayla Benefield see through the eyes of the powerless and what they see changes who they are and what they feel is right. But this change comes at a high cost, because their full-sightedness explodes the status quo.

Because the confrontations between Cassandras and the rest of the world are so profound, they are reflected back to us in stories; the conflict between a passion for truth and the desire for illusion has been a mainstay of drama since *Oedipus*. Whether it's Hickey, smashing the myths that sustain the bums of Harry Hope's bar in *The Iceman Cometh*, or Gregers Werle determined to excavate family secrets in *The Wild Duck*, or Emilia, revealing to Othello the folly of his jealousy, the bearers of truths have to be punished. All of these dramas of revealed truths – and they're all tragedies – can be at times almost unbearable to watch as one truth explodes multiple illusions. Cassandras may see the truth, but they inspire fury because those truths were so energetically and necessarily hidden, and because their revelations demand change. We side with the truth-teller but, in the comfort of the theatre, we don't have to bear the cost.

In the real world, the cost of being a Cassandra is more

ambiguous. In one study of whistleblowers, 30 per cent of them had been removed from their offices by security men carrying guns – that is how dangerous they were deemed to be. Most weren't surprised to lose their jobs but were disappointed by how hard it was to find employment subsequently. Steve Bolsin moved to Australia after his friends advised him that he was a 'marked man' and would never again find a position within the NHS. Maria Garzino often found herself sitting at her desk with nothing to do. For years, Gayla Benefield had to endure the open hostility of her neighbours, while for Frank Partnoy and Cynthia Thomas perhaps the hardest part is explaining why they've stepped out of their presumed roles. Paul Moore was fired, then castigated by an internal HBOS inquiry before the bank's collapse finally vindicated him. Harry Markopolos was so frightened by Madoff's ring of influential investors that he started carrying an airweight Model 642 Smith & Wesson everywhere he went. After successfully fighting charges that could have meant 115 years in prison, Daniel Ellsberg spent forty-two years trying to get his book on the reality of US planning for nuclear war published. For none of these Cassandras has their clear-sightedness been untrammelled.

After revealing the truth of Abu Ghraib, Joe Darby had kept a low profile, hoping to return to life in his hometown. The army had supported him in this. But once Donald Rumsfeld had named him on television, he had to relocate and assume a new identity. His old friends weren't proud that he had held America to a higher standard; for him to have looked beyond them was just a form of betrayal.

'He was a rat, he was a traitor, basically he was no good,' said Colin Engelbach, commander of the Veterans of Foreign Wars post in Darby's hometown. 'His actions were no good, borderline traitor.'[15]

But not all Cassandras are punished. The women who led #MeToo found themselves celebrated for what became a movement; Susan Fowler was named the *Financial Times*' Person of the Year for her honest revelations of sexual harassment in Silicon Valley. Steve Bolsin, eventually, received an award from the Royal College of Anaesthetists for his stand in Bristol, and Margaret Haywood was triumphantly vindicated by the High Court. In Washington, Harry Markopolos' testimony about the SEC proved a triumphant performance as he proudly demonstrated how much more one small, smart team could achieve than a vast Washington bureaucracy.

> The four of us did our best to do our duty as private citizens and industry experts to stop what we knew to be the most complex and sinister fraud in American history. What troubles us is that hundreds of highly knowledgeable men and women also knew that Bernard Madoff was a fraud and walked away silently, saying nothing and doing nothing. They avoided investing time, energy and money to disclose what they also felt was certain fraud. How can we go forward without assurance that others will not shirk their civic duty?[16]

Though many have had to wait to see their prophecies validated and to earn respect for their foresight, courage and perseverance, they have all found themselves more powerful with the truth than without it. The mother who discovered child abuse in her family found in herself a stronger, more capable parent than she knew she was. The executive who dared to resist the power of silence in a meeting can look back at a problem fixed instead of buried. The bystander who wasn't passive, the soldier who could not obey, all take as their reward a sense that what such individuals gain is the knowledge that, whatever else happens, they can live 'together with themselves', continuing in their minds a dialogue that is neither incriminating or soporific but dynamic and alive.

The greatest shock, for Cassandras and whistleblowers alike, is their revised view of the world. Having started as conformists and loyalists, they emerge from their experience wary of authority and sceptical of much that they see and read and hear. Seeing the truth, and then acting on it, changes their vision of life. This independence of mind can instil a profound sense of isolation. But setting themselves free from consolatory fictions can also reveal new allies and soulmates and inspire a vibrant and purposeful identity.

'I don't regret any of it,' says Joe Darby. 'I made my peace with my decision before I turned the pictures in. I knew that if people found out it was me, I wouldn't be liked. But the only time I have ever regretted it was when I was in Iraq and my family was going through a lot. Other than that, I never doubted that it was the right thing. It forced a big change in my life, but the change has been good and bad. I liked my little quiet town, but now I have a new place, with a new job and new opportunities.'

At Wells Fargo, Rasheeda Kamar, who had written to her CEO to protest against giving customers bank accounts they hadn't asked to pay for, was eventually driven from her job. But for Kamar, this was neither a radical protest nor a subversive act. She spoke up for what she believed to be the fundamental building block of business.

'I'm glad I did it. My heart feels good. Each of us has our own path that we have to walk. How we choose to react shows us who we are. It ultimately comes down to truth – you cannot build anything, a relationship, a company, without it. It's just fundamental: truth.'

At Fort Hood, Cynthia Thomas remembered that when, as

a child, people always asked her what she wanted to be when she grew up, she had never known how to answer.

'But now I know,' she told me. 'I found myself in this cause and I am not the same person any more.'

Such moments of glory are few and far between. But, for all the punishment and pain they sometimes endure, those who struggle to see share a core belief that seeing the truth matters and makes change possible. The most telling quality of Cassandras is that they believe they can have an impact, that nothing will change until the truth is confronted. Nobody I've spoken to has articulated that more clearly than Sherron Watkins when she talked about meeting Coleen Rowley, who revealed the FBI's failure to act on warnings before 11 September, and Cynthia Cooper, who blew the whistle on MCI/WorldCom's accounting fraud. Their actions were difficult and frequently resisted but their perseverance taught a lesson for all time.

'Cynthia Cooper of WorldCom, Coleen Rowley of the FBI and myself were all together because we had been on that cover of *TIME* magazine as Women of the Year. And we were talking about what made us do what we did, and did we have anything important in common. So, we are all three women. We're also first-born. We're also women of faith. We're also breadwinners for our families. But I think the most telling thing about us is that we grew up in tiny towns with less than 10,000 people. And in that small kind of town, there is the sense of: oh goodness, that tree fell down and knocked down that little shed, let's go call the city, or, there's trash in that vacant lot, better pick it up. There's that sense that your actions matter. What you do matters.'

12. See Better

Lear: Kent, on thy life, no more.
Kent: My life I never held but as a pawn
To wage against thine enemies; nor fear to lose it,
Thy safety being the motive.
Lear: Out of my sight!
Kent: See better, Lear . . .

King Lear, William Shakespeare

Meet Jane. The jovial executive vice president seemed to bounce, not walk. Pumped with energy and unmediated warmth, her more reserved colleagues found her a little odd but respected her expertise and experience. An engineer from a family of engineers, her career had taken her all over the world – Latin America, the United States, the Middle East and now London. She'd chosen to join the senior leadership team of a major British company just because she liked the people. The receptionist, the PAs: they all just seemed so nice. She thought it would be great working at a company full of such friendly faces.

At heart, Jane was a happy woman. But she wasn't now. For over a year, one of her senior colleagues had flaunted a series of affairs with female subordinates. It was awkward, at corporate events, when everyone else attended with their spouses. And it felt wrong, unprofessional, sleazy. Jane didn't know how much choice the women had in these relationships but she was wise enough to know that, when they were dumped, everyone in the company noticed. Apparent tolerance for such behaviour nagged at Jane. She didn't want to be associated with it – but nobody else seemed to mind. Suddenly her sense of difference became acute and it was no longer fun. She decided she had no choice but to leave.

When she discussed her decision with me, I think she expected to be congratulated for her moral stand. But I was concerned with how she left: once gone, I wanted to be sure she wouldn't have regrets. So I asked her one question: had she tried everything? Momentarily stumped, she asked: what would that entail? I didn't know – but that was what she needed to consider before leaving.

When I saw Jane next, happiness was back. What had happened? She'd sat down to consider everything she could have done, should have done. Having drawn up her list, she saw some options. She chose one. In a matter of days, everything changed: her colleague was replaced and Jane was promoted to chief operating officer. The people around her saw that problems weren't intractable; they could be faced. What identified Jane as a leader wasn't her new title; it was her action.

Jane had power; she just hadn't known how to use it. Like her colleagues, she'd been tempted by wilful blindness: tempted into conformity by the belief that, since nobody else did anything, there was nothing she could do. In this, she is far from unusual. For all that leadership has become a growth industry, perhaps the single greatest shock about leaders is how constrained they feel: in their thinking, their choices and their actions. Like Jane, they have power – but have lost sight of how to use it.

The greatest risk inherent in wilful blindness is that it is easy – and easiest of all to ignore is its cost. As I write, political parties everywhere are playing catch-up, trying to address issues they so steadfastly ignored for decades: social division, gross inequality, anachronistic bureaucracies in healthcare and education, over-mighty corporations and an under-skilled, underpaid and under-productive workforce, all confronting the remorseless threat of climate change. Why don't we get ahead of these problems? Because it was, is, always so much easier to ignore them.

We aren't sure where to start. But as we've come to understand that the world we inhabit isn't linear, that it is a complex system subject to the big impact of small changes, where to start isn't the issue; *that* we start at all is what matters most. Whether it is Jane recognising that she had influence beyond her own domain, or Cynthia Thomas seizing an opportunity to fight PTSD or Steve Bolsin saving children's lives, the positive lesson of wilful blindness is that knowledge is everywhere: everybody knows when something is wrong, everyone always knows. When just one person dares to speak up, they are never alone and change begins. Where do you start? You start where you are.

The goal of building organisations where everyone can and will speak up – with warnings, great ideas, sharp observations and incisive questions – is what lies behind the effort in institutions worldwide to dismantle their hierarchies and bureaucracies. It is not, as one corporate leader once challenged me, because the management has gone communist. Rather, the transformation companies aspire to acknowledges that their survival depends on liberating the knowledge, insight and imagination that hierarchies and bureaucracies suppress. Creativity in particular is no respecter of status: a good idea is as likely to come from a new recruit as a senior expert. Great ideas and insights can't be predicted or mandated in job descriptions or key performance indicators (KPIs). In a world where little can be foreseen and where plans can become traps, what matters most is to build febrile networks, alert to small signals, sensitive to change. Whether you inhabit a family or a multinational corporation, your health and resilience rely on staying alert, connected and aware. Leaders cannot and do not know enough or see enough. Nobody does. We need everyone.

The aviation industry recognised this decades ago. In 1972, a British European Airlines plane crashed three minutes after taking off, killing all 118 people on board. Subsequent investigations revealed classic wilful blindness: the crash had been caused by a collection of small faults and problems that many people had known about. The failure to speak up, ask difficult questions or share concerns had proved lethal. But what happened next was novel: instead of searching for a scapegoat to be publicly shamed and fired, the Civil Aviation Authority pioneered a new approach. If so many people could have prevented the crash, then what was needed was an environment in which not a few people but everyone would feel it was safe and necessary to say what was on their mind.

In 1976, the CAA started putting in place rules and processes that made it easy to speak up, ask questions, sound the alarm. Secrecy was replaced by openness. Mistakes, where they occurred, were examined and shared as a form of learning. A new test was applied to them: if the same mistake could have been made by anyone, then whoever erred could not be blamed or punished. In this way, errors and near-misses became opportunities not for recrimination but for the continuous improvement of design and processes.

Aviation is one of the most competitive and complex industries in the world, with hundreds of third-party partners and razor-thin margins. Yet those in the industry appreciated that the one area in which they could not compete was safety; when one plane crashed, everyone suffered. So everyone had to be part of the solution and the airlines agreed to share any and all information they gathered that pertained to safety. They called this new way of working 'just culture' and it transformed one of the least intuitive forms of transportation into the safest.

'If you haven't got a concept of just culture,' the CAA's Ben Alcott told me, 'then why would anyone openly report to you that they've made a mistake or that they've noticed a problem, if they feel that that might be held against them unfairly?'

By 1980, some 3,000 concerns were raised; in 2015, that number reached 14,000. The message got through: if something seems amiss, you have a responsibility to raise your concern. In some ways, this was a version of the Japanese practice of encouraging any worker on an assembly line to stop the line if they saw a fault. Both systems acknowledge that steep hierarchies encourage the delegation of responsibility, whereas for true safety what's needed is for anyone and everyone to say what they see. The just culture, which has now been written into EU legislation, isn't aimed at specialists; it is fundamentally collective, requiring that everyone – from a cleaner to a board member – report any concern they have. Implicit in that is the recognition that we each have a responsibility to keep our eyes open and to tell others what we see.

Just culture has begun to have a significant influence on global healthcare, where medical errors represent as big a problem as malaria.[1] In the United States, where 'deny and defend' had long been the standard response to any mistake, many healthcare systems have begun to experiment with greater openness and transparency. One of the new leaders of the patient safety movement is David Ring, the same physician who was so candid about the blinding impact of money. Ring first drew public attention to himself when, at Massachusetts General Hospital, he performed the wrong operation on a patient's hand. Realising the error as he wrote up his notes, he said, the floor seemed to disappear beneath his feet. But in that moment he made the decision not to defend or deny, not to hide his error but to uncover it. With painstaking research, he explored all the small slips that had led up to his major mistake. The patient had been moved to a different operating theatre at the last minute; the team was stressed as operations were running behind schedule; because the patient was Caribbean and didn't speak English, Ring spoke to her in Spanish – which a nurse interpreted as a time-out, so no formal check of the surgical site occurred. All small slips with no ill intent. Ring researched these because he wanted to understand how he'd gone so wrong. But then he went further still: at some risk to his own reputation, he published his findings in the *New England Journal of Medicine.* Why? He didn't want patients or doctors to experience the suffering he and his patient had endured. The way to prevent mistakes is to talk about them. Today, Massachusetts General Hospital and Johns Hopkins Hospital have even come together to compare the mistakes each has made, in the belief that learning shared is learning accelerated.

Some of this thinking is starting to take root in the UK, although the acute blame culture of the British media, together with deep defensiveness on the part of physicians, still makes it hard for the NHS to be as open to learning from mistakes as most of its practitioners would like. Robert Francis' creation of NHS guardians, while it is still experiencing significant teething problems, nevertheless has provoked some local successes.

'I think this role works well because it is a relatively

tangible person who can go out face to face to speak to staff, to see where problems are and report back to board,' Helene Donnelly told me. 'Problems don't get lost in translation and we've promoted it as an additional voice for front line, and all levels, to have concerns heard and act as an early warning system before things get worse.'

As a nurse at Mid Staffordshire, Donnelly had tried to raise concerns but had been steadfastly ignored, bullied and intimidated. In despair, she had left that hospital and moved to North Staffordshire where she now has a role reporting directly to the CEO. While nobody in the NHS will ever say they've solved every issue, Donnelly does feel that she's been able to demonstrate that identifying problems is how they get fixed.

'One particular shift overnight, a nurse was basically confronted with several palliative care patients and several routine patients needing insulin or intravenous antibiotics. There was a huge dilemma: how do you provide quality care to these patients, to everybody? It's so much bigger than just the patient – it's the family as well, and the nurse really felt at breaking point because she couldn't deliver the quality of care she wanted to deliver. She was so upset and disheartened that she emailed myself and the Chief Exec at 2 a.m. to explain. And by 6 a.m. the Saturday morning, the Chief Exec had responded, spoken to me and others, and we were able to make sure that that night, for the equivalent shift, more staff would be on duty and that was then going to be rolled out to make sure that it continued. It was relatively simple to resolve but it's something staff had been flagging for some time through the usual routes and they felt like nobody had listened. But I'd been promoting the fact the Chief Exec wants to hear, and you can email him directly. That empowered her to feel able to do that at two in the morning.'

Donnelly's job isn't just to fix the problems that rise to the surface; she also has to tell the story of how they come to be resolved. If people can't see that the system is safe and that it works, nobody will use it.

Failure can be a great teacher. Donnelly still vividly recalls the horrors she witnessed at Mid Staffordshire and is driven by a passion to prove that those need never be repeated. In the British civil service, the recognition that badly flawed decision-making led to the Iraq War has led to the creation of what is known as the Chilcot Checklist, named after the chairman of the inquiry into the conflict.[2]

'The idea is to make it easier to ask challenging questions,' one civil servant told me. 'To make it acceptable to ask loads of questions. Do our resources match our ambition? Do you have an exit strategy? There needs to be some preparation for worst-case scenarios even if we think they're unlikely – it makes us have to think about that. I think it also helps us move beyond a winner-takes-all mindset to specific problems that can be addressed pragmatically instead of ideologically.

'There's almost a natural cycle of moving from irrational exuberance to overcompensation. Chilcot falls on fertile ground because people remember what it came from. We have challenges in making people see things realistically and to use Chilcot, but I don't know whether its heritage means we only use it one way – against intervention – instead of both ways: to explore all the possibilities. We are still refining it, every time we use it.'

Checklists were developed in healthcare with the specific aim of disrupting hierarchy, to make it easy, even mandatory, for hard questions to be asked by even the most junior people. That should – or could – pertain as powerfully in boardrooms and government offices as in operating theatres and hospitals.

'We need to break down the hierarchy that's previously

existed, particularly in relation to raising concerns,' Donnelly insisted, 'because this is everybody's responsibility, everybody's duty, and change will only happen if everybody sees everybody being open about it and sees parity and equality in terms of response and what happens. It should be no longer that if you're a domestic or a porter or a student or a junior member of staff you won't be listened to because I'm only this or that. If we build this into the culture – making openness business as usual – people shouldn't flinch. They should get a pat on the back and support. That's the kind of response we need to have, but it will take time.'

The succession of scandals – not just in the NHS but in government and in corporations large and small – is gradually shifting how some managements come to see the whistleblowers they once despised. Executives at Tesco and leaders in the British Army tell me that there is a newfound appreciation of truth-tellers, a recognition that those who voice concerns are taking a risk that speaks more of loyalty than troublemaking. The change is long overdue and far from pervasive, even in those organisations. But the recognition that collective intelligence beats heroic, solo leadership could mark the beginning of a sea change.

Creating an environment in which everyone can and will raise issues that matter takes time; it also takes training. The best curriculum I've encountered, designed to teach people how to consider the issue or information they need to share, is Giving Voice to Values (GVV). Developed by Mary Gentile at the Aspen Institute, it started from a recognition that teaching ethics or philosophy, while enjoyable, didn't have a noticeable impact on behaviour. What was needed, Gentile argued, wasn't analysis – but action. What are the best ways to speak up and to effect change?

In essence, GVV provides a framework with which to

approach values conflicts. It walks participants through a number of steps in which they recall instances where they did, successfully, articulate their values; it encourages them to analyse how they did that and to think about how they might do so again. Central to the programme is pre-scripting and rehearsal: planning how to approach and define the problem and rehearsing (with peers or friends) how the conversation might go. How might the story end if you stay silent? How might it end if you don't? What do the key people concerned need to know – and how might they best be disposed to pay attention? Gentile put the entire programme online – she wants it to be used – and spends her time teaching her curriculum around the world, mostly to mid-level managers working in areas related to ethics and compliance. Unsurprisingly, for someone so firmly committed to keeping her eyes open, she has learned as much as she has taught.

'I was asked to do some work with Unilever in Nigeria. As usual, I was going to be working with middle managers, Change Champions. We were going to train the trainers and then they'd deliver to the rest of organisation. But then they suggested something different: why not work with the senior leaders too?

'So we put all middle managers at their own tables, figuring out how to raise an issue. And we put all the senior leaders at their own tables but asked them a different question: how could someone bring this issue to you in a way that you could respond to appropriately? We ended up with "the GVV deal", a joint commitment: you have to raise the issue in a way that's prepared and thoughtful – and leaders have to listen in a way that's open and thoughtful. Just speaking up isn't enough.'

Leaders have powerful motive to listen early and often – but are too often afraid of what they might hear. Just being called a leader can be intimidating and many of those I've worked with feel it implies omniscience – so they fear asking questions, asking for advice, asking for help. It is a profound, sometimes fatal, misconception of the role because many of their most damaging and expensive fiascos develop from the small problems that, caught early, might have redeemed reputation and costs. The general counsel of one chemical business estimated that fully 70 per cent of litigation and damages costs derived from problems that had started as minor issues. The cost had run into millions – and that was before taking reputational damage and opportunity cost into account.

It's telling that Gentile does her work in groups. When you see something that feels wrong, reaching out to other people is essential. You might have misunderstood, you could have incomplete information. Just because what you see isn't what others see doesn't guarantee you're right, so having trusted colleagues is essential. The new technologies that make it easier to build these networks of trust are powerful; #MeToo would never have gained such momentum, across industries, if individuals had not had safe, secure ways to communicate, compare notes, identify patterns. The fight for equal pay at the BBC would not have made such progress but for the men and women who volunteered to share their salary details. No single employee at Google, concerned about the ethical implication of the company's intention to provide surveillance technology to the US Department of Defense, could have changed the company's policy. Even the resignation of a few employees did not achieve that. Only when they organised across the company and the industry did they have voice and power.[3] Networks reach across silos, smashing hierarchies and stereotypes. They cannot guarantee allies, but they make it far easier to find them and to build the collective intelligence that shifts power structures. Wilful blindness is entrenched through isolation – but starts to vanish when you are no longer alone.

This can create richer dialogue than the old 'don't bring me problems, bring me solutions' mantra that silences most people. But the conversations that ensue won't necessarily be easy, because solutions are rarely obvious or simple. The search for answers always involves argument, debate, exploration. We dodge this because most people fear and avoid conflict. It's rare to grow up in families where it's easy – even normal – to argue over ideas; few of us grow up learning how to manage an argument and we rarely experience winning one. And in most families and societies, argument is interpreted as aggressive, damaging, rude. Yet argument is essential because conflict is how we (as individuals and as organisations) think. It is how weak ideas are made strong and blind spots revealed. We desperately need people who are different from us, who will ask questions and look for what we are missing. In this, there is no finer model than the collaboration between Alice Stewart and the statistician George Kneale.

'I couldn't have done anything without George,' Alice Stewart told her biographer, Gayle Greene. 'I like to think he's the power engine of our ship and that I occasionally flick the steering wheel.'[4]

Fellow scientists described Kneale's work as outstanding, elegant and exquisite, but what's most interesting is the way that Kneale himself thought about his job.

'It's my job to prove that Dr Stewart's theories are wrong. I am, in effect, trying to disprove her. Hence the strength of our long association.'[5]

Kneale was entirely different from Stewart. Stewart was outgoing, highly sociable; everyone who knew her talked of what great company she was. Kneale, by contrast, didn't like going out much and seems to have preferred numbers to people. But in that diversity lay the value of their partnership. In his seeking for *dis*confirmation, Stewart knew that Kneale protected her from blindness in her own thinking – and she was confident enough to value his challenge. They were thinking partners, not echo chambers. What both understood was that the risk of their hypothesis failing was outweighed by the danger of being blind. To paraphrase Voltaire, they understood (in ways that Alan Greenspan and the Rotherham councillors could not) that, while doubt isn't a very pleasant condition, certainty is absurd. How many of us have – or dare to have – such stringent collaborators?

'I wish someone had challenged me,' John Browne wrote when reviewing his mercurial career running BP. 'I wish someone had challenged me and been brave enough to say: "We need to ask more disagreeable questions."' Browne could have sought out more serious challenge, and he should have. That he did not says much about him and the organisation that Tony Hayward inherited.

'Once you are in a leadership position, no one will ever give you the inner circle you need,' says Saj-nicole Joni. 'You have to go out and find it.' Joni is a professional 'third opinion', a thinking partner who works with leaders and who has no agenda.

'When you are at the top of an organisation, everyone has an agenda,' she says. 'They will either be pushing forward their agenda to please you, or their own agenda to enhance themselves. So you need a third opinion which comes from someone who has nothing but your best interests, the company's best interests, at heart. That person is a thinking partner.'

What Joni is describing is that dialogue with oneself that Arendt calls thinking – except she's suggesting it doesn't have to be done alone. It is the very best leaders, she says, who recognise that they need this dialogue and who reach out and find the people with whom they can have it.

Most leaders in big positions live in a world where every

major decision is never really clearly right or wrong. And they realise that, at the level they're playing, if they don't get countervailing voices, they are personally at risk of not meeting their obligations.'

Talking to her, it's clear why Joni is a third opinion. She works hard at thinking. She comes, she says, from a family where what she was told as a child didn't fully explain what she saw. That left her with a lifelong drive to search for the full story. Joni believes that, in order not to be blind, two things are critical: unvarnished truth and unfettered exploration. One alone won't do. What thinking partners provide, and monitor, is dissonance. They don't look to quell it; rather they look to ensure that there is appropriate dissonance around critical issues.

'It's about having the right fight. Dissonance has value but it has to be practical. Leaders have to ask: what issues are so critical that we create structured dissonance around them? Using your riverbed analogy: what dissonance and third opinions offer is a tributary that takes you somewhere else, gives you a different perspective. It stops you sinking into a place where you cannot see what's happening around you.'

So-called leaders are often burdened by an expectation of omniscience, which only they can cast off. What is invisible to them may be obvious to others – but only insofar as the others are unlike them, with different biases, experiences and mental models. That's why diversity matters so much: not (as is still commonly assumed) in the interests of political correctness, but in the interest of vigorous debate and divergent thinking. If the people around you look like you, sound like you and always agree with you, then however good they are, you have a weak team that will miss all the things that you don't want to see either. On the other hand, when the people around your table come from different places – mentally, socially, intellectually – they are more likely to ask the questions which reveal something previously invisible.

In the light of so many institutional failures, it's been easy to insist that organisations just try to hire people with high standards, a deep sense of morality, ethics and integrity. That was what David Beim concluded when he investigated the failings at the Federal Bank of New York and what Dinah Rose QC suggested when reviewing the BBC in the light of the Jimmy Savile scandal. But where are all these uniquely moral people supposed to come from? Recommendations such as these are naive and wilfully blind to the psychological and physiological pressures that routinely render good, smart people oblivious to the wrongs around them.

More vigorous debate emerges from thinking partners, like Joni, or from reverse mentoring: a relationship in which junior employees are explicitly given permission to tell their bosses what is happening in their organisations, how decisions or policies are received, how the leadership is perceived. Employment lawyers tell me that this is almost the only antidote they've seen working against sexual harassment. Where I've seen this deployed in several organisations, it has been most often aimed at eliminating racial and ethnic bias and the isolation of power. That mentor and mentee are different – in age, seniority, gender, ethnicity, background – is valuable. But it takes both strong speech and hard listening to work. The formal agreement to work together – rather like Gentile's 'GVV deal' – requires that neither party shirk their commitment to keep their eyes, and ears, open and keep asking hard questions. Alternative perspectives always exist. Great questions unlock them. Where are the alternatives? Have you tried everything? Who else shares your concerns?

Constructive conflict of this kind changes what we see and how we respond. When it is normalised, the burden of challenge shouldn't fall on a few individuals but be shared across the organisation. Traditionally, however, the job of shining light on problems has been outsourced to auditors, in the hope that outsiders might see what insiders are blind to. But there is a special problem with audits, recognised as (unsurprisingly) the Auditor Problem. Every failed organisation, from the Greek government to Carillion, has been audited – and given a clean bill of health. It's well understood that auditors face two problems: they become too close to their clients to maintain objectivity, and the rest of their firm's financial fortunes depend upon keeping those clients happy enough that they will buy other, more profitable services. These close dependencies grow over time, which is why, in the UK, firms now have to rotate auditors after twenty years.[6] It doesn't appear that this new rule has made much difference. Having worked with all four of the world's leading accounting firms, I have seen none acknowledge their failure to solve this problem. They regard rotation as a nuisance, not a change – and certainly not as a safeguard. Indeed, I'm routinely told that their brands command widespread public trust and confidence, a faith that oozes wilful blindness in the absurd belief that the public has failed to notice that the fingerprints of these same firms are found at every crime scene.

To continue with audit as it is currently practised would be a form of wilful blindness in itself. Since audit is essentially a public function, designed to provide shareholders, customers, partners, employees and society at large with confidence, it might prove safer for it to become a service offered only by non-profit organisations, separate and disassociated from consulting and other practices. Others have suggested that regulators, not clients, select auditors. All of these tame proposals reflect the urgent need for organisations to be trustworthy and seen as legitimate, subjected to levels of scrutiny and critical thinking at which current audit organisations keep failing.

One proposal to fix audit is insurance: if auditors had to insure against the cost of their failure, either they would be more vigilant or the consequences would be less draconian. The essence of the proposal is resignation: a recognition that, at some point, audit will always fail. But insurance could be an interesting tool for highlighting wilful blindness. Incensed by the reckless idiocy that led to the Grenfell Tower tragedy, one group of insurance leaders recently suggested withholding insurance from buildings with inadequate sprinklers and fire safety systems. They did so in despair at the unwillingness of institutions to hold themselves to higher standards. Where insurance is withheld, failure is recognised as likely.

But insurance can't repair all forms of damage. Corporate governance in general needs a profound reappraisal; the governing boards of organisations need now to acknowledge their routine structural failures. Tesco, BHS, Volkswagen, GM, Mirror Group Newspapers, Kensington and Chelsea council, Rotherham council, the BBC, Facebook, Virgin East Coast rail, South Yorkshire Police, Uber, the Weinstein companies, Lloyds Banking Group, Carillion: these and many more had boards or trustees who failed to do their jobs. Many believed that they had to support their CEO, regardless of circumstances. However grand their membership, however élite the appointees and however expert the assembled knowledge, ultimately none of them protected stakeholders from disaster. That the boards of private companies and public organisations are filled with like-minded individuals, often selected because they can be relied upon to agree with one another, explains many institutional failures we have seen in the last twenty years. Instead of selecting the great, the good and the predictably agreeable, these bodies need to seek out the difficult and the prickly and to hold them collectively, personally and financially accountable. They also need training and practice in structuring real debate, in which hard questions are a measure of excellence, not dissidence. Board members who go for years without making a single comment shouldn't collect their pay. Apologies and offers to 'take the blame' by august chairmen who suffer nothing by their words are out of all proportion to the social harm such failed boards have perpetrated. Fostering diverse groups that can, and do, look for and debate problems is the job of governance bodies. In this issue, nothing less than the legitimacy of business is at stake.

The same problem lies at the heart of government. Where it used to be standard practice that quangos such as the British Council, Higher Education Funding Council or the Arts Council would operate independent of government control, the last decade has seen a largely invisible shift to government appointees. Whitehall routinely now refuses to approve the appointment of individuals whom the party in power regards as unfriendly – even though the premise of the structure is that it should ensure independence, diversity, debate.

While being prepared to ask hard questions doesn't guarantee enlightenment, silence always protects the status quo. The French sociologist Serge Moscovici found that just the existence of a minority opinion can have a huge impact on the direction discussions take. Subsequent researchers have found that, just knowing that there is a dissenting voice is enough to induce different cognitive processes that yield better judgements.[7] Each one of us needs to develop the courage and the ability to see these situations for what they are, to intervene while they are still easy to stop. Questions are often the gentle provocation to exploration and debate. How could we make this product safer? How do the weakest among us experience this decision? One of the best questions

I've ever encountered: If our assumptions were wrong, what might we expect to see?

That was the question Herb Meyer asked himself when, in the early 1980s, he began to intuit the collapse of the Soviet Union. Meyer's a contentious figure, then and now. Deceptively understated, he describes himself as running a small independent publishing business in Washington state. What that doesn't tell you is that, under Reagan, he served as special assistant to the director of Central Intelligence, and vice chairman of the CIA's National Intelligence Council. In that capacity, he managed the production of the US National Intelligence Estimates – which meant that, in the face of derision from the political and intelligence communities, he could test his hypothesis that the USSR was on the verge of collapse.

'Everyone was telling us the Soviet Union was fine. Our spies would bring us information about how many bombs, how many tanks. They would bring us all the data they'd always brought us. So we kept thinking what we'd always been thinking. Ask the same questions of the same people, of course you're going to get the same answers.

'So I decided to do something different. I made a list of everything I might expect to find if my hypothesis was right. If the Soviet economy was collapsing, what would you see? If it *wasn't* collapsing, what would you see? And then – this is the critical part – I made sure all the information that those questions elicited went to one guy. Just one guy. Then, if nothing comes in, you have your answer. And it doesn't get lost in all the noise.'

Meyer was doing what George Kneale did: looking for disconfirmation. One of the pieces of information that came in, Meyer told me, was news that a weekly meat train had been hijacked and all the meat stolen. The army had come out – but then the politburo had told the army to back off but tell no one. Let the people have the meat.

'Well that's not what happens when everything in the economy's just fine, is it? What's important is that, without the hypothesis, that piece of information would never *ever* have been picked up. That's what didn't happen on 9/11: we weren't looking for what we couldn't see.'

Meyer was accumulating weak signals to see if they added up to a meaningful trend. He'd had a hunch, as we all do; he might have been wrong. But, instead of giving it too much credibility, or too little, he tested it. All decisions are hypotheses and can be tested. That's what good questions do. The same kind of questioning should have been applied in Hillsborough, where the absence of disconfirming data should have rung alarm bells. The same could be said of Volkswagen: just how *was* the car company able to achieve such staggering low emissions? Someone could have, should have, asked.

Writing about groupthink, Irving Janis recommended institutionalising dissent. He used the example of the Vatican, which used to appoint a Devil's Advocate to ask hard questions during the process of canonisation. When Janis was writing, there was evidence that the role had decayed into a formality, but at least it still existed. Today, it's sad (but perhaps telling) that the post has been abolished. We would do well to resurrect it within our organisations as a means of protecting dissent and encouraging argument. Appointing one person to be the devil's advocate provides them with an unforgettable experience in critical thinking and gives permission, even reward, for awkward and difficult questions. Of course, the role has to be rotated, otherwise this voice too can get tuned out. Big strategic questions can be addressed through formal, structured exploration: what information would materially change our decision? What are the reasons not to do this?

Who benefits most – and who is harmed? Business boards, no less than government, could do with some checklist to spur serious thinking.

Nevertheless, most organisations adopt such mechanisms only when they are in trouble. But a just culture is about the routine dissemination of honest insight and information. For that, people at work need to feel safe – and mostly they don't. However hard I used to tell people in my company that I would never shoot the messenger, few believed me – not least because this was not what they'd experienced elsewhere. Generations have now grown up through education systems that define as excellent those students who know the one correct answer; schools more often produce pleasers than dissidents. Economic conditions have exacerbated the trend: anyone with a large mortgage or significant student debt is unlikely to risk voicing inconvenient truths or awkward questions. Nobody on a zero-hours contract feels safe enough, or cares enough, to draw attention to risks or problems. One of the less visible costs of persistent economic instability and inequality may be the most compliant, silent workforce in history. Where people work in fear, their leaders may be confident that they will never be told what is really going on inside their organisations.

What we know from the abundant examples of wilful blindness is that they are supported by division: by organisational silos, by hierarchies, by competition. These all divide and separate people from themselves and from each other. Creating environments of safety – not just psychological but social and economic safety too – is crucial to freeing the information, ideas and insights that want to be let loose. The deliberate fostering of social capital – the norms of generosity, reciprocity and trust that are the hallmarks of resilient communities – is a fundamental part of healthy organisations.

This means that people at work need to have time to spend together, to get to know one another as human beings – not just as widgets in a machine. When my colleagues are competitors, I will trust them with nothing. But when my colleague is a neighbour, I am more likely to ask: do you see what I see? Does it worry you too? What do you think? That aggregation of insight and awareness is what makes networks so powerful.

There is no guarantee of agreement. But we need, as Mary Gentile found, to develop in ourselves both the capacity to articulate our concerns – and to hear those raised by others. It has become fashionable of late to insist that this is a fruitless exercise, that we are all too biased, too lazy, too irrational to learn from each other. This is a self-fulfilling argument, for the less effort we expend, the less reward we are bound to receive. It's the easiest thing in the world to hide behind our own righteousness, amplified by social media, tricked into believing that posting on Facebook or Twitter is a conversation. It is, of course, nothing of the kind. Similarly, leaning on just one discipline, ideology or frame of reference means we are bound to miss much of what is important. This became painfully clear in the course of the EU referendum, all of which was framed as a simplistically economic decision. But if balance sheets are poor at reflecting the reality of companies, they are even less adequate in describing society. The failure of all political parties to see beyond the most primitive economics to the rich mix of social, cultural and historic issues at the heart of the debate left the electorate in the dark.

True dialogue, of the kind on which democracy depends, requires more: more skill, broader disciplines, more courage, richer perspectives and ample patience. If we want to say something in a way that others will hear, we have to think about *them*, about *their* values and *their* frames of reference – not just about ourselves. That means knowing people not like ourselves. Bursting our own bubbles to see what may make us uncomfortable, disoriented and uncertain. The sense of confusion, of being lost, is the evidence that you are learning something new. It's what inventors, entrepreneurs, Cassandras and whistleblowers experience: that they are exploring new territory and may need time to get their bearings. Daring to disagree and listen, to explore without preconception: this is how individuals, groups and organisations think. It can be scratchy and contentious, as all great collaboration is. But nothing less than the fate of democracy depends upon our resolve and skill in doing that work.

This is why diversity remains such a crucial concern. It isn't a matter of political correctness or simply of social justice. Making sound, wilfully sighted decisions requires multiple perspectives from a diverse range of human experience. We know that groups of people are better problem-solvers than individuals – but this is only true when the individuals bring different insights, disciplines, thinking styles and first-hand knowledge. This makes debate harder, of course. It makes blindness harder too. Especially where long-term decisions are being made, including those who won't be dead or retired before the full impact of choices is felt, seems obvious but is rare. But it is also powerful. Reflecting on the success of Citizens' Assemblies in Ireland, one citizen participant extolled at length the value of working alongside young people: suddenly, he told me, he recognised that for a democracy to work, he had to think beyond himself and his generation to the generations to come that would inhabit the world he voted for.

As I go around the world talking about wilful blindness, every country I visit recognises the phenomenon and believes that their culture is uniquely susceptible to it. In the former

Eastern bloc states, it's blamed on Soviet rule, where turning a blind eye could save your life. In Asia, the need to save face is seen as a major contributor. Americans understand that their polarised conformity makes wilful blindness more likely. The British blame the class system and British reserve. Having found nowhere that claims to be immune, I've concluded that wilful blindness is universal, that there is no society so alert, confident or open to debate as to eliminate it.

What I do believe is that certain conditions exacerbate blindness. Ideologies, narrow mental models that insist on simple solutions – whether they be markets, nationalisation or cost-cutting – discourage curiosity, imagination and creativity. Excessive focus on pay will generate perverse perspectives and behaviours. Steep hierarchies, deep inequalities, ornate bureaucracies are fertile environments in which wilful blindness clearly flourishes. Targets, KPIs, the whole managerial toolkit aimed at managing people like machines succeeds in making them as unthinking as machines. And yet, in workshops, in any industry, when I ask participants to describe the areas in which they think they or their organisations might be wilfully blind, it takes only minutes for the conversation to begin. Everyone knows. Everyone always knows. Removing the impediments to those dialogues is an essential first step.

Combating wilful blindness also requires that minds are rested, alert and focused enough to be able to function. Recent attention to the serious mental-health issues provoked by exhaustion, multitasking, long hours and stress is encouraging, insofar as it has made the problem visible. A few mindfulness or yoga sessions, however, aren't all that's needed to fix these problems. If we want healthy strong minds for vigorous productive debate, individuals and organisations alike have to celebrate the enormous capacity of the human mind by creating the physical conditions it needs to flourish.

I do not believe that new technology will eradicate wilful blindness, though it could help. Big data and data analytics can extract patterns to encourage debate – correlations are not always but can be meaningful signposts. But somebody needs to seek those patterns, ask the right questions and be prepared to explore, with rigour, what they mean. I am more concerned that artificial intelligence can exacerbate our blindness by scaling and automating our biases. We've seen this already, in cases where algorithms rejected job applicants with any history of mental illness, a form of discrimination specifically illegal if done by a person.[8] In other cases, ethnic minorities may specifically be judged differently because they don't conform to what some programmer has defined as a norm.[9] And hubristic attempts to predict abuse *before* a child is born have foundered on datasets that are themselves inadequate, incomplete and biased. As UCLA law professor Gary Blasi concluded, 'Algorithms are intrinsically stupid. You can't build any algorithm that can handle as many variables, and levels of nuance and complexity as human beings present.'[10]

But algorithms are protected as trade secrets and their authors may feel that they can't, or don't want, to explain how they work. (It's for this reason that the EU General Data Protection Regulation specifically protects workers from being subject to decisions 'based solely on automated processing'.) The arrogance with which Silicon Valley encourages consumers not to ask questions, to trust what they won't explain, is discouraging. Any new technology that consistently rejects challenge invites wilful blindness; that any industry does so should be a first warning sign. The consolatory fiction of learned helplessness – the supine belief that there's nothing we can do – is always dangerous. And machines change how we think, making it possible for us to become more blind still.

The better antidote is to remember and to celebrate all of the dissenters, debaters, challengers, guardians, Cassandras and whistleblowers who have refused such consolation, determined instead to open their own eyes and ours. We routinely celebrate as heroes those who have displayed physical courage in war; it is high time we put up monuments to those who have displayed moral courage, the people who ask hard questions and those strong enough to hear them. Where is the statue to Hugh Thompson who intervened in the My Lai massacre? To Joe Darby, Steve Bolsin, Daniel Ellsberg? Their heroic dissent sets a standard for critical thinking that is more inspiring than scepticism, and richer than doubt. Generations of lawyers had their worldview informed by Atticus Finch when they read *To Kill a Mockingbird*; generations of doctors will go into medicine inspired by the work of Paul Farmer, journalists by *All the President's Men* and around the world new voices entered politics because of Nelson Mandela. We need to celebrate the Darbys, Benefields, Bolsins, Ellsbergs and Grahams, the ordinary people who would not be blind and would not let us remain blind either. The most important thing to remember about Cassandras and whistleblowers is that they are ordinary people. They show us our own capacity to see and to act on what we see.

And we need them now. As the steep social hierarchy of inequality further separates those with power from those without, the threat of wilful blindness grows. Climate change, political volatility, an enfeebled media market, the sheer complexity of life all encourage resignation, abdication, the learned helplessness of fantasy, distraction and fatigue. It's so much easier not to ask how clothes can be so cheap, not to think about the environmental impact of our choices, not to see how much we lose when we back off, pipe down and give in to people, parties and politics we don't really understand.

When we are wilfully blind, there is information we could know, and should know, but don't know because it makes us feel better not to know. Neuroscience shows us how some of this occurs, offering a tangible reality to experiences that, heretofore, felt entirely abstract. But in the course of writing this book, I've started to wonder how far the science encourages us to see our brains as separate entities, grand machines of which we are the passive agents. We've already seen murderers plead innocence on the grounds that 'my brain made me do it'. Could the science encourage us to believe that our blindness is hardwired, inevitable, inescapable – not wilful at all?

The more crucial learning that has emerged from this science is the recognition that we continue to change right up to the moment we die. Every experience and encounter, each piece of new learning, relationship or reassessment alters how our minds work. And no two experiences are the same. In his work on the human genome, the Nobel laureate Sydney Brenner reminds us that even identical twins will have different experiences in different environments and that that makes them fundamentally different beings. Identical twins develop different immune systems. Mental practice alone can change how our brains operate.[11] The plasticity and responsiveness of our bodies and minds is what makes each of us most remarkable and unique.

In other words, however determinist the brain science may appear, we all handle our experiences in unique ways. We aren't automata serving the master computer in our heads and our capacity for change should never be underestimated. The parents and children who emerge from abusive families full of new hope and the conventional student whose college experience exposes him to dissent have a stronger sense of their own capacity because of what they've seen and overcome. Towns like Libby are not weaker but stronger because of the power to change that they discovered within themselves. Scientists are stronger when they confront disconfirmation than when they hide from it, and companies only regain respect and value when their just cultures allow them to stop defending the past and start to build safer futures.

We make ourselves powerless when we choose not to know. But we give ourselves hope when we insist on looking. The very fact that wilful blindness is willed, that it is a product of a rich mix of experience, knowledge, thinking, neurons and neuroses, is what gives us the capacity to change it. Like Lear, we can learn to see better, not just because our brain changes but because *we* do. As all wisdom does, seeing starts with simple questions: What could I know, should I know, that I don't know? Just what am I missing here?

When he received the internal audit, it showed a vast array of problems: customers badly advised, products mis-sold. Greg wasn't all that surprised; boom and bust had left financial institutions awash with legacy nightmares. Instead of viewing the audit as a report card, he decided, it would be better to see it as a to-do list. Get on and fix the problems; then they'd be gone for good. What he hadn't expected was the pushback he got: from his colleagues, from his boss who wanted him to challenge the report.

'I'd gone into the weeds and I knew the audit was accurate. I think it'd been happening for at least seven years and we needed things to change. But my boss kept pushing: stop this drama and close the thing down! There's nothing wrong.'

Greg calculated how much his bank's customers must have lost. Not just thousands of pounds each, but lost jobs. Financial distress. Divorces. Mental illness. Still his boss insisted that the problems had to be redefined so that they could be removed from the audit.

'I was one of the newest members in the executive committee. During our meetings, it was a bit like psychological bullying: "why is there all this drama going on" and "we have to look at whether he's the right person to lead this team". Absolutely no support. Every week, the Thursday meeting, it was just torture.'

Greg kept thinking that he had to leave. What stopped him was thinking about his people. He'd recruited them, they trusted him. They were, he said, great people who wanted to do the right thing.

'I thought if I left, I'd be letting the team down. No one there would take up the challenge. I am a strong believer that people get their comeuppance, that if you carry on doing the right thing, things will get better.'

A succession of audit teams were called in to try to make the problems go away, to convince Greg that the breaches weren't material. But the problems were real.

'There had been letters to the regulator, saying things had been fixed – and they hadn't been fixed! I got a call wanting to know who'd been responsible and had they been fired, had their bonuses been removed? None of that would have fixed anything. Nobody asked about whether we solved the problem or about lessons learned. It was brutal!'

Even as he recounted what was still an excruciating experience, Greg laughed. It was a relief to tell the story to someone he could trust, who knew that such tales weren't unique to him. Or to banking. Or to the UK.

'I thought the regulator was there to support me – but they were just completely focused on who can we pin this on and can we prove financial punishment? But that saves nothing – the person who went wasn't to blame at all! The root cause was a hiring freeze; we just didn't have people to do the work. By choosing a scapegoat, they thought it showed they'd addressed the problem. But I wanted to get under the skin of the problem.'

He'd built a network of people who understood what he was up against and why he wanted to do the right thing. Friendship, he said, was so important: not feeling alone, not feeling crazy.

'I have a lot of friends in banking,' he told me. 'I also have a good friend in the local NHS. We got talking – and so many issues were the same. Things she wasn't happy with, that weren't right, and how she had tried to raise them. It was so similar! Her examples were about customer care but mine were too. How do you tackle that without feeling the world is on your shoulders and nothing will get better . . .?'

Every day Greg has gone into work, cheerfully determined to shift the dial, to make things better for his customers and his team.

'I've developed a new mantra: no surprises. We changed everything about the way we worked together: fewer meetings, less formal. I didn't want people to have to call a meeting to raise an issue; they could just walk over to me, or to a colleague, and talk about it. Just ask questions. Clear things up early before it is too late. Make it easy to be open! So many issues aren't big things – but it's better to ask than to worry.'

The closer he looked, the more problems he found. Technology that didn't work as it was supposed to. Metrics that didn't match reality. Customer calls that bore no relationship to the data in front of him. And the harder he pushed to fix things, the more resistance he got. There were huge problems in the US – but nobody would let him book flights to see for himself. Problems with the technology which nobody wanted to admit they didn't understand either. In part, Greg was inspired by a former boss. He'd been in the military and loved metrics as much as anyone. But he also loved to wander around, sit in the call centre, get a feel for what was going on. Sense whether the metrics and reality had anything to do with one another. He was a far cry from the current CEO who had a private lift that went straight to his office.

'Both political parties just want the problems to disappear,' Greg said. 'Same as Carillion. A colleague there told me, months before it collapsed, that there were systemic problems, invoices not being paid on time. The company couldn't pay people! Some of those people could be our customers – what are we going to do to help them? To help the smaller companies that worked with Carillion? A lot of companies will go out of business and we could address it, and help, right away ...'

Sitting in a London cafe and hearing Greg's tale, it's easy to be in awe of him. The forces ranged against him, which would prefer a quick fix to real repair, are legion and powerful. Few understand the detail as he does, most prefer not to imagine the concrete reality of customers in trouble. Greg's gift – to see his customers as human beings, to imagine the personal suffering that the numbers symbolise – must sometimes feel like a curse. He can't just see the numbers as numbers. But he knows, as anyone hearing him would know, that keeping hold of what is human in his industry is what gives work meaning.

'When I look at segments of management, I wonder how people get to be in senior positions and lose their values. I look at them as individuals and they're not bad people – so what happened? Why don't they do the right thing? Is it the risk of losing their jobs? But if it is always like that, it won't improve! I couldn't be happy walking away and knowing I could have done something about it. With all the expertise and brainpower that we have ... we could solve these problems now.'

Notes

Introduction

1 This comes from the transcript of the court case, United States of America vs Kenneth L. Lay in the United States District Court for the Southern District of Texas, Houston Division, May 2006.

2 Marcus, J. L. (1993), 'Model Penal Code Section 2.02(7) and Wilful Blindness', *Yale Law Journal*, Symposium: Economic Competitiveness and the Law 102(8): 2231–2257.

1. Affinity and Beyond

1 Luo, S. and E.C. Klohnen (2005), 'Assortative Mating and Marital Quality in Newlyweds: A Couple-Centered Approach', *Journal of Personality and Social Psychology* 88(2): 304.

Hitsch, G.J., A. Hortacsu, et al. (2009), 'Matching and Sorting in Online Dating', *American Economic Review* 10(1): 130–63.

2 *MIT Tech Review*: https://www.technologyreview.com/s/609091/first-evidence-that-online-dating-is-changing-the-nature-of-society/ and http://uk.businessinsider.com/meeting-your-spouse-online-has-a-lot-in-common-with-arranged-marriage-2018-4

Pew Research found that 59 per cent of adults now think online dating is a good way to meet people. Even in 2005, 20 per cent of same-sex couples were meeting online. That rocketed to 70 per cent by 2010, say sociologists Michael Rosenfeld and Reuben Thomas.

3 Chandler, J., T.M. Griffin, et al. (2008), 'In the "I" of the Storm: Shared Initials Increase Disaster Donations', *Judgment and Decision Making* 3(5): 404–10.

4 Brendl, C.M., A. Chattopadhyay, et al. (2005), 'Name Letter Branding: Valence Transfers When Product Specific Needs Are Active', *Journal of Consumer Research* 32: 405–15.

5 Moreland, R.L. and R.B. Zajonc (1982), 'Exposure Effects in Person Perception: Familiarity, Similarity, and Attraction', *Journal of Experimental Social Psychology* 18: 395–415.

6 See *The Music Instinct: How Music Works and Why We Can't Do Without It* by Philip Ball, Bodley Head, 2010.

7 Pronin, E., T. Gilovich, et al. (2004), 'Objectivity in the Eye of the Beholder: Divergent Perceptions of Bias in Self Versus Others', *Psychological Review* 111(3): 781–99.

8 Macrae, C. Neil, Alan B. Milne, and Galen V. Bodenhausen (1994), 'Stereotypes as Energy-Saving Devices: A Peek Inside the Cognitive Toolbox', *Journal of Personality and Social Psychology* 66(1): 37–47.

9 Kolhatkar, Sheekah, 'The Distruptors', *New Yorker*, 20 November 2017.

10 I wrote about this phenomenon in *Women on Top*, Penguin Books, 2007.

11 Kolhatkar, 'The Distruptors', 2017.

12 Bishop, B., *The Big Sort: Why the Clustering of Like-Minded America Is Tearing Us Apart*, Boston: Houghton Mifflin, 2008.

13 Ibid, p. 5.

14 https://www.theguardian.com/society/2014/jul/25/poor-doors-segregation-london-flats. Published 25 July 2014 and accessed 10 January 2018.

15 TED Summit at Banff, June 2016. https://www.ted.com/talks/alexander_betts_why_brexit_happened_and_what_to_do_next#t-326843

16 Rank, Mark, *One Nation, Underprivileged: Why American Poverty Affects Us All*, Oxford University Press, 2004.

17 Sunstein, Cass R., *Going to Extremes: How Like Minds Unite and Divide*, Oxford University Press, 2009.

18 Albarracin, Dolores, 'Feeling Validated Versus Being Correct: A Meta-analysis of Selective Exposure to Information', *Psychological Bulletin* 135(4)

19 Massing, M., 'The News About the Internet', *New York Review of Books*, 13 August 2009.

2. Love is Blind

1 Murray, S.L., J.G. Holmes, et al. (1996), 'The Self-Fulfilling Nature of Positive Illusions in Romantic Relationships: Love is Not Blind, but Prescient' *Journal of Personality and Social Psychology* 7(6):1155–1180.
2 Kahneman, Daniel, *Judgement under Uncertainty: Heuristics and Biases*, Cambridge University Press, 1982.
3 One Plus One: *Relationships Today: Infidelity*. http://www.one-plusone.org.uk/publications/informationsheets/sexualinfidelity.pdf and http://www.savemarriage.co.uk/extramarital-fact-fantasy-the-truth-about-affairs/
4 Araton, Harvey, 'Apologizing, Woods Sets No Date for Return to Golf', *New York Times*, 20 February 2010.
5 Author interview.
6 Florian, V., M. Mikulincer, et al. (2002), 'The Anxiety-Buffering Function of Close Relationships: Evidence that Relationship Commitment Acts as a Terror Management Mechanism', *Journal of Personality and Social Psychology* 82(4): 527.
7 Bartels, A. and S. Zeki (2004), 'The Neural Correlates of Maternal and Romantic Love', *NeuroImage* 21(3): 1155–66.
8 O'Gorman, C., *Beyond Belief*, London: Hodder and Stoughton, 2009.
9 McGreevy, Ronan, 'Most people no longer trust the Church, Government or banks', *Irish Times*, 29 April 2010.
10 Author interview.
11 Author interview.
12 Sereny, G., *Albert Speer: His Battle with Truth*, London: Picador, 1996, pp. 102–3.
13 Ibid. p. 106.
14 Author interview.
15 Sereny, *Albert Speer*, p. 115.
16 Ibid. p. 368.
17 Ibid. p. 405.

3. Dangerous Convictions

1 http://www.sightline.org/research/sust_toolkit/communications-strategy/drewwestenresearch

2 Westen, D., *The Political Brain: The Role of Emotion in Deciding the Fate of the Nation*, New York: Public Affairs, 2007.
3 Greene, G., *The Woman Who Knew Too Much: Alice Stewart and the Secrets of Radiation*, Ann Arbor: University of Michigan Press, 1999, p. 57.
4 Ibid. p. 73.
5 *BMJ* video: http://www.youtube.com/watch?v=proyrn2AAMA
6 Greene, *The Woman Who Knew Too Much*, p. 82.
7 Author interview, 26 November 2009.
8 *Lancet*, 23 January 1897: 289.
9 Lowe, J.J., *Method and means for visually determining the fit of footwear*, US patent 1,614,988, Washington, DC: United States Patent Office: 1927.
10 Festinger, F. and H. W. Rieken, *When Prophecy Fails*, University of Minnesota Press, 1956, republished Pinter and Martin, 2008, p. 56.
11 Ibid. p. 138.
12 Ibid. p. 88.
13 Ibid. p. 108.
14 Ibid. p. 110.
15 Ibid. p. 161.
16 Ibid. p. 171.
17 Greenwald, A.G. (1980), 'The Totalitarian Ego: Fabrication and Revision of Personal History', *American Psychologist* 35(7): 603–18.
18 http://news.bbc.co.uk/1/hi/uk_politics/2859189.stm (accessed 4 April 2018).
19 https://www.globalpolicy.org/component/content/article/154/26026.html (accessed 3 April 2018).
20 Speech to Parliament 18 March 2003. Full text can be found at: http://www.mirror.co.uk/news/uk-news/tony-blairs-iraq-war-speech-8355646
21 https://www.globalpolicy.org/component/content/article/154/26026.html (accessed 3 April 2018).
22 MacFarquhar, Larissa, 'The Deflationist: How Paul Krugman found politics', *New Yorker*, 1 March 2010.
23 Interview with Mike Wallace, 1959. www.youtube.com/watch?v=pMTDaVpBPRO
24 Greenspan, Alan, *The Age of Turbulence*, Allen Lane, 2007, pp. 51–2.
25 Testimony before Congress, 'The Financial Crisis and the Role of Federal Regulators', 23 October 2008, House of Representatives,

Committee on Oversight and Government Reform, Washington, DC.

26 Partnoy, F. (2003), *Infectious Greed: How Deceit and Risk Corrupted the Financial Markets*, London: Profile Books, p. 114.

27 Ibid. p. 406.

28 Speaking at Bath Literature Festival, 27 February 2010.

29 Stanford alumni magazine, March/April 2009, p. 46.

30 Kirk, Michael, 'The Warning', *Frontline*, PBS, airdate: 20 October 2009. http://www.pbs.org/wgbh/pages/frontline/warning/view/

31 US Senate Hearing on the Collapse of Enron Corporation: first hearing 18 December 2001.

32 Testimony before Congress, 'The Financial Crisis and the Role of Federal Regulators', 23 October 2008, House of Representatives, Committee on Oversight and Government Reform, Washington, DC, p. 37.

33 Doll, Richard, and R. Wakeford (1997), 'Risk of Childhood Cancer from Fetal Irradiation', *British Journal of Radiology* 70: 130–139.

4. The Limits of Your Mind

1 Quotes and descriptions taken from author interviews, the TELOS report commissioned by BP before the incident and the Chemical Standard Board's report following the incident. Telos Group, 'BP Texas City Site Report of Findings: Texas City's Protection Performance, Behaviors, Culture, Management and Leadership', 21 January 2005.

US Chemical Safety and Hazard Investigation Board, 'Investigation Report: Refinery Explosion and Fire (15 Killed, 180 Injured) BP Texas City, March 23, 2005', report No. 2005-04-I-TX, March 2007. Available online: http://www.csb.gov/assets/document/ CSBFinalReportBP.pdf

2 From the CSB investigation report.

3 'EA: The Human Story' was nominated for Joel Spolsky's Best Software Essays of 2004.

4 The collected works of Ernst Abbe can be found via the Gutenberg Project: http://www.gutenberg.org/etext/19755

5 If you are interested in more technical detail, there's an interesting analysis of how productivity declines throughout the day: http://www.worklessparty.org/timework/chapman.htm

6 Tomasi, D., R.L. Wang, F. Telang, V. Boronikolas, M.C. Jayne et

al. (2009), 'Impairment of Attentional Networks after One Night of Sleep Deprivation' *Cerebral Cortex* 19(1): 233–40.

7 University of California, Berkeley: *Human Factors Curriculum for Refinery Workers.*

8 Belenky, G.M.D., 'Managing Sleep and Circadian Rhythms to Sustain Operational Performance', PowerPoint presentation given to the ALPA 52nd Air Safety Forum.

9 Some researchers speculate that the epidemic of obesity in the US and elsewhere may be related to chronic sleep loss. Fryer, B. (2006), 'Sleep Deficit: The Performance Killer', *Harvard Business Review* 84(10): 53–9.

10 Walker, Matthew, *Why We Sleep: The New Science of Sleep and Dreams*, London: Allen Lane, 2017.

11 Author interview in Urbana, Illinois.

12 Chris Chabris and Dan Simons have written an extended riff on their theme in a recent book that explores the many ways in which we make cognitive and visual errors: Chabris, Christopher, and Daniel Simons, *The Invisible Gorilla*, New York: Crown Books, 2010.

13 McCarley, Jason, 'Elements of Human Performance in Baggage X- Ray Screening', paper presented at the Fourth Annual Aviation Security Technology Symposium, Washington, DC, 29 November 2006.

14 Simons, D.J. (2007), 'Inattentional Blindness', *Scholarpedia* 2(5): 3244

Horrey, W.J., D.J. Simons, et al. (2006), 'Assessing Interference from Mental Workload Using a Naturalistic Simulated Driving Task: A Pilot Study', *Proceedings of the Human Factors and Ergonomics Society, 50th Annual Meeting*: 2003–6.

Ambinder, M.S. and D.J. Simons (2005), 'Attention Capture: The Interplay of Expectations, Attention and Awareness', *Neurobiology of Attention*, Chapter 12: 69–75.

15 Strayer, D.L., F.A. Drews, et al. (2006), 'A Comparison of the Cell Phone Driver and the Drunk Driver', *Human Factors* 48(2): 381–91.

16 https://www.rac.co.uk/drive/advice/know-how/mobile-phone-laws/

17 Grimes, T. (1991), 'Mild auditory-visual dissonance in television news may exceed viewer attentional capacity', *Human Communication Research*, 18(2), 268–98.

18 http://www.stanford.edu/group/multitasking/memos/Bergen_MultitaskingMemo.pdf

19 Kahneman, Daniel, *Attention and Effort*, New York: Prentice Hall, 1973.

Kahneman, D., and A. Treisman (1984), 'Changing views of attention and automaticity', in R. Parasuraman and R. Davies (eds), *Varieties of Attention*, New York: Academic Press.

20 Gilbert, D.T. (1991), 'How Mental Systems Believe', *American Psychologist* 46(2): 107–19.

21 Gilbert, D.T., R.W. Tafarodi, et al. (1993), 'You Can't Not Believe Everything You Read', *Journal of Personality and Social Psychology* 65(2): 221.

22 Most of the leading investment banks have worked hard to ensure that their intake of new recruits is evenly balanced, fifty–fifty men and women. But they mostly fail to maintain this balance because the women leave, recognising that this kind of work schedule is not conducive to family life – or any kind of life. But when I have confronted partners on this issue, they point out that more employees would dilute the bonus pool.

23 Finkelstein, S., *Why Smart Executives Fail*, New York: Portfolio, 2003.

24 Milgram, S. (1970), 'The Experience of Living in Cities', *Science* 167 (3924) 1461—68.

25 Zimbardo, P.G., *The Lucifer Effect: How Good People Turn Evil*, New York: Random House, 2007.

26 Zimbardo has written about the SPE extensively. Among the many accounts, perhaps the best is the most recent in his book *The Lucifer Effect*. There is also an excellent video of the experiment on his website: http://www.prisonexp.org/

27 Zimbardo, *The Lucifer Effect*, p. 344.

28 Virtanen, Marianna, Stephen A.Stansfield, Rebecca Fuhrer, Jane E. Ferrie, and Mika Kivimaki, 'Overtime Work as a Predictor of Major Depressive Episode: A Five Year Follow-up of the Whitehall II Study' (2012), *PLoS ONE* 7, No. 1 e30719;

Virtanen, Marianna et al., 'Long Working Hours and Cognitive Function: The Whitehall II Study' (2009), *American Journal of Epidemiology* 169, No. 5: 596–605.

5. The Ostrich Instruction

1 *Daily Mail*, 3 October 2009.

2 http://www.bad.org.uk/for-the-public/sun-awareness-campaign/be-sun-aware-roadshow (accessed 14 January 2018).

3 American Academy of Dermatology: http://www.skincarephysicians.com/skincancernet/whatis.html

4 Author interview.

5 Luborsky, L., and B. Blinder (1965), 'Looking, Recalling and GSR as a Function of Defense', *Journal of Abnormal Psychology* 70(4): 270–80.

6 http://www.cityam.com/1411501631/debt-map (accessed 14 January 2018).

http://themoneycharity.org.uk/money-statistics/ (accessed 14 January 2018).

7 Office for National Statistics. https://www.bbc.co.uk/news/business-44953607 (accessed 26 July 2018).

8 Hammond, John S., L. Keeney Ralph, et al. (2006), 'The Hidden Traps in Decision Making', *Harvard Business Review* 84(1): 118–26.

9 http://www.rgemonitor.com/blog/roubini/142759/

10 Author interview.

11 Author interview 18 November 2009;

Kelly, K., *Street Fighters: The Last 72 Hours of Bear Stearns, the Toughest Firm on Wall Street*, New York: Portfolio, 2009.

12 Milliken, Frances J., Elizabeth, W. Morrison et al. (2003), 'An Exploratory Study of Employee Silence: Issues that Employees Don't Communicate Upward and Why', *Journal of Management Studies* 40(6): 1453–76.

13 https://vimeo.com/142444429

14 http://www.bbc.co.uk/news/uk-42252071

15 https://www.washingtonpost.com/news/morning-mix/wp/2017/10/24/new-orleans-celebrity-chef-john-besh-steps-down-from-restaurant-group-after-sexual-harassment-allegations/?utm_term=.dc64db169b99

16 Schneider, A., and D. McCumber, *An Air That Kills: How the Asbestos Poisoning of Libby, Montana Uncovered a National Scandal*, New York: G.P. Putnam's Sons, 2004, p. 87.

17 Ibid. p. 105.

18 Ibid. p. 8.

6. Just Following Orders

1 Milgram, S., *Obedience to Authority*, New York: Harper Perennial, 1974, Preface p. xiii.

2 Ibid. p. 31.

3 According to John Darley in author interview, Princeton, September 2009.

4 Milgram, *Obedience to Authority*, p. 188.

5 Although much has been written about this experiment, there is no substitute for the first-hand account, which is lucid, accessible and thought-provoking.

6 Sheridan, Charles, and Richard G. King (1972), 'Obedience to Authority with an Authentic Victim', *Proceedings of the 80th Annual Convention of the American Psychological Association*, 165–166.

7 Blass, T. (1999), 'The Milgram Paradigm after 35 Years: Some Things We Now Know about Obedience to Authority', *Journal of Applied Social Psychology* 29(5): 955–78.

8 Burger, J.M. (2009), 'Would People Still Obey Today?', *American Psychologist* 64(1): 1–12.

9 The show was done with a live audience that shouted, 'Punishment! Punishment!' One participant, whose grandparents had died in the Holocaust, said she regretted taking part; another Romanian participant said that her experience under Ceausescu had given her the strength to say 'no'.

10 Milgram, *Obedience to Authority*, p. 8.

11 Booth, Robert, 'Grenfell: need to evacuate was "obvious"', *Guardian*, 4 July 2018.

12 Hofling, C.K., E. Brotzman, et al. (1966), 'An Experimental Study in Nurse–Physician Relationships', *Journal of Nervous and Mental Disease* 143(2): 171–80.

13 Pavlo's account of his career at MCI is told in full in *Stolen without a Gun* by Walt Pavlo and Neil Weinberg, published by Etika LLC, 2007.

14 Declassified evidence available at www.texascityexplosion.com

15 US Chemical Safety and Hazard Investigation Board, 'Investigation Report: Refinery Explosion and Fire (15 Killed, 180 Injured) BP Texas City, March 23, 2005', report No. 2005-04-I-TX, March 2007, p. 142.

16 Email dated 26 August 2004.

17 Telos Group, 'BP Texas City Site Report of Findings: Texas City's Protection Performance, Behaviors, Culture, Management and Leadership', 21 January 2005, p. 32.
18 See Morris, Erroll (2008), *Standard Operating Procedure*, USA, Sony Pictures: 111 minutes.
19 Tarnow, E., 'Self Destructive Obedience in the Airplane Cockpit and the Concept of Obedience Optimization', in Blass, T. (ed), *Obedience to Authority: Current Perspectives on the Milgram Paradigm*, New Jersey: Erlbaum Associates, 2000.
20 Martin, J., B. Lobb, G. Chapman, and R. Spillane (1976), 'Obedience under Conditions Demanding Self-immolation', *Human Relations* 29: 345–56.
21 Osiel, Mark, *Obeying Orders: Atrocity, Military Discipline and the Law of War*, Transaction Publishers, 2002, p. 8.
22 Ibid.
23 *The Army Leadership Code: An Introductory Guide* (2017). http://www.army.mod.uk/documents/general/rmas_AC72021-TheArmyLeadershipCode.pdf (accessed 10 January 2018). Also author interview.
24 Perkins, A. and Gentleman, A., 'Government knew for years of risk to Windrush children', *Guardian*, 23 April 2018.

7. The Cult of Cultures

1 Author interview, Washington, DC, September 2009.
2 Milgram, S., *Obedience to Authority*, New York: Harper Perennial, 1974, p. 114.
3 Asch, S.E. (1955), 'Opinions and Social Pressure', *Scientific American* 193(5): 3–5.
4 Larsen, K.S., J.S. Triplett, et al. (1979), 'Collaborator Status, Subject Characteristics and Conformity in the Asch Paradigm', *Journal of Social Psychology* 108: 259–63.
5 Ibid.

Berns, G.S., J. Chappelow, et al. (2005), 'Neurobiological Correlates of Social Conformity and Independence during Mental Rotation', *Journal of Biological Psychiatry* 58: 245–53.

6 Larsen, Triplett, et al. 'Collaborator Status'.
7 http://www.bristol-inquiry.org.uk/final_report/bristol_story.pdf – p. 119.

8 Ibid., p. 145.
9 Panksepp, J., S.M. Siviy, and L.A. Normansell (1985), 'Brain opioids and social emotions', in M. Reite, and T. Field (eds), *The Psychobiology of Attachment and Separation*, New York: Academic Press, pp. 3–49.
10 Panksepp, J. (2003), 'NEUROSCIENCE: Feeling the Pain of Social Loss', *Science* 302(5643): 237–9.

Baumeister, R.F., and M.R. Leary (1995), 'The Need to Belong: Desire for Interpersonal Attachments as a Fundamental Human Motivation', *Psychological Bulletin* 117(3): 497–529.
11 Stillman, T.F., R.F. Baumeister, et al. (2009), 'Alone and without Purpose: Life Loses Meaning Following Social Exclusion', *Journal of Experimental Social Psychology* 45(4): 686–94.
12 Goldie, J., L. Schwartz, et al. (2003), 'Students' Attitudes and Potential Behaviour with Regard to Whistle Blowing as They Pass Through a Modern Medical Curriculum', *Medical Education* 37: 368–75.
13 Wolf, T.M., P.M. Balson, J.M. Faucett, and H.M. Randall (1989), 'A Retrospective Study of Attitude Change During Medical Education', *Medical Education* 23: 19–23

Hundert, E.M., D. Douglas-Steele, and J. Bickel (1996), 'Context in medical education: the informal ethics curriculum', *Medical Education* 30: 353–64.
14 For reasons of confidentiality, Corden's name is a pseudonym.
15 Berns, G.S., J. Chappelow, et al. (2005), 'Neurobiological Correlates of Social Conformity and Independence during Mental Rotation', *Journal of Biological Psychiatry* 58: 245–53.
16 Ibid.
17 Janis, I.L., *Victims of Groupthink: A Psychological Study of Foreign-Policy Decisions and Fiascoes*, Boston: Houghton Mifflin, 1972, p. 13.
18 Kelly, K., *Street Fighters: The Last 72 Hours of Bear Stearns, the Toughest Firm on Wall Street*, New York: Portfolio, 2009, pp. 152–3, 160–1.

8. Complicit

1 https://www.washingtonpost.com/news/the-switch/wp/2018/04/10/transcript-of-mark-zuckerbergs-senate-hearing/?noredirect=on&utm_term=.dba9071e967d

2 The smoke-filled-room experiment can be found online: https://www.youtube.com/watch?v=KE5YwN4NW5o
3 Darley, J., and B. Latané (1968), 'Bystander Intervention in Emergencies: Diffusion of Responsibility', *Journal of Personality and Social Psychology*, 8(4): 377–83.
4 Latané, B., and S. Nida (1981), 'Ten Years of Research on Group Size and Helping', *Psychological Bulletin* 89(2): 308–24.
5 Gibb, Frances, 'Joint Enterprise Law Means Even Bystanders Can Get Life', *The Times*, 9 July 2009.
6 https://www.theguardian.com/uk/2005/aug/04/ukcrime.features11
7 Blenkinsopp, J., and M.S. Edwards (2008), 'On Not Blowing the Whistle: Quiescent Silence as an Emotion Episode', *Research on Emotion in Organizations* 4: 181–206.
8 https://www.newyorker.com/news/news-desk/after-weinstein-britains-parliament-confronts-its-own-sexual-misconduct-scandals
9 Hughes, Laura, 'Houses of Harassment' *Financial Times* magazine, 16/17 June 2018.
10 https://www.questia.com/magazine/1P4-1968444156/the-disrupters
11 Author interview.
12 https://www.nytimes.com/interactive/2014/06/05/business/06gm-report-doc.html
13 Swartz, M., and S. Watkins, *Power Failure: The Inside Story of the Collapse of Enron*, New York: Doubleday, 2003, p. 121.
14 US Department of Justice, Office of Community Oriented Policing report on Bullying in Schools, www.cops.doj.gov
15 https://www.ditchthelabel.org/annual-bullying-survey-2016/
16 Quoted in Horwitz, G.J., *In the Shadow of Death: Living Outside the Gates of Mauthausen*, London: I.B.Tauris & Co, 1991.

9. Out of Sight, Out of Mind

1 Telos Group, 'BP Texas City Site Report of Findings: Texas City's Protection Performance, Behaviors, Culture, Management and Leadership', 21 January 2005.

US Chemical Safety and Hazard Investigation Board, 'Investigation Report: Refinery Explosion and Fire (15 Killed, 180 Injured) BP Texas City, March 23, 2005', report No. 2005-04-I-TX, March 2007. Available online: http://www.csb.gov/assets/document/CSB FinalReportBP.pdf

2 CSB report p. 193.
3 http://texascityexplosion.com/etc/broadcast/files/ev5/DEPO—Manzoni,%20John.pdf

It's worth noting that John Manzoni now heads up the UK civil service.
4 Milgram, S., *Obedience to Authority*, New York: Harper Perennial, 1974, p. 38.
5 Darley, J., A. Teger, et al. (1973), 'Do Groups Always Inhibit Individuals' Responses to Potential Emergencies?', *Journal of Personality and Social Psychology* 26(3): 395–3.
6 https://www.telegraph.co.uk/news/health/news/8117727/Mid-Staffordshire-hospitals-inquiry-case-study-Julie-Bailey.html
7 https://assets.publishing.service.gov.uk/government/uploads/system/uploads/attachment_data/file/279124/0947.pdf
8 https://www.gov.uk/government/publications/report-of-the-mid-staffordshire-nhs-foundation-trust-public-inquiry
9 Ibid.
10 http://www.rotherham.gov.uk/downloads/file/1407/independent_inquiry_cse_in_rotherham
11 Ibid, 13.3.
12 Ibid, section 8.
13 Author interview.
14 http://www.rotherham.gov.uk/downloads/file/1407/independent_inquiry_cse_in_rotherham 13.28.
15 Ibid, 13.38.
16 Dixon, N.F., *On the Psychology of Military Incompetence*, New York: Futura Publications, 1976.
17 Dixon, N.F., *Our Own Worst Enemy*, London: Jonathan Cape, 1987.
18 Goodwin, S.A., A. Gubin, et al. (2000), 'Power Can Bias Impression Processes: Stereotyping Subordinates by Default and by Design', *Group Processes and Intergroup Relations* 3(3): 227–56.
19 Milliken, F.J., J.C. Magee, N. Lam, and D. Menezes (2009), *The Lens and Language of Power: Sense-making Gaps in the Aftermath of Hurricane Katrina*. Unpublished manuscript, New York University.
20 http://i.a.cnn.net/cnn/2005/images/11/03/brown.emails.pdf
21 Interview with Ted Koppel, 2 September 2005. http://espanol.video.yahoo.com/watch/223063/786068
22 Note made by Wilhelm Bonse as part of his internal inquiry into the Texas City explosion: 'Management Accountability

Project, Texas City Isomerization Explosion, Final Report', 26 June 2006.

23 http://money.cnn.com/2016/10/30/technology/facebook-advertising-discrimination/index.html?iid=hp-stack-dom

24 http://money.cnn.com/2016/11/11/technology/facebook-ads-race-targeting/index.html?iid=EL

25 http://money.cnn.com/2017/09/07/technology/business/facebook-russia-problem/index.html

26 See also https://www.theguardian.com/news/2018/mar/22/facebook-gave-data-about-57bn-friendships-to-academic-aleksandr-kogan

27 http://mattmckeon.com/facebook-privacy/

28 Feynman, R.P., *What Do You Care What Other People Think? Further Adventures of a Curious Character.* London: Unwin Paperbacks, 1988.

29 http://lightgreenstairs.com/green-choices/sigg-not-taking-responsibility/

30 Sandell, Michael, 'Markets and Morals: A New Citizenship', The Reith Lectures, transcript available: http://www.bbc.co.uk/programmes/b00kt7sh

31 Testimony before Congress, 'The Financial Crisis and the Role of Federal Regulators', 23 October 2008, House of Representatives, Committee on Oversight and Government Reform, Washington, D.C. http://oversight.house. gov/images/ stories/documents/20081024163819.pdf

32 Economics, London School of, 'Letter to the Queen in Response to Her Question: Why Had Nobody Noticed That the Credit Crunch Was on Its Way?', 2009.

33 https://www.pri.org/stories/2015-07-02/quietly-congress-extends-ban-cdc-research-gun-violence

34 Hill, Andrew, 'Amnesia dooms bankers to repeat their mistakes', *Financial Times*, 25 June 2018.

10. DE-moralising Work

1 Schwab, R.S., 'Motivation in measurements of fatigue', in W.F. Floyd, and A.T. Welford (eds), *Fatigue*, London: H.K. Lewis, 1953, pp. 143–8.

2 Vohs, Kathleen, D. (2008), 'Merely Activating the Concept of Money Changes Personal and Interpersonal Behavior', *Current*

Directions in Psychological Science 17(3): 208–12.

3 Adcock, R.A., A. Thangavel, et al. (2006), 'Reward-Motivated Learning: Mesolimbic Activation Precedes Memory Formation', *Neuron* 50(3): 507–17.

4 Pessiglione, M., L. Schmidt, et al. (2007), 'How the Brain Translates Money into Force: A Neuroimaging Study of Subliminal Motivation', *Science* 316(5826): 904–6.

5 Pink, Daniel H., *Drive: The Surprising Truth about What Motivates Us*, New York: Canongate, 2009.

6 Zhou, X., Kathleen D. Vohs, et al. (2009), 'The Symbolic Power of Money: Reminders of Money Alter Social Distress and Physical Pain', *Psychological Science* 20(6): 700–6.

7 Vohs, K.D., N.L. Mead, et al. (2006), 'The Psychological Consequences of Money', *Science* 314(5802): 1154–6.

8 Vohs, Kathleen D., Nicole L, Mead, Miranda R. Goode, 'Merely Activating the Concept of Money Changes Personal and Interpersonal Behavior': 208–12.

9 Molinsky, Andrew L., Adam M. Grant, and Joshua D. Margolis (2012), 'The bedside manner of homo economicus: How and why priming an economic schema reduces compassion', *Organizational Behavior and Human Decision Processes*, 119: 27–37.

10 https://www.thetimes.co.uk/article/keep-costs-of-cladding-down-grenfell-tower-experts-told-6qrhmwzxv

11 Paul Moore's testimony to the House of Commons Select Committee: http://ftalphaville.ft.com/blog/2009/02/11/52320/hbos-the-moore-memo/

12 The Riskminds Risk Managers Survey 2009.

13 Frey, B., S. and F. Oberholzer-Gee (1997), 'The Cost of Price Incentives: An Empirical Analysis of Motivation Crowding-Out', *American Economic Review* 87(4): 746–55.

14 Gneezy, U., and A. Rustichini (2000), 'A Fine Is a Price', *Journal of Legal Studies* 29(1): 1–17.

15 Ibid.

16 Molinsky, Andrew L., Adam M. Grant, and Joshua D. Margolis (2012), 'The bedside manner of homo economicus: How and why priming an economic schema reduces compassion': 27–37.

17 Bowles, S. (2008), 'Policies Designed for Self-Interested Citizens May Undermine "The Moral Sentiments": Evidence from Economic Experiments', *Science* 320(5883): 1605–9.

18 Greene, J.D., R.B. Sommerville, et al. (2001), 'An fMRI Investigation of Emotional Engagement in Moral Judgment', *Science* 293(5537): 2105–8.

Robertson, D., J. Snarey, et al. (2007), 'The Neural Processing of Moral Sensitivity to Issues of Justice and Care', *Neuropsychologia* 45(4): 755–66.

19 Lewis, Michael, *The Big Short: Inside the Doomsday Machine*, New York: W.W. Norton and Co., 2010.

20 Court document.

21 Gingrich, N., *To Renew America*, New York, Harper Collins, 1995. Quoted in Bandura, Albert (2007), 'Impeding Ecological Sustainability through Selective Moral Disengagement', *International Journal of Innovation and Sustainable Development* 2(1).

22 Ibid.

11. Cassandra

1 Miceli, M.P., and J.P. Near (2005), 'Standing Up or Standing By: What Predicts Blowing the Whistle on Organizational Wrongdoing?', *Research in Personnel and Human Resources Management* 24: 93–136.

2 Written testimony of Harry Markopolos, Chartered Financial Analyst, Certified Fraud Examiner before the US Senate Banking, Housing and Urban Affairs Committee, 10 September 2009.

3 Author interview.

4 http://freedomtospeakup.org.uk/wp-content/uploads/2014/07/F2SU_web.pdf

5 Author interview.

6 Author interview.

7 Markopolos, H., *No One Would Listen: A True Financial Thriller*, Hoboken, New Jersey: Wiley & Sons, 2010.

8 Hansen, J., D. Johnson, A. Lacis, S. Lebedeff, P. Lee, D. Rind, and G. Russell (1981), 'Climate Impact of Increasing Atmospheric Carbon Dioxide', *Science* 213, 957–66.

9 Lizza, R., 'The Contrarian', *New Yorker*, 2009.

10 https://www.theatlantic.com/magazine/archive/2013/01/whats-inside-americas-banks/309196/

11 Barton, L., 'On the Money', *Guardian*, 31 October 2008.

12 Tett, G., *Fool's Gold: How Unrestrained Greed Corrupted a Dream*,

Shattered Global Markets and Unleashed a Catastrophe, London: Little, Brown, 2009, p. 299.

13 A twelve-year study published in the June 2007 issue of the journal *Epidemiology and Health* clearly demonstrated that the risk of suicide among male US veterans is more than two times greater than that of the general population after adjusting for a host of potentially compounding factors, including age, time of service and health status. A report released in May 2010 by the VA inspector general noted that 'veterans returning from Iraq and Afghanistan are at increased risk for suicide because not all VA clinics have 24-hour mental care available . . . and many lack properly trained workers'.

Media reports of suicide deaths and suicide attempts among active-duty soldiers and veterans began to surface back in 2003 after a spate of suicides in Iraq during the first months of the war. Since then, both the military and the VA have stumbled and fumbled in their attempts to answer questions about the severity of this malady. For example, while all the military services maintain suicide prevention programmes, the army in its August 2007 Army Suicide Event Report acknowledged that soldiers committed suicide last year at the highest rate in twenty-six years, and more than a quarter did so while serving in Iraq and Afghanistan. The report noted 'a significant relationship between suicide attempts and number of days deployed in Iraq, Afghanistan or nearby countries where troops are participating in the war effort'. The report added that there also 'was limited evidence to support the view that multiple deployments are a risk factor for suicide behaviors'. It might be noted here that this report was released only after an FOIA request. From the Vietnam Veterans of America: http://www.vva.org/who.html

14 https://www.nytimes.com/2017/10/05/us/harvey-weinstein-harassment-allegations.html

15 CBS, *Sixty Minutes*, 25 January 2007. http://www.cbsnews.com/video/watch/?id=2972689n&tag=related;photovideo

16 Testimony of Harry Markopolos, CFA, CFE, before the US House of Representatives Committee on Financial Services, 4 February 2009.

12. See Better

1 'Physician, heal thyself', *The Economist*, 30 June–6 July 2018. See also http://www.bmj.com/content/bmj/353/bmj.i2139.full.pdf
2 https://publications.parliament.uk/pa/cm201719/cmselect/cmpubadm/708/708.pdf
3 Kuchler, Hannah, 'Tech workers of the world unite!', *Financial Times* magazine, 30 June/1 July 2018.
4 Greene, G., *The Woman Who Knew Too Much: Alice Stewart and the Secrets of Radiation*, Ann Arbor: University of Michigan Press, 1999, p. 223.
5 Ibid, p. 244.
6 Average auditor tenure in the US for the first twenty-one companies in the Dow Jones Index in 2017 was sixty-six years.
7 Nemeth, Charles, Ofra Mayseless, Jeffrey Sherman, and Yvonne Brown (1990), 'Exposure to Dissent and Recall of Information', *Journal of Personality and Social Psychology* 58(3): 429-437.
8 See Cathy O'Neill, *Weapons of Math Destruction*, Penguin Books, 2017.
9 Eubanks, Virginia, *Automating Inequality: How High-Tech Tools Profile, Police, and Punish the Poor*, New York: St Martin's Press, 2018.
10 Ibid.
11 Pascual-Leonoe, A., N. Dang, et al. (1995), 'Modulation of Muscle Responses Evoked by Transcranial Magnetic Stimulation During the Acquisition of New Fine Motor Skills', *Journal of Neurophysiology* 74(3): 1037–1045.

Bibliography

Abagnale, Frank. *Catch Me If You Can: The Amazing True Story of the Most Extraordinary Liar in the History of Fun and Profit*, New York: Broadway Books, 1980.

Adcock, R. Alison, Arul Thangavel, Susan Whitfield-Gabriel, Brian Knutson, and John D.E. Gabriele. 'Reward-Motivated Learning: Mesolimbic Activation Precedes Memory Formation', *Neuron* Vol. 50, No. 3, 507–17, 2006.

Addley, Esther. 'How Britain Fell in Love with the Tan', *Guardian*, 1 August 2009.

Ahmed, Kamal. 'Why are so many of us not saving for a rainy day?', *BBC News*, 25 July 2018.

Akerlof, George A., and Robert J. Shiller. *Animal Spirits: How Human Psychology Drives the Economy, and Why It Matters for Global Capitalism*, Princeton University Press, 2009.

Aleccia, JoNel. 'Hospital Bullies Take a Toll on Patient Safety', *MSNBC.com*, 9 July 2008.

Alford, C. Fred. *Whistleblowers: Broken Lives and Organizational Power*, Ithaca, NY: Cornell University Press, 2001.

Ambinder, Michael S., and Daniel J. Simons. 'Attention Capture: The Interplay of Expectations, Attention and Awareness', *Neurobiology of Attention* Vol. 12, 69–75, 2005.

Anderson, Cameron, and Jennifer L. Berdahl. 'The Experience of Power: Examining the Effects of Power on Approach and Inhibition Tendencies', *Journal of Personality and Social Psychology* Vol. 83, No. 6, 1362, 2002.

Anderson, Cameron, and Adam D. Galinsky. 'Power, Optimism and Risk Taking', *European Journal of Social Psychology* Vol. 36, 511–36, 2006.

Andrews, Travis M. 'New Orleans celebrity chef John Besh steps down after sexual harassment allegations', *Washington Post*, 24 October 2017.

Araton, Harvey. 'Apologizing, Woods Sets No Date for Return to Golf', *New York Times*, 20 February 2010.

Arendt, Hannah. 'Personal Responsibility under Dictatorship', in Jerome Kohn (ed), *Responsibility and Judgment*, New York: Schocken Books, 2003.

——. *The Jewish Writings*, New York: Schocken Books, 2007.

Ariely, Dan. *Predictably Irrational: The Hidden Forces That Shape Our Decisions*, New York: Harper Collins, 2008.

Aron, Arthur, Elain N. Aron, Michael Tudor, and Greg Nelson. 'Close Relationships as Including Other in the Self', *Journal of Personality and Social Psychology* Vol. 60, No. 2, 241–53, 1991.

Aronson, Elliott. 'Back to the Future: Retrospective Review of Leon Festinger's *A Theory of Cognitive Dissonance*', *American Journal of Psychology* Vol. 110, No. 1, 127–157, 1997.

Asch, Solomon E. 'Opinions and Social Pressure', *Scientific American* Vol. 193, No. 5, 31–5, 1955.

Asthana, Anushka. 'Report Reveals How Britons Were Lured into Spiral of Debt', *Observer*, 7 February 2010.

Auletta, Ken. *Three Blind Mice: How the TV Networks Lost Their Way*, Vintage Books, 1991.

Baars, Bernard J., William P. Banks, and James B. Newman (eds). *Essential Sources in the Scientific Study of Consciousness*, Cambridge: MIT Press, 2003.

Ball, Philip. *The Music Instinct: How Music Works and Why We Can't Do Without It*, Bodley Head, 2010.

Banaji, Mahzarin R. 'Foreword: The Moral Obligation to Be Intelligent', in Eugene Borgida and Susan T. Fiske (eds), *Beyond Common Sense: Psychological Science in the Courtroom*, Wiley-Blackwell, 2007.

Banaji, Mahzarin R., Max H. Bazerman, and Dolly Chugh. 'How (Un)Ethical Are You?', *Harvard Business Review*, 56–64, 2003.

Banaji, Mahzarin R., Curtis Hardin, and Alexander J. Rothman. 'Implicit Stereotyping in Person Judgment', *Journal of Personality and Social Psychology* Vol. 65, No. 2, 272, 1993.

Bandura, Albert. 'Social Cognitive Theory of Moral Thought and Action', in William M. Kurtines and Jacob L. Gewirtz (eds), *Handbook of Moral Behavior and Development*, Hillsdale, New Jersey: Lawrence Erlbaum Associates, 1991.

——. 'Moral Disengagement in the Perpetration of Inhumanities', *Personality and Social Psychology Review* Vol. 3, 193–209, 1999.

——. 'Impeding Ecological Sustainability through Selective Moral Disengagement', *International Journal of Innovation and Sustainable Development* Vol. 2, No. 1, 8–32, 2007.

——. 'The Reconstrual of "Free Will" from the Agentic Perspective of Social Cognitive Theory', in J. Baer, J.G. Kaufman and R.F. Baumeister (eds), *Are We Free? Psychology and Freewill*, Oxford University Press, 2008.

——. 'Social Cognitive Theory Goes Global', *British Psychological Society* Vol. 22, No. 6, 504–6, 2009.

Bandura, Albert, Gian-Vittorio Caprara, and Laszlo Zsolnai.'Corporate Transgressions through Moral Disengagement', *Journal of Human Values* Vol. 6, No. 1, 57–64, 2000.

Barnes, Brooks. 'Studios' Quest for Life after DVDs', *New York Times*, 25 October 2009.

Bartels, Andreas, and Semir Zeki. 'The Neural Correlates of

Maternal and Romantic Love', *NeuroImage* Vol. 21, No. 3, 1155–66, 2004.

Barton, Laura. 'On the Money', *Guardian*, 31 October 2008.

Batabyal, Amitrajeet A. 'Meeting your Spouse Online has a Surprising Amount in Common with Arranged Marriage', *Business Insider*, 8 April 2018.

Baumeister, Roy, C. Nathan DeWall, Nicole Mead, and Kathleen Vohs. 'Social Rejection Can Reduce Pain and Increase Spending: Further Evidence That Money, Pain, and Belongingness Are Interrelated', *Psychological Inquiry* Vol. 19, No. 3–4, 145–7, 2008.

Baumeister, Roy F., and Kenneth J. Cairns. 'Repression and Self-Presentation: When Audiences Interfere with Self-Deceptive Strategies', *Journal of Personality and Social Psychology* Vol. 62, No. 5, 851–62, 1992.

Baumeister, Roy F., and Mark R. Leary. 'The Need to Belong: Desire for Interpersonal Attachments as a Fundamental Human Motivation', *Psychological Bulletin* Vol. 117, No. 3, 497–529, 1995.

Baumgardner, Ann H. 'To Know Oneself Is to Like Oneself: Self-Certainty and Self-Affect', *Journal of Personality and Social Psychology* Vol. 58, No. 6, 1062–72, 1990.

Bazerman, Max H. *Negotiating Rationally*, New York: Free Press, 1993.

——. *Judgment in Managerial Decision-Making*, Wiley, 2002.

Bazerman, Max H., and Mahzarin R. Banaji. 'The Social Psychology of Ordinary Ethical Failures', *Social Justice Research* Vol. 17, No. 2, 111–15, 2004.

Bazerman Max, H., and Dolly Chugh. 'Decisions without Blinders', *Harvard Business Review* Vol. 84, No. 1, 88–97, 2006.

Bazerman Max, H., George Loewenstein, and A. Moore Don. 'Why Good Accountants Do Bad Audits', *Harvard Business Review* Vol. 80, No. 11, 96–102, 2002.

Begley, Sharon. 'Adventures in Good and Evil', *Newsweek* Vol. 153, No. 18, 46–9, 2009.

Belenky, Gregory M.D., 'Managing Sleep and Circadian Rhythms to Sustain Operational Performance', PowerPoint presentation to the ALPA 52nd Air Safety Forum.

Berns, Gregory S., Jonathan Chappelow, Caroline F. Zink, Giuseppe Pagnoni, Megan E. Martin-Skursk, and Jim Richards.'Neurobiological Correlates of Social Conformity and Independence during Mental Rotation', *Journal of Biological Psychiatry* Vol. 58, 245–53, 2005.

Betts, Alexander. 'Why Brexit Happened – and What to do Next', TED Summit at Banff, June 2016.

Bishop, Bill. *The Big Sort: Why the Clustering of Like-Minded America Is Tearing Us Apart*, Boston: Houghton Mifflin, 2008.

'Blair Loses Third Minister Over Iraq', *BBC News*, 18 March 2003.

Blair, Tony. 'The Blair Doctrine', *Global Policy Forum*, 22 April 1999.

——. Speech to Parliament, 18 March 2003.

Blake, Heidi. 'Mid-Staffordshire hospitals inquiry case study: Julie Bailey', *Daily Telegraph*, 8 November 2010.

Blakeslee, Sandra. 'What Other People Say May Change What You See', *New York Times*, 28 June 2005.

Blanchflower, David. 'My Time at Threadneedle Street Certainly Wasn't Boring', *Guardian*, 8 June 2009.

Blanford, Nicholas. 'The Admiral Ordered "Turn" and the Ships Collided', *The Times*, 2 September 2004.

Blass, Thomas. 'The Milgram Paradigm after 35 Years: Some Things We Now Know about Obedience to Authority', *Journal of Applied Social Psychology* Vol. 29, No. 5, 955–78, 1999.

Blass, Thomas (ed.). *Obedience to Authority: Current Perspectives on the Milgram Paradigm*, Lawrence Erlbaum, 2000.

Blenkinsopp, John, and Marissa S. Edwards. 'On Not Blowing the Whistle: Quiescent Silence as an Emotion Episode', *Research on Emotion in Organizations* Vol. 4, 181–206, 2008.

Bolsin, Stephen N., Tom Faunce, and Mark Colson. 'Using Portable Digital Technology for Clinical Care and Critical Incidents: A New Model', *Australian Health Review* Vol. 29, No. 3, 297–305, 2005.

Booth, Robert. 'Grenfell: need to evacuate was "obvious"', *Guardian*, 4 July 2018.

Bowen, Frances, and Kate Blackmon. 'Spirals of Silence: The Dynamic Effects of Diversity on Organizational Voice', *The Journal of Management Studies* Vol. 40, No. 6, 1393–1417, 2003.

Bowles, Samuel. 'Policies Designed for Self-Interested Citizens May Undermine "The Moral Sentiments": Evidence from Economic Experiments', *Science* Vol. 320, No. 5883, 1605–9, 2008.

BP. 'Cost Benefit Analysis of the Three Little Pigs', PowerPoint slide produced in evidence by BP, date unknown.

Brendl, C. Miguel, Amitaa Chattopadhyay, Brett W. Pelham, and Mauricio Carvallo. 'Name Letter Branding: Valence Transfers When Product Specific Needs Are Active', *Journal of Consumer Research* Vol. 32, 405–15, 2005.

Brewer, Lynn. *Confessions of an Enron Executive*, Author House, 2004.

Brooke, Heather. 'Promises of More Open Government Have Been Made Before', *The Times*, 11 June 2009.

——. 'Unsung Hero', *Guardian*, 15 May 2009.

Brown, David K. *Warrior to Dreadnought: Warship Development 1860–1905*, Chatham Publishing, 1997.

Brown, Jim. 'New Federal Whistleblower Office Off to Slow Start in First Year on the Job', *Canadian Press*, 2 May 2008.

Browne, John. *Beyond Business: An Inspirational Memoir from a Visionary Leader*, Weidenfeld & Nicolson, 2009.

Bruno, S. Frey. 'A Constitution for Knaves Crowds out Civic Virtues', *Economic Journal* Vol. 107, No. 443, 1043–53, 1997.

Burger, Jerry M. 'Would People Still Obey Today?', *American Psychologist* Vol. 64, No. 1, 1–12, 2009.

Burkin, Kevin, and Brian H. Kleiner. 'Protecting the Whistleblower: Preventing Retaliation Following a Report of Patient Abuse in Health-Care Institutions', *Health Manpower Management* Vol. 24, No. 3, 119–24, 1998.

Burton, Robert A. *On Being Certain: Believing You Are Right Even When You're Not*, St Martin's Griffin, 2008.

Cacioppo, John T., Richard E. Petty, and Mary E. Losch. 'Attributions of Responsibility for Helping and Doing Harm: Evidence for Confusion of Responsibility', *Journal of Personality and Social Psychology* Vol. 50, No. 1, 100, 1986.

Canada Safety Council. 'Don't Just Stand There – Do Something', 2004.

Cannon, M.D., and A.C. Edmondson.'Failing to Learn and Learning to Fail (Intelligently)', *Long Range Planning* Vol. 38, No. 3, 299–319, 2005.

Carey, John. 'The Unwisdom of Crowds', *Businessweek*, 7 May 2009.

Carozza, Dick. 'Chasing Madoff: An Interview with Harry Markopolos', *Fraud* Vol. 23, No. 3, 2009.

Carr, Drury Gunn, and Doug Hawes-Davis. *Libby, Montana*, a film produced by High Plains Films and distributed by Typecast Releasing, 2006.

Carville, James, and Mary Matalin. *All's Fair: Love, War and Running for President*, New York: Random House, 1994.

Cassidy, John. 'After the Blowup', *New Yorker*, 11 January 2010.

Chabris, Christopher, and Daniel Simons. *The Invisible Gorilla*, New York: Crown Books, 2010.

Chandler, Jesse, Tiffany M. Griffin, and Nicholas Sorensen.

'Improving Decision Making by Means of Dissent', *Journal of Applied Social Psychology* Vol. 31, 48–58, 2001.

——. 'In the "I" of the Storm: Shared Initials Increase Disaster Donations', *Judgment and Decision Making* Vol. 3, No. 5, 404–10, 2008.

Channel 4 Television (UK), 'Would You Save a Stranger', 2 April 2009.

Chugh, Dolly, and Max H. Bazerman. 'Bounded Awareness: What You Fail to See Can Hurt You', *Mind and Society* Vol. 6, No. 1, 1–18, 2007.

Chugh, D., Bazerman, M.H., and M.R. Banaji. 'Bounded Ethicality as a Psychological Barrier to Recognizing Conflicts of Interest', in Moore, D., D. Cain, G. Loewenstein, and M.H. Bazerman (eds), *Conflicts of Interest: Problems and Solutions from Law, Medicine and Organizational Settings*, London: Cambridge University Press, 2005.

Cohen, Stanley. *States of Denial: Knowing About Atrocities and Suffering*, London: Polity, 2001.

Cornblatt, Johannah. 'Bystanders No More: Teaching Kids to Respond to Violent Crime', *Newsweek*, 30 October 2009.

Creed, W.E. Douglas. 'Voice Lessons: Tempered Radicalism and the Use of Voice and Silence', *Journal of Management Studies* Vol. 40, No. 6, 1503–36, 2003.

'Criminal Law–Willful Blindness–Ninth Circuit Holds That Motive Is Not an Element of Willful Blindness'. *Harvard Law Review* Vol. 121, No. 4, 1245–53, 2008.

Crozier, W. Ray. *Shyness and Embarrassment: Perspectives from Social Psychology*, Cambridge University Press, 1990.

Darley, John M. 'Social Organization for the Production of Evil', *Psychological Inquiry* Vol. 3, No. 2, 199–218, 1992.

Darley, John M., and C. Daniel Batson. '"From Jerusalem to Jericho": A Study of Situational and Dispositional Variables in Helping Behavior', *Journal of Personality and Social Psychology* Vol. 27, No. 1, 100–8, 1973.

Darley, John M., and B. Latané. 'Bystander Intervention in Emergencies: Diffusion of Responsibility', *Journal of Personality and Social Psychology* Vol. 8, No. 4, 377–383, 1968.

Darley, John M., Allan Teger, and Lawrence D. Lewis. 'Do Groups Always Inhibit Individuals' Responses to Potential Emergencies?', *Journal of Personality and Social Psychology* Vol. 26, No. 3, 395–9, 1973.

DiMaggio, Paul. 'Culture and Cognition', *Annual Review of Sociology*, 1997.

Dixon, Norman F. *On the Psychology of Military Incompetence*, London: Futura Publications, 1976.

——. *Our Own Worst Enemy*, London: Jonathan Cape, 1987.

Doll, Richard and R. Wakeford. 'Risk of Childhood Cancer from Fetal Irradiation', *British Journal of Radiology* Vol. 70, No. 830, 1997.

Dorsey, David. *The Force*, New York: Random House, 1994.

Eastwick, Paul W., Jennifer A. Richeson, Deborah Son, and Eli J. Finkely. 'Is Love Colorblind? Political Orientation and Interracial Romantic Desire', *Personality and Social Psychology Bulletin* Vol. 35, No. 9, 1258–68, 2009.

Economics, London School of. 'Letter to the Queen in Response to Her Question: Why Had Nobody Noticed That the Credit Crunch Was on Its Way?', 2009.

Edelman, Aida. 'A Double Agent, That's What I Was', *Guardian*, 14 November 2009.

Edmondson Amy, C. 'Speaking up in the Operating Room: How Team Leaders Promote Learning in Interdisciplinary Action Teams', *Journal of Management Studies* Vol. 40, No. 6, 1419–52, 2003.

Edmondson, Vickie Cox, and George Munchus. 'Managing

the Unwanted Truth: A Framework for Dissent Strategy', *Journal of Organizational Change Management* Vol. 20, No. 6, 747–60, 2007.

Ehrenberg, Billy. 'World debt mapped: The UK has the fourth-highest household debt in the world', *City AM*, 23 September 2014.

Ehrlinger, Joyce, Thomas Gilovich, and Lee Ross. 'Peering into the Bias Blind Spot: People's Assessments of Bias in Themselves and Others', *Personality and Social Psychology Bulletin* Vol. 31, No. 5, 680–92, 2005.

Eichenwald, Kurt. *Serpent on the Rock:* New York: Broadway Books, 1995.

Engelmann, Jan B., C. Monica Capra, Charles Noussair, and Gregory S. Berns. 'Expert Financial Advice Neurobiologically "Offloads" Financial Decision-Making under Risk', *Public Library of Science*, 2009.

Epley, Nicholas, and Thomas Gilovich. 'Just Going Along: Non-conscious Priming and Conformity to Social Pressure', *Journal of Experimental Social Psychology* Vol. 35, No. 6, 578–89, 1999.

Eubanks, Virginia. *Automating Inequality: How High-Tech Tools Profile, Police, and Punish the Poor,* New York: St Martin's Press, 2018.

Evans, Rob. 'The Lonely Life of a Construction Industry Whistle-blower', *Guardian*, 15 May 2009.

Felblinger, Dianne M. 'Incivility and Bullying in the Workplace and Nurses' Shame Responses', *Journal of Obstetric, Gynaecologic and Neonatal Nursing* Vol. 37, 234–42, 2008.

Festinger, Leon, and James M. Carlsmith. 'Cognitive Consequences of Forced Compliance', *Journal of Abnormal and Social Psychology* Vol. 58, 203–10, 1959.

Festinger, Leon, and Nathan Maccoby. 'On Resistance to

Persuasive Communications', *Journal of Abnormal and Social Psychology* Vol. 68, No. 4, 359–66, 1964.

Festinger, Leon, Henry W. Riecken, and Stanley Schachter. *When Prophecy Fails: A Social and Psychological Study of a Modern Group That Predicted the Destruction of the World*, Harper Torch Books, 1956.

Feynman, Richard P. *What Do You Care What Other People Think? Further Adventures of a Curious Character*, Unwin Paperbacks, 1988.

Fiegerman, Seth. 'Facebook cracks down on discriminatory ads', *CNN Money*, 11 November 2016.

Fiegerman, Seth, and Dylan Byers. 'Facebook's Russia Problem: What We Know', *CNN Money*, 7 September 2017.

Finch, Julia. 'I Save Tax by Never Visiting My Family, Says Tycoon Hands', *Guardian*, 6 February 2010.

Fincher, Richard D. 'Mediating Whistleblow Disputes', *Dispute Resolution Journal*, February/April 2009.

Fine, Cordelia. *A Mind of Its Own: How Your Brain Distorts and Deceives*, W.W. Norton, 2006.

Finkelstein, Sydney. *Why Smart Executives Fail*, New York: Portfolio, 2003.

'First Evidence that Online Dating is Changing the Nature of Society', *MIT Technology Review*, 10 October 2017.

Fitzgerald, C.C. Penrose. *The Life of Vice-Admiral Sir George Tryon K.C.B.*, William Blackwood and Sons, 1897.

Florian, Victor, Mario Mikulincer, and Gilad Hirschberger.'The Anxiety-Buffering Function of Close Relationships: Evidence that Relationship Commitment Acts as a Terror Management Mechanism', *Journal of Personality and Social Psychology* Vol. 82, No. 4, 527, 2002.

Fohrman, Donald W. 'Champaign Couple Heartened by Pending Texting Law', www.illinoispersonalinjurylawyerblog.com, 2009.

Forster, Sophie, and Nilli Lavie. 'Harnessing the Wandering Mind: The Role of Perceptual Load', *Cognition* Vol. 111, 345–55, 2009.

Francis, Sir Robert, QC. 'Freedom to Speak Up: An Independent Review into Creating an Open and Honest Reporting Culture in the NHS', February 2015.

Freedman, Jonathan L., and Scott C. Fraser. 'Compliance without Pressure: The Foot-in-the-Door Technique', *Journal of Personality and Social Psychology* Vol. 4, No. 2, 195–202, 1966.

Frey, Bruno, S., and Felix Oberholzer-Gee. 'The Cost of Price Incentives: An Empirical Analysis of Motivation Crowding-Out', *The American Economic Review* Vol. 87, No. 4, 746–55, 1997.

Fryer, Bronwyn. 'Sleep Deficit: The Performance Killer', *Harvard Business Review* Vol. 84, No. 10, 53–9, 2006.

Gabor, Thomas. *Everybody Does It! Crime by the Public*, University of Toronto Press, 1994.

Garcia, Stephen M., Kim Weaver, Gordon B. Moskowitz, and John M. Darley. 'Crowded Minds: The Implicit Bystander Effect', *Journal of Personality and Social Psychology* Vol. 83, No. 4, 843, 2002.

Gentile, Mary. *Giving Voice to Values*, Yale University Press, 2012.

Gerstein, Marc. *Flirting with Disaster*, New York: Union Square Press, 2008.

Gerstein, Marc S., and Robert B. Shaw. 'Organizational Bystanders', *People & Strategy* Vol. 31, No. 1, 47–54, 2008.

Gibb, Frances. 'Joint Enterprise Law Means Even Bystanders May Get Life', *The Times*, 2009.

Gilbert, Daniel T. 'How Mental Systems Believe', *American Psychologist* Vol. 46, No. 2, 107–19, 1991.

Gilbert, Daniel T., and Randall E. Osborne. 'Thinking Backward: Some Curable and Incurable Consequences of Cognitive Busyness', *Journal of Personality and Social Psychology* Vol. 57, No. 6, 940, 1989.

Gilbert, Daniel T., Brett W. Pelham, and Douglas S. Krull. 'On Cognitive Busyness: When Person Perceivers Meet Persons Perceived', *Journal of Personality and Social Psychology* Vol. 54, No. 5, 733–40, 1988.

Gilbert, Daniel T., Romin W. Tafarodi, and Patrick S. Malone. 'You Can't Not Believe Everything You Read', *Journal of Personality and Social Psychology* Vol. 65, No. 2, 221, 1993.

Gilovich, Thomas. *How We Know What Isn't So: The Fallibility of Human Reason in Everyday Life*, New York: Free Press, 1991.

Glazer, Myron Peretz, and Penina Migdal Glazer. *Whistleblowers: Exposing Corruption in Government and Industry*, Basic Books, 1989.

Gneezy, Uri, and Aldo Rustichini. 'A Fine Is a Price', *Journal of Legal Studies* Vol. 29, No. 1, 1–17, 2000.

Goldfarb, Zachary A. 'Staffer at Sec Had Warned of Madoff', *Washington Post*, 2 July 2009.

Goldie, John, Schwartz, Alex McConachie, and Jillian Morrison. 'Students' Attitudes and Potential Behaviour with Regard to Whistle Blowing as They Pass through a Modern Medical Curriculum', *Medical Education* Vol. 37, 368–75, 2003.

Goleman, Daniel. *Vital Lies, Simple Truths: The Psychology of Self-Deception*, New York: Simon & Schuster, 1985.

Goodman, Michael J., Julie A. Barker, and Christopher A. Monk. 'A Bibliography of Research Related to the Use of Wireless Communications Devices from Vehicles', *National Highway Traffic Safety Administration*, 2005.

Goodwin, Stephanie A., Alexandra Gubin, Susan T. Fiske, and Vincent Y. Qzerbt. 'Power Can Bias Impression Processes: Stereotyping Subordinates by Default and by Design', *Group Processes and Intergroup Relations* Vol. 3, No. 3, 227–56, 2000.

Goodwin, Stephanie A., Don Operario, and Susan T. Fiske. 'Empirical Approaches to Understanding Intergroup Conflict Situational Power and Interpersonal Dominance Facilitate Bias and Inequality', *Journal of Social Issues* Vol. 54, No. 4, 677–98, 1998.

Gordon, Andrew. *The Rules of the Game: Jutland and British Naval Command*, Naval Institute Press, 2000.

Government Accountability Project, 'Internal World Bank Report Finds Staff Fear Reprisal; Corruption Inadequately Addressed', 22 April 2009. www.whistleblower.org

Gray, Judy H., and Iain L. Densten. 'How Leaders Woo Followers in the Romance of Leadership', *Applied Psychology: An International Review* Vol. 56, No. 4, 558–81, 2007.

Green, Stephen. *Good Value: Reflections on Money, Morality and an Uncertain World*, London: Allen Lane, 2009.

Greene, Gayle. *The Woman Who Knew Too Much: Alice Stewart and the Secrets of Radiation*, Ann Arbor: University of Michigan Press, 1999.

Greene, Joshua D., R. Brian Sommerville, Leigh E. Nystrom, John M. Darley, and Jonathan D. Cohen. 'An fMRI Investigation of Emotional Engagement in Moral Judgment', *Science* Vol. 293, No. 5537, 2105–8, 2001.

Greenspan, Alan. *The Age of Turbulence*, Allen Lane, 2007.

Greenspan, Alan. 'The Financial Crisis and the Role of Federal Regulators', testimony before US Congress, House of Representatives, Committee on Oversight and Government Reform, Washington, DC, 23 October 2008.

Greenwald, Anthony G. 'The Totalitarian Ego: Fabrication and Revision of Personal History', *American Psychologist* Vol. 35, No. 7, 603–18, 1980.

Greenwald, Anthony G., and Mahzarin R. Banaji. 'Implicit

Social Cognition: Attitudes, Self-Esteem and Stereotypes', *Psychological Review* Vol. 102, No. 1, 4–27, 1995.

Grimes, T. 'Mild auditory-visual dissonance in television news may exceed viewer attentional capacity', *Human Communication Research* Vol. 18, No. 2, 268–98, 1991.

Groopman, Jerome. 'Diagnosis: What Doctors Are Missing', *New York Review of Books*, 5 November 2009.

Grover, Steen L., and Chun Hui. 'How Job Pressures and Extrinsic Rewards Affect Lying Behavior', *International Journal of Conflict Management* Vol. 16, No. 3, 287–300, 2005.

Gruenfeld, Deborah H. 'Status, Ideology and Integrative Complexity on the Supreme Court: Rethinking the Politics of Political Decision Making', *Journal of Personality and Social Psychology* Vol. 68, No. 1, 5–20, 1995.

Hammond, John S., L. Keeney Ralph, and Howard Raiffa. 'The Hidden Traps in Decision Making', *Harvard Business Review* Vol. 84, No. 1, 118–26, 2006.

Hansen, J., D. Johnson, A. Lacis, S. Lebedeff, P. Lee, D. Rind, and G. Russell. 'Climate Impact of Increasing Atmospheric Carbon Dioxide', *Science* Vol. 213, No. 4511, 957–66, 1981.

'Harassment survey: "I'm a waitress but I feel like a sex worker"', *BBC News*, 11 December 2017.

Harris, Gardiner. 'Prosecutors Plan Crackdown on Doctors Who Accept Kickback', *New York Times*, 4 March 2009.

Hawkins, Peter. 'Organizational Culture: Sailing between Evangelism and Complexity', *Human Relations* Vol. 50, No. 4, 417–40, 1997.

Heffernan, Margaret. *Women on Top*, Penguin Books, 2007.

Henriksen, Kerm, and Elizabeth Dayton. 'Organizational Silence and Hidden Threats to Patient Safety', *Health Services Research* Vol. 41, No. 4, 1539, 2006.

Hester, Robert, and Hugh Garavan. 'Working Memory and Executive Function: The Influence of Content and Load on the Control of Attention', *Memory & Cognition* Vol. 33, No. 2, 221–33, 2005.

Heyman, James, and Dan Ariely. 'Effort for Payment', *Psychological Science* Vol. 15, No. 11, 787–93, 2004.

Hilberg, Raul. *Perpetrators, Victims, Bystanders: The Jewish Catastrophe 1933–1945*, New York: Harper Collins, 1992.

Hill, Andrew. 'Amnesia dooms bankers to repeat their mistakes', *Financial Times*, 25 June 2018.

Hillman, Charles H., Kirk I. Erickson, and Arthur F. Kramer. 'Be Smart, Exercise Your Heart: Exercise Effects on Brain and Cognition', *Nature Reviews Neuroscience* Vol. 9, 58–65, 2008.

Hills, Stuart L. (ed). *Corporate Violence: Injury and Death for Profit*, Lanham, Maryland: Rowman and Littlefield, 1987.

Hitsch, Gunter J., Ali Hortacsu, and Dan Ariely. 'Matching and Sorting in Online Dating', *American Economic Review* Vol. 10, No. 1, 130–63, 2009.

Hofling, Charles K., Eveline Brotzman, Sarah Dalrymple, Nancy Graves, and Chester M. Pierce. 'An Experimental Study in Nurse–Physician Relationships', *Journal of Nervous and Mental Disease* Vol. 143, No. 2, 171–80, 1966.

Hogan, Linda. 'Confronting the Truth: Conscience in the Catholic Tradition', Lahwah: New Jersey, Paulist Press, 2000.

Horrey, William J., Daniel J. Simons, Evan G. Buschmann, and Kevin M. Zinter. 'Assessing Interference from Mental Workload Using a Naturalistic Simulated Driving Task: A Pilot Study', *Proceedings of the Human Factors and Ergonomics Society, 50th Annual Meeting*, 2006.

House of Commons Public Administration and Constitutional Affairs Committee. 'Lessons still to be learned from the

Chilcot inquiry: Government Response to the Committee's Tenth Report of Session 2016–17: Third Special Report of Session 2017–19', 10 January 2018.

Horwitz, Gordon J. *In the Shadow of Death: Living Outside the Gates of Mauthausen*, London: I.B. Tauris & Co., 1991.

Hough, Richard. *Admirals in Collision*, London: Hamish Hamilton, 1959.

Howard, John W., and Myron Rothbard. 'Social Categorization and Memory for in-Group and out-Group Behavior', *Journal of Personality and Social Psychology* Vol. 38, No. 2, 301–10, 1980.

Hughes, Laura. 'Houses of Harassment', *Financial Times* magazine, 16 June 2018.

Hundert, E.M., D. Douglas-Steele, J. Bickel. 'Context in medical education: the informal ethics curriculum', *Medical Education* Vol. 30, 353–64, 1996.

'Independent Inquiry into Child Sexual Exploitation in Rotherham 1997–2013', August 2014.

'Info Overload Can Kill'. *The Star-Ledger News*, 1 October 2006.

Jackson, Maggie. *Distracted: The Erosion of Attention and the Coming Dark Age*, Prometheus Books, 2008.

Janis, Irving L. *Victims of Groupthink: A Psychological Study of Foreign-Policy Decisions and Fiascoes*, Boston: Houghton Mifflin, 1972.

——. *Crucial Decisions: Leadership in Policymaking and Crisis Management*, Free Press, 1989.

Janis, Irving L., and Robert F. Terwilliger. 'An Experimental Study of Psychological Resistances to Fear Arousing Communications', *Journal of Abnormal and Social Psychology* Vol. 65, No. 6, 403–10, 1962.

Joint Commission, 'Behaviors That Undermine a Culture of Safety', *Joint Commission*, 2008.

Kahneman, Daniel. *Attention and Effort*, New York: Prentice Hall, 1973.

Kahneman, Daniel, Alan B. Krueger, David Schkade, Norbert Schwarz, and Arthur A. Stone. 'Would You Be Happier If You Were Richer? A Focusing Illusion', *Science* Vol. 312, No. 5782, 1908–10, 2006.

Kahneman, Daniel, Paul Slovic and Amos Tversky, *Judgement under Uncertainty: Heuristics and Biases*, Cambridge University Press, 1982.

Kahneman, D., and A. Treisman. 'Changing views of attention and automaticity', in R. Parasuraman and R. Davies (eds), *Varieties of Attention*, New York: Academic Press, 1984.

Kantor, Jodi and Megan Twohey. 'Harvey Weinstein Paid Off Harassment Accusers for Decades', *New York Times*, 5 October 2017.

Karabell, Zachary. 'The One Who Saw It Coming', *Newsweek*, 19 January 2009.

Kegan, Robert, and Lisa Laskow Lahey. 'The Real Reason People Won't Change', *Harvard Business Review*, 85–92, 2001.

——. *Immunity to Change: How to Overcome It and Unlock Potential in Yourself and Your Organisation*, Harvard Business Press, 2009.

Kelly, Kate. *Street Fighters: The Last 72 Hours of Bear Stearns, the Toughest Firm on Wall Street*, New York: Portfolio, 2009.

Kerber, Ross. 'The Whistleblower: Dogged Pursuer of Madoff Wary of Fame', Boston.com, 8 January 2009.

Kida, Thomas. *Don't Believe Everything You Think: The 6 Basic Mistakes We Make in Thinking*, Prometheus Books, 2006.

Kirk, Michael. 'The Warning', *Frontline*, PBS, 20 October 2009.

Knight, Sam. 'After Weinstein, Britain's Parliament Confronts its own Sexual-misconduct Scandals', *New Yorker*, 21 November 2017.

Knutson, Brian, Andrew Westdorp, Erica Kaiser, and Daniel Hommer. 'Fmri Visualization of Brain Activity During a Monetary Incentive Delay Task', *NeuroImage* Vol. 12, 20–7, 2000.

Kohn, Nicholas W., and Steven M. Smith. 'Collaborative Fixation: Effects of Others' Ideas on Brainstorming', *Applied Cognitive Psychology* Vol. 25, No. 3, 2010.

Kolb, Bryan, and Ian Q. Whishaw.'Brain Plasticity and Behavior', *Annual Review of Psychology*, No. 49, 43–64, 1998.

Kolbert, Elizabeth. 'The Catastrophist', *New Yorker*, 29 June 2009.

Kolhatkar, Sheekah. 'The Distruptors,' *New Yorker*, 20 November 2017.

Krackow, Annamarie, and Thomas Blass. 'When Nurses Obey or Defy Inappropriate Physician Orders: Attributional Differences', *Journal of Social Behavior and Personality* Vol. 10, No. 3, 585–94, 1995.

Krugman, Paul. 'How Did Economists Get It So Wrong?', *New York Times*, 6 September 2009.

Kuchler, Hannah. 'Tech workers of the world unite!' *Financial Times* magazine, 30 June 2018.

Kunda, Ziva. 'The Case for Motivated Reasoning', *Psychological Bulletin* Vol. 108, No. 3, 480–98, 1990.

Kunst-Wilson, William Raft, and R.B. Zajonc. 'Affective Discrimination of Stimuli That Cannot Be Recognized', *Science* Vol. 207, 557–8, 1980.

Larsen, Knud S., Jeff S. Triplett, William D. Brant, and Don Langenberg.'Collaborator Status, Subject Characteristics and Conformity in the Asch Paradigm', *Journal of Social Psychology* Vol. 108, 259–63, 1979.

Larson, Selena. 'Facebook's Ad Options Could be Discriminatory', *CNN Money*, 30 October 2016.

Latané, Bibb, and John Darley. 'Group Inhibition of Bystander Intervention in Emergencies', *Journal of Personality and Social Psychology* Vol. 10, No. 3, 215–21, 1968.

——. 'Apathy', *American Scientist* Vol. 57, 244–68, 1969.

Latané, B., and Steve Nida. 'Ten Years of Research on Group Size and Helping', *Psychological Bulletin* Vol. 89, No. 2, 308–24, 1981.

Latané, B., and J. Rodin. 'A Lady in Distress: Inhibiting Effects of Friends and Strangers on Bystander Intervention', *Journal of Experimental Social Psychology* Vol. 5, No. 2, 189–202, 1969.

Layton, Deborah. *Seductive Poison: A Jonestown Survivor's Story of Life and Death in the Peoples Temple*, Aurum Press, 1999.

Lazear, Edward P. 'Performance Pay and Productivity', *American Economic Review* Vol. 90, No. 5, 1346–61, 2000.

Lea, Stephen E.G., and Paul Webley. 'Money as Tool, Money as Drug: The Biological Psychology of a Strong Incentive', *Behavioral and Brain Sciences* Vol. 29, 161–209, 2006.

Lee Hamilton, V., and Joseph Sanders. 'Personality and Social Psychology Review', *Personality and Social Psychology Review* Vol. 3, 222–233, 1999.

Lewis, Michael. *The Big Short: Inside the Doomsday Machine*, New York: W.W. Norton and Co., 2010.

Liu, James H., and Bibb Latané. 'Extremization of Attitudes: Does Thought- and Discussion-Induced Polarization Cumulate?', *Basic and Applied Social Psychology* Vol. 20, No. 2, 103–10, 1998.

Lizza, Ryan. 'The Contrarian', *New Yorker*, 6 & 13 July 2009.

Long, Jennifer. 'Testimony at the Oversight Hearing on the Internal Revenue Service', *US Senate Committee on Finance*, 1997.

Luborsky, Lester, and Barton Blinder. 'Looking, Recalling and GSR as a Function of Defense', *Journal of Abnormal Psychology* Vol. 70, No. 4, 270–80, 1965.

Lundberg, George D. 'How Will Changes in Physician Payment by Medicare Influence Laboratory Testing?', *Journal of the American Medical Association* Vol. 258, No. 6, 803–9, 1987.

Luo, Shanhong, and Eva C. Klohnen. 'Assortative Mating and Marital Quality in Newlyweds: A Couple-Centered

Approach', *Journal of Personality and Social Psychology* Vol. 88, No. 2, 304, 2005.

MacFarquhar, Larissa. 'The Deflationist: How Paul Krugman found politics' *New Yorker*, 1 March 2010.

Mack, Arien. 'Inattentional Blindness: Looking without Seeing', *Current Directions in Psychological Science* Vol. 12, No. 5, 180–4, 2003.

Macrae, C. Neil, Alan B. Milne, and Galen V. Bodenhausen. 'Stereotypes as Energy-Saving Devices: A Peek inside the Cognitive Toolbox', *Journal of Personality and Social Psychology* Vol. 66, No.1, 37, 1994.

Makary, Martin A., and Michael Daniel. 'Medical error – the third leading cause of death in the US', *BMJ* Vol. 353, i2139, 2016.

Manz, Charles C., Vikas Anand, Mahendra Joshi, and Karen P. Manz. 'Emerging Paradoxes in Executive Leadership: A Theoretical Interpretation between Corruption and Virtuous Values', *Leadership Quarterly*, No. 19, 385–92, 2008.

Marcus, Jonathan L. 'Model Penal Code Section 2.02(7) and Willful Blindness', *Yale Law Journal* Vol. 102, No. 8, 2231–57, 1993.

Marcus, Jonathan L. 'Symposium: Economic Competitiveness and the Law', *Yale Law Journal*, Vol. 102, No. 8, 2231–2257, June 1993.

Markey, P.M. 'Bystander Intervention in Computer-Mediated Communication', *Computers in Human Behavior* Vol. 16, No. 2, 183–8, 2000.

Markopolos, Harry. *No One Would Listen: A True Financial Thriller*, Hoboken, New Jersey: Wiley & Sons, 2010.

——. Written testimony before the US Senate Banking, Housing and Urban Affairs Committee, Thursday 10 September 2009.

——. Testimony before the US House of Representatives Committee on Financial Services, Wednesday 4 February 2009.

Marsh, Jason. 'We Are All Bystanders', *Greater Good*, Fall/Winter, 2006.

Marsh, Stefanie, and Bojan Pancevski. *The Crimes of Josef Fritzl: Uncovering the Truth*, London: Harper Element, 2009.

Martin, J., B. Lobb, G. Chapman, and R. Spillane. 'Obedience under conditions demanding self-immolation', *Human Relations* Vol. 29, 345–56, 1976.

Martz, John M., Julie Verette, Ximena B. Arriaga, Linda F. Slovik, Chante L. Cox, and Caryl Rusbult. 'Positive Illusion in Close Relationships', *Personal Relationships* Vol. 5, 159–81, 1998.

Maslach, Christina, and Michael P. Leiter. *The Truth About Burnout: How Organizations Cause Personal Stress and What to Do About It*, Jossey-Bass, 1997.

Massing, Michael. 'The News About the Internet', *New York Review of Books*, 13 August 2009.

McCarley, Jason. 'Elements of Human Performance in Baggage X-ray Screening', paper presented at the Fourth Annual Aviation Security Technology Symposium, Washington, DC, 29 November 2006.

McCartney, Tara. 'I Kept Saying, "Help Me, Help Me." But No One Did', *Guardian*, 4 August 2005.

McClellan, Scott. *What Happened: Inside the Bush White House and Washington's Culture of Deceptions*, New York: Public Affairs, 2008.

McGreevy, Ronan. 'Most people no longer trust the Church, Government or banks', *Irish Times*, 29 April 2010.

McLaughlin, Brian P., and Amelie Oksenberg Rorty (eds). *Perspectives on Self-Deception*, University of California Press, 1988.

McTague, Jim. 'Looking at Greenspan's Long-Lost Thesis', *Barron's*, 28 April 2008.

Mead, Nicole L., Roy F. Baumeister, Francesca Gino, Maurice E. Schweitzer, and Dan Ariely. 'Too Tired to Tell the Truth: Self-Control Resource Depletion and Dishonesty', *Journal of Experimental Social Psychology* Vol. 45, No. 3, 594–7, 2009.

Mele, Alfred R. *Self-Deception Unmasked*, Princeton University Press, 2001.

Mendelson, Sarah E., and Theodore P. Gerber. 'Failing the Stalin Test', *Foreign Affairs* Vol. 85, No. 1, 2006.

Mesmer-Magnus, Jessica, Chockalingam Viswesvaran, Jacob Joseph, and Satish P. Deshpande. 'The Role of Emotional Intelligence in Integrity and Ethics Perceptions', *Emotions, Ethics and Decision-Making: Research on Emotion in Organizations* Vol. 4, 225–39, 2008.

Miceli, Marcia P., and Janet P. Near. 'Standing up or Standing By: What Predicts Blowing the Whistle on Organizational Wrongdoing?', *Research in Personnel and Human Resources Management* Vol. 24, 93–136, 2005.

Milgram, Stanley. 'The Experience of Living in Cities', *Science* Vol. 167, 1970.

——. *Obedience to Authority*, Harper Perennial, 1974.

Milkman, Katherine L., Dolly Chugh, and Max H. Bazerman. 'How Can Decision Making Be Improved?', *Perspectives on Psychological Science* Vol. 4, No. 4, 379–83, 2009.

Miller, Dale T., and Cathy McFarland. 'Pluralistic Ignorance: When Similarity Is Interpreted as Dissimilarity', *Journal of Personality and Social Psychology* Vol. 53, No. 2, 298–305, 1987.

Miller, Rowland S. *Embarrassment: Poise and Peril in Everyday Life*, Guilford Press, 1996.

Milliken, Charles S., Jennifer L. Auchterlonie, and Charles W. Hoge. 'Longitudinal Assessment of Mental Health Problems among Active and Reserve Component Soldiers Returning from the Iraq War', *Journal of the American Medical Association* Vol. 298, No. 18, 2141–8, 2007.

Milliken, Frances, J., and Elizabeth Wolfe Morrison. 'Shades of Silence: Emerging Themes and Future Directions for Research on Silence in Organizations', *Journal of Management Studies* Vol. 40, No. 6, 1563–8, 2003.

Milliken Frances, J., Elizabeth W. Morrison, and Patricia F. Hewlin. 'An Exploratory Study of Employee Silence: Issues that Employees Don't Communicate Upward and Why', *Journal of Management Studies* Vol. 40, No. 6, 1453–76, 2003.

Milliken, F.J., J.C. Magee, N. Lam, and D. Menezes. 'The lens and language of power: Sense-making gaps in the aftermath of Hurricane Katrina', New York University, 2009 (unpublished).

Molinsky, Andrew L., Adam M. Grant, and Joshua D. Margolis. 'The bedside manner of homo economicus: How and why priming an economic schema reduces compassion', *Organizational Behavior and Human Decision Processes*, Vol. 119, 27–37, 2012.

Moll, Jorge, Frank Krueger, Roland Zahn, Matteo Pardini, Ricardo de Oliveira-Souza, and Jordan Grafman. 'Human Fronto-Mesolimbic Networks Guide Decisions About Charitable Donation', *Proceedings of the National Academy of Sciences* Vol. 103, No. 42, 15623–8, 2006.

Moore, Carter & Associates with Prof. Andrew Kakabadse. 'The Riskminds Risk Managers Survey 2009: The Causes and Implications of the 2008 Banking Crisis', March 2010.

Moore, Don A., and George Loewenstein.'Self-Interest, Automaticity, and the Psychology of Conflict of Interest', *Social Justice Research* Vol. 17, No. 2, 189–202, 2004.

Moreland, Richard L., and Robert B. Zajonc. 'Exposure Effects in Person Perception: Familiarity, Similarity, and

Attraction', *Journal of Experimental Social Psychology* Vol. 18, 395–415, 1982.

Morewedge, Carey K., Daniel T. Gilbert, and Timothy D. Wilson. 'The Least Likely of Times', *Psychological Science* Vol. 16, No. 8, 626–30, 2005.

Morris, Errol. *Standard Operating Procedure*, Sony Pictures, 2008.

Morrison Elizabeth, W., Sara L. Wheeler-Smith, and Dishan Kamdar. 'Speaking up in Groups: A Cross-Level Study of Group Voice Climate', *Journal of Applied Psychology* (read under review), 2009.

Moscovici, Serge, and Marisa Zavalloni. 'The Group as a Polarizer of Attitudes', *Journal of Personality and Social Psychology* Vol. 12, No. 2, 125–35, 1969.

Murray, Sandra L., John G. Holmes, Gina Bellavia, Dale W. Griffin, and Dan Dolderman. 'Kindred Spirits? The Benefits of Egocentrism in Close Relationships', *Journal of Personality and Social Psychology* Vol. 82, No. 4, 2002.

Murray, Sandra L., John G. Holmes, and Dale W. Griffin. 'The Self-Fulfilling Nature of Positive Illusions in Romantic Relationships: Love Is Not Blind, but Prescient', *Journal of Personality and Social Psychology* Vol. 7, No. 6, 1155–80, 1996.

National Safety Council, 'National Safety Council Calls for Nationwide Ban on Cell Phone Use While Driving' Press Release, 12 January 2009.

National Sleep Foundation, '2009 Asleep in America: Poll Highlight and Findings', 2 March 2009.

Nedd, Council A. II. 'When the Solution Is the Problem: A Brief History of the Shoe Fluoroscope', *American Journal of Roentgenology* Vol. 158, 1270, 1992.

Nemeth, Charles, Ofra Mayseless, Jeffrey Sherman, and Yvonne Brown. 'Exposure to Dissent and Recall of Information', *Journal of Personality and Social Psychology* Vol. 58, No. 3, 429–437, 1990.

Newrx.com. 'Women Whistleblowers Suffer More Discrimination Informs-Published Study Suggests', *Integrity International website*, 28 May 2008.

Nobuyuki, Chikudate. 'Collective Myopia and Disciplinary Power Behind the Scenes of Unethical Practices: A Diagnostic Theory on Japanese Organization', *Journal of Management Studies* Vol. 39, No. 3, 289–307, 2002.

Norton, Michael I., Jeana H. Frost, and Dan Ariely. 'Less Is More: The Lure of Ambiguity, or Why Familiarity Breeds Contempt', *Journal of Personality and Social Psychology* Vol. 92, No. 1, 97–105, 2007.

Norton, Michael I., Benoit Monin, Joel Cooper, and Michael A. Hogg. 'Vicarious Dissonance: Attitude Change from the Inconsistency of Others', *Journal of Personality and Social Psychology* Vol. 85, No. 1, 47–62, 2003.

O'Gorman, Colm. *Beyond Belief*, Hodder and Stoughton, 2009.

O'Neill, Cathy. *Weapons of Math Destruction*, New York: Penguin Books, 2017.

O'Neill, Sean and Fariha Karim. 'Keep costs of cladding down, Grenfell Tower experts told', *The Times*, 30 June 2017.

Osborne, Hilary. 'Poor doors: the segregation of London's inner-city flat dwellers', *Guardian*, 25 July 2014.

Osiel, Mark J. *Obeying Orders: Atrocity, Military Discipline and the Law of War*, New Brunswick, New Jersey: Transaction Publishers, 2002.

Panksepp, Jaak. 'Neuroscience: Feeling the Pain of Social Loss', *Science* Vol. 302, No. 5643, 237–9, 2003.

——. *Affective Neuroscience: The Foundations of Human and Animal Emotions*, Oxford University Press, 1998.

Panksepp, J., S.M. Siviy, and L.A. Normansell. 'Brain opioids and social emotions', in M. Reite, and T. Field (eds), *The Psychobiology of Attachment and Separation*, New York: Academic Press, 3–49, 1985.

Paperny, Justin M. *Lessons from Prison: Bear Stearns, UBS Stockbroker Muses on Ethics and Provides Guide through Criminal Justice System*, APS Publishing, 2009.

Parker-Pope, Tara. 'A Problem of the Brain, Not the Hands: Group Urges Phone Ban for Drivers', *New York Times*, 2009.

Partnoy, Frank. *Infectious Greed: How Deceit and Risk Corrupted the Financial Markets*, Profile Books, 2003.

——. 'The Case against Alan Greenspan', *Euromoney* Vol. 36, No. 437, 90–6, 2005.

——. *F.I.A.S.C.O.: Blood in the Water on Wall Street*, W.W. Norton, 1997, 2009.

Partnoy, Frank, and Jesse Eisinger. 'What's Inside America's Banks?', *The Atlantic*, January/February 2013.

Pascual-Leonoe, Alvaro, Nguyet Dang, Leonardo G. Cohen, Joaquim P. Brasil-Neto, Angel Cammarota, and Mark Hallett. 'Modulation of Muscle Responses Evoked by Transcranial Magnetic Stimulation during the Acquisition of New Fine Motor Skills', *Journal of Neurophysiology* Vol. 74, No. 3, 1037–45, 1995.

Pavlo, Walter Jr, and Neil Weinberg. *Stolen Without a Gun*, Tampa, Florida: Etika LLC, 2007.

Pearson, Mary. 'An Overview of the Enron Collapse', US Senate Hearing, 18 December 2001.

Pelham, Brett W., Matthew C. Mirenberg, and John T. Jones. 'Why Susie Sells Seashells by the Seashore: Implicit Egotism and Major Life Decisions', *Journal of Personality and Social Psychology* Vol. 82, No. 4, 469, 2002.

Pennebaker, Ruth. 'The Mediocre Multitasker', *New York Times*, 30 August 2009.

Perkins, Anne, and Amelia Gentleman. 'Government knew for years of risk to Windrush children', *Guardian*, 23 April 2018.

Perry, David L. 'Why Hearts and Minds Matter', *Armed Forces Journal*, September 2006.

Pessiglione, Mathias, Liane Schmidt, Bogdan Draganski, Raffael Kalisch, Hakwan Lau, Ray J. Dolan, and Chris D. Frith. 'How the Brain Translates Money into Force: A Neuroimaging Study of Subliminal Motivation', *Science* Vol. 316, No. 5826, 904–6, 2007.

Petty, Richard E., Gary L. Wells, and Timothy C. Brock. 'Distraction Can Enhance or Reduce Yielding to Propaganda: Thought Disruption Versus Effort Justification', *Journal of Personality and Social Psychology* Vol. 34, No. 5, 874–84, 1976.

Phillips, Katherine W., and Robert B. Lount. 'The Affective Consequences of Diversity and Homogeneity in Groups', *Affect and Groups: Research on Managing Groups and Teams* Vol. 10, 1–20, 2007.

'Physician, heal thyself', *The Economist*, 30 June 2018.

Piderit, Sandy Kristin, and Susan J. Ashford. 'Breaking Silence: Tactical Choices Women Managers Make in Speaking up About Gender-Equity Issues', *Journal of Management Studies* Vol. 40, No. 6, 1477–1502, 2003.

Pink, Daniel H. *Drive: The Surprising Truth about What Motivates Us*, New York: Canongate, 2009.

Premeaux Sonya, Fontenot, and G. Bedeian Arthur. 'Breaking the Silence: The Moderating Effects of Self-Monitoring in Predicting Speaking up in the Workplace', *Journal of Management Studies* Vol. 40, No. 6, 1537–62, 2003.

Prentice, Deborah A., and Dale T. Miller. 'Pluralistic Ignorance and Alcohol Use on Campus: Some Consequences of Misperceiving the Social Norm', *Journal of Personality and Social Psychology* Vol. 64, No. 2, 243, 1993.

Proctor, Robert N., and Londa Schiebinger (eds). *Agnotology: The Making and Unmaking of Ignorance*, Stanford University Press, 2008.

Pronin, Emily, Thomas Gilovich, and Lee Ross. 'Objectivity in the Eye of the Beholder: Divergent Perceptions of Bias in Self Versus Others', *Psychological Review* Vol. 111, No. 3, 781–99, 2004.

Proulx, Travis, and J. Heine Steven. 'Connections from Kafka: Exposure to Meaning Threats Improves Implicit Learning of an Artificial Grammar', *Psychological Science* Vol. 20, No. 9, 1125–31, 2009.

'Quietly, Congress extends a ban on CDC research on gun violence', *The Takeaway*, Public Radio International, 2 July 2015.

Rank, Mark. *One Nation, Underprivileged: Why American Poverty Affects Us All*, Oxford University Press, 2004.

Reite, M., and T. Field (eds). *The Psychobiology of Attachment and Separation*, New York: Academic Press, 1985.

'Report on the Mid Staffordshire NHS Foundation Trust Public Inquiry: Executive Summary', February 2013.

Richtel, Matt. 'U.S. Withheld Data on Risks of Distracted Driving', *New York Times*, 21 July 2009.

Robertson, Diana, John Snarey, Opal Ousley, Keith Harenski, F. DuBois Bowman, Rick Gilkey, and Clinton Kilts. 'The Neural Processing of Moral Sensitivity to Issues of Justice and Care', *Neuropsychologia* Vol. 45, No. 4, 755–66, 2007.

Robinson, Evan. 'Why Crunch Mode Doesn't Work: 6 Lessons', *International Game Developers Association*, 2005.

Rosenhan, D.L. 'On Being Sane in Insane Places', *Science* Vol. 179, No. 4070, 250–8, 1973.

Rosin, Hanna. 'When Joseph Comes Marching Home: In a Western Maryland Town, Ambivalence About the Son Who Blew the Whistle at Abu Ghraib', *Washington Post*, 17 May 2004.

Rost, Peter. *The Whistleblower: Confessions of a Healthcare Hitman*, Soft Skull Press, 2006.

Rothschild, Jeffrey M., Carol A. Keohane, Selwyn Rogers, and Charles A. Czeisler. 'Risks of Complications by Attending Physicians after Performing Nighttime Procedures', *Journal of the American Medical Association* Vol. 302, No. 14, 1565–72, 2009.

Roubini, Nouriel. '"The Biggest Slump in US Housing in the Last 40 Years" … Or 53 Years?', *RGE Monitor*, 23 August 2006.

Rowe, Mary. 'Dealing with – or Reporting – "Unacceptable" Behavior (with additional thoughts about the "Bystander Effect")', *Journal of the International Ombudsman Association* Vol. 2, No. 1, 2009.

Sandel, Michael. 'Markets and Morals: A New Citizenship', The Reith Lectures, 2009.

Sanders, William Gerard, and Donald C. Hambrick. 'The Effects of CEO Incentive Compensation on Subsequent Firm Investments and Performance' (unpublished).

Sands, Philippe. 'Polished, Assured … But Was He Persuasive? No', *Guardian*, 28 January 2010.

Schmitt, Rick. 'Prophet and Loss', *Stanford*, 2009.

Schneider, Andrew, and David McCumber. *An Air That Kills: How the Asbestos Poisoning of Libby, Montana Uncovered a National Scandal*, G.P. Putnam's Sons, 2004.

Schwab, R.S. 'Motivation in measurements of fatigue', in W.F. Floyd and A.T. Welford (eds), *Fatigue*, London: H.K. Lewis, 1953.

Schwartz, Barry. 'Incentives, Choice, Education and Well-Being', *Oxford Review of Education* Vol. 35, No. 3, 391–403, 2009.

Seager, Ashley. 'Method of Inflation Targeting Was Wrong', *Guardian*, 2009.

Seligman, Martin E.P. *Authentic Happiness*, Nicholas Brealey Publishing, 2003.

Sereny, Gitta. *Albert Speer: His Battle with Truth*, Picador, 1996.
——. *The German Trauma: Experiences and Reflections 1938–2001*, Penguin, 2001.
Sheridan, Charles L., and Richard G. King. 'Obedience to Authority with an Authentic Victim', *Proceedings, 80th Annual Convention, APA*, 165–6, 1972.
Shermer, Michael. 'The Political Brain', *Scientific American*, 26 June 2006.
Simons, Daniel J. 'Inattentional Blindness', *Scholarpedia* Vol. 2, No. 5, 3244, 2007.
Simons, Daniel J., and Christopher F. Chabris. 'Gorillas in Our Midst: Sustained Inattentional Blindness for Dynamic Events', *Perception* Vol. 28, 1059–74, 1999.
Smith, J. Walker, Ann Clurman, and Craig Wood. *Coming to Concurrence: Addressable Attitudes and the New Model for Marketing Productivity*, Racom Communications, 2005.
Snow, John. 'The Financial Crisis and the Role of the Federal Regulators', testimony before Congress, House of Representatives, Committee on Oversight and Government Reform, 23 October 2008.
Sophocles. *The Theban Plays*, Penguin, 1947.
Sorkin, Andrew Ross. *Too Big to Fail: Inside the Battle to Save Wall Street*, Allen Lane, 2010.
Stanovich, Keith E., and Richard F. West. 'Individual Differences in Reasoning: Implications for the Rationality Debate?', *Behavioral and Brain Sciences* Vol. 23, 645–726, 2000.
Staub, Ervin. 'The Roots of Evil: Social Conditions, Culture, Personality, and Basic Human Needs', *Personality and Social Psychology Review* Vol. 3, 179–92, 1999.
——. *The Psychology of Good and Evil: Why Children, Adults, and Groups Help and Harm Others*, Cambridge University Press, 2003.
Stewart, Alice, Josefine Webb, and David Hewitt. 'A Survey

of Childhood Malignancies', *British Medical Journal*, 1495–508, 1958.

Stillman, T.F., R.F. Baumeister, N.M. Lambert, A.W. Crescioni, C.N. DeWall, and F.D. Fincham. 'Alone and without Purpose: Life Loses Meaning Following Social Exclusion', *Journal of Experimental Social Psychology* Vol. 45, No. 4, 686–94, 2009.

Stone, Jeff, and Joel Cooper. 'A Self-Standards Model of Cognitive Dissonance', *Journal of Experimental Social Psychology* Vol. 37, 228–43, 2001.

Strayer, David L., Frank A. Drews, and Dennis J. Crouch. 'A Comparison of the Cell Phone Driver and the Drunk Driver', *Human Factors* Vol. 48, No. 2, 381–91, 2006.

Sunstein, Cass R. *Going to Extremes: How Like Minds Unite and Divide*, Oxford University Press, 2009.

Swartz, Mimi, and Sherron Watkins. *Power Failure: The Inside Story of the Collapse of Enron*, Doubleday, 2003.

Taleb, Nassim Nicholas. 'David, You're Right', *Observer*, 16 August 2009.

Tangirala, Subrahmaniam, and Rangaraj Ramanujam. 'Employee Silence on Critical Work Issues: The Cross Level Effects of Procedural Justice Climate', *Personnel Psychology* Vol. 61, 37–68, 2008.

Tangney, June Price. *Self-Conscious Emotions: The Psychology of Shame, Guilt, Embarrassment and Pride*, Guilford Press, 1995.

Tarnow, Eugen. 'Self Destructive Obedience in the Airplane Cockpit and the Concept of Obedience Optimization', in Thomas Blass (ed), *Obedience to Authority: Current Perspectives on the Milgram Paradigm*, New Jersey: Erlbaum Associates, 2000.

Tavris, Carol, and Elliot Aronson. *Mistakes Were Made (But Not by Me): Why We Justify Foolish Beliefs, Bad Decisions and Hurtful Acts*, Harcourt Inc., 2007.

Tedlow Richard, S. 'Leaders in Denial', *Harvard Business Review* Vol. 86, No. 7–8, 18–19, 2008.

Tedlow, Richard S., and David Ruben. 'The Dangers of Wishful Thinking', *American*, 86–90, 2008.

Telos Group. 'BP Texas City Site Report of Findings: Texas City's Protection Performance, Behaviors, Culture, Management and Leadership', 21 January 2005.

Tenbrunsel, Ann E., Kristina A. Diekmann, Kimberly A. Wade-Benzoni, and Max H. Bazerman. 'The Ethical Mirage: A Temporal Explanation as to Why We Aren't as Ethical as We Think We Are', Harvard Business School Working Paper 08–12, 2007.

Tenbrunsel, Ann E., and David M. Messick.'Ethical Fading: The Role of Self-Deception in Unethical Behavior', *Social Justice Research* Vol. 17, No. 2, 223–36, 2004.

Tett, Gillian. *Fool's Gold: How Unrestrained Greed Corrupted a Dream, Shattered Global Markets and Unleashed a Catastrophe*, London: Little, Brown, 2009.

Thaler, Richard H. 'From Homo Economicus to Homo Sapiens', *Journal of Economic Perspectives* Vol. 14, No. 1, 133–41, 2000.

Thompson, Courtenay. 'Willful Blindness', *Internal Auditor*, 71–3, June 2003.

Thornberg, Robert. 'A Classmate in Distress: Schoolchildren as Bystanders and Their Reasons for How They Act', *Social Psychology of Education* Vol. 10, 5–28, 2007.

Tierney, John. 'How to Concentrate in a World of Distractions', *New York Times*, 31 May 2009.

Tomasi, D., R.L. Wang, F. Telang, V. Boronikolas, M.C. Jayne, G.-J. Wang, J.S. Fowler, and N.D. Volkow. 'Impairment of Attentional Networks after One Night of Sleep Deprivation', *Cerebral Cortex* Vol. 19, No. 1, 233–40, 2009.

'Tragedy of Sun-loving Air Hostess who Died from Cancer Aged Just 25', *Daily Mail*, 3 October 2009.

Treanor, Jill. 'Bankers Admit They Got It Wrong', *Guardian*, 11 February 2009.

——. 'Shown the Door – Brown's Banker Falls Victim to the Whistleblower', *Guardian*, 12 February 2009.

United States of America vs Kenneth L. Lay, United States District Court for the Southern District of Texas, Houston Division, May 2006 (transcript).

University of California, Berkeley. *Human Factors Curriculum for Refinery Workers.*

US Chemical Safety and Hazard Investigation Board. 'Investigation Report: Refinery Explosion and Fire (15 Killed, 180 Injured) BP Texas City, March 23, 2005', report no. 2005-04-I-TX, March 2007.

Van Dyne, Linn, Soon Ang, and C. Botero Isabel. 'Conceptualizing Employee Silence and Employee Voice as Multidimensional Constructs', *Journal of Management Studies* Vol. 40, No. 6, 1359–92, 2003.

van Straaten, Ischa, Rutger C.M.E. Engels, Catrin Finkenauer, and Rob W. Holland. 'Meeting Your Match: How Attractiveness Similarity Affects Approach Behavior in Mixed-Sex Dyads', *Personality and Social Psychology Bulletin.* Vol. 35, No. 6, 685–97, 2009.

van Veen, Vincent, Marie K. Krug, Jonathan W. Schooler, and Cameron S. Carter. 'Neural Activity Predicts Attitude Change in Cognitive Dissonance', *Nature Neuroscience* Vol. 12, No. 11, 1469–74, 2009.

Vermeulen, Freek. 'Why Stock Options Are a Bad Option', *Harvard Business Review* (website), 21 April 2009.

Virtanen, Marianna, Stephen A. Stansfield, Rebecca Fuhrer, Jane E. Ferrie, and Mika Kivimaki. 'Overtime Work as a Predictor of Major Depressive Episode: A Five Year

Follow-up of the Whitehall II Study', *PLoS ONE* 7, No. 1, e30719, 2012.

Virtanen, Marianna et al. 'Long Working Hours and Cognitive Function: The Whitehall II Study', *American Journal of Epidemiology* Vol. 169, No. 5, 93–605, 1 March 2009.

Vohs, Kathleen, D. 'Merely Activating the Concept of Money Changes Personal and Interpersonal Behavior', *Current Directions in Psychological Science* Vol. 17, No. 3, 208–12, 2008.

Vohs, Kathleen D., Nicole L. Mead, and Miranda R. Goode. 'The Psychological Consequences of Money', *Science* Vol. 314, No. 5802, 1154–6, 2006.

Walker, Matthew. *Why We Sleep: The New Science of Sleep and Dreams*, London: Allen Lane, 2017.

Walker Report, 'Psychological and Behavioural Elements in Board Performance', Annex 4, 2009.

Webb, Tim. 'Sun King Reveals His Darker Side', *Guardian*, 9 February 2010.

Webb, Tim, Robert Booth, Justin McCurry, and Paul Harris. 'How World's Biggest Carmaker Managed to Veer So Far Off Course', *Observer*, 7 February 2010.

Weinberger, Joel, and Drew Westen. 'Rats, We Should Have Used Clinton: Subliminal Priming in Political Campaigns', *Political Psychology* Vol. 29, No. 5, 631–51, 2008.

Weisbuch, Max, Stacey A. Sinclair, and Jeanine L. Skorinko. 'Self-Esteem Depends on the Beholder: Effects of a Subtle Social Value Cue', *Journal of Experimental Social Psychology* Vol. 45, No. 1, 143–9, 2009.

Werner, Anna. 'Oakland Bank's Lending Sparks Ex-Employee Lawsuit', *CBS.com*, 21 May 2008.

Wertz, Adam T., Joseph M. Ronda, and Charles A. Czeisler. 'Effects of Sleep Inertia on Cognition', *Journal of the American Medical Association* Vol. 295, No. 2, 2006.

Westen, Drew. *The Political Brain: The Role of Emotion in Deciding the Fate of the Nation*, New York: Public Affairs, 2007.

Westen, Drew, Pavel S. Blagov, Keith Harenski, Clint Kilts, and Stephan Hamann. 'Neural Bases of Motivated Reasoning: An fMRI Study of Emotional Constraints on Partisan Political Judgment in the 2004 U.S. Presidential Election', *Journal of Cognitive Neuroscience* Vol. 18, No. 11, 1947–58, 2006.

White, Jenny, Albert Bandura, and Lisa A. Bero. 'Moral Disengagement in the Corporate World', *Accountability in Research* Vol. 16, No. 1, 41–74, 2009.

Wispe, Lauren. *Altruism, Sympathy and Helping: Psychological and Sociological Principles*, Academic Press, 1978.

Wolf, T.M., P.M. Balson, J.M. Faucett, and H.M. Randall. 'A retrospective study of attitude change during medical education', *Medical Education* Vol. 23, 19–23, 1989.

Wong, Julia Carrie, and Paul Lewis. 'Facebook gave data about 57bn friendships to academic', *Guardian*, 22 March 2018.

Woodward, Bob. *Maestro: Greenspan's Fed and the American Boom*, Simon & Schuster, 2000.

——. *State of Denial: Bush at War, Part III*, Simon & Schuster, 2006.

Young-Bruehl, Elisabeth. *Hannah Arendt: For Love of the World*, New Haven: Yale University Press, 1982.

Zerubavel, Eviatar. *The Elephant in the Room: Silence and Denial in Everyday Life*, Oxford: Oxford University Press, 2006.

Zhou, Xinyue, Cong Feng, Lingnan He, and Ding-Guo Gao. 'Toward an Integrated Understanding of Love and Money: Intrinsic and Extrinsic Pain Management Mechanisms', *Psychological Inquiry* Vol. 19, 208–20, 2008.

Zhou, Xinyue, Kathleen D. Vohs, and Roy F. Baumeister. 'The Symbolic Power of Money: Reminders of Money Alter Social Distress and Physical Pain', *Psychological Science* Vol. 20, No. 6, 700–6, 2009.

Zimbardo, Philip G., 'Discontinuity Theory: Cognitive and Social Searches for Rationality and Normality May Lead to Madness', *Advances in Experimental Social Psychology* Vol. 31, 345–413, 1991.

——. *The Lucifer Effect: How Good People Turn Evil*, Random House, 2007.

——. 'The Heroic Imagination Project', Planning documents, 2009.

Zuckerberg, Mark. Senate's Commerce and Judiciary Committee hearing, 10 April 2018.

Index

Acknowledgements

Had it not been for the commissioning courage of the BBC's Jeremy Howe, Clare McGinn and Sara Davies, I would never have found myself submerged in the transcript of Ken Lay's trial. Encountering the legal doctrine of wilful blindness felt like introducing a magnet to a mess of iron filings. Without Fiona Wilson, I would not have had access to that transcript and without a timely conversation with Joelle Delbourgo, my ensuing thoughts might have gone nowhere. If it weren't for Alan Weber and Claire Alexander, I might not be writing at all. Since then, Suzanne Baboneau and Mike Jones have proved staunch supporters of my work. My agent, Natasha Fairweather, has been incredibly tolerant of my impatience and generous with her kindness, time and insights.

One of the glories of American academic life has been the openness and enthusiasm with which scholars generously share their work and insights with curious investigators. I am immensely grateful to all of those who appear in this book, who gave their time generously and were always prepared to engage with my questions and challenges. If their work is imperfectly articulated, that is my fault, not theirs. I'd also like to thank Beth Edwards for guiding me through the legal nuances of wilful blindness. In Texas, the attorneys Brent Coon and Eric Newell were thoughtful and generous in sharing with me their years of insight into the workings of BP. They will, alas, be at work for many years to come.

I would also like to thank the people of Libby, Montana, who were open, hospitable and generous. Their character is more impressive even than the stunning surroundings in which they live.

In the United Kingdom, I am especially grateful to the London Library and the library at the University of Bath, without whose resources I would have been blind indeed. I would also like to thank Don Honeyman and the late, great Gitta Sereny for being prepared to share their memories of Speer after all these years. I will always be indebted to Donna Banks and Nancy Coveney, whose obsessive fact-checking made me a more fastidious writer. I'd also like to thank my colleagues at Merryck & Co. and in Jericho Chambers for letting me share some of my thinking with them.

I'd like to thank Jenni Waugh for her research support and Stephanie Cooper-Lande for her help in keeping other commitments at bay. In tracking down a strange array of experts, fraudsters and Cassandras, Isobel Eaton proved fearless and determined, regardless of time zone. Crossing the United States in what sometimes felt like a tour of industrial disasters, I was hugely encouraged and energised by the hospitality, generosity and kindness of Paul Muldoon, Jean Hanff Korelitz, Rob and Fiona Wilson, Donald Low, Geeta Sheker, Tatiana Bicât, Cindy Solomon, Juliet Blake, Beth and Chuck Finkle. I'd also like to thank Nick Bicât and Philip Ridley for writing, in 'Lie to Me', the wilful blindness theme song.

Updating this book has been an ambivalent experience. Every writer wishes their thesis to be vindicated; I found myself wishing mine had been less so. But I am deeply grateful to all of those individuals, corporations and institutions that have embraced my argument and deepened my understanding. Around the world, many individuals from all walks of life have sent me information about new examples of wilful blindness. Not all wish to be mentioned but I would like to thank, in particular, Bryony Kendall and Helene Donnelly in the NHS and Ben Alcott at the CAA.

If at times writing this book made me wilfully blind to the needs and wants of my two children, Felix and Leonora Nicholson, I hope it's also left me more appreciative of their stamina and self-sufficiency. And once again my husband Lindsay has proved stalwart in his arguments, in his support of my work and sacrifice of time together. My trip into the land of wilful blindness was a long one and it's good to be home.

This new edition is dedicated to my colleagues at the Forward Institute, for which this book is the only textbook. Their embrace of my ideas has been heartening and I'm grateful to them for taking seriously and enacting the premise that argument, dissent and debate are how good ideas and good people get better. Scratchy colleagues are always the best. Jonathan Gosling, Adam Grodecki, Cleo Sheehan and Ruth Turner have been that and more. I also owe a great deal to the openness and honesty with which the institute's fellows have shared their experiences, insights, doubts and daring with me. That so many experienced and seasoned leaders identify wilful blindness in themselves and their institutions and are determined to see better must give us all hope.